CHARLES DICKENS

JACK LINDSAY

Charles Dickens

A BIOGRAPHICAL AND CRITICAL STUDY

ANDREW DAKERS LTD
39 STORE STREET, LONDON, W.C.1

KRAUS REPRINT CO.
New York
1970

FIRST PUBLISHED 1950

LC 50-13629

Reprinted with the permission of the Licensor
KRAUS REPRINT CO.
A U.S. Division of Kraus-Thomson Organization Limited

Printed in U.S.A.

NOTE

★

My main excuse for this book is a great love of Dickens and a failure to find any book about him which made a serious attempt to grapple with his creative processes.

For reasons which I give in my study I believe that Blake and Dickens are the two writers who hold the key to the nature of our cultural crisis to-day—that is, the national key, the signposts to the resolutions needed by British culture in its last stages of nationhood.

By making the attempt to relate Dickens's work to the processes of history I have found that the pattern of his life assumes forms and colourations invisible to his biographers and critics, and that various episodes, often written about, take on quite new contours.

I should like to pay a special tribute to Edmund Wilson's essay on Dickens's last years in *The Wound and the Bow*, which, I think, was what made me turn my attention afresh with increasing interest to Dickens's work and life.

In the biographical sphere I should like to express thanks to Thomas Wright, who had the courage to make the first breach in the Dickensian Lie, and to Miss Gladys Storey, whose excellent book *Dickens and Daughter* showed much valuable research as well as the extremely important records of Katey Dickens's conversation. The abuse that the official Dickensians have showered on this devoted pair, especially on Miss Storey, is an astonishing exposure of the power of the Lie.

Miss Storey tells me that Ellen Ternan, after Dickens's death, married and bore children. In that fact no doubt lies some of the reasons for the determined efforts to hush up her part in Dickens's life. But in such a matter the claims of truth are paramount. What is at stake is not the unimportant question whether Dickens did or did not take a girl to bed, but the whole meaning of his life and work. For, as I have tried to show, the marital crisis and Ellen's part in it are only one aspect of a crisis in the whole man. The understanding of that crisis throws light backward over his life and work as well as forward; and the degree to which we grasp what then happened is the extent to which, in the last resort, we grasp the creative struggle of Dickens.

5

What value my book has will be found to lie in the extent to which I have been able to define the unity of development in Dickens's life and work, and the decisive shift of levels as he strives on. It is only when the unity is realized that the remarkable drive from level to level can be seen. Then Dickens appears what he was, one of the greatest of creative writers, taking into himself a whole epoch of human development. There is a sense in which, it is then understood, he, and he alone, stands near Shakespeare in our literature.

JACK LINDSAY

CONTENTS

★

7

for
EDITH SITWELL
who also has carried on the great tradition
in a dark age

I

Childhood

You have seen my works many a time, though it's
fifty thousand to one if you have seen me. You say
you don't want to see me? You say your interest is in
my works, and not in me? Don't be so sure about
that. (Charles Dickens in *Somebody's Luggage*.)

I

WHEN Mrs. Elizabeth Dickens, widow, retired
with a pension from her position as housekeeper of Crewe Hall in 1820, she was visited
at her lodgings in Oxford Street by her
grandchildren, among whom was a quick-
eyed youngster, Charles. He remembered her warm, kindly,
talkative presence, and thirty years later sketched her out as
Mrs. Rouncewell, house-keeper of Chesney Wold, in his novel
Bleak House.

The children of Crewe Hall also remembered her gossipy
readiness to spin yarns, especially fairy stories, and the excitement of visits to her room. Annabella (later Lady Houghton),
born in 1814, recorded her memories of the vivacious old lady;
no one, she declared, had ever had greater powers of improvis-
ing a tale. Elizabeth Dickens had been a Miss Ball, housemaid
to Lady Blandford of Grosvenor Square, till, in 1781, at the
mature age of thirty-six, she married William Dickens at St.
George's, Hanover Square. William served John Crewe, M.P.
for Chester (made Lord Houghton in 1806), who also had a
house in Grosvenor Square; and rose in time to the rank of
steward of Crewe Hall. He may or may not have belonged to a
poor branch of the Staffordshire Dickenses; but when his
grandson Charles wanted a crest, the obliging College of
Heralds, after due application and payment of fees, awarded
him their coat-of-arms.

At Crewe Hall, William, a thrifty fellow who twice made

9

investments in Consols, paid out the wages and board-wages of the staff. Elizabeth bore him two sons, William and John; and then, in October 1785, the year of John's birth, he died. The Crewes, however, kept Elizabeth on as housekeeper for some thirty-five years, and took a paternal interest in her sons. They saw to their education and found them jobs. John was appointed, through the patronage of Crewe's friend, Canning, to the Navy Pay Office on April 5, 1805. Aged nineteen, he began at Somerset House with a salary of five shillings a day. By June, 1807, he received as fifteenth assistant clerk in the Pay Branch, a salary of £70 a year, with two shillings extra for every day he actually turned up for work. And despite ups-and-downs of fortune he held his civil-service position till 1825, when he was pensioned off.

Thomas Culliford Barrow gained a clerkship in the office about the same time as John Dickens, through his father, a senior supervisor in the department. The Barrows were a cut above the Dickenses, and very aware of it. They were related to Sir John Barrow, Second Secretary to the Admiralty from 1804 to 1845, and Arctic explorer; and Thomas's father, Charles, as Chief Conductor of Money in Town, at a salary of £350 a year, held the responsible job of sending out cash under armed escort to the outports. For this purpose he used large imprest bills, himself signing the accounts and the Paymaster of the Navy Board endorsing.

Thomas, the eldest son, starting as a Navy Pay clerk, ended by qualifying for a pension of £710 a year. Edward, the next, married Janet Ross, a miniaturist; and John Henry became a barrister of Gray's Inn, dabbled in verses, did law-reporting for *The Times*, and founded a rival to *Hansard*. Of the daughters, Mary married Allen, a naval lieutenant, and Elizabeth married John Dickens.

She was still a minor; but John Dickens dashingly won her heart, and the Barrows gave in. They agreed to an early marriage as John was about to be detached from Somerset House. On June 13, 1809, the couple were wedded at St. Mary le Grand, opposite the main entrance of John's old place of work. The bride's father and mother with a relative Sarah, but no Dickenses, signed the register in the vestry as witnesses; and John, possibly excited and nervous, more likely well-flushed with wine, started signing in the wrong place, till the bride or the curate jogged him and he signed higher up, leaving room for Elizabeth.

Then, eleven days later, the Dickenses moved off by stage-coach to Portsmouth, where John was to pay off various men-of-war. They stayed there for some five years.

Elizabeth was a small, pretty girl, with a good education and a strong sense of the ridiculous. No doubt what attracted her to John was a kindred appetite for living and aptitude for fun, an equal readiness to put up with many inconveniences as long as existence held a core of laughter and glancing enjoyment. Her son guyed her as Mrs. Nickleby, seizing on to the careless chatterbox aspects of her character, which tended to seem silly after the brave gaieties of youth had gone; but it is clear that there was much more to her than the caricature allowed. And since Charles Dickens's life was in many ways from first to last dominated by his relationship to his parents, their characters and actions must be thoroughly understood if we are to understand the son and his work.

Elizabeth Dickens was a light-hearted woman, who brought up her children and held her household together under extremely difficult conditions. Doubtless, when the first ardours and laughters wore a little thin, and the children and the bills accumulated in her lap, she developed her own garrulous stridencies; and Charles witnessed many a shouting match between his indomitably voluble mother and his jovially smug father. His ingrained tendency to depict marriage as a confusion of nagging wills was certainly not simply derived from his own married life, where Kate was not so easily roused from her acquiescent amiabilities; its roots lie rather in his childhood's memories of endless squabbles, altercation and accusation and reconciliation. From those early levels he took a bias to disharmony into his own personal love-relations.

A pencil-drawing, made in middle-age, shows Elizabeth as a slight woman shawled in a box at the opera, regarding the house with a mild and slightly quizzical composure. Her mouth, generously large and even somewhat coarse, droops at the corners but is humorously tense. Her irregular features, once merged in a general sketch-effect of impulsive girlish charm, have become more obviously irregular as her energies slacken; and her nose suggests a sharpness belied by the drowsy eyes. But even as she ages, she keeps a quality of mercurial interest in life, a bird-like element, which shows a far deeper intelligence than her husband's multiple layers of capable complacence.

John's gaiety was more superficial. He was the kind of person who ripens fruitily with the years, but does not gain any new resources. The gay lad becomes a gay man, and finally a gay old man. He may turn out more obstinately irritating for all his dependents as he matures his ingratiating manners towards the rest of the world; but the heart of the man is doggedly the same. A cold egotism underlies the warm exterior; and the pleasant notes, indefinitely repeated, become madly jarring. What has been a careless and charming refusal to take life too seriously turns into a settled trick for evading responsibilities. But the man himself feels rightly enough that nothing has changed. If he was a good fellow then, he is a good fellow now; and of course he is. Everyone except his worried wife in her tantrums admits it, and even she caves in after he has made a sufficiently dignified show of displeasure.

Mrs. Christian, depicting the family in the late 1830's, declared that John "appeared younger than his wife," a plump, good-looking man, rather an "old buck" for dress, who "indulged occasionally in fine sentiments and long-winded sentences, and seemed to take an airy, sunny-sided view of things in general." He had a habit of importantly fingering his watch seals as he delivered his comments on life. W. T. Wright, for some years head of the Navy Pay Office at Chatham, described him "a fellow of infinite humour, chatty, lively and agreeable; and believed him capable to have imparted" to his son Charles the material for some of his sketches on men and manners. Another acquaintance told Langton that J. D. was a thorough good fellow, and the family a most genial lovable family.

A later friend, who knew him at Alpington, saw him as "a chatty, pleasant companion, possessing a varied fund of anecdote, and a genuine vein of humour. He was a well-built man, rather stout, of very active habits, a little pompous, and very proud (as well he might be) of his talented son." He still played with his goodly bunch of seals, and dressed with care. Charles no doubt had this aspect in mind when he wrote of Mr. Dobble, "We know the face by the cut of his coat, the tie of his waistcoat, and the self-satisfaction of his gait—the very green blinds themselves have a Somerset House air about them."

A pencil sketch, made about the same time as that of his wife, shows him a well-preserved beau with a stock round his thick neck, hair beginning to retreat, a small nose in a large naked-looking face, a battering-ram of a face which, however, has a slight frowning tension of anxiety, a fear of affront, a fear that

the world may at any moment not take him at his own estimate
of hail-fellow bravado.

One side of his character was depicted at length by Charles
in Mr. Micawber: his amiable pomposity, his shabby gentility
which sees itself in mirrors of semi-aristocratic delusion, his
dauntless trust in something turning up—a trust which had as
its twin the determination to make others responsible for his
shortcomings. Though Charles almost uniformly protested an
affectionate regard for him, he could not help depicting the less
pleasant elements of his character. John Dickens is Old Dorrit
as well as Micawber; and there is probably more than a touch of
him in Pecksniff and Turveytop. Indeed a hint of him pervades
all his son's incessant studies of the parasitic shabby-genteel,
the "ghosts of gentility" and the shameless hangers-on.

His mother seems to have had no illusions about him. She
described him (Arabella Crewe says) as "that lazy fellow John,
who used to come hanging about the house," and added, with
satisfaction, "and many a sound cuff in the ear I've given him."
That this was her considered judgment is shown by her constant distrust of him in all financial matters.

At Portsmouth the Dickenses found a neat little house with
two storeys and an attic, with back and front gardens, at 387
Commercial Road (then Mile End Terrace), Landport, Portsea.
The yearly rental was £35, paid quarterly. As John's salary had
not risen past £110, it looks as if he was basing his domestic
budget on help from his prosperous father-in-law.

They settled proudly in, and on December 21st Elizabeth
celebrated her twenty-first birthday. Portsea was entered via
the Landport Gates, at which guards were stationed; and a ferry
ran between it and Gosport or Portsmouth, charging a penny in
good weather for the crossing, threepence in foul. Otherwise,
to get over the four miles to Portsmouth, you went by a single-
horse chaise. But Portsea had its own resources, its chapels, and
its busy assembly hall.

In February 1810 disturbing news came from London.
Elizabeth's father was in bad trouble. For many years the Paymaster had been countersigning his imprest warrants without a
murmur; then someone grew suspicious or accidently did some
arithmetic in the account books. Charles Barrow put in his
usual bills for cash, but no money arrived. Instead, a Writ of
Extent. Normally he handled the money for paying out at the
outports (Portsmouth, Plymouth, Sheerness, Chatham), hiring

the armed guards, attending to repairs, furniture, coals, oil and so on at the offices, and the rates. But this time when he made his request for £900, the Navy Board wrote to the Navy Treasurer, complaining that as Mr. Barrow had seemed to have a balance of £51 odd, they had referred to his 1808 account and found that in December he'd had a balance of £3,713 14s. 10d. They therefore suggested an inquiry.

The inquiry showed that ever since 1803 Charles Barrow had been stating a false balance and that the deficit was at least £5,689 3s. 3d. Called before the Treasurer, he respectfully pleaded guilty with the extenuating circumstances of ten children and bad health. He also begged the Treasurer not to communicate with the Navy Board for a few days, as he had hopes of getting his brother to make up the missing sum. But a few days later he admitted that these hopes were baseless and that after what had happened he could not expect the Treasurer to have confidence in him; he therefore reluctantly tendered his resignation with a request that the Board would not press for settlement. "The demand might drive me into gaol, strip my family of what little furniture, clothes, or other resources they possess" and "confound us all in one overwhelming calamity."

The Treasurer then set the situation before the Board; and the Admiralty seems to have lost interest in the whole sordid thing. At least they took no proceedings against Barrow. This attitude annoyed the Treasurer, who expressed his low opinion of them in a letter and himself gave orders for a criminal prosecution. Barrow promptly absconded, "Supposed to have left England." All that the Middlesex sheriff could find to seize were goods (presumably furniture too heavy for quick shipment to France) worth some £499 9s. 0d.

It is clear, then, that John Dickens was not the only example of a happy-go-lucky mode of living in the Civil Service or among Charles Dickens's close relations.

Barrow's behaviour does not seem to have prejudiced the career of his son Thomas in the Service; and John Henry went on calmly with his legal and literary pursuits. The other son Edward, however, was more of a chip off the old block; in 1838 we find Charles Dickens paying a £57 debt for him.

II

Later on in 1810, on a Friday in November, a few minutes before midnight, a girl was born to the Dickenses: Frances

14

Elizabeth, known to the family as Fanny; and on the 23rd she was baptized. Then on February 7, 1812 came the second child, Charles.

The manner of his birth reveals Mrs. Dickens's tenacity of enjoyment. Though near her time, she was determined to attend the ball that evening at the Beneficial Society's Hall, in Rope Walk. She went to the ball and had her money's worth, and then before daybreak she bore her son in the small bedroom (seventeen and a half feet by thirteen feet seven inches to be precise) where a few hours before she had been admiring her dance frock by candlelight.

On March 2nd the child was baptized by the curate in the ancient parish church of Kingston, Portsea, with the name of Charles John Huffam (Huffham in the register). The church lay about fifteen minutes' walk across the fields; and in the family party went the sprightly and vigorous godfather, Christopher Huffam, come specially down from London to please his friend John.

Huffam, now about thirty-eight, was a comely and swash-buckling fellow, though a tradesman; he and his wife at one time were described as the handsomest couple in London. His father Solomon had founded the business of ship chandlers and sailmakers; and he, Christopher, and his brother carried on. Their men made sails and stored rope, lifebuoys, and other ship materials in the brick-walled workshop and cellar; and above, they themselves lived. Masts of eighteen feet length could be brought down through the street door into the workshop; for themselves they had a door cut in the panelling that reached to the top of the narrow stairs. Outside, at the back, flowed the Thames. Christopher, after the death of wife and brother, moved on to Limehouse Hole. Later, in February 1823, he applied to the Admiralty for leave to rig navy ships; but as already three sailmakers were employed at Deptford Docks, he was refused. In 1826, however, when Deptford was building a brig-sloop of ten guns, he supplied rigging and took the title of Rigger to His Majesty's Navy. He fitted out privateers against the French and was offered a knighthood, declined but accepted the position of First Gentleman in Waiting. The painting by the court artist shows him indeed handsome with large eyes and shapely mouth, very alert, very manly—and yet with a touch of feminine charm. His high stock is white and his hair is fashionably brushed forward. He lived till May 1839. That John Dickens should gain the friendship of such a man certainly testifies to his hearty *bonhomie*, his drinking powers, his conversational versatility.

Charles's birth coincided with a decline in the family fortunes. John Dickens's easy habits made for hard living; and the rich father-in-law had vanished overseas in disgrace. So the Dickenses on June 24th moved to a cheaper house, in Hawke Street. Here was no garden in front, though a small space at the back provided somewhere to put the children. You went straight up from the paving stones on two little wooden steps; and a small bay window looked out from the cramped sitting-room on to the dingy street. Here was born the third child, Alfred, who died young.

A naval officer recalled Charles as "a babe in long petticoats in their lodging in Portsea," and Charles himself had a dim remembrance how, "watched by a nurse through a low kitchen window almost level with the gravel walk, he trotted about with something to eat, and his little elder sister with him." He also recalled watching the soldiers exercise. Revisiting Portsmouth with Forster he recognized "the exact shape of the military parade seen by him as a very infant, in the same spot, a quarter of a century before."

But Portsmouth days were soon to end. John was transferred back to Somerset House in 1814. The family lodged at 10 Norfolk Street, and John's salary was raised—from June 1815 to 1819 he got £200 a year. Charles was now able to note things and people; he met his godfather and got on good terms with him at Church Row, Limehouse. Huffam, chuckling, liked to put the boy on the dining-room table and draw him into reciting poems. The frail, slightly precocious child already knew how to attract attention, and enjoyed the noisy admiration of Huffam and his cronies.

They stayed in London till 1817. Alfred died and Letitia was born. Then, probably through Huffam's influence, John Dickens was transferred to Chatham Dockyard.

III

The Dickenses, with the optimism of a new start, set up in the best house they had so far rented: at 2 (later 11) Ordnance Terrace, a comfortable, three-storeyed house with hayfields opposite, on the boundaries of Chatham and Rochester. Here they stayed till Lady Day, 1821. From 1820 John's salary went up to £350; but to a man of his temperament an increase in salary was an incitement to an increase in debts.

At Ordnance Terrace two more children were born—Harriet Ellen, born in the autumn of 1819, who died young; and Frederick William, born in 1820, who lived to become as shiftless as his father.

With the family now lived Elizabeth's sister, Mrs. Mary Allen, whose husband, risen to the rank of commander, had been drowned at Rio. For some reason she was called Aunt Fanny. She shared expenses and her presence made the whole household run more smoothly. Now was the happy period of the Dickenses. John was expanding amiably, showing all his paces as an entertainer and raconteur; and Elizabeth wasn't the one to spoil a good time with counsels of caution. This is the place that Charles idealizes in *David Copperfield*:

. . . the outside of our house, with the latticed bedroom-windows standing open to let in the sweet-smelling air, and the ragged old rooks' nests still dangling in the elm trees at the bottom of the front garden. Now I am in the garden at the back . . . where the fruit clusters on the trees, riper and richer than fruit has ever been since, in any other garden, and where my mother gathers some in a basket, while I stand by, bolting furtive gooseberries, and trying to look unmoved.

At peace with his mother, enjoying a warm sense of security, with no danger in the forbidden fruit at her shielding apron.

Charles and Fanny learned to read from a primer with fat black letters, first with the aid of their mother alone, and then with the aid of both mother and Aunt Fanny. "The easy good nature of O and S always seem to present themselves before me as they used to do." Mrs. Dickens taught Charles the rudiments of Latin. He told Forster that she taught him "regularly every day for a long time, and taught him, he was convinced, thoroughly well." She was "a dear, good mother," said Mary, the servant girl, "and a fine woman."

Then Charles, still a weakly boy with very fair hair, was sent with Fanny to a Dame's School over a dyer's shop in Rome Lane (later Railway Street), kept by a hard-knuckled old lady who inculcated the first principles of education at ninepence a week. When in doubt she poked his head "by way of adjusting the confusion of ideas in which he was generally involved."

He still did much reciting. Mary the servant remarked that his favourite piece was *The Voice of the Sluggard* by Watts, and he

gave it "with great effect, and with *such* action and *such* attitudes."
Forster recounts:

He told a story offhand so well, and sang comic songs so specially
well, that he used to be elevated on chairs and tables, both at home
and abroad, for more effective display of these talents; and when he
first told me of this, at one of the twelfth-night parties on his eldest
son's birthday, he said he never recalled it that his own shrill little
voice of childhood did not again tingle in his ears, and he blushed
to think what a horrible little nuisance he must have been to many
unoffending grown-up people who were called upon to admire him.

He liked sea songs; and he and Fanny used to sing love duets.
The landlord of the Mitre Inn, Chatham, Mr. Tribe, a close
friend of John Dickens, recalled a party at which Charles and
Fanny stood on the dining table and sang the following duet:

> Long time I've courted you, miss,
> And now I've come from sea;
> We'll make no more ado, miss,
> But quickly married be. *Sing fal de ral*, etc.
>
> I ne'er will wed a tar, sir,
> Deceitful as yourself;
> 'Tis very plain you are, sir,
> A good-for-nothing elf. *Sing fal de ral*, etc.
>
> I ne'er deceived you yet, miss,
> Though like a shrew you rave;
> But prithee, scold and fret, miss, . . .
> A storm I well can brave.
>
> False man, you courted Sally,
> You filled with vows her head;
> And Susan in the Valley,
> You promised you would wed.

The song ended with a display of mutual forbearance and
forgiveness.

Mary the servant, whom Robert Langdon fortunately ferreted
out in his quest for Dickens's childhood, said that "little Charles
was a terrible boy to read." He sat with the book in his left hand,
holding his wrist with his right and constantly moving it up and
down, and at the same time sucking his tongue. "Sometimes,
Charles would come downstairs and say to me, 'Now, Mary,
clear the kitchen, we are going to have such a game,' and then
George Stroughill would come in with his magic lantern, and

they would sing, recite, and perform parts of plays. Fanny and Charles often sang together at this time, Fanny accompanying on the pianoforte. Though a good and eager reader in those days (about 1819) he had certainly not been to school, but had been thoroughly well taught at home by his aunt and mother." He was, she added, "a lively boy of good, genial, open disposition, and not quarrelsome, as most children are at times."

Now this Mary herself was an important factor in Charles's childhood, and needs some close attention. Her name was Mary Weller; and though she is called the nurse, we must not think of her as a grown-up woman. In 1817 she was only about thirteen or fourteen years old (she died at the age of eighty-four in April 1888); and after Mrs. Dickens and Fanny, she was perhaps the most important person of these years in Charles's thoughts and feelings. He not only gave her name to the character who made the success of *Pickwick* and established him as a popular writer; he also married Sam Weller off to a Mary. In *Sketches of Young Couples* he brings her in for pathos. "She once nursed the children on her lap . . . as neat a girl as you'd wish to see," and drops a tear over the change wrought by the years. In *The Uncommercial Traveller* (xi and xiv) he deals at length with her. She must be the "very sympathetic nurse" who takes him round to visit her married friends who are lying-in; and he specially recalls a greengrocer's shop set below street level, where they went to see a woman who had born four or five children in one birth. ". . . the four (five) deceased young people lay, side by side, on a clean cloth, on a chest of drawers: reminding me by a homely association, which I suspect their complexion to have assisted, of pigs' feet as they are usually displayed at a neat tripe shop." Caudle was handed round, and he resisted an attempt to draw on his pocket-money for the subscription entered into among the company.

Again, the nurse girl who tells him stories at bedtime can hardly be other than Mary Weller. She belongs to Chatham, and no one else but Mary fits the role. The whole of this account of child terrors is of the utmost importance in any understanding of Dickens, and makes clear how deeply affected he was by the events of these years. "If we all knew our own minds (in a more enlarged sense than the popular acceptation of that phrase)," he says, "I suspect we should find our nurses responsible for most of the dark corners we are forced back to, against our wills." And he reveals some of his own dark corners.

The first story he dredges up from the lost years is one of cannibalism and murder. A Captain Murderer used to marry girls and then eat them up. One bride asks about the flowers he has planted on both sides of the way to church. "They are called garnish for house-lamb," he answers and laughs ferociously, showing his fine teeth. His coach-and-twelve has milk-white horses, each with one red spot on its back, which the harness hides. "For the spot *would* come through . . . and the spot was young bride's blood. (To this terrific point I am indebted for my first personal experience of a shudder and cold beads on the forehead.)" At last he weds a twin. Taking her home, he makes her roll out a huge pie crust, chops her up in it, peppers and salts her, and sends her out to be baked. He then proceeds to marry the other twin, who, however, has suspicions, climbs up to his window, and sees him sharpening his teeth. He goes through his cannibalistic routine with her; but she has taken the precaution of swallowing a dreadful poison. So, "Captain Murderer had hardly picked her last bone, when he began to swell, and to turn blue, and to be all over spots, and to scream. And he went on swelling and turning bluer and being sore, all over spots and screaming, until he reached from floor to ceiling and from wall to wall; and then, at one o'clock in the morning, he blew up with a loud explosion. At the sound of it, all the milk-white horses in the stables broke from their halters and went mad, and then they galloped over everybody in Captain Murderer's house (beginning with the family blacksmith who had filed the teeth) until the whole were dead, and then they galloped away."

The next tale has a strong Chatham flavour. It deals with a shipwright who worked in the Government Yard, named Chips, son of Chips and grandson of Chips; and all the Chips sold their souls to the Devil for an iron pot, a bushel of tenpenny nails, half a tin of copper and a rat that could talk. The point of the complicated plot is the way in which the present Chips, though trying to break the fate of the Chipses, succumbs and brings a nemesis on himself. Driven from his carpenter's job, he becomes a sailor, and perishes with the ship that his own misdeeds have doomed.

The swarming of the rats is told with a fine effect of environing evil, the result of the fated greed that Chips tries to escape from but cannot:

And they got into his lodging, and into his bed, and into his teapot, and into his boots. And he was going to be married to a corn-

chandler's daughter; and when he gave her a workbox he had himself
made for her, a rat jumped out of it; and when he put his arm round
her waist, a rat clung about her: so the marriage was broken off. . . .
(By this time, a special cascade of rats was rolling down my back,
and the whole of my small listening person was overrun with them.
At intervals ever since, I have been morbidly afraid of my own
pocket, lest my exploring hand should find a specimen or two of
those vermin in it.)

Throughout, Dickens emphasizes the enduring effect of
horror:

Hundreds of times did I hear the legend of Captain Murderer, in
my early youth, and added hundreds of times was there a mental
compulsion upon me in bed, to peep in at his window as the dark
twin peeped, and to revisit his horrible house, and look at him in his
blue and spotty and screaming stage, as he reached from floor to
ceiling and from wall to wall. The young woman who brought me
acquainted with Captain Murderer, had a fiendish enjoyment of
my terrors, and used to begin, I remember—as a sort of introductory
overture—by clawing the air with both hands, and uttering a long
low hollow groan.
So acutely did I suffer from this ceremony in combination with
this infernal Captain, that I sometimes used to plead I thought I was
hardly strong enough and old enough to hear the story again just yet.
But she never spared me one word of it, and indeed commended the
awful chalice to my lips as the only preservative known to science
against "The Black Cat"—a weird and glaring-eyed supernatural
Tom, who was reputed to prowl about the world by night sucking
the breath of infancy, and who was endowed with a special thirst
(as I was given to understand) for mine.

The full effect of these stories on Dickens will appear as we go
on; but I shall reach ahead for a moment, to point out that the
awful figure of Captain Murderer, swelling till he bursts in his
foul glut of poison, reappears in *Bleak House* in the grim figure
of the mock Chancellor, who bursts in spontaneous combustion
through his own inner corruption.

The ambivalent nature of the image of Mary Weller for
Dickens appears when we contrast the above picture of her as
the fiend turning the edge of sleep into a torment with the
picture given in a letter of September 24, 1857, where she is
found as the kindly guardian of sleep, easing the sense of guilt:

I shall cut this letter short, for they are playing Masaniello, in
the drawing-room, and I feel much as I used to do when I was a

21

small child a few miles off, and Somebody (who, I wonder, and which way did She go, when she died) hummed the evening tune to me and I cried on the pillow—either with the remorseful consciousness of having kicked Somebody else, or because Somebody else had hurt my feelings in the course of the day.

Langdon asked Mary Weller, "Did you ever sing the evening hymn to the children?" After a little reflection, she replied, "Yes, many a time," and "seemed very much surprised by so unexpected a question."

IV

The days at Ordnance Terrace left a deep impress on Charles's work at all levels. He drew directly on his memories of them throughout his writing years, and certain tensions derived from the pattern of experience at this time persist, deeper down, right up to the end. From the *Sketches by Boz* we gain much factual information of the neighbours. The old lady of *Our Parish*, for instance, was Mrs. Navisham who lived at No. 5 and was very kind to the children, especially to pretty little Letitia; she lived in a parlour full of knick-knacks, many of which were "presents from little girls—Fanny being among them." The half-pay captain lived nearby, breeding silkworms, bringing them in three or four times a day to show the old lady and dropping a few each visit on the floor.

Charles had many friends here. The Stroughills: George, "a fresh, open, and charming boy" (the original of Steerforth), and Lucy his sister, the peach-faced angel in a blue sash and blue shoes who seemed entirely reared on seed cake and sweet wine in an everlasting birthday. He supposed birthdays a special favour bestowed by heaven on so distinguished a child, and retired with her into a bower far from the world (under the table), where they ate and drank all manner of sweetnesses. She, his constant companion, became later the heroine, the Golden Girl, of *The Wreck of the Golden Mary*, where he killed her sanctimoniously off; and she, like the other small girls of these years, contributed her portion to the image of Little Em'ly.

Then there was the daughter of Tribe of the "Mitre," another sweetheart. Noble parties were given at the inn, which had pleasant grounds and showed the cabin where Nelson had put up, and had a bar "the next best thing to a bishopric it was so snug," (William IV and the Duke of Clarence had also stayed there, and so it had a second name, "The Clarence Arms").

I loved the landlord's youngest daughter to distraction—but let that pass. It was in this inn that I was cried over by my rosy little sister [Fanny], because I had acquired a black eye in a fight. And though she had been, that holly-tree night, for many a long year where all tears are dried, the Mitre softened me yet.

And then there was Mary Ann Mitton, another of these sweethearts, whom he met again in Rochester when a young man and told that he'd write a book about her and call it *Little Dorrit*.

Charles was still liable to "spasms" (apparently attacks of giddiness) and at times suffered pain. He was thus debarred from rough games, and was often left alone to his own resources: a "very small and not-over-particularly-taken-care-of boy," he said years later. As so often when his deepest emotions are stirred, we meet an ambivalence, a flat contradiction. He describes his childhood as a period of loneliness and also as the one period of completely satisfying comradeship. He and the others were always learning the "merriest games that ever were played." Rowing in summer, skating in winter. "Holidays and Twelfth Night Cakes and parties dancing till midnight. And friends! more and more friends!" They went on picnics, and played fiercely at pirates.

Here, in the haymaking time, had I been delivered from the dungeons of Seringapatam, an immense pile (of haycock), by my countrymen, the victorious British (boy next door and his two cousins), and had been recognized with ecstasy by my affianced one (Miss Green), who had come all the way from England (second house in the terrace) to ransom me, and marry me.

Here had I first heard in confidence, from one whose father was greatly connected, being under Government, of the existence of a terrible banditti, called "The Radicals," whose principles were, that the Prince Regent wore stays, and that nobody had a right to any salary, and that the army and navy ought to be put down— horrors at which I trembled in my bed. . . .

When in middle age he returned, he found the playground swallowed up by the railway station. Hawthorn hedge and turf with daisy and buttercup had gone down before a stony road, "while, beyond the station, an ugly monster of a tunnel kept its jaws open, as if it had swallowed them and was ravening for more destruction." The engine that had brought him "was spitting ashes and hot water on the blighted ground." And he contrasts the blithe games of prison-and-escape with the fact of his emergence from the carriage "like a prisoner whom the turnkey grudgingly released."

He romped, too, in Fort Pitt Fields, while Mary Weller sat with Tom Gibson, the shipwright whom she later married. Here in autumn they watched the soldiers at their sham fights and siege operations in Tom-all-alone's. This area took its name from one Thomas Clark, who about 1747 moved out from the part of Chatham now called Old Brompton, to escape from people; he bought the waste about half a mile from the town and built a house on it; and for twenty-five years he lived alone. Coming home of an evening, he sang to himself *Tom's All Alone*. So the house was given that name. Later, however, he married and begot a large family, which colonized the area, until the military took it over and a convict prison was built there.

If we consider the use to which Dickens put this name, Tom-all-alone's, we get a clue to the way in which his deepest images in work are images drawn from his childhood and subtly transformed in the process. Thus, in *Bleak House*, he uses Tom-all-alone's to express the utter desolation of the London slums, the rotten forces of greed caught in a material effluvium of decay and darkness. A benighted and corrupted area inhabited by the lost child, Joe. "Twice, lately, there has been a crash and a cloud of dust, like the springing of a mine, in Tom-all-alone's, and, each time, a house has fallen."

Now, at Chatham, in the real Tom-all-alone's, Dickens had often seen the soldiers at their operations blow up a house. The springing of the mine, which was there an observed fact, has been changed into a symbol of the inner forces of self-destruction in the night of decay. And what links the actual experience and the symbolic recreation is the tale of the lonely man, turning away from the defiled world and crying eerily in the dark of the eve. This man is the Bedlamite, the poor Tom of *Lear*, the folk-image of the prophet in all his scared and pitiful isolation steadfast against the world. Woe, woe. The lost child, the sacrificed child, poor shivering Joe. Tom's a cold, Joe's all alone.

No important writer has drawn so continuously and directly on his personal experience as Dickens. There is scarcely any gap between the experience and the creative image. That is why the industrious commentators have been able to link almost every person, however unimportant, in Dickens's work with a person whom he met or heard of; every place with some place which he saw or heard of. The names of the people in his books are almost always woven out of names which for some reason or other assumed an emotional significance for him. The slow process of absorption and redefinition which is usually found in a novelist has little relevance to his method. All the while he is consciously or unconsciously moving over the narrow ground of certain key experiences of childhood. Sometimes the material comes in quite rawly; sometimes there is the great poetic leap which turns Captain Murderer into the Lord Chancellor or the mined house outside Chatham into a whole world of ominous decay. But the filament is never broken; the connection between image and experience is naïvely left intact. All the weaknesses and strengths of Dickens reside in this fact.

The industrious commentators have thus been heaping up evidence of considerable importance, though they have not understood its meaning.

Aunt Fanny had grown friendly with the garrison doctor, Dr. Matthew Lamert, and his son James, a Sandhurst Cadet, had a turn for private theatricals. The doctor's quarters in the Ordnance Hospital were large and rambling, almost empty, excellently suited for putting shows on. Plays were staged, and Dr. Lamert contributed his exuberant share to their performance. James Lamert, who had taken a fancy to Charles, introduced him not only to these private plays but also to the professional ones given at the Theatre Royal at the foot of Star Hill, Rochester.

About this time (1819–20) Charles and Fanny were taken to see the great clown Grimaldi (perhaps on a visit to London); and on St. Clement's Day they witnessed a surviving piece of folk ritual. The dockyard blacksmiths then held a pageant in honour of their patron saint. Led by one of themselves masked as Old Clem, who was carried in a chair of state, they paraded the town and collected drink money. *Great Expectations* borrowed their refrain, "Beat it out, beat it out, Old Clem! with a clink for the stout, Old Clem."

On March 3rd, 1820, an exciting event occurred. A fire destroyed thirty-eight houses at Chatham and left many families homeless. John Dickens was an active member of the Relief Committee, subscribed two guineas to the fund, and was thanked in the printed report for his services. (His name indeed was prominent in local subscription lists all the while the family lived at Ordnance Terrace). He also showed his literary powers. He sat down at once after the fire and wrote out a lengthy account which he sent on to *The Times*, in which it appeared on March 4th. The promptness and thoroughness of the account, rather than its literary virtues, were what called for praise; but Mr. Dickens must certainly have plumed himself on the achievement. (He uses phrases like "the devouring element" and "a sacrifice to its rage"; but it is of interest to learn that "at an early hour of the day the news of the fire reached London, from which some engines were despatched; but before their arrival the flames had been subsided.")

Charles was now in better health, and could go for walks with his father into the surrounding country, to Gadshill, Snorridge Bottom, Tom-all-alone's, Findsbury, and Rochester. As they strolled, John Dickens talked to his small admiring son. These walks left a deep impression.

In *Copperfield* Dickens wrote, "If it should appear from anything I may set down in this narrative that I was a child of close observation, or that as a man I have a strong memory of my childhood, I undoubtedly lay claim to both these characteristics." From this passage and others of the same sort Dickens may be thought to describe himself as consciously noting down and observing. That, however, would be a great mistake. His observation was of a peculiar kind, emotionally selective, intensely aware of certain movements and interconnections in a given field of contacts, but blind to all others. What it had been in childhood it remained throughout life. Its action, or failure to act, is always linked with the key impulses of his life, his quest for certain definite patterns and clues of union and separation. No one was ever farther from the naturalistic observer or cataloguer.

His daughter Mamie wrote, "He believed the power of observation in very young children to be close and accurate, and he thought that the recollection of most of us could go back further than we suppose." And his comments bring out the way in which he felt this intense awareness by the child of its world to be based on its emotional relation to that world, its pervasive need of harmony, its continual scrutiny of the parental sphere for any signs of discord, anything liable to upset the fine balance of its fears and desires.

In the little world in which children have their existence, whosoever brings them up, there is nothing so finely perceived and so finely felt as injustice. It may be only small injustice that the child is exposed to; but the child is small, and its rocking-horse stands as many hands high, according to scale, as a big-boned Irish hunter.

And again:

It would be difficult to overstate the intensity and accuracy of an intelligent child's observation. At that impressible time of life it must sometimes produce a fixed impression. If the fixed impression be of an object terrible to the child, it will be (for want of reasoning upon) inseparable from great fear. Force the child at such a time, be Spartan with it, send it into the dark against its will, and you had better murder it.

Dickens was throughout his life deeply aware of the basis of his art in his early memories: the "great fears" which kept on working underneath the conscious levels ("responsible for most of the dark corners we are forced back to, against our wills"), and the equally great loves in which the child found escape from fear.

But once more John Dickens was finding that debts have a way of accumulating; and Aunt Fanny had no intention of staying a widow. In 1821 she agreed to marry Surgeon Lamert, a kindly man with an odd short way of expressing himself (who became Dr. Slammer in *Pickwick*); and on December 11th the marriage came off. Charles and Fanny were present; and John Barrow, their literary uncle, who was to become a member of Gray's Inn two years later, was a witness. The Lamerts then went off to Ireland, taking with them the second serving girl, Jane Bonny; and James, the surgeon's son, waiting for his Army commission, came to lodge with the Dickenses.

The family had already moved, on Lady Day, into a new house, 18 St. Mary's Place, the Brook, near the parish church. They had come down in the social scale, though no doubt John Dickens explained to everyone that the place gave him a much easier walk to his office. The house, however, was neat enough, with its whitewashed plaster front and its small back and front gardens. Next door stood the Providence Baptist Chapel under Mr. Giles. From the upper window on one side of the house the parish church and churchyard could be seen.

John Dickens could find a further excuse for the move in the fact that the elder children simply must go to school, and here a school was handy. (Charles was now nine, and his long tuition with Fanny at his mother's side had had a profound emotional effect on him.) Things suddenly became drabber all round for the children. "There were no such entertainments at this house," said Mary Weller, "as I have seen at the Terrace."

27

Charles and Fanny went together to the school of William Giles, son of the Baptist minister. A not-too-expensive preparatory school attended by the master's own brothers and sisters, and the children of officers and naval officials. The boys all wore white beaver hats; and the school, once situated in Clover Lane, now expanded to the corner house of Rhode and Best Streets.

Thus Charles and Fanny became Cats of Giles. For a derisive Chatham rhyme gives the nicknames of the scholars of the four main schools: Baker's Bulldogs, Giles's Cats, New Road Scrubbers, Troy Town Rats. Giles, now about twenty-three, had been ordained in 1817 after a good education at Oxford, and thus had claims for scholarship unusual in the master of such a school. He had the intelligence to recognize a distinctive quality in Charles's mind, did his best to make him appreciate good English, and emphasized the virtues of Goldsmith's style. He often made Charles his evening companion; and his eldest sister (some fifteen years Charles's senior) remembered him as a handsome boy with light curly hair and an agreeable disposition, who was already capital company.

At the year end, at the examinations, Charles recited a poem from the *Humorists' Miscellany* about Doctor Bolus, which gained (says Forster), "unless his youthful vanity bewildered him, a double encore." His group experience was widened and strengthened. He played cricket and other games; and if Langdon is right, he now picked up a sort of lingo, useful in giving schoolboys a sense of secrecy and superiority. About this time, "a not very robust child sitting in by-places near Rochester Castle," he heard about a very different sort of school—his impressions of which "were somehow or other connected with a suppurated abscess that some boy had come home with, in consequence of his Yorkshire guide, philosopher, and friend having ripped it open with an inky penknife. The impression made upon me, however made, never left me," and led in time to *Nicholas Nickleby*.

Now, under the stimulus of a fuller group-life, Charles made his first ventures into writing and discovered new worlds in reading. In a room upstairs where no one else went he came on some of his father's books. He browsed through the novels of Smollett and Fielding, *The Vicar of Wakefield*, *Don Quixote*, *Gil Blas*, books of travel, *The Arabian Nights* and its imitation in *Tales of Genii* by the Rev. J. Ridley. For weeks on end he lived through the excitement of the reading and then of day-dreams based on what he had read. He enacted the roles of Tom Jones or Gil Blas. "I can remember to have gone about my region of the house, armed with the centrepiece out of an old set of boot trees: the perfect realization of Captain Somebody, of the Royal British Navy, in danger of being beset by savages, and resolved to sell his life at a great price." Or he sat on his bed reading, able to get glimpses of the other children at play in the church-yard.

More, in roaming about alone in the neighbourhood, he relived in fantasy the stories he had read, giving the events a local habitation in the dream-world of play. "Every barn in the neighbourhood, every stone in the church, and every foot of the churchyard, had some association of its own, in my mind, con-nected with these books, and stood for some locality made famous in them. I have seen Tom Pipes go climbing up the church steeple; I have watched Strap, with the knapsack on his back, stopping to rest himself upon the wicker gate; and I *know* that Commodore Trunnion held that club with Mr. Pickle, in the parlour of our little village alehouse." This fantasy-weaving of the book themes into his play-life, into the whole environment of these years of childhood, was of crucial importance for the artistic method he later developed. Throughout, what he did was to redefine the fantasy-life of these years in terms of the new pressures invading his adult experience. While this method produced certain limitations and weaknesses, it gave his work its tremendous dynamic, its great poetic sweep and depth.

One tale of Ridley's especially affected him. It tells of a hag who hobbled out of a chest and terrorized Abudah, a Bagdad merchant. The story hovered long at the back of his mind, and lies at the heart of his *Haunted Man* (and indeed many of the novels). On another of Ridley's tales he now tried to found a tragedy, *Misnar*, about an Indian Sultan. His fantasy-life was already issuing in direct dramatizations, in which it linked with his group-life, the schoolboy passion for play-acting and miming. Mrs. Inchbald's *Collection of Farces*, apparently read about this time, helped to give a direction to his need for expression.

VI

These years when Charles, a sickly and delicate child, was growing up in the warm shadow of his mother, built up a permanent bias in his temperament. His relation to his mother was a dominant factor throughout his life, his memory of the blessed years of harmony and protection, his agonized resentment against all that broke the bond. But in such a relationship there are sure to be other figures, who play their part in the drama of love and fear, and who are to some extent mother-substitutes. As far as one can see, the surrogates for the mother who exercised a potent effect over Charles's development were his sister Fanny and his nurse Mary Weller. In particular Fanny, his sister a couple of years older, was in a position to attract much of the emotion born out of his intense and strained desire to monopolize his mother's attention. She often looked after him; she was his one constant companion; she shared his fate in many ways and sang love songs with him.

In order to estimate the significance of Fanny's part in Charles's life we have to look at the stories he wrote around the time of her death in 1848. He and she had largely drifted apart for many years; Charles had had his excruciating love affair with Maria Beadnell, had married Kate Hogarth, and had idealized Mary Hogarth; Fanny had been apparently pushed far from the centre of his emotional life. But the shock of her death, coming at a moment of considerable stress, broke through the accumulated layers of experience and stirred the deep patterns. Charles was driven to express what she had meant for him, and to realize, at least while he wrote, how the later heroines of love had been to some extent wearing her mask. The pattern of hope and fear, powerfully arrested and entangled with Fanny, had never been successfully carried forward into adult resolutions of love.

In *The Haunted Man*, begun shortly after her death, he tells of a chemist visited on Christmas Eve by his spirit double, who reminds him of the afflictions which have blighted his life. These are two. First, the death of his sister. She had been the one gleam of happiness in his early years, had been entirely wrapped up in him, had lived on to see him famous (his ambition rewarded after its spring was broken), and then died, gentle, happy, concerned only for her brother. (In point of fact, Fanny had been for years concerned only for her husband and children; and this bland displacement of the real objects of her devotion by the neglected brother in his day-dream gives the measure of his resentment. It also reveals the central place of Fanny in his emotional hierarchies.)

Secondly, the nature of his parents. He blames them for his sense of loss, his homelessness in the world. They were "of that sort whose care soon ends, and whose duty is soon done;

who cast their offspring loose, early, as birds do theirs; and, if they do well, claim the merit; and if ill, the pity."

And so his sweetheart, for whose sake he strove upwards, has married someone else.

The story is a fantasy-reconstruction of the facts, of course. But so is all Dickens's work where it is creatively alive. It is precisely by reason of the distortions that we can evalue the pressures, and determine how the day-dream beats against the contrary movements of actuality. In such a story there is no pretence of artistic detachment; there is an agonized attempt to break through the superficies of experience into the determining patterns. The observant child, torn by suspicions, is re-enacting the events of family life, trying to get them fully into focus, to find the flaw, the source of discord. To find what has made things go wrong and broken up the original harmony.

The hidden logic of the day-dream brings together the loving sister who unavailingly died, and the sweetheart who proved faithless or failed to love. To make this identification consciously is impossible; for it is true only of the infantile levels. Yet, because the sufferer has been unable to proceed with steady resolution from those levels into a fully integrated adult experience, he can only look back to the agitation in the depths; and the pattern which he drags out as artist is a pattern in which the fall into individual misery from family unity is imaged as a split between the loving sister and the faithless sweetheart.

In the second issue of *Household Words*, 1850, Charles published *The Child's Dream of a Star*, in which he pursued the theme. The story tells of a brother and sister, inseparable child companions, who made friends with a star. They watched it together till they knew when and where it would rise, and always said good night to it. Then the sister died. The desolate brother still connected her with the star, which he now saw as a world of light, its rays a road stretching from earth to heaven. Angels waited in it to receive the traveller up the bright road, his little sister among them. So he began to think that he belonged less to the earth than to the star where his sister stood. He grew up, lived his life through, aged. All the while he was consoled under a succession of domestic bereavements by a renewal of his childhood's vision. At last on his deathbed he felt himself moving as a child to his child sister and thanked his heavenly father that the star had so often opened before to receive the dear ones who now awaited him.

"His sister Fanny and himself," Forster records, "he told me long before this paper was written, used to wander at night about the churchyard near their house, looking up at the stars; and her early death . . . reawakened all the childish associations which made her memory dear to him."

The significance of this story, in which we find the key to all Dickens's most perverse sentimentalities, lies in the way in which the day-dream displaces the date of Fanny's death. He is blaming the actual Fanny because she failed to remain the pure and blessed Fanny of the child relationship. The only way to keep her in the relationship he wants is to kill her off at that point. Then, he feels, life would have been happier. True, the perfect happiness of the union in the starry night of the churchyard would be lost; but its memory would stay unimpaired to lend a radiance to all later relationships. Those relationships would then be purged of the discord which Charles feels all too present in his own adult life, somehow spoiling everything.

Thus, the image of a perfect love relationship, a perfect union, is given the death setting, and is in fact identified with the image of death. The only wholly desirable girl is the dead girl, the dying girl. Only in that death-throe is pure contact established and a safeguard set up against the corruptions and distortions that seem fated in adult developments.

This story then gives us the key to Dickens's obsession with the image of Little Nell. But the response of the public to such sentimentalities, with its flood of tears over the biers of the dying heroines, shows that Dickens was not expressing a mere neurotic idiosyncrasy in such matters. He was expressing something which went deep down into the whole historical situation, into the pang of growth at this moment. That is a matter we shall have to explore more fully later. For the moment it is enough to point to the way in which an essential element of Dickens's creative dynamic is bound up with the death-wish aimed against Fanny. The wish that she had died in pure and happy childhood.

For then all the later miseries would have been avoided, the day-dream logic argues. Her death is also his death. In the death image he feels only the ceaseless union, the arrest of time at the moment of pure harmony.

But here the ambivalence of the death-wish intervenes. It cannot entirely escape from the world of actual consequences. As soon as the external world looks in on it, it reveals itself as a murder impulse. And so it gives a vehement push to the whole mechanism of guilt, fear, shame—everything that it most wants to pacify and nullify.

Further, behind the sister stands the mother. Ultimately it is a harmony with her that is desired, and so the death-wish is aimed at her too. In *David Copperfield* there is a very revealing passage in which Dickens brings out the link of these death-wishes with resentment against the pregnant and child-bearing mother. David returns from school to find his mother nursing a new baby—as Charles himself had so often done.

> I spoke to her, and she started and cried out. But seeing me she called on her dear Davy, her only boy! and coming half across the room to meet me, kneeled down upon the ground and kissed me, and laid my head in her bosom near the little creature that was nestling there, and put its hands up to my lids. I wish I had died. I wish I had died then, and with that feeling in my heart! I should have been more fit for Heaven than I have ever been since.

Here the death-wish is directed finally against himself in a moment of supreme union when all emotions of jealousy and resentment have been overcome.

Yet another story, written towards the end of his days, has direct bearing on his relations to Fanny, and shows a more extended working out of the day-dream. It is *George Silverman's Explanation* (published 1868), and earned him a thousand pounds. So deeply moved was he by the writing of it, so hypnotically absorbed within its movement, that he declared to a friend, W. H. Wills, "I feel as if I had read something (by somebody else), which I should never get out of my mind."

It opens with a statement of the strong resistances that the writer feels against getting his story out. Then he manages to begin. He was reared in a cellar in Preston by a screaming mother, who told him, when cold or hungry, that he was a worldly little devil. His lazy, hopeless father sat by the empty grate till the woman pulled his stool from under him and sent him out to bring some money home. These parents die of starvation. George is looked after by a rascally dissenting lay-preacher, who cheats him out of a fortune left by his grandfather. George falls in love with a little girl, but, so affected is he by his mother's accusations, he fears to contaminate her. So he shuns her and lives sad and lonely among the happy country folk. He lies brooding in bed while they sing and dance. Managing to get to Cambridge, he enters the Church and gains a living—always alone: "I myself am always in the shadow looking on." Then he renounces his beloved Adelina, daughter of baleful Lady Fareaway, and gets her married off to his rival, the bold and energetic Granville (Stroughill again). He himself carries out the secret ceremony, and Lady F. denounces him to the bishop as having been bribed. For years a cloud rests on him; but at long last it clears away, and he is given a living in a sequestered place. There he sits brooding at a window which opens out on a churchyard, "equal resting place for sound hearts, wounded hearts, and broken hearts."

Here the sense of guilt has taken charge and pervades the story. The boy feels outcast, and all his love relations are broken by guilt-fear. Here we get the obverse to the picture of *The Child's Story of a Star*. If the sister beloved lives, she must be renounced.

Two further points in this version of the fantasy are worth noting. The hero gets the full education that Charles lacked; but it doesn't make any difference, the inner flaw still rends his life. Thus Charles consoles himself at the same moment as he exploits to the full his pang of self-pity. Also, he opens by identifying himself with the poor broken children of the industrial areas—an unusual note for him, and significant of changes in his outlook towards the end of his life.

The story ends in the churchyard where *The Child's Story* began. George, looking out sadly on the churchyard, is Dickens looking sadly back on his childhood; on the place of laughter and guilt, of love and sin. The spot which brings a sudden intrusion of self-pity into his account of David Copperfield's world: "There is nothing half so green that I know anywhere, as the green of that churchyard; nothing half so shady as its trees; nothing half so quiet as its tombstones."

Here is both the lost Eden, and the dark spot of the death-wish. A locality we shall find continually reappearing in Dickens's life and work.*

VII

Mrs. Dickens went on being prolific. Alfred Lamert Dickens was baptized on April 3, 1822, at St. Mary's Church. Charles himself was getting to know Chatham and Rochester inside out.

* The name Fanny is given to at least eleven characters in his stories and novels. Some of these Fannies are of much importance in clarifying further his relations to the sister, and we shall deal with them as we come to them. (Aunt Fanny as a mother-surrogate may have helped to intensify the magical virtue of the name.)

A great walker in his dark clothes and white hat, he breathed happily the smell of oak chips, oakum, pitch, tarred ropes, canvas, familiar long past at Huffam's works. He walked with his father to the Navy Pay Office, now close at hand, a plain red-brick building with heavy barred windows, which impressed him with its gravity and staid pretence of having nothing worth mentioning to do. Inside, connected with his father's mysterious work, were strong rooms lined with iron. All around was a roving population in oilskin hats, marine-store dealers peering cunningly out of crammed shops, drunken bargees in steady influx, and other maritime advantages.

In *Pickwick* Chatham appears mainly associated with soldiers, sailors, shrimps, dockers, oysters, tobacco. Charles loved to watch the rope-makers, the block-makers, the anchor-smiths (nine of them in a ring like the Muses), the men-of-war on the slips; the sailors and all great sea-porkypines. He had been born near the sea, and at Chatham grew up in earshot of "the great voice of the sea, with its eternal nevermore" (as it sounded to David), the voice which mixed up its enigma with the death of Paul Dombey.

Off the dockyard lay the convict hulk roofed like a Noah's Ark; a receiving ship. Convicts with great numbers on their backs as if they were street doors, were seen going back after the day's work with oak planks on their shoulders (the small man in the middle escaping the weight), with soldiers on guard; and on the London coach they troubled passengers on the box-seat with stench of bread poultice, baize, rope-yarn, hearthstone. Charles always had a keen sense of smell, of characteristic odours.

Sometimes, as a treat, he and Fanny were taken aboard the Navy Pay (or Commissioners') Yacht *Chatham*, down the Medway to Sheerness. The *Chatham* was a high-sterned cutter-rigged craft with big round ports, dating from the time of the Commonwealth; a sluggish boat, but capable of a speed that astonished sailors in a stiff breeze. She wasn't broken up till 1868.

Across the Medway stood the cathedral town of Rochester, a contrast to busy Chatham. Here Charles could day-dream of the past. The walls of the castle keep were reflected in the broad Medway out of a medieval romance; the glooms of the past still hung chilly round the nooks of the cathedral with its sculptured western front; and High Street with its archways and gables retreated some six hundred years with darkness. In *Pickwick* Rochester plays its part as a background for high jinks, Tupman and his widow, Winkle and his difficult horse, pleasant times at the Bull Inn, and a quiet moment as Pickwick leans over the bridge balustrade to look at the waters. It comes up again strong in *Great Expectations,* when Dickens tries to look clean through his illusions. It looms strange and heavy with cloistral shadows of decay in *Edwin Drood* as he faces up to death. That view over the Medway, which for Pickwick was a passing glimpse of the picturesque, deepened with romantic tones as Dickens stared back into the penumbra of his lost days. The sunset-track glimmering redly over the waters came to represent the passage back into the mystery, into death and birth, into the deep patterns.

And so, when many years later all the accepted supports of his life began to fall away, he turned back to Rochester and Chatham, and moved there from the London which now increasingly represented his defeat. For long his thoughts had kept homing that way, building up a day-dream story out of some chance occurrence in the walks with his father. They often used to go up to Gadshill, a spot of high ground on the main road between Rochester and Gravesend, from which they could look down on the sea and its sailing ships. An itinerary which gave John Dickens a chance to call in at the delectable Falstaff Inn. On the hill stood a fine red-brick house with magnificent cedars.

In a fantasy of the 1860's, when Gadshill was his own residence, he wrote as follows.

"Halloa!" said I, to the very queer small boy, "where do you live?"
"At Chatham," says he. . . .
I took him up in a moment, and we went on. Presently, the very queer small boy said, "This is Gadshill we are coming to, where Falstaff went out to rob those travellers, and ran away."
"You know something about Falstaff, eh?" said I.
"All about him," said the very queer small boy. "I am old (I am nine), and I read all sorts of books. But do let us stop at the top of the hill, and look at the house there, if you please."
"You admire that house?" said I.
"Bless you, sir," said the very queer small boy, "when I was not more than half as old as nine, it used to be a treat for me to be brought to look at it. And now, I am nine, I come by myself to look at it. And ever since I can recollect, my father, seeing me so fond of it, has often said to me, 'If you were to be very persevering and were to work hard, you might some day come to live in it.' Though that's impossible!" said the very queer small boy, drawing a long breath, and now staring at the house out of the window with all his might.
I was rather amazed to be told this by the very queer small boy;

for that house happens to be my house, and I have reason to believe that what he said was true.

No doubt something like that happened. John Dickens was not the man to miss a chance for pontifical effects of rhetoric. But he must have improved the shining hour by hundreds of such moralizing comments. The reason why this one stuck and became portentous was because it chimed with something deep in Charles himself.

Forster mentions that he and Dickens passed the place by often in the years before Dickens bought it, and Dickens never failed to repeat the anecdote. Mamie Dickens says, "I have heard him tell this story over and over again, when he had become the possessor of the very place which had taken such a hold upon his childish affections. Beyond this I cannot recall a single instance of any allusion being made by him to his early childhood."

VIII

It was at Chatham also that Charles developed his main bias in religion, a hatred of Nonconformity—to which was later added an equal hatred of Catholicism. The mainspring of this attitude seems to have been his revulsion from the discomfort and terror of services in the Baptist Chapel. He tells how as a child he went off on a Sunday to steam in the unventilated bath of the powerful Boanerges Boiler, till all his small mind was steamed out.

In which pitiable plight I have been haled out of the place of meeting, at the conclusion of the exercises, and catechized respecting Boanerges Boiler, his fifthly, his sixthly, and his seventhly, until I have regarded that reverend person in the light of a most dismal and oppressive character. . . .

I have sat under Boanerges when he has specifically addressed himself to us—us, the infants—and at this present writing I hear his lumbering jocularity (which never amused us, though we basely pretended that it did), and I behold his big round face, and I look up the inside of his outstretched coat-sleeve as it were a telescope with the stopper on, and I hate him with an unwholesome hatred for two hours.

This kind of picture is repeated again and again. We meet it in the cramped Bethel to which Kit and his mother go; or the room where Mrs. MacStinger listens to the Rev. Melchisedeck Howler (discharged from the docks on suspicion of making gimlet holes into puncheons) when the rapturous behaviour breaks the floor down and throws the congregation into the kitchen below, to the detriment of a mangle. Its smell clings to Chillop and Murdstone in *Copperfield*, or the Doubly Seceding Little Emanuel Persuasion in a Christmas Story. Mrs. Varden was "most devout when most ill-tempered." Stiggins and Chadband are oily characters of unmitigated hypocrisy and greed, crooks and parasites of the most revolting kind; and Hawkyard and Gimlet of *George Silverman's Explanation* are no better. Here we find a savagely hostile account of the rolling of the converted brothers and sisters on the floor amid the self-righteous shrilling of hymns. But the climax comes in the terrible picture of religious hatred and gloom surrounding Mrs. Clennam in *Little Dorrit*; for now the attack on puritanism and its commercial ethic is not incidental. It stands right at the heart of the whole definition of contemporary society.

Dickens's attitude to Nonconformity is thus entwined with his essential judgments on life. Since it exists strongly from the outset of his career, it represents a primary point of critical dissent from the lower middle-class world out of which he comes. A point of dissent to which he holds fast in his early years and which ultimately widens into a complete break between him and the values of the money world. To understand the integrity of his art and life we must grasp this fact.

In his early pamphlet, *Sunday under Three Heads* (1836) he makes an uncompromising assault on Nonconformist values. He depicts at bitter length a chapel Sunday.

There is something in the sonorous quavering of the harsh voices, in the lank and hollow faces of the men and the sour solemnity of the women, which bespeaks this a stronghold of intolerant zeal and ignorant enthusiasm. . . .

The preacher is a coarse hardfaced man of forbidding aspect, clad in rusty black as he calls upon the Sacred Founder of the Christian faith to bless his ministry, in terms of disgusting and impious familiarity not to be described. . . .

He stretches his body half out of the pulpit, thrusts forth his arm with frantic gestures, and blasphemously calls upon the Deity to visit with eternal torments those who turn aside from the word, as interpreted and preached by—himself. A low moaning is heard, the women rock their bodies to and fro, and wring their hands.

The preacher goes on wallowing in his lurid account of hell. "A great excitement is visible among his hearers, a scream is heard, and some young girl falls senseless on the floor."

His anger at the deadening way in which the poor were forced to spend Sunday remained undiluted to the end of his days. Once, when dining with Lord John Russell, he seized a chance to make a fierce attack on the Lord's Day Observance Act, "giving them a little truth about Sunday that was like bringing a Sebastopol battery among the polite company." Meyerbeer, who was there, couldn't control his delight and cried out, "*Ah, mon ami illustre! que c'est noble de vous entendre parler d'haute voix morale à la table d'un ministre!*"

Catholicism did not come his way during childhood; but as soon as he reaches intellectual maturity, he classes it with Non-conformity as a regressive force. He sees it mainly as a form of political and economic reaction. Since it does not belong to his childhood world, it scarcely enters his novels; but his letters and his pictures from Italy state scathingly his utter abhorrence of all its forms. His *Child's History*, crude and summary as it is, treats the Catholic Church consistently as a strange and ugly remnant of barbarous times.

The Anglican Church comes off better, but largely because he sees no reason for taking it seriously at all. He makes fun of curates in *Boz*, and has a nastily obsequious Rev. Timson. *Sunday under Three Heads* mocks at the fashionable clergy, and is caustically dedicated to the Sabbatical Bishop of London. Of the same ecclesiastic he later wrote, "I cannot but bethink me that it was not until this year of grace 1848 that a Bishop of London first came out respecting something wrong in poor men's social accommodations." And his general attitude remained always detached and strongly critical. Thus he wrote in 1864 to Cerjat, "As to the Church, my friend, I am sick of it. The spectacle presented by the indecent squabbles of priests of most denominations, and by the exemplary unfairness and rancour with which they conduct their differences . . . utterly repel me." He disliked missionaries, "who," he said, "(Livingstone always excepted) are perfect nuisances, and leave every place worse than they found it."

Anglicans do not figure importantly in his books. There is a harmless clergyman with a large family in *Our Mutual Friend*; and *Edwin Drood*, amid its imagery of decay draped round the cathedral, has one sympathetic ecclesiastic, who holds a hint of Kingsley's muscular and socially-conscious Christianity. But for him the more typically Anglican figure is the Dean advising, "Do nothing emphatically."

39

For a short while, partly under Forster's influence, Dickens became a Unitarian. But he preferred not to make the question of creed a conscience matter. His own position was simple. He saw Christ as a morally perfect person, and praised the Bible "because it teaches the best lessons" (so he wrote to a son going off to Australia) "by which any human creature who tries to be truthful and faithful to duty can possibly be guided." And his Will, drawn up in his last years, reiterates his impatience with any theological discussion whatever.

The Rev. Boiler, who seems to have started off this revulsion from church services, was presumably Mr. Giles of Chatham; but Charles may well have been taken to other chapels than his at Portsmouth or Chatham, and it would therefore be unfair to make a flat identification. The family life of the Dickenses, whatever its shortcomings, was easy-going and lacking in compulsions. Charles did not go to school till he was about nine, and then studied under the friendly William Giles. Only, then, in the chapel did he come up against a form of authority full of threats and violences. Therefore it is easy to understand why the child's fears gathered round a resistance to the claims of the preacher as the only obvious menace, the only dangerous authority, within view. Boanerges Boiler comes to represent the external world in its dark and repressive aspect, threatening to come with hell fire between the child and its enjoyments, its claims to the mother. All the fears in the child, which have already, for one reason or another, come to look on those enjoyments as entailing something forbidden, are given a new force by the shouting preacher.

Hence the central part played by Charles's hatred of Nonconformity in his life and work. From the first it is the one point at which he is at odds with the respectabilities of his world, and it gradually broadens until it embraces his whole critique of Victorian society, his final condemnation of its basic values. Further, in his fidelity to this attitude, which might so easily have broken his close link with his public, we touch his fundamental honesty, his artistic sincerity. He had his problem of resistances and conformities like any other artist, and sometimes he ran into confusions and made mistakes; but his conformity was never mercenary or insincere. And his development was a steady breaking down of what was false (because imperfectly realized); a steady breaking through into a fuller truth, human and artistic.

The origins of his attitude to religion thus lie early and deep;

but a later contributory attitude was perhaps the antagonism he felt to the pious singer whom Fanny married.

And so we come near the end of Charles's Chatham days. The question he kept on asking, in later life, was the question which the ghost asked in the story, *The Ghost in Master B's Room*: "Where is my little sister, and where is the boy I went to school with?" And it was no use for him to answer jestingly, "I entreated the phantom to be comforted, and above all things to take heart respecting the loss of the boy he went to school with. I represented to him that probably that boy never did, within human experience, come out well." For the phantom wasn't so easily put off. In *The Haunted House*, 1859, Charles wrote, "Ah, me! ah, me! no other ghost has haunted the boy's room, my friends, since I occupied it, than the ghost of my childhood, the ghost of my own innocence, the ghost of my own airy belief." But that wasn't any more effective as a complete answer. A ghost of innocence and a ghost of guilt equally haunted that room, and made it impossible for him to forget. He, like the ghosts, went on returning to find out.

"Every little incident, and even slight words and looks of those old days," he wrote in *Nickleby*, "came fresh and thick before him many and many a time, and, rustling above the dusty growth of years, came back fresh green boughs of yesterday." There in the past, in the dead years, were the green shoots, the sources of life and renewal. "Memory," he insisted, "however sad, is the best and purest link between this world and a better." That better world was for him childhood, "when everything was happy," as he said in *Chuzzlewit*, "when there was no distance and no time."

41

2

Boyhood: London

I

IN the winter of 1822–23 John Dickens was transferred back to Somerset House, with salary unchanged. The family sold some of its heavier goods—Mary Weller's sweetheart bought some of the parlour chairs—and the rest of the things were sent off by water. They themselves, all except Charles, went off by stagecoach to settle in 16 Bayham Street, Camden Town, with a small unnamed slut from Chatham Workhouse (original of the Marchioness) and James Lamert, who still hadn't got his commission. Charles was left with Giles to finish the term.

In *Copperfield* he describes the scene, with a characteristic touch of yearning and resentment towards the mother:

I think, as Mrs. Micawber sat at the back of the coach, with the children, and I stood in the road looking wistfully at them, a mist cleared from her eyes, and she saw what a little creature I really was. I think so, because she beckoned to me to climb up, with quite a new and motherly expression in her face, and put her arm round my neck, and gave me just such a kiss as she might have given to her own boy. I had barely time to get down again before the coach started, and I could hardly see the family for the handkerchiefs they waved. It was gone in a minute.

In the day-dream of the novel the excluded boy is left with the Orfling from St. Luke's Workhouse: in fact the orphan went off with Fanny, Letitia, Harriet, Fred, and baby Alf. The displacement is made because it helps to emphasize the sense of Charles's own fear and loss. For the first time he was parted from his mother, and he didn't like it, even though he was being left in the best of hands for the best of reasons.

He seems to have stayed on till the term ended in early spring, though the death of Harriet through smallpox may have called him away prematurely. The night before he left, Giles came flitting among the packing cases, with a set of Goldsmith's *Bee* as a present: a work that had considerable effect on Charles's style. And then Charles was put, he says, into Timpson's (actually Simpson's) coach, the *Blue-eyed Maid*—which, in retrospect, he compared with Locomotive No. 97 that brought him back later to Chatham. As this coach started from Brompton, it was more convenient than the *Commodore* (which Forster cites) driven by Old Chumley, who was to some extent the original of Old Weller in *Pickwick* and who appears in Nimrod's *Northern Tour* with the argument: "If the Railway blows up, where are you? Now if a coach overturns, *there* you are!"

Through all the years that have since passed, have I ever lost the smell of damp straw in which I was packed—like game—and forwarded, carriage paid, to the Cross Keys, Wood-street, Cheapside, London? There was no other inside passenger, and I consumed my sandwiches in solitude and dreariness, and it rained hard all the way, and I thought life sloppier than I had expected to find it.

In London he arrived in time to share another decline of fortune. The house, with four rooms as well as basement, garret and outhouse, was on the outer fringe of the city, near the arboured tea gardens of Chalk Farm, not yet spoiled (as Forster, writing after the railways had blighted the area, imagined). Country walks ran between little groups of town houses; and close by was a field, inviting in hay-time. Mrs. Dickens liked to visit Mother Redcap's tea gardens, with its odd little watchman's box near at hand. The view was pleasant, "with delightful vistas of far-distant hills and vales" dotted with mansions. Dairy farms and drinking wells attracted London visitors. But the house, despite the walks and the view, was a come-down, a cheap out-of-the-way ramshackle place.

But there were consolations. Charles liked to go to the head of the street, where a row of almshouses stood, and look over at London. Through the scarfing veils of smoke he could make out the dome of St. Paul's; and he felt a keen curiosity about the great city.

Here, indeed, we touch Dickens's basic attitude to London. For some uncritical reason he has been often written about as a great Cockney, as pre-eminently a Londoner. Nothing could be farther from the truth. He is the lad from a country town—from Dullborough, as he calls it in *The Uncommercial Traveller*, seeking a generic term. The lad from a country town who comes up to know and master the metropolis. The interest he had shown in

Chatham and Rochester and their environs, the way in which he had woven the towns and the landscape into his inner drama and its multiple perspectives of fantasy, he now transferred to London. He is approaching puberty, and the need to know and master is sharpening, coming to a more intense focus. On the one hand, the few months when he has been left alone at Chatham, removed for the first time from the mother-warmth that meant so much to him, have strengthened his fears. On the other hand, he has returned to the maternal bosom, in the bewildering circumstances of the new London environment, to find an increasing shadow of distress on the family. His extreme sensitiveness to such family tensions, his sudden sense of Time dragging him away from the old securities into new dark pressures of fear, his inability and his need to grasp what is endangering the united family life—all this conspired to make him want to know and master London, to plant his fantasy-life as richly and satisfyingly inside it as he had planted it inside Chatham and Rochester. "Neglected and miserable as he was," says Forster acutely, "he managed gradually to transfer to London all the dreaminess and all the romance with which he had invested Chatham."

And so he climbs the slope to look out over the roof-tops and fields at the vast, smokily monstrous city, in which his fears and his hopes are both lodged.

I was taken home, and there was Debt at home as well as Death, and we had a sale there. My own little bed was so superciliously looked upon by a power unknown to me, hazily called "The Trade," that a brass coal-scuttle, a toasting-jack, and a bird-cage, were obliged to be put into it to make a Lot of it, and then it went for a song—so I heard mentioned, and I wondered what song—and I thought what a dismal song it must have been to sing.

But there was the city on which to pour out his speculations; and now and then the intensely absorbing experience of a walk into it. He especially liked to loiter round Covent Garden and the Strand; and St. Giles exercised a fascination of fear. "Good heavens," he exclaimed to Forster, "what wild visions of prodigies of wickedness, want and beggary, arose in my mind out of that place."

But he was still subject to fits of illness, and that circumscribed his movements. Also, in the sinking household, he was left to do much of the housework, clean boots and brush clothes. School seemed forgotten; and now, compared with his menial tasks, it shone as a place of freedom and honour. In the forbearing way he generally wrote about his father in later years, he said:

I know my father to be as kindhearted and generous a man as ever lived in the world. Everything that I can remember of his conduct to his wife, or children, or friends, in sickness or affliction, is beyond all praise. By me, as a sick child, he has watched night and day, unweariedly and patiently, many nights and days. He never undertook any business, charge or trust, that he did not zealously, conscientiously, punctually, honourably discharge. His industry has always been untiring. He was proud of me, and had a great admiration of the comic singing. But, in the ease of his temper, and the straitness of his means, he appeared to have utterly lost at this time the idea of educating me at all, and to have utterly put from him the notion that I had any claim upon him, in that regard, whatever.

In fact this zealous, conscientious, etc., man had simply washed his hands of family responsibilities altogether, was affably waiting for something to turn up, and had handed the situation over to his worried wife.

James Lamert was still with the family, and in his leisure he made a small theatre for Charles, painted it and fitted it out. They played old farces and dramas with puppets; and into this game of make-believe Charles could release all the emotions and needs for which there was now no outlet in play with other boys. To make things worse, Charles lost the companionship of Fanny for the first time. She had shown considerable aptitude for music, and was entered on the books of the Royal Academy of Music— "for the piano," recommended and nominated by T. Tomkisson, a pianoforte maker of Dean Street, who had perhaps been teaching her. She was admitted April 9, 1823, and continued her studies, uninterrupted by the family vicissitudes, until midsummer 1827.

The blow of losing Fanny's close companionship was exacerbated by the circumstances in which Charles lost her. While he was declining into a household drudge, she was being petted, praised, and advanced on to a lofty level of study. "He has told me what a stab to his heart it was," said Forster, "thinking of his own disregarded condition, to see her go away to begin her education, amid the tearful good wishes of everybody in the house."

To help him to acclimatize his emotions to the London scene, Charles had visits to pay to his grandmother in Oxford Street, where he heard her fairy stories and her homely wisdoms, and to two admiring gentlemen, uncle and godfather. The uncle was Tom Barrow, who with his wife lived over a bookshop in Gerrard Street, Soho. He had injured his leg in an accident, and ended by losing it. Charles spent much time in attending to him, acting as "his little companion and nurse"; and he also came to know the woman who ran the bookshop, the widow of a Mr. Manson. She lent him books which included Holbein's *Dance of Death* and George Colman's *Broad Grins*. Forster tells us that Colman's poems "seized his fancy very much" and were the cause of his intense interest in Covent Garden. So interested was he that "he stole down to the market by himself to compare it with the book. He remembered, as he said in telling me this, snuffing up the flavour of the faded cabbage-leaves as if it were the very breath of comic fiction." One more example of the way in which characteristic smells left a strong impress on Dickens's memory.

But his reaction to Colman was more than a matter of cabbage smells. *The Elder Brother*, the piece that so interested Dickens, throws much light on the boy's emotions at the time. Not so much for the description of Covent Garden itself, which is slight:

> Centrick, in London noise, and London follies,
> Proud Covent Garden blooms, in smoky glory;
> For chairmen, coffee-rooms, piazzas, dollies,
> Cabbages, and comedians, fame'd in story!

Nothing much there to strike the imagination of Charles with such a powerful effect. What struck him was the story of the poem, and it was that story which made Covent Garden so significant. For it tells of a collision in the dark between a child-birth doctor who specializes on unmarried mothers and a "staid young man," an orphan. Crow was the doctor:

> He was *obstetrick*;—but, the fact is,
> He didn't in Lucina's *turnpike* practise;
> He took *bye-roads*,—reducing Ladies' shapes,
> Who had secure'd themselves from leading apes
> But kept the reputation of virginity.

In the same house lodged Shove, the orphan, who had high expectations from "a fusty, canting, stiff-rump'd Maiden Aunt." He puts in a bell, with a notice *please to ring*, so that he won't be disturbed by the callers for Dr. Crow. One night, as he prepares to go to bed, "as naked as his mother bore him: barring his shirt and night-cap on his head," a drunken Jolly Dog or Choice Spirit sees the notice and thinks it a joke to take it at its word. He rings; then after an exchange of words with the annoyed Shove, gives a thunderous knock. Dr. Crow takes the knock as a call from one of his clients, goes down and collides with Shove, whom he takes to be a person sent from Shove's maiden aunt, who is with child. In the confusion he gives away his mistake.

> "Zounds!" bellows Shove, with rage and wonder
> wild,
> "Why then, my *maiden* Aunt is *big with child*!"

He goes off to take up the matter with the aunt in person, thinking that his fortunes are ruined. She however quietens him by saying:

> "Your fortune will continue much the same;
> For,—keep the Secret—you're his *Elder Brother*."

An odd poem indeed to have so fascinated the boy aged about twelve. It is full of equivocal jests, e.g. "He had one foot in bed, More certainly than cuckolds go to heaven." Shove, on the stairs, cries out, "From all such plagues I'll quickly be deliver'd," and the puzzled Dr. Crow takes him up:

> "You be deliver'd?" says the Doctor,—"Sblood!"
> Hearing a man's gruff voice—"You lout! you lob!
> You be deliver'd!—Come, that's very good!"
> Says Shove, "I will, so help me Bob!"

Clearly, the poem appealed to Charles because of his own bewildered resentment at his mother's pregnancies, a resentment now brought to a head by his own apparent neglect and exclusion (in comparison with the lucky Fanny or the more indulged small children). And his nearing puberty has quickened his interest in matters of sex and child-bearing. The orphan, who turned out to have a rich "maiden aunt" or true mother, was a figure which could slip into his day-dreams with ease. His strong reaction to this rather poor poem, which has been entirely undiscussed by biographers, reveals the turmoil in his mind and heart. His anxious eagerness to see Covent Garden had in it a hope to find there some answer to the question: What was dislodging him from the safe lap of his mother's protection? What hope was there for him? What was the truth

of relationship under his own quivering emotions and the concentrated tumult of London activities?

That he was perhaps stylistically affected by Colman's type of
humour can be seen by considering a passage from the poem:

> These spendthrifts, who Life's pleasures, thus, out-run,
> Dozing, with head-aches, till the afternoon,
> Lose half men's regular estate of Sun,
> By borrowing, too largely, of the Moon.
>
> . . . And being *Bacchus plenus,*—full of wine,—
> Although he had a tolerable notion
> Of aiming at progressive motion,
> 'Twasn't direct,—'twas serpentine,
> He worked, with sinuosities, along,
> Like Monsieur Corkscrew worming thro' a Cork;
> Not straight, like Corkscrew's proxy, stiff Don Prong,
> A Fork.

Now Charles made his first efforts at writing about the world
round him. His uncle was shaved by an old barber of Dean
Street, who had a passion for reviewing Napoleon's mistakes
and rearranging his life on better lines. Charles composed a
sketch about him, but was too shy to show it round. Also,
basing himself on the account of the canon's housekeeper in
Gil Blas, he described an old lady who waited on the family at
Bayham Street, and made delicate hashes with walnut ketchup.

He was also visiting his godfather Huffam and reviving his
memories of Limehouse. Huffam still delighted in the boy's
comic songs; and through him Charles came to know the
Thames, its wharfs and odd craft, its watermen and its houses
on the bank, half afloat at high tide. And he loved the journeys
home from Limehouse, through a London strange in its glooms
and flaring lights.

II

Under the shadow of the Debt and a mysterious Composition
Deed which accompanied it, Charles fell ill with fever. When he
recovered the Deed was still hovering about. Then in Michaelmas
1823, Mrs. Dickens had a brave idea. As John Dickens was doing
nothing about the burden that was crushing the family, she
herself would turn money-earner. In short, she'd start a school.
The family, in a sudden burst of confidence and decision,
moved from its obscure locality to a good house at 4 Gower

Street North (later 147 Gower Street); and the tenancy was taken in Mrs. Dickens's name. The rate books show that she held it from March 1823, to Lady Day 1824, at £50 a year. Possibly Huffam had been drawn in as a part-guarantor.

Somehow she managed to furnish a portion of the house and put up a brass plate on the door: MRS. DICKENS'S ESTAB-LISHMENT. Handbills were printed, and hopes ran high for a while. Charles says that he felt "perhaps even I might go to school myself." He and the little workhouse girl went round pushing the handbills into letter-boxes and under doors.

But nothing happened. Nobody came; and Charles could not recollect "that the least preparations were made to receive anybody." What he ignored in his satirically bitter account of this venture of his mother's was the fact that she had been relying on Huffam to use his connections at court and in commerce and to gain her the nucleus of pupils she needed for a start. And Huffam chose this moment to go bankrupt. No further help could be looked for from him, and so her attempt foundered.

The episode, which Charles used to mock at his mother's incompetence, was in fact a tribute to her courage and her capacities. But its failure meant that nothing except collapse lay ahead for the family. In all his comments on the situation Charles shows not the least inkling of the way in which his mother must have been at her wit's end; he has much sympathy for his father, who is ignoring the whole problem, but none for his mother's gallant efforts to grapple with things. In his self-pitiful refusal to see anything of her dilemma he exposes the deep pang of exclusion that obsesses him.

James Lamert was unable to stand the miseries of the household any longer, and left to go into business, relinquishing his commission to a younger brother. Charles's little library was taken from the chiffonier and sold, book by book, to a book-seller in Hampstead Road. The stall-man lived in a little house at the rear, got drunk every night, and was fiercely abused next morning by his wife. Charles used to arrive early enough to find the man in his turn-up bedstead with a cut brow or a black eye and to watch him looking with shaky hands for the needed coins in the pockets of his clothes, while the wife, with baby in arms and trodden-down slippers, ceaselessly went on scolding. Often as not, there'd be nothing, and the man would say call again; then the wife would intercept Charles on the stairs and give him the money from her own hidden stock.

Charles also came to know the inside of a pawnbroker's shop, where the assistant, while making out the duplicates, liked to hear him conjugating his Latin verbs. At last only a few chairs and beds, with one kitchen table, were left at Gower Street; and the family camped in two parlours of the big empty house.

Then came the blow which left a lifelong bruise, seeming to bring his worst fears and suspicions true. James Lamert had gone into partnership with his cousin George, who was running a blacking factory at 80 Hungerford Stairs, Strand, near Charing Cross. George had bought the firm from Jonathan Warren for an annuity, despite the fact that the more prosperous concern of Robert Warren contested Jonathan's claim to have invented the blacking. In the easy-going manner of the period, Jonathan's firm purloined the advertisements and trademarks of Robert's, and in its address printed Hungerford Stairs very small and STRAND very big, since Robert's factory was in the Strand itself. James now, knowing the collapse of the Dickenses' fortunes, offered to take Charles in to do odd jobs in packing the blacking; and Mrs. Dickens snatched at the chance.

To her it meant a chance to get a small bit of order into the lost household and to put Charles on comparatively solid ground. To Charles it meant the final betrayal. He never forgave his mother for accepting the offer, and round his sudden violent anger there gathered all the past elements of fear and distrust. Under the shock he revalued the whole of the past. Emphasis now swung on to the aspects of loss and loneliness; and he saw his childhood as the churchyard garden in which he and Fanny had wandered in their small pathetic love, homeless on earth but united in a star of longing.

The blow was made all the dramatically worse by being timed for his twelfth birthday, February 7, 1824. The day which should have happily celebrated his link with the mother had been made the occasion of his cruel cutting off.

How correct was Mrs. Dickens's estimation of the family impasse was shown by what happened about a fortnight later. John Dickens was arrested at the suite of one James Karr for a £40 debt and carried off to the Marshalsea. He was entered in the Day Book of Commitments as Dicken, on February 20, 1824, and stayed in the prison till his discharge on May 28th. His last words, as he went, were that the sun had set on him for ever. "I really believed at the time," commented Dickens to Forster, "that they had broken my heart." Not a word about his mother and her troubles.

In *Copperfield* he tells the story, though throwing a faint veil over the facts by changing the Marshalsea into the King's Bench Prison. However, we also have his personal statement of the period; and since the whole episode was so crucial in his development, we had better follow closely his own words.

My father was waiting for me in the lodge, and we went up to his room (on the top story but one) and cried very much. And he told me, I remember, to take warning by the Marshalsea, and to observe that if a man had twenty pounds a year, and spent nineteen pounds nineteen shillings and sixpence, he would be happy; but that a shilling spent the other way would make him wretched. I see the fire we sat before, now; with two bricks inside the rusted grate, one on each side, to prevent it burning too much coal. Some other debtor shared the room with him, who came in by-and-by; and, as the dinner was a joint-stock repast, I was sent up to "Captain Porter" in the room overhead, with Mr. Dickens's compliments, and I was his son, and could he, Captain P, lend me a knife and fork?

Captain Porter lent the knife and fork, with his compliments in return. There was a very dirty lady in his little room; and two wan girls, his daughters, with shock heads of hair. I thought I should not like to have borrowed Captain Porter's comb. The Captain himself was in the last extremity of shabbiness; and if I could draw at all, I would draw an accurate portrait of the old, old, brown great-coat he wore, with no other coat below it. His whiskers were large. I saw his bed rolled up in a corner; and what plates, and dishes, and pots he had, on a shelf; and I knew (God knows how) that the two girls with the shock heads were Captain Porter's natural children, and that the dirty lady was not married to Captain P. My timid, wondering station on his threshold, was not occupied more than a couple of minutes, I dare say; but I came down again to the room below with all this as surely in my knowledge, as the knife and fork were in my hand.

Here, as in so many passages, he harps on his powers of observation as a child, and we see clearly revealed the reasons for this claim. He is insisting that he sees through the adult world and its tricks and devices; he is not being taken in. The child is not deceived, he keeps insisting. You may pretend as much as you please, but the child sees the truth. He, Charles, was never deceived.

The remarks about the Porter family give all this away. He didn't in fact know anything about them, and he still didn't know anything while he was writing so confidently about the

bastardy of the girls. He simply palms off his suspicions as a
proof of his insight, his refusal to be taken in. What he is saying
is no more than this: I have been aware all the while of the network of falsity and lies which surrounds me—you may snare
me in it, but you can't fool me.

He started off on a Monday morning at the factory—if one can
dignify the small workshop with that name—at six shillings,
soon (it seems) raised to seven.

It is wonderful to me how I could have been so easily cast away
at such an age. It is wonderful to me, that, even after my descent
into the poor little drudge I had been since we came to London, no
one had compassion enough on me—a child of singular abilities,
quick, eager, delicate, and soon hurt, bodily or mentally—to suggest
that something might have been spared, as certainly it might have
been, to place me at any common school. Our friends, I take it,
were tired out. No one made a sign. My father and mother were
quite satisfied. They could hardly have been more so, if I had been
twenty years of age, distinguished at a grammar school, and going to
Cambridge.

This is not simply a restatement of his boyish emotion; it is
his mature judgment on the situation. (And it is of interest that
in the *George Silverman* story, written many years after the
autobiographical notes, he does send his day-dream self to
Cambridge.)

The blacking warehouse was a tumbledown house overrun
with rats and abutting on the river. "Its wainscotted rooms and
its rotten floors and staircase, and the old grey rats swarming
down in the cellars, and the sound of their squeaking and
scuffling coming up the stairs at all times, and the dirt and decay
of the place, rise up visibly before me, as if I were there again."
Always that insistence on immediacy of memory, on a clarity of
observation that can't be deceived! The swarming of the rats
could not but have revived the horrors of Mary Weller's tale
of Chips, in which the rats symbolize the loss of one's soul to
the devil, the dreadful nemesis coming on the person guilty of
cheating, of surrender to the money-ways of the world.

In a recess in the counting-house on the first floor he sat and
worked, looking out over the coal-barges. His job was to tie up
the blacking-pots neatly in oil-paper and blue-paper; then to
paste the labels on. Two or three other boys did the same job
downstairs; and one of these, Bob Fagin (whose name was used
in *Oliver Twist*), showed him how to do the tying-up. Lamert

had promised to give Charles some lessons around noon, but he soon found that he couldn't squeeze them in. And soon, too, Charles's gentlemanly seclusion on the first floor was ended, and he had to join the other boys below—Fagin and Paul Green (called Poll, like Sweedlepipe of *Chuzzlewit*). "Bob Fagin was an orphan, and lived with his brother-in-law, a waterman. Poll Green's father had the additional distinction of being a fireman, and was employed at Drury Lane Theatre; where another relation of Poll's, I think his little sister, did imps in the pantomimes."

Not such uncongenial company, one would think. But for Charles they represented a fall into the hopeless morass of the dispossessed, the broken, the brutalized.

No words can express the secret agony of my soul as I sunk into this companionship; compared these everyday associates with those of my happier childhood; and felt my early hopes of growing up to be a learned and distinguished man, crushed in my breast. The deep remembrance of the sense I had of being utterly neglected and hopeless; of the shame I felt in my position; of the misery it was to my young heart to believe that, day by day, what I had learned, and thought, and delighted in, and raised my fancy and emulation up by, was passing away from me, never to be brought back any more; cannot be written.

My whole nature was so penetrated with the grief and humiliation of such considerations, that even now, famous and caressed and happy, I often forget in my dreams that I have a dear wife and children; even that I am a man; and wander desolately back to that time of my life.

Fanny was safe at the Academy. Charles and the rest of the family, except John Dickens, were still living at Gower Street North. As it was a long way to tramp back from Charing Cross, he generally took his dinner with him or went to a shop for a saveloy and penny loaf, or a fourpenny plate of beef. Sometimes he had bread and cheese with beer at a pub. Once he ventured with his own bread into an alamode beef-house in Clare Court and magnificently ordered "a small plate of alamode to eat with it." The waiter fetched another waiter to have a look at the odd customer. "I gave him a halfpenny, and I wish, now, that he hadn't taken it."

On Saturday nights he walked home with his wages proudly jingling, looked into the shop windows, and bought Hunt's Roasted Corn (a British and patriotic substitute for coffee), which he roasted on Sunday. He also bought periodicals, in

53

chief the *Portfolio of Entertaining and Instructive Varieties in History, Science, Literature, the Fine Arts, etc.*, for twopence, attracted by its burlesques of well-known plays.

John Dickens's negotiations with his creditors had had no success; and in consequence, as the future looked very dark indeed, Mrs. Dickens decided to give up the Gower Street house and go into the Marshalsea with all the children except Fanny and Charles. She may well have breathed a sigh of relief over having one of the family freed to some extent from the general misery; but to Charles he was the only really miserable and lost one of the group.

I (small Cain that I was, except that I had never done harm to any one) was handed over as a lodger to a reduced old lady [Mrs. Roylance], long known to our family, in Little-college-street, Camden-town, who took children in to board, and had once done so at Brighton; and who, with a few alterations and embellishments, unconsciously began to sit for Mrs. Pipchin in Dombey when she took me in.

She had a little brother and sister under her care then; somebody's natural children, who were very irregularly paid for; and a widow's little son. The two boys and I slept in the same room. My own exclusive breakfast, of a penny cottage loaf and a pennyworth of milk, I provided for myself. I kept another small loaf, and a quarter of a pound of cheese, on a particular shelf of a particular cupboard; to make my supper on when I came home at night.

He bought this food himself, but his mother paid for his lodging. "No advice, no counsel, no encouragement, no consolation, no support, from any one that I can call to mind, so help me God." On Sundays he went to the Academy in Tenterden Street at nine o'clock, to fetch Fanny; and they walked to the Marshalsea, where they stayed for the day. Often on a weekday he spent his dinner-money on stale half-price pastry on his way to work, and then had only a roll or slice of pudding at midday. Pudding indeed was a great problem, as he had to choose between the shop with a cheap article, heavy and flabby, with sparse raisins, and the shop with a more expensive well-curranted product. At the half-an-hour off for tea, he bought half-a-pint of coffee and a slice of bread-and-butter, or, if hard up, stared at the pineapples in Covent Garden. At the coffee-shop in St. Martins Lane:

in the door there was an oval glass-plate, with COFFEE-ROOM painted on it, addressed towards the street. If I ever find myself in a very different kind of coffee-room now, but where there is such an inscription in glass, and read it backward on the wrong side MOOR-EEFFOC (as I used to do then, in a dismal reverie), a shock goes through my blood.

He had by now become as handy at the work as the other boys; but prided himself on being spoken of as "the young gentleman." The foreman and a carter named Bob sometimes went so far as to call him Charles—"but I think it was mostly when we were very confidential, and when I had made some efforts to entertain them over our work with the results of some of the old readings, which were fast perishing out of my mind. Poll Green uprose once, and rebelled against the 'young-gentleman' usage; but Bob Fagin settled him speedily." He felt himself hopeless and abandoned for life, and felt the ache of his fall every minute of the day.

That I suffered in secret, and that I suffered exquisitely, no one ever knew but I. How much I suffered, it is, as I have said already, utterly beyond my power to tell. No man's imagination can overstep the reality.

One day, however, he burst out to his father about his unhappiness at the lodgings. His mother then promptly found him a back-attic "at the house of an insolvent court agent, who lived in Lant Street in the Borough, where Bob Sawyer lodged many years afterwards. A bed and bedding were sent over for me, and made up on the floor. The little window had a pleasant prospect of a timber-yard; and when I took possession of my new abode, I thought it was a Paradise."

Now he could breakfast with the family in the Marshalsea, where Mrs. Dickens had finally found a calm refuge. At last he had something on which to build a sound resentment; for in jail (where the £6 salary was being duly paid by the benevolent Civil Service) the family weren't doing so badly. "They had no want of bodily comfort there," he noted. The Chatham maid-of-all-work still came in to tidy up; and as he lounged by London Bridge, waiting for the jail gates to open, she often joined him. He passed the time by telling her remarkable tales about the wharves and the Tower. "But I hope I believed them myself."

He had supper as well as breakfast in the jail, and so was in no sense parted from the family. In his lodgings, too, he had a pleasant couple to look after him, a fat good-natured lame old fellow, with a quiet old wife and "an innocent grown-up son also lame." Once when Charles had a spasm in the night, the three of them sat up till morning at his bedside. Bob Fagin, too, was very kind to him when an attack of his disorder came on. He made a straw-bed for him in the first-storey recess and filled blacking bottles with hot water and kept applying them to his side half the day. Then he embarrassed Charles by refusing to let him go home alone. Charles could not bear to let him know about the jail, so at last in desperation he pretended to go up the steps of a house near Southwark Bridge on the south side and knock on the door. When a woman opened, he asked if Robert Fagin lived there,

He still enjoyed his Saturday nights. Often on his way home a show-van seduced him and he went in to see the Fat Pig, the Wild Indian, the Little Lady. Again we find his strong sense of smell associations:

> There were two or three hat-manufacturers there, then (I think they are there still); and among the things which, encountered anywhere, or under any circumstances, will instantly recall that time, is the smell of hat-making.

John Dickens for a while had hoped to escape having to ask the benefit of the Insolvent Debtors' Act; but in vain. It was then necessary to have his entire property sworn at £10, and Charles had to go before an appraiser near the Obelisk and have his clothes valued. He had in his pocket a large silver watch his grandmother had given him, and he feared it might be valued at £20; but the beery official merely smiled at his white hat, jacket and corduroy trousers, and said "That'll do."

A few times he played in the dinner-hour with Green and Fagin on the barges; but mostly he strolled about the back streets and explored the Adelphi arches. One of his discoveries was a little pub by the river called "Fox Under the Hill," which was gained via an underground passage. There he had the vision he mentions in *Copperfield* of sitting eating something on the bench outside, one fine evening, and watching the coal-heavers in a dance. "I wonder what they thought of me." Another evening after going on an errand for his father he entered a pub in Parliament Street and for some festive reason asked "What is your very best—the VERY *best*—ale, a glass?" The landlord said twopence. "Then just draw me a glass of that, if you please, with a good head on it." The man, queerly smiling, called his wife, who came out with her work in hand.

> Here we stand, all three, before me now, in my study in Devonshire-terrace. The landlord, in his shirt-sleeves, leaning against the bar

window-frame; his wife, looking over the little half-door; and I, in some confusion, looking up at them from outside the partition. They asked me a good many questions . . . to all of which, that I might commit nobody, I invented appropriate answers . . . and the landlord's wife, opening the little half-door and bending down, gave me a kiss that was half-admiring and half-compassionate, but all womanly and good, I am sure.

Again the moment of "observation," in which he is suddenly aware of everything going on, is one of self-pity, of doubt and scrutiny into relationships. He feels quite outside himself, and sees the scene from some external point, floating about himself, like some detached spirit of judgment, like a criminal investigator.

During these months he certainly often thought about running away, back to Chatham, back to the garden of childhood. The day-dream took the form of running off from the present unsatisfactory parents to the loving ones of the past. It is writ large in *Copperfield* and its anxiety-aspect provides the whole dynamic of *Oliver Twist*. Further, one of Dickens's stories, as usual, gives us the fantasy in simplified form. Here it is *The Perils of Certain English Prisoners* (1857), told by a Foundling Child who is employed to scare birds at Snorridge Basin (one of the spots taken in by the Chatham walks). The narrator lives with a shepherd who is perhaps his father, who keeps him in conditions of extreme hardship, and who beats him. The boy at last, unable to bear his miseries any longer, runs away. "Which was what he'd wanted all along, I expect." That is the typical suspicion of the child who feels unwanted and hardly-treated. They want to make me run away, to get rid of me.

During his last days at the Marshalsea John Dickens organized a petition among the prisoners. In *Copperfield* the petition has a noble aim, praying for the abolition of imprisonment for debt. The actual petition was for leave to drink the King's health on his birthday. John Dickens was far-sighted at least in matters concerning drink; for the birthday was not till August 12th. Charles sat in a corner of the room and observed the prisoners while Captain Porter read the petition out—"my poor father listening with a little of an author's vanity, and contemplating (not severely) the spikes on the opposite wall." When he visited the prison after work, he used to get his mother to tell him all she knew about the various prisoners;

and on the occasion of the petition he was able to look them all over. All the details "were written indelibly upon my memory."

Then came the one chance which could have rescued John Dickens. His mother died in April 1824; and William, the trusted son, arranged for the service in the church where she had been married. She had been quietly living on the interest of her savings and her Crewe pension, and left an estate sworn at £20 with £750 stock which she had transferred to William in 1813. Her settled distrust of John is shown by the fact that she appointed William her sole executor, and, in the event of his death before hers, his wife and a T. Paul. She wasn't going to let John have a finger in anything. That she had lost all patience with him is proved by her failure to intervene when he was jailed. Knowing John, we cannot doubt that he made application for aid to her as to the Barrows, and that he was turned down. However, now she was dead, and she left £250 to him, explaining the discrepancy between the shares of the two brothers in her money by the fact that John had had "several sums of money some years ago."

William at once paid £40 into court, and John was discharged on May 28th. He had been in the Marshalsea less than a hundred days.

Either near the end of 1823 or some time during the Marshalsea days, Fanny had won a prize at the Academy, and Charles was taken along to witness the presentation. He felt utterly humiliated. "I could not bear to think of myself—beyond the reach of all such honourable emulation and success. The tears ran down my face. I felt as if my heart were rent. I prayed, when I went to bed that night, to be lifted out of the humiliation and neglect in which I was. I never had suffered so much before. There was no envy in this." Envy in it there certainly was, but indeed envy was far too meagre a term to express the anguish which he felt. Fanny's glory was in every way for him a riveting of his own conviction of loss and rejection.

III

The family now went to live in Little College Street with Mrs. Roylance; but in their uncertain circumstances Charles was left at his job. John Dickens, during his jailing, had petitioned the Hon. W. Huskisson, asking to be recommended for a superannuation grant on the grounds of ill-health, enclosing a medical certificate that he had a chronic affliction of the urinary organs. Now his whole position was in doubt, for he had taken advantage of the Insolvent Debtor's Act and should in consequence lose his Civil Service position. On the other hand, there were the couple of hundred pounds that had come out of the blue.

The blacking works was prospering and there were a couple of new boys. Fagin and Charles had grown very dexterous at tying the pots up. They worked near a window, and people used to stop and watch them.

Then one day, soon after the release from jail, John Dickens picked a quarrel with James Lamert. Charles himself took the letter which caused the explosion. "It was about me. It may have had some backward reference, in part, for anything I know, to my employment at the window." John Dickens, it would seem, didn't mind his son tying up pots, but he wouldn't have people knowing about it. Possibly, however, the quarrel was about a more serious matter, Lamert's inability to carry out his promise of giving Charles some lessons. Anyway Lamert told Charles that "he was very much insulted about me; and that it was impossible to keep me, after that. I cried very much partly because it was so sudden, and partly because in his anger he was violent about my father, though gentle to me."

What seems certain is that John Dickens's new-found dignity was hurt at seeing his son doing a manual job in public—though a streak of kindness may well have mingled with the egotism. But for Charles all that mattered was that his father had come to the rescue. His father had understood; his father had shown himself a true father.

This emotion was strengthened by the fact that Mrs. Dickens, facing the economic issues, was upset and wanted to have the boy sent back to his job. She went to see Lamert, patched things up, and returned with the request that Charles should resume work. "My father said I should go back no more, and should go to school. I do not write resentfully or angrily: for I know now all these things have worked together to make me what I am: but I never afterwards forgot, I never shall forget, I never can forget, that my mother was warm for my being sent back."

Thus the drama of his childhood, his fears and hopes centring round his mother, came to a head, to this apparently rather ordinary anger, a banal bit of egotism. However we look at it,

59

we cannot but be struck by the extreme overvaluation of his misfortune—or rather the disproportion between the external causes and the anguish that he undoubtedly experienced. Most analysts have either taken his bitterness at its face-value—have seen in the small boy the great Charles Dickens with all his claims on special treatment. Or they have dismissed the emotion as sadly unbalanced, almost megalomaniac. Both judgments are equally irrelevant.

To understand his sufferings we must see them in terms of his previous childhood drama, his enormous powers of fantasy-projection and the complicated way in which he had woven his day-dreams round his mother and Fanny. His whole sense of worth, his whole claim to security, had been staked on his ability to command his mother's attention and love; and when she seemed to cast him out and yet to cherish Fanny, he felt his very identity obliterated.

No other understanding can make sense of the episode or explain that obviously sincere agony of his. No other under-standing can explain how the tensions of this moment enter into all his works and determine his fundamental attitudes.

At no time was he really cut off from the family. His worst period was that at Mrs. Roylance's, which can have lasted, however, only a few weeks. Yet Mrs. Roylance, grim as she was, was a friend of the family; and at the first hint that he was unhappy, he was found new lodgings, which he liked. He started work in February, and stopped shortly after his father's release in April. But he—and Forster following his lead—wrote about the episode as if it took years. Charles himself says, "I have no idea how long it lasted; whether for a year, or much more, or less." And telling about the time he asked for the Very Best Ale, he adds, "It may have been my birthday, or some-body else's." Yet he could not have forgotten that he started on his twelfth birthday, so that his comment suggests that he imagined the job lasted well over into 1825. And these con-fusions are those of a person who prided himself on his clear memory of childhood.

While he was at work, his mother visited the establishment continually; but his father came only a few times.

Another important aspect of the episode was the deep emotion of shame and fear it left him with. Obviously, some of the roots of this were social in the simple sense; he was snobbishly ashamed of admitting the lapse from middle-class gentility. And from this angle we can judge something of the terrible fear of the lower middle-class that they would fall back into the struggling miserable mass of the proletariat of those years. But any examination of the terms of Charles's statements will make clear that the fear had deep psychic causes, which went beyond any conscious social attitudes, any simple issues of prestige.

Charles's desperate effort to whelm the whole episode in darkness and silence is the measure of the awful defeat it represented for him. It was his period of hell; and though it haunted him throughout his days, it involved him in a passionate need of secrecy. In the personal notes which he found it impossible to publish he wrote:

From that hour until this at which I write, no word of that part of my childhood which I have now gladly brought to a close, has passed my lips to any human being. I have no idea how long it lasted. . . . From that hour, until this, my father and my mother have been stricken dumb upon it. I have never heard the least allusion to it, however far off and remote, from either of them, I have never, until I now impart it to this paper, in any burst of confidence with anyone, my own wife not excepted, raised the curtain I then dropped, thank God.

In fact, he never told his wife. She and everyone else knew nothing about the blacking works till Forster told the story in his *Life* after Dickens's death. The autobiographical fragment goes on with an astonishing statement of phobia:

Until old Hungerford-market was pulled down, until old Hungerford-stairs were destroyed, and the very nature of the ground changed, I never had the courage to go back to the place where my servitude began. I never saw it. I could not endure to go near it. For many years, when I came near to Robert Warren's in the Strand, I crossed over to the opposite side of the way, to avoid a certain smell of the cement they put upon the blacking corks, which reminded me of what I was once. It was a very long time before I liked to go up Chandos-street. My old way home by the borough made me cry, after my eldest child could speak.

In my walks at night I have walked there often, since then, and by degrees I have come to write this. It does not seem a tithe of what I might have written, or what I meant to write.

Note there once more the peculiar sensitiveness to smell-associations.

He told Forster about the blacking factory against his will. Forster made a chance enquiry about a C. W. Dilke. Charles said at once that he had met Dilke only at his uncle Tom Bar-row's rooms in Gerrard Street. Never anywhere else. Forster then remarked that there must have been some mistake, for Dilke had seemed to refer to some job Dickens had had as a boy in a warehouse near the Strand. There Dilke, happening to be with John Dickens, had given the person in question half-a-crown and received a very low bow in return. Dickens was silent for several minutes, but did not resume the subject. Then some weeks later he confessed to Forster about "a time of which he could never lose the remembrance while he remem-bered anything, and the recollection of which, at intervals, haunted him and made him miserable, even to that hour."

Yet though he zealously guarded his secret in all personal relations, in his work he found himself compelled to return to it again and again. How could it be otherwise? His roots as a creative writer lay in the enigmatic Eden of his Chatham days; he had to keep on continually returning to it, probing it for its sources of lyrical delight and trying to grasp its tragic conse-quences. Socially he was almost as ashamed about his father's jailing as he was about his own warehouse job; the two matters were closely entwined. Yet he found it difficult to keep away from the subject; and throughout, in dealing with the forbidden personal material, he left the most glaring clues, the most obvious trails of personal connection with supposed fictional events and persons. Even the name of Warren's Blacking keeps on intruding, or a reference to the blacking trademarks. Thus in *Hard Times* Bounderby refers to one of the famous Warren advertisement devices, bragging that the only pictures he'd looked at as a boy were the illustrated labels of "a man shaving himself in a boot on the blacking bottles." And Henry (Charles's son) mentions an episode that occurred one Christmas night shortly before his father's death. At Gadshill they had been playing a memory game. One person named an object, the next person repeated the word and named something else, and so on, till the list gaew too long for someone's memory-powers. Dickens, whose leg had been giving him trouble, was lying on a sofa. At his turn, he repeated the list and added, with "a strange twinkle in his eye and a curious modulation in his voice": *Warren's Blacking, 30 Strand*. At the time none of his children knew the point of the phrase. But when they read Forster's *Life*, they understood. The name of the game, Memory, had brought out from their father his most rankling image.

Dickens himself never wavered in his belief that the sufferings of 1823 left a permanant bias in his character. In June 1862 he wrote to Forster, at the time when his marriage had collapsed and he was proceeding to outrage the core of Victorian morality:

I must entreat you to pause for an instant, and go back to what you know of my childish days, and to ask yourself whether it is natural that something of the character formed in me then, and lost under happier circumstances, should have reappeared in the last five years. The never to be forgotten misery of that time, bred a certain shrinking sensitiveness in a certain ill-clad ill-fed child, that I have found come back on the never to be forgotten misery of this later time.

What was at fault in his analysis was his isolation of that period of unhappiness as a disaster unrelated to the whole set of tensions operating through his childhood days. But where his conscious analysis failed, his creative intuition picked up and went on reviving the old day-dreams, expanding them in terms of his adult experience, using them to provide a focus for penetrating into the inner meaning of the historical movement entangling him.

What, then, in the final analysis gave the terrible urge to secrecy (coupled with an equal urge to blab everything)? If the account of Charles's childhood given above is correct, then the death-wish was central. The wish to arrest life at the point of maximum harmony, maximum unity. To possess the mother in perfect security and peace, to abide at the source of life, holding its horn of plenty. And because this wish stirred up a sense of antagonism to the father, who kept on spoiling its fruition, there was set into motion a secondary drama, which came more and more to the forefront: the wish to find in union with the sister the peace, plenty, harmony, which had been denied by the mother. Then the union of brother and sister would be a perfect moment of love, rooted in defiance of parental authority but thriving because of that very defiance.

The dramatization of Charles's baffled love for his mother thus worked itself out in his relations to Fanny. But now, in 1823, when the Chatham delights were finally ended and he moved towards puberty, the mother rejected him in a way that cut him to the heart and at the same time the dramatization of union with Fanny was rudely shattered. Fanny went off into a life of seeming satisfaction and high prestige, solving her own problem of contact and conflict; Charles was left alone, in a desecrated earth, to confront the full retort of affronted authority. The desperate desire to have the mother all his own in her role of protector and sustainer became an unavailing but passionate death-wish directed towards her. It failed, and the retort it seemed to provoke was thus all the more terrifying. This retort took the form of Charles being thrown aside out of the family circle, to fend for himself while paralysed with fear.

Hence the joy he feels when at last his father seems to relent and to remove the curse, the judgment of death. He has finally lost the mother, but a new basis of union has emerged between himself and his father. Hence the lenient view he takes in his judgments of John Dickens. And hence, too, the way in which his future work will show an enduring resentment against his mother and Fanny—whether this resentment takes direct form in the depiction of nagging and idiot women, or veiled form in the glorification of young girls or women whom the death-wish successfully lays out. Mrs. Nickleby, on the one side, and Little Nell on the other.

But in order to break through into those resolutions of the deep guilt-sense apparent in his bleak terror during 1823 he had to make several efforts to find stable relations with other women; and the story of his success and failure in that respect will be told later. For the moment we must return to his boy-hood.

IV

After perhaps a brief stay at Hampstead, the family rented a house in Johnson Street, Somers Town. The tenancy lasted from July 1824 to July 1827. Tenancies are now taken in the name of Mrs. Dickens, and by an accident (the striking out of only the surname of the previous tenant) she appears in the rate-book as Caroline Dickens. On July 30, 1827, we find Caroline Dickens "applied for time to pay, or relief." They were in difficulties once more.

Meanwhile they were living in Johnson Street and managing to pay the rates. The house was poor, but near it lay the fields between Somers and Camden Town; an air of faded gentility make it unlike the others, which were nearly all built "in a monotonous pattern." The locals tended to throw out into the roads any odd trifles they didn't want, such as old shoes, bonnets, umbrellas, and bent saucepans.

Mr. Dickens's case went through all the necessary channels. It passed from the hands of the Treasurer of the Navy to Croker, Admiralty Secretary, who laid it before the Commissioners and the First Lord. Croker told Huskisson (December 1, 1824) that Mr. D. had gone Insolvent and so must depart from the Navy Pay Office. Still, in consideration of six children and twenty years of service he was given on compassionate grounds a retired allowance of £145 a year. ("A yearly saving of £114 13s. 4d. will be for some time affected to the public by the difference between a new Clerk at £90 and Mr. Dickens's salary of £350." This logic had been accepted, but the 13s. 4d. was knocked off in the interests of book-keeping.)

Mr. Dickens decided to follow up his literary bent. He applied to his brother-in-law, John Barrow, now editor and owner of *The Mirror of Parliament*, for work as a political reporter. Now, oddly, near the age of forty he appears proficient in shorthand—possibly aided by Barrow—and in January 1825 was parliamentary reporter for *The British Press*.

The glimpse we have had of his style in the report on the Chatham fire is confirmed by remarks which Charles made later. Thus, speaking of a doctor's departure from Genoa, Charles said:

We are very sorry to lose the benefit of his advice—or, as my father would say, to be deprived, to a certain extent, of the concomitant advantages, whatever they may be, resulting from his medical skill, such as it is, and his professional attendance, in so far as it may be so considered.

And he cited as examples of his father's style:

(*a*) I must express my tendency to believe that his longevity is (to say the least of it) extremely problematical.

(*b*) The Supreme Being must be an entirely different individual from what I have every reason to believe Him to be, if He would care in the least for the society of your relations.

Charles was now able to go to school again. S. C. Hall, connected with *The British Press*, saw him about this time and described him as "a handsome lad gleaning intelligence in the byways of the metropolis." The school chosen was Mr. Jones's Classical and Commercial Academy in Granby Street, Mornington Crescent—Wellington House Academy, according to the notice-board over the door. Charles, sent to get the card of terms, found Jones a portly man, carving at the table with a pair of holland sleeves on his arms. Jones turned out a teacher addicted to the rod, heavy-footed, and no scholar: but with the sense to choose capable assistants. He was always ruling copy-books with a bloated ruler that he used on offending small boys, viciously drawing their pantaloons tight with one hand and hitting with the other; and he made vacation visits to parents in a yellow hackney.

Charles naturally arrived with a strong sense of contrast between the school and the Marshalsea or the blacking works. "My mind ran upon what they would think," he wrote in *Copperfield*, "if they knew of my familiar acquaintance with the King's Bench? Was there anything about me which would reveal my proceedings in connection with the Micawber family —all those pawnings and sellings and suppers—in spite of myself?"

One of the boys, Dawson, wrote later that it was "a very superior sort of school, one of the best indeed in that part of London; but it was most shamefully mismanaged, and the boys made but little progress." They said that the head knew nothing and one of the ushers knew everything. The schoolroom was a detached wooden structure, with three rows of desks—the boys sitting each side and facing one another. An excellent arrange-ment for tricks as soon as the master's eye strayed. The play-ground was spacious. When Dickens visited the place later, he found that the schoolroom had been sliced off by the Birming-ham Railway; the playground had been swallowed and a corner of the house pared off.

The railway, in fact, seemed following up his past, turning his Chatham playing fields into a waste, devastating the green of Camden Town, and then smashing up his London school. This feeling of pursuit by the railway was to have an important effect on his later life.

He was advanced enough to be put into Virgil, gained some prizes, rose to be first boy. (This rosy account was to some extent contested by his school-fellows.) In *Copperfield* he refers to embellishments in copybooks where the titles of elementary rules of arithmetic diverged into swans, eagles, griffiths, and capital letters went ecstatically out of their minds.

The boys had their own systems of amusement and edifica-tion. They trained white mice better than the masters trained the boys. Also bees, red-polls, linnets, and canaries were kept in desks, drawers, boxes. But white mice were the favourites. One grew so learned as to trot up ladders, draw Roman chariots, shoulder muskets, turn a wheel, and act creditably on the stage as the Dog of Montargis; and might have risen even higher if in a triumphal progress it had not fallen into an inkwell and been drowned. Pumps and boats were constructed, driven by mice-power.

One of the boys remembered Charles as a "healthy-looking boy, small but well-built, with a more than usual flow of spirits, inducing to harmless fun, seldom if ever to mischief." He held himself unusually erect and had an air of smartness; wore a weekly suit of pepper-and-salt, with turndown collar instead of usual frill—which made him look older than others of his age. Nothing suggested his coming literary fame. He invented, or brought with him a lingo, made by adding a few letters of the same sound to every word. "And it was our ambition, walking and talking thus along the street, to be considered foreigners." (Another boy calls it simply gibberish and says Charles spoke it before he came to the school.)

A second description from this time runs: "A handsome, curly-headed lad, full of animation and animal spirits" who "probably was connected with every mischievous prank in the school. I do not think he came in for any of Mr. Jones's scourging propensity." It was the boarders like the Keys, mulatto boys, especially Frederick, who got the beatings, as they couldn't run home with tales. There were some Key girls too, under Mrs. Jones's control; and Frederick and his sister have been thought the originals of Neville Landless and his sister Helena in *Edwin Drood*.

For a while Charles took lessons in violin playing, but soon dropped them. Theatricals, however, as throughout Dickens's life, turned up and became of absorbing interest.

We were very strong, too, in theatricals. We mounted small theatres, and got up very gorgeous scenery to illustrate the *Miller and his Men* and *Cherry and Fair Star*. I remember the present Mr. Beverley, the scene painter, assisted us in this. Dickens was always a leader at these plays, which were occasionally presented with much solemnity before an audience of boys, and in the presence of the ushers.

Young Beverley made a mill in such a way that an explosion of crackers would blow it into pieces. Once, the blast was so loud that the police came knocking on the door.

Another boy recalled a play performed in the back kitchen of one of them, Tobin; and thought it wasn't written out and learned. Only the rough plot was settled, and the play was then developed extempore.

They carried their miming high spirits into actual life.

I quite remember Dickens on one occasion heading us in Drummond-street pretending to be poor boys, and asking the passers-by for charity—especially old ladies; one of whom told us she "had no money for beggar boys." On these adventures, when the old ladies were quite staggered by the impudence of the demand, Dickens would explode with laughter and take to his heels.

Here we catch him in the act of miming the part of the Lost Child, the Orphan, which held so central a place in his day-dream fears and hopes. And the next anecdote brings out his resistance to the atmosphere of chapel.

I met him one Sunday morning shortly after he left the school, and we very piously attended the morning service at Seymour-street chapel. I am sorry to say Master Dickens did not attend in the slightest degree to the service, but incited me to laughter by declaring his dinner was ready and the potatoes would be spoiled, and in fact behaved in such a manner that it was lucky for us we were not ejected from the chapel.

He was reading penny-dreadfuls and Saturday magazines with avidity. In a letter he says, "I used, when I was at school, to take in the *Terrific Register*, making myself unspeakably miserable, and frightening my very wits out of my head, for the small charge of a penny weekly; which considering that there was an illustration to every number, in which there was always a pool of blood, and at least one body, was cheap." Once again he was himself making an attempt to write. Bowden, a boarder, and Charles used to issue weekly *Our Newspaper*, written out on bits of copybook paper and pinned together; and lend it round on payment of marbles or slate-pencils. It contained comic advertisements and scraps of news, such as:

Lost.—Out of a gentleman's waistcoat pocket, an acre of land; the finder shall be rewarded on restoring the same.

Lost.—By a boy with a long red nose, and green eyes, a very bad temper. Whoever has found the same may keep it, as the owner is better without it.

Another boy says, "I think at that time Dickens took to writing small tales, and we had a sort of club for lending and circulating them."

Thus, outwardly enduring a classical education that left little marks on him, he was in fact being given by the school routine the group-contacts and the leisure for the release of fantasy in group-forms of play.

It went on till some date before Easter 1827.

NOTE.—The relations of course did all they could from simple snobbishness to hush up or lie about the blacking firm. Thus, when Charles was seeking a newspaper-job, his uncle John Barrow, replied to an enquiry, "At one time he had assisted Warren the blacking man in the conduct of his extensive business among other things had written puff verse for him. In this way as well as others he had shown ability." Note the attempt even to suggest that it was the *big* Warren firm.

3

Youth

I

WHILE Charles was still at school, his uncle, William Dickens, died at the age of forty-three (in December 1825). Thriftily unlike John, he left some £1,300, to be shared after his wife's death among his nephews and nieces. Yet another nephew turned up with a claim on this testament, when Mrs. Dickens bore Augustus, her last child, in 1827.

Charles took a job in the offices of Charles Molloy, solicitors, of 6 Symonds Inn, but stayed only for six or seven weeks. He wanted something better, and his father tried to help him. Someone asked, "Pray, Mr. Dickens, where was your son educated?" John replied, "Why, indeed, Sir . . . ha! ha! . . . he may be said to have educated himself." An aunt of Mrs. Dickens, Mrs. Charlton, kept, with her husband, a boarding house in Berners Street, and Mrs. Dickens often visited her with the children. Among the boarders was Edward Blackmore, junior partner of Ellis and Blackmore, solicitors of Gray's Inn; he knew the Dickenses and was asked to help Charles.

"He was a bright clever-looking youth," he said later, "and I took him for a clerk. He came to me in May 1827, and left in November, 1828." The salary was 13s. 6d. a week, raised after the first month to 15s. Charles kept the petty-cash books and did odd jobs, registering wills and serving processes.

In *Pickwick* Charles retails the various grades of attorney's clerk. His own present status was below that of the articled clerk who had paid a premium and had an attorneyship in sight, below that of the full-salaried clerk who could afford 30s. a week on his pleasures, even below that of the seedy middle-aged copying clerk. Rather on the level of the office boys who in their first surtout feel contempt for schoolboys, club together on their way home for saveloys and porter, and think there's nothing like life. He told Wilkie Collins later that he "didn't much like it."

His interest in theatricals revived as soon as he was at home in his job. A fellow clerk named Potter abetted him. "They took every opportunity," said Blackmore, "then unknown to me, of going to a minor theatre, where (I afterwards heard) they not infrequently engaged in parts." No evidence of these parts has been forthcoming. Dickens himself never mentioned them, and biographers have tried to pooh-pooh the whole idea. But Dickens was never voluble (except in his writings) about his shabby past; and probability is on the side of Blackmore's account. Old Tom Didbin, for instance, was having trouble in making ends meet at Sadler's Wells and was ready to use amateurs for odd parts. Certainly Charles's interest in private theatricals never wavered.

In one of the *Boz Sketches* Charles appears (as Smithers) having a night out with the more adventurous and obstreperous Potter. "There was a spice of romance in Mr. Smithers's disposition, a ray of poetry, a gleam of misery, a sort of consciousness of he didn't exactly know what, coming across him he didn't precisely know why—which stood out in fine relief against the off-hand, amateur-pickpocket-sort-of-manner, which distinguished Mr. Potter. . . ." Together, they wandered about London, its fashionable and its disreputable haunts, and knew all its theatres, from Covent Garden to the dingy suburban halls.

But all the while he was studying hard at shorthand, stimulated by his father's example and aided by his uncle John Barrow (now reporting for *The Times* and *The Morning Herald* and meditating his *Mirror*, which began in January 1828). He bought Gurney's *Brachygraphy*, costing 10s. 6d., and went through the agonies of mastering the system, which are recounted in *Copperfield*. Yet something in him enjoyed the mastery of such mysteries—the part which kept watching people for the secret clue, which had carried on the school lingo, and which made him later quickly adept in French and Italian. There is a verve of excitement in his words. "The wonderful vagaries that were played by circles; the unaccountable consequencies that resulted from marks like flies' legs; the tremendous effects of a curve in the wrong place; not only troubled my waking hours, but reappeared before me in my sleep." He ended by becoming the finest shorthand reporter in England.

But meanwhile the family, having applied for relief from rates at Johnson Street, had to get out, perhaps were thrown out. In November 1828 they moved to The Polygon, in the higher-class part of Somers Town; and in the same month Charles took the important decision to leave his clerk's job. He set up as a free-lance reporter in one of the offices in Doctors' Commons, joining his cousin Tom Charlton in the Consistory Court. They rented a box and sat waiting for custom: also sharing the costs of a private room or transcribing office in Bell's Yard, Paul's Chain.

Paul's Chain, on the south side of St. Paul's Church, led through an archway into a shady stone courtyard overlooked by red-brick houses. A green baize door with brass nails admitted to Doctors' Commons and a huge tangle of obscure legal survivals. Attached to the place were various sinecure appointments in the gift of the Lord Chancellor. And here, more than in the solicitor's office, Dickens came to know his legal types. Here was the Court of Arches, with bewigged counsel in red gowns and proctors in fur collars, dealing with various ecclesiastical matters; the Consistory Court of the Bishop of London; the Prerogative Court covering testimentary matters in the dioceses, with its office for registering and filing the wills; and the Admiralty Court. The proctors were a sort of monkish attorney (according to *Copperfield*) whose contact with reality ended a couple of centuries earlier; and Doctors' Commons was there to play all sorts of tricks with obsolete old monstrous Acts of Parliament. "A cosey, dosey, old-fashioned time-forgotten, sleepy-headed little family party," with an ancient monopoly in suits about wills and shipping disputes. (It was abolished in 1857, and its jurisdiction taken over by the new Probate Court.) The reports were taken in a room like a dis-senting chapel, with doctors in grey wigs and red gowns and the judge blinking over a small pulpit-desk. Some of those reported by Charles are extant in the archives of St. Bartholomew's Church, in his transcripts: cases of trouble over the church rates and uproars in the vestry.

He gained a very low opinion of the law indeed; and to the end of his days he considered it largely made up of unnecessary formalities and organized injustice. Shortly before his death, on May 2, 1870, he reiterated his conviction that our legal system was fundamentally warped and unjust, based on the need to preserve inequalities and maintain greed. "I have that high opinion of the law of England generally, which one is likely to derive from the impression that it puts all the honest men under the diabolical hooves of all the scoundrels."

Here, then, arrives his second point of break with contemporary society. As a child he rebelled against the one form of threatening authority which he came up against—religion in the guise of the dissenting chapel—and never thereafter relented in his resistance to what he looked on as a darkening and distorting force. Now, his first proper job of work brought him up against another form of authority, the law, and he decided that it, too, was essentially a form of considered and organized oppression.

But he was enjoying himself, getting at grips with the world. He said these were the two most useful years of his life. He soon established his reputation as a first-rate reporter, but as yet there was no vacancy in the ranks of parliamentary reporting.

His interest in the stage was unabated. He used to study the playbills, and went to see a show almost every night, especially never missing the comedian C. Mathews. At the same time he was scribbling. He wrote an adaptation of Goldoni's play, *La Vedona Scoeton*, calling it *The Stratagems of Rozanza: A Venetian Comedietta* by C. J. J. Dickens. The manuscript seems in his mother's hand, but has little drawings which may be by Charles—he later had a habit of scrawling such in his letters. The play opens with a song, *Long live the bottle! Long live mirth!*, but entirely lacks any original flavour.

His restless uncertainty of aim appears in his wish to get away from England altogether. An aunt from Demerara visited England; and he sounded her for possibilities in the West Indies. This was the first of the many semi-projects of emigration that caught him up. The aunt didn't encourage him, but the thought of the West Indies remained, to come in *Barnaby Rudge*; Joe the hero loses his arm "at the defence of the Sal-wanners" and would have gone back but for Dolly, and his old father dies with the utopian cry—the cry of the realized day-dream, "I'm a-going, Joseph, to the Salwanners."

John Dickens was continuing with his journalistic career; but its ups and downs are hard to follow. He seems to have shown much energy of mind in acquiring shorthand; but he could not sustain effort, and no doubt his reporting jobs were not so satisfying to his literary ambition as he had imagined.

73

However he now got a job on *The Morning Herald*, and the family moved to Fitzroy Street.

Charles was seriously applying himself to his work, but he wasn't sure what he wanted to do. The one obvious goal ahead was the position of parliamentary reporter. Meanwhile as soon as he was eligible, on his eighteenth birthday, he applied for a reader's ticket to the British Museum, and did some assiduous studying.

Fanny was now a lovely intelligent girl, with access to more cultured society than Charles had. Serjeant Ballantyne wrote of her as "a young lady of great talents and accomplishments who unfortunately died when still quite young." And on January 10, 1838: "Evening party at Leviens. Met Boz—looks quite a boy. His sister with him; she sang beautifully, is pretty, and I should think clever." At the Academy she had the chance to meet musicians and artists; and through her a group collected round the Dickenses. To some extent thus the deep breach between brother and sister was covered up, and Charles once more spent much time in her company; but things were not as they had once been, and Charles in the rapid expansion of his interests and capacities had no need that they should be. Only in so far as that romantic gleam of misery, which troubled Smithers, still shot across Smithers's creator, was the pang active—and with it the whole tangle of fears and baffled desires which collected in guilt and delight round the Eden of Chatham and still earlier times.

Among the friends thus gathered, for merry and musical evenings, at the Dickenses, were John Hullah (pioneer of music for the masses) and J. P. Harley, ex-pupils of the College of Music, Henry Austin, an artist, and Henry Kolle, who from the status of bank clerk rose to that of a business man dealing in quilt prints at Addle Street, Aldermanbury, and who liked singing. There were also the Rosses—two sons, John and William (later knighted) and three girls, Georgina, Janet, and Thomasina. The girls had charm and talent. In 1830 Janet painted a miniature of Charles; she married his uncle, Edward Barrow, and had a fair skill, gaining the praise of Benjamin West. For Georgina (apparently the eldest Miss Larkins of *Copperfield*) he wrote a poem *The Ivy Green*. Thomasina later contributed to *Household Words*.

Through Kolle, Charles Dickens was introduced into the family of a bank manager, George Beadnell, who also had three charming daughters. With one of these girls, who was a close friend of Fanny's, Charles fell head-over-heels in love. He was ready for such a passion. Family tradition had it that he began to feel love for Georgina Ross, but received no encouragement. He then transferred his emotions to Maria Beadnell.

II

Mr. Beadnell worked at Smith, Payne and Smith's Bank at No. 1 Lombard Street, and lived over the bank. The three daughters were Margaret, engaged to David Lloyd, a tea merchant, who was married on April 20, 1831; Anne, with auburn curls, who played the lute and was engaged to Kolle; and Maria, small and gaily pretty, so small and pretty that her friends called her the Pocket Venus. Her eyebrows tended to come together; she played the harp in a raspberry-silk dress cut at the top into vandykes, singing to it *Meet Me by Moonlight Alone*. She was friendly with Fanny Dickens and had a pet dog Daphne (the Gip of *Copperfield*).

Charles had grown quite friendly with Kolle (whose name he first mis-spelled Kollie). In an early letter he invited him to a ride and promised him a mount. "I am a poor judge of distance, but I should certainly say that your legs would be off the ground when you are on his back."

For some two years, at times with Kolle's complicity, the love of Charles for Maria went on. All the passion, all the love was on his side. Maria no doubt encouraged him to some extent, and enjoyed his wooing in its earlier phases. Letters to Kolle in 1830 give us glimpses of Charles getting a bad 5s. piece from a cabby, arranging parties for "knocking up a song or two," and giving a Christmas party at the end of 1830 at Fitzroy Street. Early in January there was a sickness in the Dickens family, and they all went for a fortnight to Highgate, to a house next door to the "Old Red Lion." Charles writes to suggest Kolle gives them a look up there. All the while, keenly in love, he was singing and acting with Fanny and her friends, going to the theatre, and perfecting his shorthand.

The musical parties had canalized his hopes of literary fame into attempts at verse. *The Ivy Green* which he had written for Georgina Ross was set to music at his own request by Henry Burnett, a staid young singer, who was fluttering round Fanny, and proved very popular. Later, the lines having been inserted into *Pickwick*, text and music were published, with a romantic cover of Gothic ruins in moonlight, and went into many editions. For the moment Charles had only the plaudits of the family group, but he was trying hard.

Mr. and Mrs. Beadnell did not look on him with much favour. Mr. Beadnell had somehow found out about John Dickens's period in the Marshalsea, and Mrs. Beadnell had definitely decided that she didn't want one of her girls marrying into the unreliable family. Margaret and Anne had married solid business men, and Maria was to do the same. Mrs. Beadnell therefore carefully found herself unable to remember the egregious young man's name, and called him Mr. Dickon, and otherwise showed her active lack of interest. But Charles was persistent.

April 1832 had seen the marriage of Margaret and Lloyd. In May there was a dinner at Lombard Street, to which Charles managed to get an invitation. Charles wrote a long poem, which he duly recited at the meal. Entitled *The Bill of Fare*, it was in part an imitation of Goldsmith's *Retaliation*. In it Charles gives a clear though artless picture of the group and of himself.

Mr. Beadnell appears as a fine sirloin of beef ("Though to see him cut up would cause no small grief")—and so on, each person present is equated with some food. The two unmarried girls are nice little ducks, very well dressed. Willie Moule is a trifle. But these culinary jokes are feeble, and can be passed over. Of more interest are the character sketches which follow. By an odd transition, Charles passes from the fancy of the people as various edible objects on the dinner table into a fancy of them all dead. They have rolled on to the floor one by one, and there they lie, not flattened with indigestion, but simply dead. "We'll say they're all dead." So he composes their epitaphs.

Mr. B. is praised as "beyond contradiction, an excellent man, and a good politician," a consistent reformer, friend of freedom and the ballot. Mrs. B. is perfection. She was "the means of first bringing me out." She is faultless and kind-hearted.

After this rather weak effort to curry favour with the hard-eyed Mrs. B., he escapes into the easier praises of the girls. Anne is "a truly delightful, and sweet-tempered girl." She is well-read—but this point is made only to drag in a wretched pun on Kolle as Collie Cibber, her favourite author. She sometimes wears her hair *à la chinoise*.

Then comes Maria, and he lets himself go.

I might tell you much, and I say it with a sigh,
Of the grace of her form, and the glance of her eye
I might tell of happy days now pass'd away
Which I fondly hoped they would never decay
But 't were useless—I should only those times deplore
I know that again I can see them no more.

Behind the fancy pretence that he is lamenting her decease on the dining-room carpet we catch a deeper note of regret; she is already pulling away from him, and he is pleading with her.

I linger here now, and I hardly know why,
I've no wish, no hope now, but this one—to die.
My bright hopes and fond wishes were all centred here
Their brightness has vanished, they're now dank and drear.
The impression that mem'ry engraves in my heart
Is all I have left, and with that I ne'er part.

Those lines were to become truer than he had meant them to be.

Has Maria left this world of trouble and care
Because for us she was too good and too fair,
Has Heaven in its jealousy ta'en her away
As a blessing too great for us children of clay.
All ye fair and beautiful, sadly come here,
And spring's early flowers strew over her bier.
Fit emblems are they of life's short fleeting day,
Fit tributes are they to her mem'ry to pay;
For though blooming now, they will soon be decayed,
They blossom one moment, then wither and fade.

She clasps to her heart a small form—a little white and liver-coloured dog that "would eat mutton chops if you cut off the fat." He is ready to change places with it. But in vain. And so, with this long funeral elegy, he leaves Maria flat on the floor and proceeds to the other corpses.

There is William Moule, an elegant young chap whom the lads envy and the girls anxiously await at parties. If he is late, it's not his fault. He lives fashionably "in the West" ("N.B.— The purlieus of Tottenham Court Road! ! !").

Then there are the Leighs of Clapton, a solid suburban family. Mr. Leigh, who likes his bottle and has a good-humoured face, is not drunk, just dead. Mrs. Leigh, friendly, good-hearted, intelligent in heedless scandal; and her daughter Mary Anne, "the greatest tormentor that I e'er knew," (who seems

to have been rather in love with Charles or who liked causing
mischief for its own sake):

> Whenever she met you, at morn, noon, or night,
> To tease and torment you was her chief delight.
> To each glance or smile she'd a meaning apply,
> On every flirtation she kept a sharp eye.
> Though,—tender feelings I trust I'm not hurting—
> She ne'er herself much objected to flirting. [A singular fact.]
> She to each little secret always held the candle,
> And I think she liked a small bit of scandal.
> I think, too, that she used to dress her hair well,
> Although Arthur said—but that *tale* I won't tell.
> In short she was always so terribly teasing
> So pretty she looked, her ways were so pleasing
> That when she had finished I used to remain,
> Half fearing, half hoping to be teased again.

Then came the elder Moules, more solid suburbanites. Mr.
Moule, hospitable (at whose board Charles has often dined),
never put out except by a rubber of whist; his wife amiable and
kind; her girl Louisa, the same pattern, only smaller in size;
the younger Moule girl, Fanny, with head turned by romance
or sentiment, who sits by herself in a corner and sighs, and who
lets you talk for an hour without taking a word in. Is it love,
hesitation, affectation? A remarkable thing that a girl should
take so much trouble to spoil her charms. And then, last of the
Moules, Joe, mad about soldiering, gold lace and redcoats,
battles and military bands.

Next, the Lloyds. Charles pauses to envy Mrs. Lloyd's fate:

> And I wish when with death I've my tete a tete,
> He'd do me the favour to take my away,
> When my prospect [*sic*] here were bright bloomy and gay.

Lloyd is a good fellow, but with a touch of the Tory since he
returned from Paris last summer. Finally come three odd male
guests. Dr. Beetham, a fanatic in buttoning himself up against
colds; Francis M'Namara, a good client of the florists, a fellow
with yellow gloves and wonderful waistcoats; and then Charles
himself:

> Last, here's Charles Dickens, who's now gone for ever
> It's clear that he thought himself very clever
> To all his friends' faults;—it almost makes me weep;
> He was wide awake—to his own fast asleep!
> Though blame he deserved for such wilful blindness
> He had one merit,—he ne'er forgot kindness.

His faults—and they were not in number few,
As all his acquaintance extremely well knew,
Emanated—to speak of him in good part,
I think rather more from his head than his heart,
No mortal means could this young fellow save,
And a sweet pair of eyes sent him home to his grave.

A poor enough poem, despite some touches of character-humour. But it gives quite a sidelight on his feelings at this rather obscure phase of his life. In view of what we know of his deep-rooted death-wish towards the beloved, it is surely of interest that this poem, starting off with an apology for imitating Goldsmith, goes on to forget all about Goldsmith's poem. *The Retaliation* appears in fact in the fantasy-act of killing off the entire company, after presumably eating them up as slices of beef, duck, trifle, and gooseberry fool.

In short, the emotional basis of the poem is crude and infantile, and in the key of the fancies of fear and hope we have found continually emanating from his childhood and carried on into his adult life. It can be no accident that he, who was to set the image of the dying young girl at the heart of his emotional stimulations, is met here at the outset of his adult love-life with an elaborated day-dream of not only the beloved lying lovely in death but also all the group who come between him and her equally prostrate. Finally, he lays himself out in order to be united with her. (The thought of her sister Anne in her honeymoon evokes the same death-wish: "And I wish when with death . . .").

The poem is so weak that one does not like to press any analysis of it too far. By itself, it would hardly amount to evidence of anything much, except of a very immature talent; but when we fit it into the general pattern of Charles's life it, too, yields its secret. In the first flushes of youthful passion Charles may be using very slight literary counters to express his inner life; but when we wash away their trivial exterior we find the same complex of forces, of hopes and fears, as we find everywhere else in his life and work. Under the pressure of frustration in his love he is reverting to his child-attitudes.

That he thought highly of the poem is shown by the fact that the copy we have of it is in John Dickens's handwriting. Charles must have read it out with much pride in the family circle. And in view of the romantic core of the death-wish in it, we may find some significance in the melancholic tone of the one earlier poem of his we have, the song he wrote for Georgina

Ross, which is all about ivy crawling over mouldering graves and bones of the dead.

He still went on wooing Maria with verses. "A sincere friend" had given her an album on November 17, 1827, probably her seventeenth birthday. Bound in dark green morocco, it had 140 pages for paintings, drawings, verses. Austin, the artist, was in love with Maria like Charles, and he did several pictures of her. She appears as a dumpling milkmaid with dangling sun-bonnet, as an untragical Dido (with her brother as Ascanius), and as the delectably enticing landlady of *Lodgings to Let*. A small, sweet, plump, kittenish thing enclosed in small sensuous vanities.

She herself wrote two poems in the book, glib and weak. "So I think that for lovers the summer is best," and "Happy a man may pass his life, If freed from Matrimonial chains." The latter poem hypocritically describes the female sex as addicted to "hypocrisy, deceit and pride." Her sisters and George her youngest brother, the Lloyds, Louisa and William Moule, and the naughty Mary Anne Leigh, all contributed. A poem signed F. E. D. is in the hand of Fanny Dickens; and there is music by J. H(ullah).

Charles wrote several poems for the book in 1831-32. A laborious *Acrostic* begins, "My life may chequered be with scenes of misery and pain." Then in November 1831 he breaks in with *The Devil's Walk* and *The Churchyard*. The former is a politically satirical poem, of the same sort as Coleridge's *The Devil's Thoughts*, Southey's *The Devil's Walk*, and Byron's *The Devil's Drive*. No doubt Dickens's inspiration came from the fact that in 1830-31 the general political agitation made Southey's poem topical once more, and many versions, some incorrect, with illustrations by Robert Cruikshank or T. Landseer, were issued. Dickens makes his devil visit the House of Lords, which he heard with hatred and pleasure:

> For he saw a few Nobles rich and proud
> War 'gainst the people and Prince,
> And he thought with pain though he laughed aloud
> Of the Wars in Heav'n long since.

Then he goes to Irving's Chapel, which fills him with pleasure and pride at being "among the Maniacs." After that he walks to Bristol "And he gaily laughed as he slowly stalked o'er a scene of desolation." Back in London he strolls in Regent Street "as some other great folk do," and is glad to meet his lying old friend, the Member for Preston. But passing down Lombardy Street he sees a lovely girl at a window, and weeps for "days now past recall." He thinks "of the bright angelic train and of his own wretched fall." He groans at "a dim cold feeling of what he had been"; and looks for the album to find the girl's name. Reading Charles's lines, he says with glee that they're worthy of himself, "for I'm sure they're *devilish bad.*"

This mixture of radical politics and romantic tears over a lost heaven of love is already highly typical of Dickens. He is here picking up a theme of the romantic poets, and giving it his own characteristic development.

The Churchyard is less interesting. It contrasts the slave of money-making and the true Christian, moralizes over the churchyard and the ruin of an innocent girl who dies. "But why pursue the painful theme?" A day of ultimate judgment will come. Even here, however, the theme of money against love, of love-guilt and the young dying girl, are indicative of his bent.

For the *Landlady* sketch by Austin, Charles contributes a poem wishing to have his home in this charming spot, with the key kept by Maria; and he copies out ten lines by Thomas Moore, "Here is one spot reserved for me."

So far he is still hoping strongly, despite a certain unease and a hearkening back to happier times. More and more he feels his whole sense of personal worth is bound up with the winning of the lovely elusive babbling pocket Venus.

III

Meanwhile Charles was tiring more and more of Doctors' Commons and impatient about getting a good chance as a newspaper reporter. After discussions with Fanny, he decided to turn to the stage. He had memorized a large number of parts by means of "a sort of Hamiltonian system"; practised at home before a mirror how to enter a room, sit down, or bow; and took lessons from an actor, Robert Keeley. In February–March, 1832, he wrote to Bartley, the manager of Covent Garden:

and told him how young I was, and exactly what I thought I could do; and that I believed I had a strong perception of character and oddity, and a natural power of reproducing in my own person what I observed in others. This was at the time when I was at Doctors'-commons as a shorthand writer for the proctors. And I recollect I wrote the letter from a little office I had there, where the answer came also.

There must have been something in my letter that struck the authorities, for Bartley wrote to me almost immediately to say that they were busy getting up the Hunchback (so they were), but that they would communicate with me again, in a fortnight.

Punctual to the time another letter came, with an appointment to do anything of Mathews's I pleased, before him and Charles Kemble, on a certain day at the theatre. My sister Fanny was in the secret, and was to go with me to play the songs.

I was laid up when the day came, with a terrible bad cold and an inflammation of the face; the beginning, by the bye, of that annoyance in one ear to which I am subject to this day. I wrote to say so, and added that I would resume my application next season. . . . See how near I may have been to another sort of life.

For the last time he was trying to carry on in his collaboration with Fanny. The cold, inflammation and ear-trouble, coming at such a moment of drastic choice, can hardly be other than a nervous affliction expressive of an intensely divided will. Something of him was resisting strongly the decision he had made in his discussions with Fanny.

This episode occurred in the middle of his agitation over Maria. He wanted very much to vindicate himself, to show that he had a superior talent of some sort, and to get revenge for Mrs. Beadnell's snubs and prove he could do more than sing comic songs in a drawing-room.

Close on the heels of his collapse over the theatre project, Charles at last found an opening in the reporting world. He joined the staff of *The True Sun*, a sevenpenny, which was appearing on March 5, 1832; and reached the House of Commons in time to take down the last speeches made during the committee stage of the Reform Bill—the third reading was passed on March 23rd, and the Bill was sent to the Lords three days later. The crisis about it in the Lords went on in May. Charles said that he wore out his knees by writing on them in the old House, and his feet in the temporary House (after the fire) by standing to write in "a preposterous pen where we used to be huddled together like so many sheep kept in waiting, say —until the woolsack might need restuffing." The reporters had to crush in at the back of the Strangers' Gallery, with no facilities for writing and with the mutter of visitors between them and the speakers in the House.

During recess Charles was probably still carrying on with work in Doctors' Commons; but he was also soon taking a prominent part in the newspaper world. On *The True Sun* was a young dramatic critic from Newcastle, John Forster, soon to be one of Dickens's best friends; and he records his first view of Charles. A general strike of reporters broke out:

and I well remember noticing at this dread time, on the staircase of the magnificent mansion we were lodged in, a young man of my own age whose keen animation of look would have arrested attention anywhere, and whose name, upon enquiry, I then for the first time heard. It was coupled with the fact which gave it interest even then, that "young Dickens" had been spokesman for the recalcitrant reporters, and conducted their case triumphantly.

Partly to separate Maria from the assiduous Charles, the Beadnells sent her off to a finishing school at Paris; and her absence at least gave him the chance to concentrate on his new work. On August 7, 1832, began the first session after the passing of the Reform Bill, and Charles reported it for *The Mirror of Parliament*, a well-printed summary of parliamentary proceedings in grey paper covers, which had its offices in Abingdon Street. John Barrow was still running it. He had written a dull poem in imitation of Scott's narrative method, *The Battle of Talavera*, had managed to make himself an authority on Indian affairs, and was still on the staff of *The Times*. He had taken up his bright nephew and asked him out to his house at Norwood for week-ends. For the moment he was the great man, whose favour meant a great deal to Charles, who made the most of the invitations. (Sixteen years later Charles wrote to Tom Beard to mention that Barrow was coming to dine next Sunday: "Will you come and meet the little man?" Barrow died at Stoke Newington, in March 1858, apparently in poverty.)

Charles reported three important measures: the Bill for the Preservation of Peace (in Ireland), the Bill for the Abolition of Slavery in the Colonies, and the measure turning the British East India Company by charter into a trustee of the Crown. He was supremely unimpressed. Or rather he was indelibly impressed with contempt for Parliament as an institution.

Early in 1833 the family moved to Bentinck Street. On January 5th Charles wrote to Kolle, "The piano will most likely go to Bentinck Street to-day, and, as I have already said, we cannot accompany it, so that the piano will be in one place and we in another." The piano had become an integral part of the family group. He renewed his ticket at the British Museum with the change of address on February 2nd; and five days later he

came of age. The party was on Monday, the 11th, and constituted a house-warming, too. "Quadrilles 8 o'clock," ran the
invitation. Tom Beard of the Reporters' Gallery came and congratulated his colleague, who, by an expenditure of "celestial
or diabolical energy" had qualified as a first-rate hand at the job.
Kolle and his two brothers were also invited. Charles wrote, "I
do not like, after partaking so liberally of your hospitality, to
leave any one out." Fanny was now twenty-three and Letitia
was seventeen. Henry Austin, baffled like Charles in his attempts
on Maria Beadnell, was present at the party, and was making up
to Letitia, with whom he was soon engaged.

Soon after getting his new work Charles had found himself
able to indulge at least a few of his clothing ambitions. "He
bought a new hat and a very handsome blue coat," says J. P.
Collier, "with black velvet facings, the corners of which he
threw over his shoulder *à l'espagnole.*" He had embarked on the
sartorial ventures which were to lead him into many flamboyant
garbs. (In 1836 he has become a "dapper little being" whose
delight is "crimson velvet waistcoats, multi-coloured neckties
with two breast-pins joined by a little gold chain and yellow kid
gloves." Carlyle in 1840 described him as dressed "à la D'Orsay
rather then well.")

Charles was reporting the Coercion Bill drafted in Stanley's
Dublin offices and approved by Lord Grey, which replaced trial
by jury in Ireland with courts-martial and in general set up
dragooning measures. His own sympathies were shown by the
fact that when reporting a speech by O'Connell, in which an
account of an Irish anti-tithe riot was given, he broke down and
wept and had to drop his pencil.

Stanley, moving the second reading, spoke at some length.
The Mirror reporters worked on shifts of three-quarters of an
hour each. Charles did the first and last parts of the speech. The
middle part was full of mistakes, and Stanley asked the editor to
send along the man who had done the other sections. He wanted
the whole speech taken down for circulation in Ireland. Barrow
asked John Dickens to fetch Charles from the country, to which
he had rushed for a rest; and Charles duly went along to Carlton
House Terrace. Stanley, coming into the waiting-room, remarked, "I beg pardon, but I had hoped to see the gentleman
who reported part of my speech." Dickens said that he was the
man. "Oh, indeed," replied Stanley, looking down to hide his
half-smile; then he paced the room, declaiming his speech.

Afterwards he wrote to Barrow a note of thanks for the smart reporter. Dickens, always on the look-out for chances, wrote to Stanley's secretary, Earle, who had praised his skill, with a request to be recommended as a reporter to a Commission or Board.

This Irish Bill then shows us Dickens with his ready response to all appeals against tyranny, his efficiency, his boyish charm, his quickness in following up any opening.

He was convinced that Parliament was a sham, a façade of free discussion and decision behind which various sections of the ruling and owning classes got on with the real business of quarrelling over the plundered country's body. This conviction had been completed by his observations during the time of the Reform Bill and the first activities of the Reformed Parliament. So far from the Reformed House giving him any better hopes of the future, it finally clarified his viewpoint that Parliament could never be an adequate form for the expression of the people's will; various abuses might be modified or cut away, but the central disability would remain. He had no ideas now, or at any time, what kind of institution should take the place of Parliament in order to make the people masters of their own house and country; but from now on he remained steadfast in his belief that Parliament was a contaminated system, which could never overcome the limitations enforced by its origin as an organ of class domination. In the days following the Reform Bill he saw a new quarrel developing over the plunder as the more important sections of the middle-class claimed their right to a share in government; but it was this very extension of franchise rights which convinced him of the corruptness of the Parliamentary method. After four years' experience his suspicion and contempt were unshakable.

And so he made his first tentative movement into a new sort of writing, a mixture of satire and fantasy, which dealt with basic social or political issues. Drawing on his memories of Eastern fable, he wrote a tale about Howsa Kummauns and the odalisque Reefawm. For the time being, he did not quite know what to do about this new turn in his interests; and he put the sketch aside. Then later, in 1855, he turned it up, found that it expressed what he was still feeling, and remodelled it with Palmerston (Parmastoon or Twirling Weathercock) as Prime Minister, calling it *The Thousand and One Humbugs*. It tells how the Sultan, Taxedtaurus (Fleeced Bull), has many loves whom he raises to the dignity of Howsa Kummauns or Peerless

Chatterer; but the inhabitants of his harem prove faithless, idle, boastful, extravagant, chattering, useless. So the various Howsas generally die a sudden and violent death. The youngest charmer was Reefawm (Light of Reason), and Taxedtaurus hoped she would make up for all his disappointments; but she turned out as bad as all the others. The Sultan cries, "Every Howsa Kummauns has deceived me, every Howsa Kummauns is a Humbug, I must slay the present Howsa Kummauns as I have slain so many others, I am brought to shame and mortification, I am despised by the world." Listening to Reefawm talking away about her virtues and telling all sorts of lies ("Which she always did all night"), he decides to put her to the sword. But the Grand Vizier Parmastoon hurries up to distract him and tells stories. First he tells about a poor man who meets the monstrous Genie of the Law and lets himself be slaughtered without resistance. Then, finding the Sultan still angry, he brings in his lovely daughter Hansardade to seduce the Sultan; and she sings a long song in prose, "I am the recorder of brilliant eloquence, I am the chronicle of patriotism," and so on. She tells a story about the Forty Thieves, and the Robbers' Cave that opens at the magic word *Debrett's Peerage*. Intrigues go on with the result "that there are now two bands of robbers" instead of one. Finally the robbers agree to work together. "There is plunder enough in the cave. So that it is never restored to the original owners and never gets into other hands but ours, why should we quarrel overmuch!" The jobbers and the robbers all talk loudly of patriotism and conscience, and those who dispute their right to control things to the end of the world correctly "receive the bastinado as atheists and rebels."

To realize how thoroughly Dickens reached an early detached and hostile attitude to the State, we must see his emergence into adult attitudes taking place at a chaotic moment of transition when all the old loyalties and habitual acceptances had been torn apart. A good observer such as Plumer Ward wrote of the period that "the spirits of men seem either fermenting in discontent or deadened to all feeling of interest about *any* government." Dickens could not have matured in the way he did out of any other phase of the century.

IV

Maria Beadnell had come home some time during the vacation; and some time later in 1832 Charles managed to get in touch with her again. He used Kolle as his stalking-horse and postman. In one letter he says, asking Kolle to deliver a note to Maria, "You know so well my existing situation that you must be almost perfectly aware of the general nature of the note." He would have delivered it verbally, but "I lost the opportunity of keeping the old gentleman out of the way as long as possible last night." He adds, "Perhaps you will accompany the delivery by asking Miss Beadnell only to read it when she is quite alone. Of course in this sense I consider you as nobody."

The next letter, written probably the next day, asks for the handing-on of yet another note "when you practise your customary duet this afternoon."

These notes to Maria, and others, were no doubt destroyed or returned during a tiff; no copies or originals are known.

In January 1833, came the family move already mentioned; during this winter Charles was apparently managing somehow to meet Maria. But with the first gleams of spring the affair is clearly collapsing. Maria has grown afraid of her ardent lover, or tired of him. Paris and parental homilies have succeeded in giving her ideas well above the station of the young reporter with his pleasant but feckless family. Charles was forced to face the breakdown of his great love at the same time as he was organizing a super-example of their private theatricals. The love broke down, but the theatricals came off.

Five of the letters he wrote in the bitter tailing-off of his relations with Maria have been preserved. The first we have in her handwriting: when she had to return the original, she took a careful copy, preserving the evidence of his devotion and her hard little wilful vanity. "Dear Miss Beadnell," he begins, on March 18, 1832, with a fine show of detached pomposity and dignified suffering:

Your own feelings will enable you to imagine far better than any attempt of mine to describe the painful struggle it has cost me to make up my mind to adopt the course which I now take—a course than which nothing can be so directly opposed to my wishes and feelings, but the necessity of which becomes daily more apparent to me. Our meetings of late have been little more than displays of heartless indifference on the one hand, while on the other they have never failed to prove a fertile source of wretchedness and misery; and seeing, as I cannot fail to do, that I have engaged in a pursuit which has long since been worse than hopeless and a further perseverence in which can only expose me to deserved ridicule, I have made up my mind to return the little present I received from you some time since (which I have always prized, as I still do, far beyond anything I ever possessed) and other enclosed mementos of our past correspondence which I am sure it must be gratifying to you to receive, as after our recent situations they are certainly better adapted for your custody than mine.

As lumbering a pair of painful and pained sentences as one could expect to meet in the correspondence of adolescent lovers. Love and indignation have certainly not winged Charles's style with any fire. Such brief eternal farewells have a tendency to avoid briefness, and this one goes on for many more heavy sentences, in which a deep anger struggles with a poor feeble hope and self-pity bears down the wish to utter a manly rejection.

. . . I feel that this is neither a matter nor a time for cold, deliberate, calculating trifling. *My* feelings upon any subject, especially upon this, must be to you a matter of very little moment; but I *have* feelings in common with other people—perhaps as they relate to you they have been as strong and as good as ever warmed the human heart, and I do feel that it is mean and contemptible of me to keep by me one gift of yours. . . .

He affirms his own truth in such a way as to hint at slyness and deceit on her part.

I have ever acted without reserve. I have never held out encouragement which I knew I never meant; I have never indirectly sanctioned hopes which I well knew I did not intend to fulfil. I have never made a mock confidante to whom to entrust a garbled story for my own purposes, and I think I never should (though God knows I am not likely to have the opportunity) encourage one danger as a useful shield for—an excellent set off against—others more fortunate and doubtless more deserving.

He ends, "If you are as happy as I hope you may be, you will indeed possess every blessing that this world can afford. C.D."

This letter may have led to some slight patching-up of their differences; for there followed a lull of some weeks, during which the theatricals were held and were attended by Maria. Kolle's marriage with Anne Beadnell was near, and Kolle failed to take as keen an interest in the show as a distracted stage-manager would have liked. On April 15th Charles wrote, "You ask whether I do not congratulate you." And proceeded with a tortuous exclamation that of course he did, though of course he lacked fellow-feeling and had "no cause to sympathize with your past causes of annoyance, or your present prospects of happiness." Then he comes to business:

Now turning from feeling and making oneself miserable, and so on, may I ask you to spare one evening this week for the purpose of doing your two pair of side scenes. I would not ask you, but I really have no other resource. The time is fast approaching and I am rather nervous.

No wonder. "An immense audience are invited, including many judges." Whoever these judges were, their inclusion makes clear that Charles was still keeping the stage up his sleeve as a last hope. "The family are busy. The corps dramatic are all anxiety. The scenery is all completing rapidly, the machinery is finished, the curtain hemmed, the orchestra complete and the manager grimy." How often was he to repeat those words.

Next Tuesday a much more testy letter is written. Perhaps the grimy manager finds it harder to forgive a defaulter who is marrying the sister of his own lost beloved.

My dear Kolle, I will not say that I have been surprised at our not hearing from or seeing you, either on the day you mentioned in your note or any other time since its reception, because of course we know from practical experience in other cases that a little flow of prosperity is an excellent cooler of former friendships, and that when other and more pleasant engagements can be formed, visits, if not visits of convenience, become excessively irksome.

And so on, ending with the stern request:

Now, as Saturday is fast approaching, I should really be much obliged to you if you will (if you can find the time) write me a word in answer to these two questions. In the first place, do you play the Nobleman? . . . In the second place, when may I send for your scene, as it requires fitting up, lighting, etc.? Believe me (in great haste) Very truly yours.

But with or without Kolle as the Nobleman and his side-scenes, the show was staged. The play-bill was headed PRIVATE THEATRICALS. STAGE MANAGER, CHARLES DICKENS, and advertises four pieces: an *Introductory Prologue*, *Clari*, the Interlude of *The Married Bachelor*, and Finale, *The Farce of Amateurs and Actors*. The players listed included Edward Barrow, John Dickens, Henry Austin, Miss Dickens (Fanny), Letitia, Mrs. Austen, and a Miss Urquhart (in a letter to whom Charles complains of the trouble of making moonlight); and in the audience were Maria Beadnell and Mary Anne Leigh.

Clari, by J. H. Payne, first given at the Theatre Royal, Covent Garden, in May 1823, was a popular play with the song *Home, Sweet Home* in it. Charles was the Farmer Father of Clari; he acted in the prologue, he was Sir Charles Countall in the interlude, and An Actor in the farce; and, of course, stage-manager. Fanny had almost as arduous a set of roles: she was in the prologue, acted and sang the part of Clari, was Grace in the interlude, and Miss Mary Hardacre in the farce. In the latter piece John Dickens appeared as a retired manufacturer, "simple of wit and manners, and utterly unacquainted with Theatricals." He also appeared as a farmer in the episode in *Clari*. Mrs. Dickens, we presume, did the catering and talked to the guests whenever there was no acting going on. The performance, if on time, started at seven o'clock; and went on until it stopped.

The presence of Maria Beadnell in his own home, watching the result of his endeavours, must have spurred Charles to attempt his best; but whatever satisfactions he may have felt were spoilt by the behaviour of Mary Anne Leigh. This teasing girl wouldn't leave his side. Even after they all went upstairs, no doubt to eat and drink, she clung to him. It is, of course, possible that she was so overcome by Charles's performance that she didn't see how she was upsetting things for him with Maria. But she may well have been acting a malicious part on her own initiative or in complicity with Maria.

Then Fanny came into the picture. She knew more about what was going on, it seems, than Charles himself; and she disclosed something of what she knew. Mary Anne told a false story about herself and Charles to Maria, and a false story of something Maria said to Charles, and a false story or a true story about it all to Fanny; and Maria blamed Charles, and Charles blamed Mary Anne and Maria and finally Fanny. Blamed Fanny with an intense bitterness.

The confused story is told in the remaining three love-letters to Maria and an enclosure of the copy of a letter to Mary Anne. Charles met Maria on May 13th, Monday; and denied he had ever made any confidences to Mary Anne, of whose duplicity he'd heard only that day. He seems then to have talked the matter over with Kolle, and felt that he ought to write to Mary Anne in protest—but not without Maria's permission.

He wrote to Maria on Tuesday, May 14th, sending the letter on to Kolle and begging for immediate delivery. In it at excited length he denies ever having made a confidante of Mary Anne,

gives a sad glance back at the "happy hopes" which in miscarriage have turned him to a "miserable reckless wretch," and
adds that Mary Anne said Maria had made her the confidante
of "all that had ever passed between us without reserve"
(underlined). "On hearing this yesterday (and no consideration
on earth shall induce me ever to forget or forgive Fanny's not
telling me of it before) my first impulse was to go to Clapton."
Then to write, then to consult Maria first. Obviously, the stoical
lover is only too glad to have a valid chance of writing to Maria;
some tiny spark of hope refuses to go out. "I have no hopes to
express, no wishes to communicate," and so on. "Though surprised at such inconceivable duplicity, I can express no pleasure
at the discovery, for I have been so long used to inward
wretchedness. . . ."

Two days later Maria's reply was received, with some in-
nuendoes of her own. Charles at once replied, at 4 o'clock, with
another long epistle, in which once more a stilted diction of
hurt dignity struggles with a genuinely deep suffering. He hotly
denies that there has been any love-making between him and
Mary Anne. "That she has for some reason to suit her own
purposes, of late thrown herself in my way, I could plainly see,
and I know it was noticed by others. For instance, on the night
of the play, after we went upstairs I could not get rid of her.
God knows I have no pleasure in speaking to her or any girl
living, and never had. May I say that *you* have been the sole
exception." He accuses Maria of changing from kindness to
unkindness "as your will altered and your pleasure changed."
He protests the deep mark she has left on his life—and in this
he said little less than the facts were to warrant.

He goes on to correct Maria's idea that he is complaining of
Maria running him down to Mary Anne. What he complains
about is simply that Maria confided to her the story of their
love. "I reflected upon it. I coupled her communication with
what I saw (with a jaundiced eye perhaps) of your own conduct;
on the very last occasion of seeing you before writing that note
I heard even among your own friends (and there was no Mary
Anne present), I heard even among them remarks on your own
conduct and pity—pity, Good God!—for my situation. . . ."
He then complains that Maria had returned a previous letter in
a small loose piece of paper. He then comes to the point at issue.
He is visiting Kolle at ten o'clock the next evening and will
hand to him a copy of the proposed note to Mary Anne. He
doesn't want any advice; he merely wishes to know if Maria

has any reason to object to the note. Then he hits again at Fanny:

With regard to Fanny if she owed a duty to you she owed a greater one to *me* and yet for this reason *because she knew* what Marianne Leigh had said of *you*; she heard from you what she had said of *me*, and yet she had not the fairness, the candour, the feeling to let me know it—and if I were to live a hundred years I never would forgive it.

Maria had written about sending his last note back; he tells her to consult her own feelings, not his. He asks her to consider if it is cold, unkind, hasty, or conciliatory and deliberate. He declares that he has no doubt been too open for her liking; and that he can never feel anger towards her.

If you had ever felt for me one hundredth part of my feeling for you there would have been little cause for regret, little coldness, little unkindness between us. My feelings on one subject was early roused; it has been strong, and will be lasting.

He ends by saying that he has borne much and no doubt can bear more.

Next day, Friday, he sent the letter for Mary Anne, with a short note of explanation which begins formally and tumbles over itself a little in asking Maria to make any observations she likes. He promises to adopt them. Then, "I find I have proceeded to the end of my note without even inserting your name. May I ask you to excuse the omission and to believe that I would gladly have addressed you in a very, very different way."

The letter to Mary Anne is somewhat rambling, but reaches its point as follows:

The remark to which I allude however is one which if it had the slightest foundation in truth—would so strongly tend to implicate me as a dishonourable babbler, with little heart and less head, that in justice to myself, I cannot refrain from adverting to it—You will at once perceive I allude to your giving them to understand (if not directly by implication) that I had made you my confidante with respect to anything which may have passed between Maria B. —and myself. Now passing over any remark which may have been artfully elicited from me in any unguarded moment, I can safely say that I never made a confidante of any one.

He then tries some heavy sarcasm, saying that if he had wanted one with candour, secrecy and honour he would of course have wanted no one better; but he declines the relationship. "A proof of self denial in which so far as I learn from other avowed confidantes of yours, I am by no means singular." He is still a fumbler with the satirical touch, or perhaps the strength of his emotion disturbs his literary capacities. He goes on to protest his own unimportance:

and it is solely because I am so; because I would rather mismanage my own affairs, than have them ably conducted by the officious interference of anyone, because I do think that your interposition in this instance, however well intentioned, has been productive of as much mischief as it has been uncalled for; and because I am really and sincerely desirous of sparing you the meanness and humiliation of acting in the petty character of an unauthorized go-between that I have been induced to write this note.

These events had been going on on the eve of Kolle's marriage to Anne Beadnell. On Saturday Kolle gave a bachelor supper to which Charles went, partly in order to receive Maria's reply. Kolle's brother provided a large quantity of choice hock; and Charles tried to escape his misery by drinking. Next morning he wrote to Kolle, "Yesterday I felt like a maniac, to-day my interior resembles a lime basket." He had written again to Maria, whose interest in the Mary Anne episode he seems to have hoped was a reviving interest in himself. "A very conciliatory note. *Sans* Pride, *Sans* Reserve. *Sans* anything but an evident wish to be reconciled." And he wanted Kolle to deliver it while there was yet time.

In the letter he says that there was no need for Maria to ask to see any reply from Mary Anne; of course, he'd send it to her at once. "If I know anything of her art and disposition however you are mistaken in supposing that her remarks will be directed against yourself. I shall be the mark. . . ." But he declares that he has no intention of communicating with Mary Anne again, personally or in writing. Then he comes to the point. He makes a plea for reconciliation and promises on his side to bury the past without reserve. He protests his earnest and sincere desire to be reconciled, and hints at his hopes of rising in the world. "All that any one can do to raise himself by his own exertions and unceasing assiduity I have done, and will do." Then yet again he insists on the enduring nature of his emotion.

I never have loved and I can never love any human creature breathing but yourself. We have had many differences, and we have lately been entirely separated. Absence, however, has not altered my feelings in the slightest degree, and the Love I now tender you is as pure and lasting as at any period of our former correspondence. I have done all I can to remove our most unfortunate and to me most unhappy misunderstanding. The matter now of course rests wholely with you. . . .

He begs her not to let the excitements of the marriage get in the way of a speedy reply during the coming week.

Mary Anne seems not to have obliged with a reply to his letter of sarcastic disavowal; and so Maria's interest languished. But she had enough pride in her conquest to make a copy of the letter to Mary Anne, as well as of the earlier letter to herself, which she returned. Charles, perhaps, made one more effort, as a note to Kolle on Tuesday, the eve of the wedding, mentions, "I am very much obliged to you for performing my commission in the midst of your multifarious concerns so kindly and punctually." But this may be a belated reference to the commission of the week-end; and there was no further letter in Maria's careful collection. He was Kolle's best man at the wedding, calling at Kolle's place at ten o'clock in the morning; and in the excited marriage-group he saw Maria with the other Beadnells and exchanged, perhaps, some polite words. And then he lost sight of her.

So the great love fades out. Charles did not altogether break his relations with the Beadnells. In July 1837, he had some correspondence with Mr. Beadnell about a Mr. Clark who wanted to provide material for *Pickwick* about prison life. In December 1839, he wrote to Mr. Beadnell in condolence over his son Alfred, who had died in India: a letter all about angels and bright forms. Beadnell called at Dickens's house when the latter was out, and invited him to dinner; Charles went, but Maria wasn't there. Then, in January 1846, he wrote in connection with tickets for a benefit stage-show: "with all earnest wishes for you and yours in the years to come—for the love and remembrance of the years that are gone." In October 1849, he wrote to condole about the death of Mrs. Beadnell. Beadnell went to live in the north of England, and in May 1852, hearing that Charles was coming to Manchester and Liverpool with a show, he invited him to a visit. Charles replied that a manager was too madly busy for visits. (Anne Beadnell had died a couple of years before.) "Your handwriting is like a breath of my hobbledehoyhood and is delightful to remember." He ended, "Pray give my love to Margaret and ask her to give the same to Maria if she should see her. (I am exactly nineteen when I write these names)".

Maria had married a business man named Winter. The dream-picture of her turned into the Dora of *Copperfield*, in which Charles released his emotions by a characteristic use of the death-wish. He blended together his dream-definition of a lyric union with the sweet young thing and his imagery of ecstatic death. The death of Dora was thus both an act of revenge against Maria for the suffering and ignominy she inflicted on him, and a dream-compensation for loss, a compensation in which he emotionally achieved a sense of union with the beloved at the highest point of imaginable intensity.

Dickens had protested to Maria that she had filled his life and emotions so entirely that he would never be able to love anyone else. There was a deep truth in this protest, though not exactly what Dickens had intended. Maria was the first girl with whom he fell strongly in love in adult life; and the drama of acceptance and rejection which he played out with her was both a repetition of the drama of his childhood, his relations with his mother and with Fanny, and the riveting of that drama-pattern on his life. Because he was never quite able to rise above the set of tensions which Maria had evoked in his life, he was never able to "love anyone else"—though he was to make a desperate attempt later on. Maria still haunted the relationship, the image of desire which made it lovely and the flaw of loss which turned it into ugliness.

Dickens himself never wavered in his knowledge that his experience with Maria had been fundamental, had stirred his spirit to its ultimate depths. Here, as in most things, he was wiser than his biographers, even if he did not consciously know all the reasons for his insistence. When Forster, in 1855, ridiculed his belief that the young love could have left such marks upon him, he wrote:

I don't quite apprehend what you mean by my over-rating the strength of the feeling of five-and-twenty years ago. If you mean of my own feelings, and will only think what the desperate intensity of my nature is, and that this began when I was Charley's age [Charley: his eldest son]; that it excluded every other idea from my mind for four years, at a time of life when four years are equal to four times four; and that I went at it with a determination to overcome all the difficulties, which fairly lifted me up into that newspaper life, and floated me away over a hundred men's heads: then you are wrong, because nothing can exaggerate that.

I have positively stood amazed at myself ever since!—And so I

95

suffered, and so worked, and so beat and hammered away at the maddest romances that ever got into any boy's head and stayed there, that to see the mere cause of it all, now, loosens my hold upon myself. . . . No one can imagine in the most distant degree what pain the recollection gave me in *Copperfield*. And, just as I can never open that book as I open any other book, I cannot see the face (even at four-and-forty), or hear the voice, without going wandering away over the ashes of all that youth and hope in the wildest manner.

The Dickens family did their best to pooh-pooh the idea that Maria had ever really meant much to Charles. His son Charley wrote, "She can have had in reality very little to do with Dora Spenlow," and Georgina Hogarth, always on the look-out for a chance to muffle up the truth, spoke of Maria as "a very dear friend of Charles Dickens in his youth" and did her best to make Maria out a simpering fool who could not possibly have been the object of anyone's devotion.

But the facts were as Dickens himself set them forth. Maria had brought to a head his deepest capacities for love, and thus had inevitably, by the drama of her relations with him, stimulated and fixed a certain pattern of love and loss in his spirit. Twenty years later, when Maria had come to his notice again, he couldn't stop talking about her in the trip he had taken to Paris. Lady Oliffe asked him if it was true he used to love Maria so very much. He replied that there was no woman in the world, and very few men, who could imagine how much. He paused and conjured up the distant days. "When we were falling off each other, I came from the House of Commons many a night at two or three o'clock in the morning only to wander past the place she was asleep in."

The part that Maria played spiritually in Dickens's life went on to his last moment. And Maria in person was to turn up again later and play a crucial part in the period of decisive change in his life and attitudes. That crisis, however, was twenty years ahead, something quite unimaginable by the suffering lad of 1833.

4

First Writings

I

CHARLES had struggled hard to do well in the world through his need to vindicate himself in Beadnell eyes. A lad who enjoyed the theatre and the gatherings for song and music at home and at friends' houses, who could so easily get absorbed in the excitement of meeting people and taking part in the scurry of events—such a lad had distractions enough; and one reason why he threw himself into his passion for Maria was because it helped him to canalize his energies. The deeper part of himself that responded to the girl was also the deeper part which wanted to get at grips with life and find some satisfying form of self-expression. In one way his passion carried him away and made him waste an apparently endless time in day-dream, in planning to see Maria, in trying to impress her; but this waste of time was ancillary to a deeper concentration of purposes, and without it that concentration could never have come about.

"It was the hope of winning her that led me to make the most desperate efforts to succeed in life."

When he had to face up to the fact that he had lost her, he must have felt all those efforts going flat and pointless. But he fought on; and gradually the inner emptiness fell away. He began to get the full advantage of his canalization of energy. For the moment, however, he still didn't know what shape his expression was to take. That he did not yet feel any certainty of literary success can be gauged from the letters to Maria. There he is agonized with an anxious need to grapple her, to overcome the low opinion which he knew her parents had of him; but though he hints that there may be better things ahead, he does not make the least suggestion that he anticipated literary fame of any sort. Clearly, he is still very vague as to whether he is going to succeed as a journalist, an actor, a writer, or as something that he hasn't even yet thought of.

In 1833 he wrote a travesty of *Othello, The O'Thello*, for performance by his family and friends. The only link between it and his future work is the fact that his father appears as one of the characters in it, "The Great Unpaid." Its level can be guessed from a solo by Cassius (to the tune from one of Moore's melodies, *When in death I shall calm recline*):

> When in sleep I shall calm recline,
> Oh! take me home to my missus dear;
> Tell her I've taken a little more wine
> Than I could carry, or very well bear;
> Bid her not scold me on the morrow
> For staying out drinking all the night;
> But several bottles of soda borrow,
> To cool my coppers and set me right.

So far Charles certainly seems cut out for nothing higher than a hack job at burlesques on the stage. And he is in his twenty-first year, recuperating from a *grande passion*.

John Dickens seems to have treasured the travesty. At least he kept the script and later gave away (or sold) the pages as precious souvenirs of the great writer, his son.

We have a couple of anecdotes of John, which fit in about this time. Letitia was given to virginal fainting fits, and went to stay with some girl friends for a change, which made her feel stronger without removing her pallor. Word came that Pa would arrive to observe progress. The girls got together and squeezed geranium blossoms to yield a cosmetic juice for Letitia's cheeks. Pa came and beheld his rosy daughter. He wept for joy and cried on heaven to witness his everlasting gratitude to the house and inmates, etc. Letitia went into hysterics and had to be led from the room.

Again, one day at Bentinck Street, the kettle was on, but was it boiling? John Dickens rose and addressed the family. "My dears, you seem to have some doubts as to whether the water boils. Now, by what test, what proof, can we ascertain whether it boils or not?" Across the table came the voice of one of the girls, "Put your finger in it, Pa."

Charles had a friend Wiffin, a gold and silversmith's apprentice; and the two of them, being given to reading, frequented a circulating library in Fetter Lane kept by a printer and curio dealer, Haines. The library was in an old house full of tarnished silver, cracked paintings and foxed engravings—a house which no doubt reappeared in *The Old Curiosity Shop*. Haines recalled later Charles's pleasant face, his way in laughter of throwing up his upper lip, his passion for sensational novels, which he carried off in piles. Once Wiffin attacked Fennimore Cooper's *Red Rover* (1828) in which the American cause was upheld against England (and in which there are Smollett-based sailors, Dick Fid the old tar and Scipio Africanus, a negro). Charles, as a Radical, supported the American Revolution, and the dispute grew warm, till Charles finished the matter by flinging the book at Wiffin's head.

But left without his obsession for Maria to control his thoughts, Charles was able to give himself up to his efforts to write with a new persistence. He had been a year in the Gallery, and all his interests seemed to his colleagues wrapped up in reporting; but in spare moments he was scribbling in a note-book, trying to follow up on those sketches of people which he had begun as a boy after the return to London. At last he had one which pleased him enough to seem worth submitting to an editor. It was *A Dinner at Poplar Walk* (later called *Mr. Minns and his Cousin*), and told about a wealthy middle-aged man, a clerk at Somerset House, who held two classes of object "in the deepest and most unmingled horror"—dogs and children. Nothing could please him more than "the execution of a dog, or the assassination of an infant." His cousin draws him from his rooms in Tavistock Street, Covent Garden, to a visit to Stamford Hill, where he is afflicted by a spoiled child, an obstreperous dog, and toasts at dinner, and has by a mishap to walk all the way home. He then cuts the cousin and family from his will.

One November twilight in Fleet Street, Charles dropped the manuscript into the box of the *Monthly Magazine*, which a Captain Holland from South America had bought recently for £300. Then, one day, on his way to the House, he stopped at Chapman and Hall's double-fronted shop in the Strand to buy the December issue for half a crown, and found his sketch in it. With tears in his eyes he walked into Westminster Hall, to gain time for mastering his emotion before he went to the House.

He wrote at once to ask Kolle's verdict. "I am so dreadfully nervous that my hand shakes to such an extent as to prevent my writing a word legibly." He asks specially for Mrs. Kolle's criticism, and dares to speak of the "little paper" as "the first of a series." Clearly he wants Anne to write about the triumph to Maria.

He lost no time in following up with six more sketches, content to be unrecognized and unpaid (for Captain Holland had no cash for contributors) as long as he saw himself in print. His second sketch was *Mrs. Joseph Porter*, an account of private theatricals which shows his characteristic gusto already well developed. The amateurs present *Othello*. The stage manager has to beg the "kindness of a British audience" with a confession that Iago is detained at the Post Office; then as a substitute is hastily dressing up, the original Iago arrives and the substitute has to get all the clothes off. When the play does start, Uncle Tom insists on holding up the performance as he corrects and prompts; the piano-player faints through the heat, and so on—the whole affair concluding about four o'clock in the morning.

The third sketch deals with a young fellow taken up by the family of a city man with a couple of daughters looking out for an eligible suitor. They romanticize "Horatio Sparkins" till he is found out as an imposter, a mere draper's assistant.

Oddly enough, the theme of hatred of children, especially infants, turns up in the fourth sketch, *The Bloomsbury Christening*. Nicodemus Dumps, its main character, "adored King Herod for his massacre of the Innocents; and if he hated one thing more than another, it was a child." And he is drawn into all the horrors of a christening. Finally he ruins the ceremony by a speech in which he pictures the probable death, early decay by lingering disease, or gracelessness of the child.

The fifth and sixth sketches dealt with the goings-on in a boarding house, and ended with a confused tangle in which Mr. Tibbs is found trying to seduce the servant Agnes in the storeroom one night. " 'Be quiet, sir, will you?' (Another bounce and scuffle.)"

Charles is drawing on his own experiences of London society; but his method is still too new, and he is too close up against the material, for his originality to come through as yet with anything like its full power. He is concerned with small moments of discomfort and collision. In *Horatio Sparkins* he draws directly on the sense of being an imposter that the superior Mr. and Mrs. Beadnell had continually inflicted on him, and satirizes Mr. Malderton with his narrow interests as a City man. There is not a hint of sentimentality, not the glint of one self-pitiful tear. And no prudishness. The *Boarding House* shows that he would have had no objections to carrying on the broad humour of the eighteenth century with touches of lewdery. Only in the first and fourth sketches we find an element intruding from his childhood conflicts in the two characters who abominate children and christenings.

Already we cannot miss the joyous impact of his humour, his capacity to strike out vivid phrases in which character and action appear defined with creative verve and concentration on essentials: a definition of the internal motive force in terms of visual imagery. What is lacking is any central impulsion, any deep pattern of significance.

II

The letter to Kolle drawing attention to the December issue of the *Monthly Magazine* was followed a month or so later by another, in which Charles, asked to stand as godfather to Kolle's daughter, excused himself from calling in person. He was busy at work—and also at some agreeable relaxations: pleasure "in the shape of a very nice pair of black eyes" was luring him to Norwood, and he couldn't very well disobey the summons. Having conveyed the news of his first literary success to Maria via Anne, he now wanted to convey that others were finding valuable the heart she had scorned.

But at Norwood he seems to have been thinking more of his career than of new loves. One of Barrow's friends was John Payne Collier, in charge of parliamentary reporting on *The Morning Chronicle*; and Barrow now asked him to give Charles a letter of introduction to the editor. "I myself taught my nephew shorthand," Barrow wrote, calling him an extremely clever youth, and adding that if there'd been a vacancy he'd have liked to get him a job on *The Times*. Could Collier introduce him to the new stock-broker proprietor of the *Chronicle*, John Easthope?

Collier, in reply, wanted to know where Dickens had been educated and what his record was. Easthope was a very irascible man, and his harried employees called him Blasthope. As Barrow's remarks were not quite satisfactory, Collier decided to meet young Dickens himself. Barrow recommended him as "cheerful company, and a good singer of a comic song," and arranged a meeting at Norwood in July 1834.

Charles chatted and sang his best after dessert and much pressing, and won Collier's heart. He was so delightfully young: "no vestige of beard or whiskers." However, the charming was in vain. Collier wrote a note for him to John Black, the *Chronicle's* editor, who had been brought in by East-hope to find staff capable of standing up against *The Times*; but it had no effect. Black wanted sure names. Eyre Crowe had been gained as Paris correspondent, and George Hogarth as theatrical and musical critic. Thackeray offered himself as sub-editor; but Collier and Charles Mackay were preferred as men of more experience (and later *The Times* took him on). Tom Beard, the reporter friend of Charles, had, however, been engaged, and he vouched for Charles as "the fastest and most accurate man in the Gallery." This support got Charles the job at last.

He was taken on at some five pounds a week: a salary which he got all through the year (whereas on *The Mirror* he was paid only during sessions). And now his centre of work shifts to the offices in the Strand, over which Black had his residence.

On *The Mirror* Charles had reported the Poor Law Bill, and was familiar with its hundred clauses on guardians, parishes, paupers. He recognized in it the grand result of the Reform Ministry and it completed his contempt of Parliament and of the State machine. He felt in its key idea (no outdoor relief) the perfect exposure of the basic inhumanity of all measures concerned with furthering the money ethic. Throughout his life its clauses rang in his mind as the deadly condemnation of all theories of political or economic expedience which set property before persons.

As a reporter on the *Chronicle* he had a far more busy time than on *The Mirror*. Expense didn't matter, as long as records in speedy reporting were established. Charles spent days on end in express and post-chaise.

I have had to charge for half-a-dozen break-downs in half-a-dozen times as many miles. I have had to charge for the damage to a great-coat from the drippings of a blazing wax-candle, in writing through the smallest hours of the night in a swift-flying carriage and pair. I have had to charge for all sorts of breakages fifty times in a journey without question, such being the ordinary results of the pace which we went at. I have charged for broken hats, broken luggage, broken chaises, broken harness—everything but a broken head, which is the only thing they would have grumbled to pay for.

In September 1834 he and Beard went to Edinburgh to report the banquet for the retiring Lord Grey. Sailing to Leith, he was delighted to find a bagman on the boat reading *The Bloomsbury Christening* and chuckling as he read. In the reports of the dinner, at which, the Earl being a few minutes late, some of the gentlemen rushed the viands, he shows his satirical power with strengthened thews.

In August he had hit upon the name *Boz* for his sketches—using the adenoidal version of the nickname *Moses* which young Augustus, his brother, applied to himself. Editor Black, and Hogarth the theatre critic, were let into the secret, and Black agreed to print some sketches in the *Chronicle*. The first appeared on September 26th, and Charles wrote his first four London sketches for the same columns. Now he was beginning to attract the attention of editors and critics. His verse straggled on in a fable written in the album of Beard's sister, Ellen; but now he knew where his talent lay—in prose.

In October 1834, the House of Commons was burned down; and to Charles the tale of the fire was an allegory of Parliament itself. Exchequer accounts had long been kept on the antediluvian method of notched sticks, splints of elm called tallies. In George III's reign ordinary paper accounts were suggested, but a long fight was put up against the innovation. Not till 1826 were tallies abolished. Eight years later it was noted that many were worm-eaten and perished; and so the decision was taken to destroy them "privately and confidentially" instead of offering them to the poor for fuel. Burned in the stove of the House of Lords, they set fire to some panelling. As some guards were coming up to help in putting the fire out, Joseph Hume, reformer, called to the officer, "There ought to be ten pioneers to each regiment. I see only eight. How is this, Lord Hill?"

Charles drew this moral from the tale: "All obsolete rubbish which the time has long outlived is certain to have in the soul of it more or less what is pernicious and destructive, and will some day set fire to something or other."

In that moral we touch a fundamental aspect of his thinking, and at the same time a fundamental aspect of his artistic method, which works by allegorizing such an event as this of the fire and its causes, until the particular event becomes an all-embracing symbol of the society begetting it. I have already mentioned how the blown-out houses in Tom-all-alone's (because of the deep-going folk-symbol of Tom crying in the dusk) become in due time the symbols of the inner corruption of Victorian society. In Charles's treatment of the Parliament fire we see his key method arriving in something like mature form.

From now on he was going to see less of the inside of the House as his reporting work hustled him all over the country; but the impression was indelible. Night after night he had sat recording predictions that were never to come to pass, professions never to be fulfilled, explanations that explained nothing. "A conglomeration of noise and confusion to be met with in no other place in existence not even excepting Smithfield on a market day or a cock-pit in its glory." His books are thick with corrupt, imbecile politicians, but not one Member of Parliament is shown as admirable. The *Sketches* start off the gallery with Dingwell, portentously working up a Bill for the Better Observance of Easter Monday. *Pickwick* in its picture of elections utters Charles's belief that parliamentary government was rooted in stupidity, chicanery, and class exploitation. *Nickleby* shows us Gregsburg, the windbag type of new imperialist. Then in the following books we get an extended picture of Parliament as a committee-form of class exploitation, in which disputes are over the allocation of power and plunder between contending factions of the ruling class. Warming Pan Adams, Boots and Brewer, Boodle, Doodle and Foodle, Cuffy, Duffy and Fuffy: these are the types. Against their obsessed playing round with the shuttlecock of inner power-politics stands Gradgrind, the type of capitalist M.P. whose power is rooted in his economic grip on the lives of men and represents for Dickens the abomination of desolation.

Charles had moved into lodgings of his own in October, near the office; then soon after moved into some others close by. The discomforts made him think about a house of his own. John Dickens, however, distracted him by yet another downfall. His erratic journalistic career, aided as it was by the pension, did not suffice to keep him out of trouble. Charles wrote to Mitton (a friend from his early clerk days), "My father went out yesterday accompanied by Alfred to endeavour to get some money as Burr refused to wait beyond last evening. He sent the boy home to say he had been unsuccessful and has not made his appearance all night or forwarded a message of any kind." Next day, "on waking this morning I was informed that my father has been arrested by Shaw and Maxwell, the quondam wine people." He did not know how far his father had managed to get into debt and feared he might be himself involved. "I have not yet been taken, but no doubt that will be the next act in this domestic tragedy."

What had happened was merely the coming true of a fear that had long haunted the family. When debt pressures became too bad, John Dickens had a simple habit of vanishing from home. Thus we find Charles writing, "I own that at present his absence does not give me great uneasiness, knowing how apt he is to get out of the way when anything goes wrong." But this time the net had closed. Charles had to hurry off to Sloman's sponging house before going to work. Money was at once needed to provide the "Governor" with his keep; and Charles asked Mitton for five pounds against an enclosed "money order from my French employer."

The Dickenses took counsel together and decided that as John might be unable "to rejoin his family for some time," the best thing was to scatter. Charles rented cheap lodgings for his mother, Fanny and the younger children, and himself went with Frederick to some rooms at Furnival's Inn, which had recently been rebuilt by Peto (the contractor whose statue stood in the square) in pale brick diversified by stucco pilaster and cornice.

His salary was "completely mortgaged for weeks to come," but he was "determined to see everything in as bright a light as possible."

He needed all his determination. John kept on blandly draining his son. Charles was reduced to borrowing four shillings to get cash for him; and John went on borrowing from Tom Beard himself at the same time—or from anyone else who would listen. At Furnival's Inn, in a "three-pair-back" at twelve shillings a week, Charles had no curtains or crockery. In January 1835 he records, "I have just returned from accompanying father to Coldbath Fields"—the prison. The gloom was no doubt all on his side. John Dickens knew that he now had a son capable of earning good money; and it was up to that son to pinch and scrape till he could buy his father out of captivity.

III

In January 1835 there was a General Election. Charles rushed off in a gig to Ipswich; then on to Sudbury, and, through a night of heavy rain, to Bury St. Edmunds.

But he was also looking for a money-making outlet other than

in this hard-going work of reporting. He had become friendly
with George Hogarth on the *Chronicle*, yet another father with
three charming girls. (A fourth, Helen Isabella, was born in
1833; but she was a mere baby.) Mrs. Georgina Hogarth was
daughter of George Thomson, with whom Burns as song-writer
had had so much to do. Hogarth himself, a writer to the *Signet*,
had been Sir Walter Scott's law agent and knew many of the
literary figures of the day; he is mentioned in Christopher
North's *Noctes Ambrosianae*. Now the editor Black had placed
in his hands the project of an evening paper; and as Black
thought highly of Charles's sketches, he asked him to contribute
some to the new venture.

Charles replied on January 20th. He was pleased to write
the sketches but hoped he was not "unreasonably or improperly
trespassing," if he asked *some* extra pay for them. As a result his
salary was raised from five to seven guineas; and the first sketch,
Hackney Coach Stands, was printed on January 31st. A series of
twenty was written, earning Black's praise. "It was John Black
that flung the slipper after me, dear old Black! My first hearty
out-and-out appreciator."

He now felt in a strong enough position to ask the *Monthly
Magazine* to pay at least half a guinea a page. A new editor,
James Grant, had to refuse and so lost his contributor.

Lord John Russell, having accepted the office of Home
Secretary from Lord Melbourne, was standing for re-election
in South Devon. Charles and Beard dashed off and followed the
campaign through unending rain. In the Castle Yard at Exeter,
amid a free fight and a pelting rain, "two good-natured colleagues who chanced to be at leisure held a pocket handkerchief
over my notebook, after the manner of a state canopy in an
ecclesiastical procession," while another gave his shoulder as a
writing desk. The platform collapsed before the end of the
meeting. But by bribing the postboys "tremendously" he got
his report to London so quickly that the *Chronicle* was able to
describe the meeting ahead of *The Times*—and to give a longer
and more correct account than any of the other papers into the
bargain. Black clapped Charles on the back; and Charles replied
that the rain had made him deaf and rheumatic, Lord John was
defeated, and the whole thing had been immensely enjoyable.

But Charles didn't want to go on with that sort of thing
indefinitely. He had fallen in love again, with one of Hogarth's
girls, the eldest, Catharine; and she returned his affection enough

to agree to an engagement. As a betrothal gift Charles had his own portrait painted on ivory by Rose Drummond (original of Miss La Creevy of *Nickleby*).

Kate Hogarth was small like Maria Beadnell. She was very pretty, with small, red, round mouth, weak chin, and big, heavy-lidded blue eyes. Her nose was slightly retroussé, and she had a quiet, sleepy air about her, almost a touch of voluptuousness. Her typical pose seems one of repose: she leans a little forward, with a dreamy look, half-listening for something. In the portrait painted of her in 1846 by Maclise (who was much attracted by her) she shows a graceful, slightly-drooping figure, with dark hair flowing to her shoulders and flowers closing her deep-cut dress. More like a southern beauty from one of the *Keepsakes* than a Scottish girl, a capricious and petulant note could intrude upon her somnolent charm; and when excited she could reveal a considerable animation and sweetness. She came from a far more cultured milieu than Charles. Her second name was Thomson to commemorate her grandfather who had had dealings with Burns and Beethoven; and she remained on lifelong close terms with her aunt Helen Thomson. Charles was doubtless at this stage drawn towards the Hogarth household with its pretty girls and its breath of a richer life than any he had known. In sending Kate a *Life of Savage* he asks her to read it carefully: "if you do, I know from your excellent understanding you will be delighted." Through his relations with the Hogarths he read Scott more closely, with lasting effects. Mrs. Hogarth and the elder girls, Kate and Mary, spoke with something of a Scotch accent.

Kate herself seems to have a taste for girlish puns and for plain, broad jokes. We possess two of them. She liked to tell of the woman who said, in Scots, "Eh mon, it would be nae temptation to me to gae rinning about a gairden stairk naked 'ating green apples." And of an old, confused woman who, very fond of sweetbreads and seeing them at dinner, clapped hands, "Turnpikes again, this is kind!"

IV

Charles had now taken the plunge; but his prospect was a somewhat chequered one. He had made his name as a journalist, and shown that he could earn a few extra pounds by sketches of people and scenes; but no one could have yet suspected that he was to become a novelist at all, let alone a great one. Nat

Willis, a feline American gossip writer, visited him in his early days at Furnival's Inn, Holborn, and found him in a bleak, uncarpeted room, with a deal table, two or three chairs, and a few books, not to mention a small boy (Fred, his brother). Charles in haste tried to get out of his ragged office coat into a blue surtout and stood "collarless and buttoned up" before the visitors. Willis had with him the publisher Macrone and he attributed Charles's embarassment to an "English obsequiousness to employers." He describes his cropped hair and his clothes "scant, though jauntily cut"—much as "he has since described Dick Swiveller, *minus* the swell look." And he declares that he said to himself, "My good fellow, if you were in America with that fine face and your ready quill, you would have no need to be condescended to by a publisher."

This account, though pettily malicious, is no doubt correct enough in its physical facts. Forster insisted it had hardly a true word and was "no unfair specimen of the kind of garbage" written since Dickens's death; and Dickensians have followed his lead in asserting it was pure fabrication. A small example of the way in which assiduous efforts have been made to obscure the truth of Dickens's life and works. But what Willis took for obsequiousness was merely annoyance at being caught at a difficult moment when his denuded rooms expressed the money troubles he was having over John Dickens. Charles, always the man to make the best financial bargain possible, might well have disliked appearing before a publisher even harder up than he actually was.

But hard up he was, with the burden of the family moving more and more on to his shoulders. And he was looking round to find ways of getting better payment for his *Sketches*. He was working hard at them, and moving back at moments from the immediate scene to earlier days: thus the first series in *The Evening Chronicle* ended in August with *Our Parish*, which goes back to Chatham memories.

And he wanted a publisher. Hence the appearance of Macrone with Willis in the visit to Furnival's Inn. Macrone, an amiable chap, borrowed money from his fiancée, Sophie, and started publishing with offices in St. James's Square (after a brief partnership with one Cochrane, during which he became connected with the *Monthly Magazine*); and soon Charles was discussing with him the publication of the *Sketches* in book form.

The association with Macrone was linked in turn with the

acquaintance which Charles had struck up with Harrison Ainsworth. Ainsworth, seven years his senior, had read the *Sketches* as they appeared and got in touch with their author. For the first time Charles met an established author and was asked to his house. A very handsome fellow (called by women the Antinous of Literature), Ainsworth had come from Manchester to finish off his legal training, and had entered publishing. Then he turned to writing himself, and published the best seller, *Rookwood*, through Macrone. Separated from his wife, he was living with his small daughters and a Mrs. Le Touchet and her sister near the village of Willesden.

At this place, Kensal Lodge, he gave literary parties on Sunday afternoons; and Charles rode out to them. But he feared the keen eye of Mrs. Le Touchet, a Cheshire hunting-woman, and dismounted well before he came in sight. Here it was that he met Macrone; and on a return journey found that both were making for Furnival's Inn. In his expansive way he offered to help Macrone with proofs, and the project of the volume of *Sketches* came up. "Capital value," said Macrone. Cruikshank, the artist, with whom they had been chatting at the Lodge, was the very man to illustrate the book. A suggestion that must have delighted Dickens, for Cruikshank, some twenty years his senior, had already made his name and would ensure sales.

Charles was becoming friendly also with Edward Bulwer (later Lord Lytton), already well-known as author of *Paul Clifford* (1830), *Eugene Aram* (1832) and *The Last Days of Pompeii* (1834). He was in touch, too, with one of his old journalist colleagues, Vincent Dowling, who was now editing *Bell's Life in London*, and contributed twelve sketches to his popular sporting journal, signing them "Tibbs." These began in September 1835, and went on to January of the next year. Another acquaintance gained somehow about this time was Edward Marjoribanks, partner in Coutts's Bank, who late in 1835 invited him to dinner to meet Miss Angela Burdett—soon to be known as Miss Burdett Coutts, the heiress. Later, recalling the event, he wrote, "It must have been on a Friday, for I was born on a Friday and never began a book or began anything of interest to me or [have] done anything of importance to me, but it was on a Friday."

To get an effective volume together, Charles was sketching anything Macrone thought a suitable subject. He visited the House of Correction at Coldbath Fields and asked Black to get an alderman to take him over Newgate. "I think it would sell extremely well." Cooks' shops and Bedlam, banks and hospitals, the jail-van and Covent Garden. He is rushing round looking for good subjects everywhere. Cruikshank is definitely drawn in. On November 7th he writes that he can't see the artist as arranged because he's off to Bristol; shivering in chilly candle-light with a kettle that won't boil and no cabs on the foggy cab-stand. Nothing for it but to heave the portmanteau up on his own back and trudge to catch the coach.

Beard went with him to Newbury. There, from the "George and Pelican," Charles wrote to his sub-editor; then he and the *Herald* man made for the Bush Inn, Bristol, to attend a dinner given for Lord John Russell. After the dinner he wrote a report to catch the coach at half-past six. Beard went over to Bath to do the Bath dinner. Charles himself returned via Marlborough. He wrote that if Lord John made a speech of ordinary dimen-sions, he could have it written out by the time he reached Marl-borough, "and taking into consideration the immense impor-tance of having the addition of saddle horses from thence, it is, beyond all doubt, worth an effort. . . . I need not say that it will be sharp work and will require two of us; for we shall both be up the whole of the previous night, and shall have to sit up again all night to get it off in time." Then, as soon as they've had a bit of sleep, they'll return to London—stopping at various places to pay charges for the express that has gone on ahead.

A strenuous life. To some extent it helped him to form the habit of making furious dashes at writing-jobs and then turning away into busy distractions.

Back in London he found that Hogarth had corrected his book-proofs; but the pugnacious and bibulous Cruikshank lingered with the illustrations. Charles made an effort to work himself up to writing the *Visit to Newgate*, which he managed at last by November 20th. In December he took another look at Coldbath Fields, to get more vividness into his sketch. "The treadmill will not interest men like the gallows."

The gallows was in his mind, and he made an attempt at a serious story, *The Black Veil*. This is set at Christmas time, and tells of a young surgeon waiting for his first patient. A woman in a black veil mysteriously calls and takes him into a horrible slum region; a body is brought in and he inspects it in a dark-ened room; he finds it the body of a hanged man. The mad mother has hoped he will somehow find or give life to it.

Both Macrone and Ainsworth praised the story, and Charles

must have found increased confidence in his powers of invention.

But all the while his reporting work was getting in the way of his attempts to write and to achieve a settled personal life. In December he had to dash off to Hatfield to cover a fire, and wrote to Kate from the "Salisbury Arms": "Here I am waiting until the remains of the Marchioness of Salisbury are dug from the ruins of her ancestor's castle." He also went on December 18th to Kettering, where an election was proceeding. He wrote from the *White Hart* to Kate, "Damn the Tories! They'll win here I am afraid."

Charles and the *Globe* man went early to the ground where voting was to take place. The Whig supporters were all on foot and good order existed till a body of Tory horsemen rode up and tried to force their way to the front of the hustings. The men on foot, to save themselves from being trampled, caught the reins; and the horsemen produced large sticks and heavy whips, which they used on everyone handy. One of the Tories even lugged out a pistol; but a man of his own party caught his hand. The Tories, including the candidate, refused to refer to this incident, and the candidate simply remarked that the Whigs had taken the field first. "The pistol was a double-barrelled one," said Dickens, "and was *loaded*."

The Tory candidate won, and in offering thanks attacked *The Morning Chronicle* reporter for calling his supporters "the most brutal, the most drunken, and most ignorant set of electors in the kingdom." (A passage certainly by Dickens.) The candidate was then chaired to shouts of "No Popery! Church and State! Mr. Maunsell the Farmers' Friend!"

In Dickens's account we read:

The noise and confusion here this morning—which is the first day of polling—is so great that my head is actually splitting. There are about forty flags on either side, two tremendous bands, one hundred and fifty constables, and vehicles of every kind, sort and description . . . conveying voters to the Poll; and the voters themselves are drinking and guzzling and howling. . . .

Such a ruthless set of bloody-minded villains I never set eyes on. . . . All agricultural places at election times are as bad; but beastly as the electors usually are, these men are superlative blackguards.

At Christmas Charles moved from 13 to 15 Furnival's Inn, into the "three pair floor south" at £50 a year. There, a few days later, called Hall, a partner in the recently-formed publishing firm of Chapman and Hall. Charles recognized him as the man who had sold him the copy of the *Monthly Magazine* with his first-printed sketch in it. Hall explained that his visit had been suggested by Charles Whitehead, who was editing a *Library of Fiction* for them. Charles had written for Whitehead two sketches (which dealt with Ramsgate and sweeps, and appeared in the following March); and Hall wanted more work of the same sort, but this time in a continuous series dealing with the same characters. The firm would provide illustrations based on the adventures in the field of sport.

Charles was a little dashed at the reference to sport, about which he knew so little. But Hall argued. His firm had already done the *Squib Annual*, illustrated by Robert Seymour; and now the artist wanted to do "something superior in the same line." The idea was to take an amateur group of sportsmen, who called themselves the Nimrod Club; and the remuneration would be £14 a month, with extra on sales. Charles could not resist an opening of any sort, and agreed.

Then he wrote off at once to tell Kate about it all. The work would be "no joke," but he couldn't resist the money. At some date before this he must have managed to raise the cash to get his unabashed father out of jail; but with a sponging family and an impending marriage he couldn't afford to pick and choose his jobs.

V

The year 1836 thus opened with a medley of hopes and fears. Charles was in the foremost rank of reporters, and his sketches were having a rapid success; but was he yet out of the journalistic level? He had attained the acquaintance of men like Ainsworth and Bulwer, but was he himself a man of letters? The shadow of his feckless family weighed on him, and at the same time the joys and anxieties of his betrothal with Kate drew him another way, in the dream of a happy home-life untouched by any of the sordidness and worry associated with his own parents. What lay ahead?

The book was progressing. On January 7th he told Macrone that he had been asked to Cruikshank's house to see the plate and was very gratified at Ainsworth's appreciation of the Newgate sketch. He was still in touch with the man who had first printed his work, for eight days later he wrote, "Captain

Holland invited himself here to-morrow night to take a glass of grog and some oysters. Will you meet him? I shall be most happy to see you in my new quarters."

He was busy thinking up characters for the Seymour series and hit at last on a Mr. Pickwick as the central butt. Much argument has gone on as to who invented this Pickwick, a figure hardly original at all in his general contours—just another of the amiable slightly-odd slightly-foolish old gentlemen who wander through eighteenth-century fiction and are made, with variations on the amiability and the foolishness, the picaresque centre of various incidents of a satirical or humorous nature. Spiritual Quixotes or Dr. Syntaxes. And, indeed, when the first issues of *Pickwick* appeared nobody turned a hair. Nothing unusual had happened. It was when the Wellers irrupted, and the gusto of Charles's vision of men and things got under way, that *Pickwick Papers* were recognized by the public as something new.

While *Pickwick* was going through its first throes of birth, the *Boz* book was nearing its appearance, and Charles was worrying about its reception. When would Macrone send the first advertisements to the *Chronicle*? "I can hardly begin to puff it till then." In point of fact he shrank from a self-puff when the time did come, and wrote a quite modest paragraph. We next find him expressing his sympathies over the death of Macrone's baby and proceeding with the task of extracting the last illustration from Cruickshank. Then, on his twenty-fourth birthday, the book surprisingly appeared: *Sketches by Boz. Illustrative of Every Day Life and Every Day People.*

He need not have feared the reception, which was kindly and encouraging. The *Morning Post* noticed the book under the heading of "Literature"; and Hogarth did the puffing from which Charles himself had shrunk. In his review he compared the style with that of Washington Irving at his best and said that the Newgate sketch reminded one of Victor Hugo's *Dernier Jour d'un Condamné.*

Whitehead, who had suggested Charles for Pickwick, was a tall, dark, diffident fellow, with hollow chest and stooping walk. His poem *The Solitary* (1831), was admired by Rossetti; and in 1834 he had published the *Autobiography of Jack Ketch* and *Lives of the Highwaymen*, sensational and successful works that strengthened the vogue for tales of criminal low-life—a vogue on which both Ainsworth and Bulwer had cashed in, and which had not a little effect on Dickens. The writings of Whitehead, Ainsworth, Bulwer, strongly influenced Charles at this phase.

The first issue of *Pickwick*, which was to appear in monthly parts, was announced on March 31st at the price of a shilling: "*The Posthumous Papers of the Pickwick Club*, containing a faithful record of the Perambulations, Perils, Travels, Adventures and Sporting Transactions of the corresponding members. Edited by Boz. Each monthly part embellished with four illustrations by Seymour." The title seems suggested by a passage in Whitehead's *Ketch* where a jesting reference is made to a publication of the subject's "more mature experiences under the unambitious title of *The Ketch Papers*."

The original idea had merely been to find a good journalist who could write catchily around Seymour's drawings of the mishaps of the Nimrod Club; but this idea did not fit in with Charles's confidence in his own capacities. "It would be infinitely better," he considered, "for the plates to arise naturally out of the text." He wrote the first sketch, and Seymour seems to have illustrated it with a long, thin Pickwick. Chapman then suggested as model a man he knew at Richmond, "a fat old beau, who would wear, in spite of the ladies' protests, drab tights and black gaiters." And so Seymour drew the familiar plump old fellow perched on a chair with his left hand under his coat-tails and his right hand raised as he holds forth.

Charles's engagement was now drawing to a close. It had had its difficult moments. Kate moped at times, had unexplained depressions and caprices. He accused her of "a sullen and obstinate temper." "I hope you will not get low again," he wrote. And, "You are in better spirits than yesterday, I hope?" Indeed there are many such hopes in his letters to her during the months of their engagement. "I hope your cold is better and that you have no other complaint bodily or mental." There the loving inquiry turns a trifle tart.

Early in the engagement he wrote to her in terms which show the strain that existed in their relationship:

It is with the greatest pain that I sit down before I go to bed to-night, to say one word which can bear the appearance of unkindness or reproach; but I owe a duty to myself as well as to you, and as I am wild enough to think that an engagement of even three weeks might pass without any such display as you have favoured me with already I am the more strongly induced to discharge it.

The sudden and uncalled-for coldness with which you treated me before I left last night surprised and deeply hurt me—surprised because I could not have believed that such sullen and inflexible obstinacy could exist in the breast of any girl in whose heart love had found a place; and hurt me because I feel for you far more than I have ever professed, and feel a slight from you far more than I can tell.

It is, however, only fair to Kate to point out that here as throughout their relationship we have only his voice putting the case; and we must reconstruct her almost entirely from his statements and addresses. There was amusement and tenderness enough in their courting; and she is his "dearest Life," "dearest Wig," "dearest Pig," and "dearest Mouse." He tells her how "warmly and deeply attached" he is; and insists "I have never ceased to love you for one moment since I knew you; nor shall I." He can't see enough of her. "I have not seen you, you know, dearest, since seven o'clock yesterday morning. It seems an age." He sent his brother Fred with messages, with black-currant jam for her throat, with offers of service. At one time he took rooms in Chelsea, at Selwood Place, to be near; and astonished the Hogarths by appearing in sailor's rig outside their window and dancing a boisterous hornpipe—then hastily changing his clothes he gravely called as his normal self, shook hands, "and then at the sight of their puzzled faces, burst into a roar of laughter."

But he finds it difficult to make her grasp that his work can interfere with their pleasures. He tries to tell her that his "composition is peculiar," that he can't write till he gets his steam up, and that once he does work himself up to that pitch he is "so excited with" his subject that he can't leave off. Again the tart note intervenes: "If the representations I have so often made to you, be not sufficient to keep you in good humour . . . why then my dear you must be out of humour, and there is no help to it."

That sounds as if it were written, not three weeks before marriage, but three years after it. Still, when she caught scarlet fever, something deep was stirred in him and he sat with her daily at the risk of being infected.

One's final judgment, derived from the letters, is that Charles was strongly attracted by Kate, but did not know how to get into living touch with her. His remarks, even at the moment of love-declaration, have often a note of smugness:

If you could only determine to *shew* the same affection and kindness to me, when you feel disposed to be ill-tempered, I declare unaffectedly

I should have no one solitary fault to find with you. Your asking me to love you "once more" is quite unnecessary. I *have never ceased to love you for one moment*. . . .

Kate felt a deep distrust of him and his love. He writes:

I am most happy, when you have not been "coss"—though I perceive you have not subdued one part of your disposition—your distrustful feelings and want of confidence. However this may be, you may rest satisfied that I love you dearly—far too well to feel hurt by what in anyone else would have annoyed me greatly. . . . God bless you, Pig, and believe me (if you have any faith in your nature). Ever yours.

Kate was a dreamy sort of girl, with a suppressed energy which only a lover of patience and penetration could have brought to a flowering of character. Her strengths were veiled by a superficial passivity, which became heavily riveted through the sort of married life Charles offered her.

On the day before *Pickwick's* publication Charles wrote to his uncle Tom Barrow saying that the success of *Boz* enabled him to get married earlier than he had expected. "I have therefore fixed Saturday next for my marriage with Miss Hogarth—the daughter of a gentleman who has recently distinguished himself by a celebrated work on Music." He wanted to introduce his bride to Barrow; but John Dickens's behaviour had scandalized the Barrows and he was excluded from their house. Charles himself had therefore seen little of them for some time. "Nothing that has occurred to me in my life," he wrote with humble exaggeration, "has given me greater pain than thus denying myself the society of yourself and aunt."

But though Charles felt that the publication of *Pickwick* made marriage with Kate possible he could not have been anticipating much more than the agreed payments. The publishers had had only 400 copies of the first issue stitched at first; and then they sent out, for the first five issues, a mere fifteen hundred each. The reception was discouraging. Charles, however, managed to get the sums due for the first two issues paid over to meet his marriage expenses.

Charles did not want any publication of banns, and so had to apply to Doctors' Commons for licence. The wedding took place at St. Luke's Church, Chelsea, on April 2nd, with Tom Beard as best man. Henry Burnett, the mild singer friend of Fanny, described the ceremony:

The wedding breakfast was the quietest possible. The Hogarth family and Mr. Beard comprised the whole of the company. A few common, pleasant things were said, and healths drunk, with a few words—yet all passed off very pleasantly, and everybody seemed happy, not the least so Dickens and his young wife. She was a bright, pleasant bride, dressed in the simplest and neatest manner. . . .

I can see him now helping his young wife out of the carriage after the wedding and taking her up the steps of quiet, intellectual, unobtrusive Mr. Hogarth in the Fulham Road, then standing opposite orchards and gardens extending as far as the eye could reach.

For honeymoon, Charles turned in the direction of his childhood, and went to Chalk, some five miles from Rochester—"at Mrs. Nash's." Then after what were perhaps the only few days they ever spent alone together, the young couple returned to the rooms in Furnival's Inn. Charles was just twenty-four and Kate just twenty-one. In their rooms they had Fred with them; and soon there was Mary, the second of the Hogarth girls, living with them too. At once the inner conflict of Charles's sexual life began to express itself in his emotionally divided condition, which went on hovering between Kate and Mary.

A short while before the marriage Charles, asking Kate to breakfast, had sent his love to Mary and added, "I rely on her characteristic kind-heartedness and good-nature to accompany you." She could hardly have known that the invitation to Mary was one for life; and that her sister was going to accompany her married days and nights, first in person and then as a ghost.

VI

Kate liked the country, Charles didn't; and that diversity of taste perhaps provided their first theme of dissent. Kate could have lived at Chalk for ever, but Charles wanted to get back to London. (However, occasionally in their early married life he went back with her for a few days at Mrs. Nash's.)

Back in London, Charles had his hands full. He was still a working journalist; he had *Pickwick* to carry on; and he needed to consolidate his position by writing more and more sketches. At this point his future must have seemed an infinity of sketches, with odd journalistic work thrown in.

His first troubles occurred over Seymour, who wasn't at all pleased at Dickens's dominating role in the *Pickwick* series. After all, such sales as the series had could be attributed to Seymour's drawings. Yet Dickens didn't like the drawing for

The Stroller's Tale, and wrote politely asking the artist to do another and bring it to Furnival's Inn next Sunday. Chapman and Hall were to be there too, and over a glass of grog everything could be smoothed out. Seymour came, but no publishers. This was the first time author and artist had met. Seymour, trained in his father's workshop as a pattern-draughtsman, had aspired to serious art; he hired a room on the top of Canonbury Tower and studied there; then gave up his high ambitions, took some lower residence in Islington, and illustrated books. He achieved something like fame with his drawings for *Figaro in London*, the *Book of Christmas*, and other works.

This frustrated successful man, twelve years older than Dickens, now found himself confronted with a confident young journalist-author determined to have his own way in the most charming way possible. But Seymour, no doubt made suspicious by the absence of the publishers, resisted the blandishments of Charles and grog, cut things short, and went off. Next day, April 20th, he shot himself in his Islington garden.

Burnett, who visited the Dickenses once or twice a week about this time, wrote later, "I well remember the consternation, disappointment and anxiety at the melancholy news."

Seymour, in fact, had knocked off in the middle of a new design for *The Stroller's Tale* to commit suicide. Dickens's attitude had certainly been the final straw breaking his back; but it would be ridiculous to blame Dickens in any way. He could not possibly have known anything of Seymour's state of mind, and he was right enough from his own angle in fighting for a more serious part being allotted to the author in the venture. No doubt he now felt regret and pain at the news of Seymour's death, but he was also worried about the future of the series, which mattered so much for his new establishment.

Seymour had completed three of the plates for the second number; but a successor must quickly be found if the whole thing were not to collapse. R. W. Buss, who had illustrated the sketch about sweeps in *The Library of Fiction*, was called on; but he was inexpert in etching and had to hand the plates over to a professional engraver. The result was not satisfactory; and the hard-pressed publishers and author could not pause to give him time to work up the craft. Meanwhile Leach and Thackeray had applied for the job; but they were turned down in favour of Hablot Knight Browne, a young artist who had just won a medal for a large etching, *John Gilpin*. His first signature was "Nemo," but he soon took up "Phiz." His success as an illustrator coincided with Dickens's success as author; for *Pickwick* leapt into popularity with the sixth number, where Sam Weller appears, and it was Browne's plate of Pickwick's introduction to Sam in the yard of the "White Hart" that revealed his powers of humorous characterization.

In May another death distressed Charles with its agitation of old griefs. Anne Kolle died, after writing a poem *Farewell Bequests*, in which she bequeaths one of her auburn curls in a locket to her mother, her diamond ring to her "stainless" father, her lute to Maria.

Charles was in a whirl of journalism and literature. He was still struggling on as a reporter. In May he went to Ipswich to report O'Connell's speech. In June, he wrote to Macrone, "I am tired to death to-night, though I have been in bed all day. Melbourne *v.* Norton has played the devil with me." The reference is to the divorce case that was shaking fashionable society to the roots. Captain Norton was accusing Lord Melbourne of adultery with his lovely literary wife, who came into court on Samuel Rogers's arm. All the upper-class world was there to hear the servants testifying to Mrs. Norton's goings-on, her paintings and powderings to receive Lord M. in her house with two entrances, the Lord's visits to her bedroom, and her tell-tale disorders, her calls at South Street. The demolition of the character of these witnesses, however, won her the case. Captain Norton had hoped to blackmail Melbourne, who, Home Secretary in 1833, was Prime Minister in 1836.

Dickens determined to trust his luck and give up reporting. He signed a contract to write Macrone a novel within six months for £200. In a letter written shortly after the trial he declared:

I see a decent prospect of the House being up at last, and I devoutly hope ere next Session I may make some arrangements which will render its sittings a matter of indifference to me—as the books say—for ever after.

By July he had decided finally to abandon reporting and to escape from having to listen to the House of Commons any more. Years later he told the wife of a Boston publisher that since he left that House as a reporter he had never entered it again, and that his hatred of the falsity of its talk and the horror he had felt for the bombastic eloquence he had had to record made it impossible for him to listen to another speech there. (In 1854 he had the idea of a series of papers for *Household Words* called *The*

Member for Nowhere, which were to show up the lie and corruption of Parliament; but he was dissuaded. "I give it up reluctantly and with it my hope to have made every man in England feel something of the contempt for the House of Commons that I have. We shall never begin to do anything until this sentiment is universal.")

Before he left, however, he wrote a work derived from his experiences in the House. He had reported a Bill for the stricter observance of Sunday (sponsored by Sir Andrew Agnew), against which Bulwer argued vigorously as a thing anti-Christian and anti-social. Under the name Timothy Sparks he wrote his pamphlet *Sunday Under Three Heads* (June 1836), which I have already cited. The work is dedicated to the Bishop of London who had attacked the lower classes for their Sunday excursions; and Charles makes great play with the Bishop's readiness to accept without rebuke the rich church-goers with their carriages and attendants—"powdered minions" who even have to put the prayer-books in the comfortable pews. All denominations are attacked, but the Dissenters with special fury.

In July Charles tried to get his brother Fred into a job. He wrote to Macrone, "If you will give him a stool, he shall sit himself upon it forthwith." But Fred (now about sixteen) was no more a sticker at work than his father; and from now on he meanders weakly through life, parasitizing where possible.

Charles was himself eagerly keeping an eye open for work. He was hoping to get £100 for a children's Christmas book, *Solomon Bell: the Raree Showman*, from T. Tegg, a Cheapside publisher; but the project fell through. He wrote *The Hospital Patient* in August for the *Carlton Chronicle*, hoping that its circulation among "the nobs" would help his book sales. And a sketch on hackney cabs in September. In September and October he gave sketches to the *Morning* and *Evening Chronicle*.

Meanwhile he was looking round also for new worlds to conquer, and turned back to the theatre. Even during his brief honeymoon he had scribbled away at a play, and he had worked it up into *The Strange Gentleman* (a stage-version of his story *The Great Winglebury Duel*). He had then hurried on into *The Village Coquettes*, a burletta, for which Hullah wrote the music.

The family got together once more to sing and act; and Charles asked "a few confidential friends literary and musical" to see the burletta—at seven o'clock on Saturday evening, July 23rd. He read the words, and the music was tried out. The audience applauded, and Macrone, who was there, wanted to buy the copyright. At first Dickens was inclined to accept, but then he wrote that he and Hullah had decided to publish the books of the songs themselves, and that as the books would be sold in the theatre no bookseller was needed.

Then came the success of *Pickwick*. On July 27th Charles wrote in a postscript to Macrone: "PICKWICK TRIUMPHANT." And triumphant it was, through the pert chatter of Sam Weller. Charles's pay was raised; and in August he rented a furnished house, Elm Lodge, at Petersham. There the important singer Braham visited them from the new and splendid St. James's Theatre, with his stage-manager—both keen on the burletta. "A sure card," said the manager, and prophesied a run of fifty nights. Bentley, the Savile Row publisher, short, pink and bristly-whiskered, also came out for a talk. He made the staggering offer of £500 for "entire copyright" of a novel, without need of specifying subject, title, or date of completion.

Charles signed a contract at once without bothering about the June contract with Macrone, and offered to do a second novel on the same terms. Bentley had just dissolved a partnership with Colburn, who had set up his own firm and was trying to snaffle some of Bentley's authors. Bentley was thus keen to grab any new talent. A sort of publishing war was working up. Bentley announced a comic miscellany; Colburn planned in retort to produce a similar monthly edited by T. Hook of *The Joker's Magazine*. Colburn's threat made Bentley change the name of his periodical from *Wits' Miscellany* to *Bentley's Miscellany*. ("But why go to the other extreme?" asked Barham.)

On their return to Furnival's Inn the Dickenses were still saddled in their small apartment with Mary Hogarth, a sort of angelic incuba, now aged about sixteen. She decisively wrecked Kate's happiness and ensured the failure of her marriage. Not, of course, that we can blame the small adoring girl with a plain face and slightly large nose. She merely brought out in Charles the inner conflict which had been obviously twining its tensions round Kate even during the engagement. If she hadn't been there, something else would have served to focus Charles's divided state of spirit. All we can say is that her intrusion into his married life at such an early stage and the facts of her close relationship to Kate facilitated the fixation of a certain sort of emotional discord and wrecked any possibility of a balanced adult relationship between Kate and her husband.

Kate had promptly become with child and was expecting the baby by Christmas. She stayed at home, left to thoughts which her husband had no wish to share; and Charles took the angelic incuba, whose pure adoration intoxicated him, all round with him. When alone with her he felt himself returned to his own innocent childhood, before the forces of alienation had spoiled his life. Mary was Mary Weller, his young nurse, and Fanny his young sister, and with her he could throw off all the burden of heavy responsibility, all the deadly pretences of the world, and retreat into a romping sweetness. His achievement of Kate had pleased and confirmed his manhood, the part of him that faced the world and mixed with it and made money; his companion-ship with Mary went deep down, to the creative depths of childhood fantasy and the union of the star in the churchyard. In his divided loyalty between Kate and Mary, the two parts of him were each given its mate, wife and sister; and while he could feel Kate and Mary in harmonious alliance and balance he could feel perfectly happy, utterly himself.

In fact, for the first time since the early Chatham days he was quite happy—happy in the whole man.

That is the essential point to grasp. Unless it is grasped—and we cannot grasp it unless we understand the magical potence of the Chatham relationship to Fanny—we can follow nothing of the inner truth of Charles's development.

About few things in his life has more nonsense been written than about his relations to Kate and Mary (which includes his later relation to Georgina Hogarth, the third sister). The earlier biographers preferred to hush the matter up as gently as pos-sible. Chesterton irrupted with the idiotically bluff declaration that Charles fell in love with the whole family of Hogarth girls and simply in his excitement married the wrong one.

In fact, Mary was a girl of about fourteen when Charles fell in love with Kate, and Georgina about six. Chesterton's sug-gestion that Charles was in love with all these girls, and drunken with "an abstract femininity" happened to grab the wrong one, is peculiar to say the least. It is, however, the best that most later biographers can offer:

. . . as alike as chestnuts; they were small, sweet and pretty in a generally rather characterless way. So unindividualized were they that when Dickens came to feel he could love every one of them in turn, one is not at all surprised. (Una Pope-Hennessy.)

Psychological frivolity can hardly go further. And yet here is the key problem in Dickens's character which if unsolved bars our understanding of his whole life and work.

Dickens plays out the odd drama of marrying one sister and falling in love with the other two sisters in turn, because thus he is able to actualize the division in his own soul. The desire that he feels for Kate conditions and creates the desire that he feels for her sisters. In his diffused emotion for the Hogarth sisters (without apparently committing any "sin," without actually doing anything that infringes the Victorian marriage-taboos) he is able to satisfy both his physical and his psychic desires—to hold the permitted and the forbidden in a single nexus of relationships. He is a normal, good husband, and yet he is one with Fanny in the enchanted garden, which has now become the sphere of the forbidden; he inhabits the Eden from which he has been excluded; he defies the ruling powers which have cut him off and prohibited return to the primary satisfactions, and yet he cannot be accused by those powers. He is both adult and child; working for money and drawing on the pure sources.

But this happy balance is dependent on both Kate and Mary playing their parts without discord or conflict or displacement in the delicately-adjusted set of responses.

Charles took Mary with him when he visited Macrone's offices, which were decorated with busts of Distinguished Men (Macrone himself and John Sadleir, M.P., the fraudulent business man whom Dickens turned into Merdle of *Little Dorrit*) which had been given John Strang, wine-merchant author. Some had been made by Angus Fletcher, of Oxton, who charmed Dickens and was taken into his friendship as *Kindheart*. In Charles's gay company Mary let herself go in demure fun, and left an impression. Strang, who met her at the offices, wrote on New Year 1837, to Macrone, "How does his (Boz's) pretty little sister-in-law get on? She is a sweet interesting creature. I wonder some two-legged monster does not carry her off. It might save many a yonker losing his night's rest."

Looking back later in agonized regret on these months with Mary, Charles felt that he had been living a life of incredible sweetness, bathed in sympathy and laughter.

VII

Among the persons to whom Charles had sent a copy of the *Sketches* was Thomas Noon Talfourd. He had met Talfourd some time ago when he was law reporting for *The Times*, and had seen him enter the House as Member for Reading. Talfourd, a generous man, was fond of writers, and he soon introduced Charles to Lady Blessington and Lady Holland, and later managed to wangle his early election to the Athenaeum. He had written *Memorials of Lamb*, aspired to become a playwright, and (like his wife) sat at dinner with a cat on his knees. In 1835 he had had his verse-drama *Ion* played, and followed it up with *The Athenian Captive*. He revised for Charles the court scene of Bardell *v.* Pickwick; and Charles dedicated *Pickwick* in book form to him.

A very different person, though also with his stage connection, was Henry Burnett, who has already turned up as an admirer of Fanny. Burnett had had a devout grandmother and had been brought up under the influence of R. Knill, who became a missionary. Before Knill went to India (he went later to Russia) he said to small Henry, "Now, I am going away, and may never see you again. I want you to make me one promise, and that is, that you will pray for me every day as long as you live, if I am still alive." The boy kept his promise. Owning a very fine voice, he studied first at Brighton, where he stood on a table and sang for gouty, flannel-swathed George IV. He was with Fanny at the Royal Academy of Music; then sang at the Theatre Royal, Edinburgh, and elsewhere. Braham, the famous tenor, used to say, "If I can't come, send for Burnett, he will do as well." But Burnett's religious temperament was at odds with the theatre.

Soon he was to marry Fanny and draw her entirely outside the sphere of Charles's influence. The Rev. James Griffin, whose chapel in Manchester Fanny and Henry then attended, wrote in *Memories of the Past*, "The evenings of the Sunday were usually spent at the house of Mr. Dickens in a manner which, though strictly moral, were not congenial with his feelings." That a man with these evangelical attitudes should take Fanny away must have been repugnant to Charles, and certainly helped to strengthen his hatred of Nonconformity as a divisive repressive force.

Both *The Strange Gentleman* and the operetta were booked for production. The play came on on September 29, 1836, announced as by Boz, with Madame Sala in the part of Julia Dobbs. There is a Charles in the play, who is in love with a Fanny. (Different types with other names take their places in the story on which the play was based.) In a scene where Fanny thinks Charles mentally deranged, he grows jealous and bursts into a fury. He protests that he arrived brimful of hope and finds her "cold, reserved, and embarrassed." Later, she means to come and see how he is during the night: "I tremble at the idea of going into his room, but surely at such a moment as this . . . the strict rules of propriety . . . may be dispensed with." She goes into the wrong room, No. 23, and Charles sees her. "What an ass I must have been ever to have loved that girl.—It *is* No. 23 though.—I'll throttle him presently."

When one thinks how extremely important names are to Dickens and the way he continually gives away by his choice of them the relation to his real life which he does not want to disclose, it is not too much to see significance here. Forster tells how surprised Charles was to find that *David Copperfield* had his own initials reversed, and found a deep meaning in the fact. Right at the end of his life Charles, wanting to hide nothing from the world so much as his relations to Ellen Lawless Ternan, couldn't help introducing Helena Landless into *Edwin Drood*. This fascination with names, which has helped in making practically every one of the thousand names in his books traceable to some original, is linked with the whole complex of childish curiosity which I have discussed as the key to his powers of "observation." It extends even to a fascination in the forming of letters and the shape of names as revelations of character: Pip in *Great Expectations* declared:

The shape of the letters on my father's [tombstone] gave me an odd idea that he was a square, stout, dark man, with curly black hair. From the character and turn of the inscription, "*Also Georgiana, Wife of the Above,*" I drew a childish conclusion that my mother was freckled and sickly. To five little stone lozenges, each about a foot and a half long, which were arranged in a neat row beside their grave, and were sacred to the memory of five little brothers of mine. . . I am indebted for a belief I religiously entertained that they had all been born on their backs with their hands in their trouser-pockets, and had never taken them out in this state of existence.

And when David Copperfield is sent away in disgrace to school, he looks at the names carved on the door in the playground and guesses:

There was one boy—a certain J. Steerforth—who cut his name very deep and very often, who, I conceived, would read it in a rather strong voice, and afterwards pull my hair. There was another boy,

Tommy Traddles, who I dreaded would make game of it, and pretend to be dreadfully frightened of me. There was a third, George Demple, who I fancied would sing it.

Such passages show his strangely deep awareness of the subtle net of association in form and sound, and indeed give us a very important clue to his whole creative method.

The Strange Gentleman was so successful through Madame Sala that the operetta had to be postponed till December 6th. It had been developed out of a part of an opera by Hullah, *The Gondolier*, for which Charles agreed to write the libretto. Charles, however, had declared, "while I am at home in England, I am in Venice abroad indeed," and so *The Gondolier* became *The Village Coquettes*. At the rehearsals Squire Norton (Hullah) had to sing a song at Lucy (Miss Rainforth), and the actress (like her colleague the fat Julia Smith) was dreadfully upset by the lines: "A Winter's night has its delight, Well warmed to bed we go." Dickens replied to Hullah:

I . . . cannot give up (what I consider) the best verse in the best song in the whole piece. If the young ladies are especially horrified at the bare notion of anybody's going to bed, I have no objection to substitute for the objectionable line, Around, old stories go.

But you may respectfully signify to Cramers that I will see them d—d before I make any further alteration. . . .

We ought not to emasculate the very spirit of a song to suit boarding schools.

But the ladies gave in, and allowed the song to make a public statement of the fact they went to bed. A large claque clapped the performance and called for Boz, who made his bow and surprised the audience by his neat smallness of stature. The critics were mostly adverse. "All blow their little trumpets against unhappy me," Charles complained, and must have been specially hurt by the suggestion that the plays would "blast his reputation as a periodical writer."

The operetta's theme is that of two village girls who flirt with gents in superior stations, and then, learning their lesson, return to their humble but faithful swains. Its one virtue is its effort at the start to give an effect of harvest-home.

Scene I.—A Rick-yard, with a cart laden with corn-sheaves. John Madox and labourers, unloading it. Implements of husbandry, etc., lie scattered about.

And the labourers sing a harvest-round.

On December 11th Burnett took over from Hullah, and made his first appearance on the London stage.

Later Charles was very ashamed of these stage works, especially the operetta. When asked if he had a copy of the latter, he said, "No, if I knew it was in my house and if I could not get rid of it in any other way, I would burn the wing of the house where it was."

VIII

In September of 1836 his aunt Sarah Dickens married a widower; and so, under the terms of her husband's will, each of the nephews and nieces inherited about £100 each. Later in the year Charles met at Ainsworth's house a man who was to play a large part in his life, John Forster; and (though Forster had not been at all polite about the opera in the *Examiner*) sent him a copy of the printed text, begging for a closer acquaintance. In recalling the period Forster emphasized how different Charles looked from the grizzled Dickens of later years. "A capital forehead, a firm nose with full wide nostril, eyes wonderfully beaming with intellect and running over with humour and cheerfulness, and a rather prominent mouth strongly marked with sensibility" in the beardless face. But what struck was the air of animation:

... the quickness, keenness, and practical power, the eager, restless, energetic outlook on each several feature, that seemed to tell so little of a student or writer of books, and so much of a man of action and business in the world. Light and motion flashed from every part of it. It was as if made of steel, was said of it, four or five years later ... by ... Mrs. Carlyle. "What a face to meet in a drawing-room!" wrote Leigh Hunt to me, the morning after I made them known to each other. "It has the life and soul in it of fifty human beings."

Meanwhile Charles was working at the *Miscellany* for Bentley, whom he admired as a go-getter scattering on all walls his six-foot orange posters printed red and black. During the autumn he had made a new contract—£20 a month with a £2 extra for the sixteen pages of original material he put into each number. Contract to run for twelve months, renewable by Bentley for three years; copyright entirely Bentley's.

Bentley was pleased. He put Charles up for the Garrick Club. And Charles was pleased. From the *Miscellany* he was now to get nearly £500 a year; from *Pickwick*, about £300. The first issue of the new venture came out on January 2, 1837, and was a success. To the first number Charles contributed what became the first of *The Mudfrog Papers*, a skit on the Royal Association meeting at Mudfrog (Chatham). It told of Tulrumble's attempts to stage a Lord Mayor's Show at Mudfrog and to reform the town's morals. The satire is feeble, but shows Charles no friend of Victorian moral reformers.

In the February issue appeared the first instalment of *Oliver Twist*, which he meant at first to link with the Mudfrog-Chatham series. In the third issue, besides carrying on *Oliver*, he wrote *Pantomimes*, which tries to debunk the opening of Parliament.

Among contributors to the *Miscellany* under Charles's editorship were Samuel Lover, T. Hook, Whitehead, Fennimore Cooper, Maginn, Morier, W. Jerdan, and Hogarth. Lover's *Handy Andy* ran as a serial.

In March 1837, he signed a new contract with Bentley, promising two novels—the first to be delivered at "an early specified date": £500 apiece was to be paid to him (and soon the price was raised to £750).

But he was already running up against trouble through this reckless signing of contracts. Macrone had kept quiet, though he had been surprised at hearing from Ainsworth that Dickens had linked up with Bentley as well as Chapman and Hall. In November, however, he naturally wanted to know what had happened to the novel now due to him. Whatever Dickens replied was unsatisfactory—and indeed anything he could have replied would have been unsatisfactory—and Macrone wrote several impolite letters. Ainsworth told him not to make things worse, and reminded him of the August warning:

I differ from you in thinking you have kept your temper, though I own the circumstances are sufficient to endanger one's equanimity; and I find it hard to blame Mr. Bentley or any other spirited publisher (yourself, for instance) for patronizing rising talent.

Still, Dickens had flatly broken his contract, and near the middle of November Ainsworth wrote "in the strictest confidence," advising legal action.

Your reply to him ought simply to have been—My dear D—, in reply to your note I beg to state that I shall hold you to your agreement. Nothing more. The allusion to Mr. Bentley was (pardon my frankness) in extremely bad taste, and the whole tone of the note betrayed irritability and weakness. This I state that you may judge of its effect on the opposite party! He who is firm is always calm: and in the present matter you must be firm.

Ainsworth has been blamed for duplicity over this letter. True, he was advising hostile action to Dickens behind his back; and Dickens was his friend. But he had known Macrone before Dickens, and he had been responsible for introducing and recommending the latter. His position was difficult. Macrone took his advice and threatened legal action; and Dickens proposed a compromise, under which the novel contract was cancelled and Macrone got the copyright of both series of *Sketches*. The matter seems to have dragged on into early 1837.

Meanwhile Charles felt that he could dispense with all newspaper connections, and gave final notice to the *Chronicle*. Easthope was annoyed, and suggested that Dickens, having been paid in advance to supply weekly sketches, was behaving not too honourably. Charles replied that he would return the six guineas with the utmost pleasure and reminded Easthope of the slogging work he had put in to break reporting records for the *Chronicle*. "Instead of an appreciatory farewell letter, he gets a reminder that he has been overpaid by six guineas!"

But, worse, Chapman and Hall were discontented over the failure of *Pickwick* instalments to turn up in time and their proving somewhat tedious when they did turn up. Charles replied with assurances that "the disease has reached its height and that it will now take a more favourable turn." He pleaded "many occupations" and that "spirits are not to be forced up to *Pickwick* level every day." He declared (what did not turn out to be correct) that if he lived till a hundred and wrote three novels a year "I should not be so proud of any of them as I am of *Pickwick*."

Also, his private life was getting more tangled up. On twelfth night 1837, his first child, a son, was born and named Charles Culliford Boz. Mrs. Elizabeth Dickens and Mrs. Hogarth both settled in and pushed Charles and Mary out of the centre of things into an uncomfortable and cramped looking-after-themselves. Charles decided to find a house, and went joyously gadding round with Mary on the quest. Before getting rid of his rooms he signed the three-year lease for a twelve-roomed house in Doughty Street, a gated no-thoroughfare with liveried watchmen at either end.

In February Charles and Kate, with the inevitable Mary tagging ecstatically on, went to the honeymoon cottage at

I

Chalk. Tom Beard, too, was invited from Saturday to Monday, February 25th to 27th; and on Saturday the four of them went off to have a look at the fortifications at Chatham, and had "a snug little dinner" at "The Sun." On Sunday Charles left the ladies and the cigars with Beard for a few hours while he went off to dine at the Marine Barracks.

In March *Is She His Wife?*, another burletta, was sold for £100 and performed at St. James's Theatre, with Madame Sala again acting a leading role. The story deals with a set of marital confusions, in which jealousy plays the major part. The only interest lies in the way in which Charles's own bickerings with Kate seem to have got into sections of the dialogue. The play was written six months after his marriage, and Mrs. Lovetown in it says to her husband, "How little did I think when I married you, six short months since, that I should be exposed to so much wretchedness." Charles seems to have written the thing mainly to score off Kate's liking for the country. It opens:

Mrs. L. I wish, Alfred, you would endeavour to assume a more cheerful appearance in your wife's society. If you are perpetually yawning and complaining of ennui a few months after marriage, what am I to suppose you'll become in a few years?

Mr. L. The fact is, my love, I'm tired of the country—green fields and blooming hedges and feathered songsters are fine things to talk about, and write about, but I candidly confess I prefer paved streets, area railings and dustmen's bells after all.

They wrangle away; and he, reading the newspaper, gives distracted answers to her complaints.

In late March the family moved into Doughty Street; Charles and Kate, Mary and Fred. Charles took a room overlooking the small back garden as study, and here he was to write *Pickwick* and *Oliver* in fortnight turns. When stimulus flagged, he could go for long walks or hire a horse and ride to Richmond or Highgate.

Forster had been making various efforts to meet Dickens, which circumstances defeated. After the move to Doughty Street Charles twice called on him with Kate, but found him out; and then in reply to Forster's invitation pleaded a prior engagement, the dinner which the publishers were giving to celebrate *Pickwick's* first year of life, and at which a cheque for £500 was to go in Charles's pockets. Then, before other arrangements could be made, a disaster darkened Dickens's life and left an indelible mark.

Mary died. Suddenly, and for no apparent reason, died.

IX

On Saturday night, May 6th, Charles and Kate and Mary, John Dickens and his wife were at St. James's Theatre. After the return home Mary was taken suddenly ill. Apparently Charles heard her give a stifled cry and ran into her room. He found her in a bad way, hardly able to breathe. Kate came in to see what was happening. Fred was sent for a doctor.

But nothing helped. Mary died in Charles's arms, at five o'clock. In his anguish he pulled a ring from one of her fingers and put it on his own little finger, where he kept it till his death.

Kate, whom he had lost no time in impregnating again, had a miscarriage; but that was only a minor unpleasantness for him in the shattering shock he had experienced.

In a letter to a friend Cox, who had been connected with the production of *The Strange Gentleman*, he wrote on Monday, "A sister of Mrs. Dickens, a young and lovely girl, who had been the grace and ornament of our home for the whole time of our marriage, died here yesterday." He took charge of the funeral in the new cemetery at Kensal Green, and composed the epitaph: "Young, beautiful and good, God in his mercy numbered her among his angels at the early age of seventeen." After the funeral he left a note with Ainsworth, asking him to have a rose tree planted on the grave, and rushed off with Kate to the "country," Collins's Farm, North End, a fifteenth-century farmhouse with a lean-to verandah along the front and a cherry tree built into one angle of the house, where Forster, Phiz, and Maclise visited and tried to console him.

He found it impossible to work. He had to give up trying to write his instalment of *Pickwick* or *Oliver Twist*. The *Miscellany* of June 1st had the notice: "Since the appearance of the last number of this work the editor has to mourn the sudden death of a very young relative to whom he was most affectionately attached and whose society has been for a long time the chief solace of his labours."

He yearned to be buried beside her. In 1841, when Mary's brother died, he declared:

It is a great trial to me to give up Mary's grave; greater than I can possibly express. I thought of moving her to the catacombs, and saying nothing about it; but then I remembered that the poor old lady (Mary's grandmother) is buried next her at her own desire, and could not find it in my heart, directly she is laid in earth, to take her grandchild away.

The desire to be buried next her is as strong upon me now, as it was five years ago; and I know (for I don't think there ever was love like that I bear her) that it will ever diminish. I fear I can do nothing. Do you think I can? They would move her on Wednesday, if I resolved to have it done. I cannot bear the thought of being excluded from her dust; and yet I feel that her brother and sisters, and her mother, have a better right than I to be placed beside her. It is but an idea. I neither think nor hope (God forbid) that our spirits would ever mingle *there*. I ought to get the better of it, but it is very hard. I never contemplated this—and coming so suddenly, and after being ill, it disturbs me more than it ought. It seems like losing her a second time.

He wrote the next morning:

No, I tried that. No, there is no ground on either side to be had. I must give it up. I shall drive over there, please God, on Thursday morning, before they get there; and look at her coffin.

Forster adds, "He suffered more than he let anyone perceive, and was obliged again to keep his room for some days." Finally, feeling better, he went to Richmond and Windsor with Kate and Georgina, "But it was not till near the close of that month he could describe himself as thoroughly on his legs again." And this, remember, was five years later.

In April, 1842, while at Niagara Falls in America, he wrote "What would I give if the dear girl whose ashes lie in Kensal Green, had lived to come so far along with us—but she has been here many times, I doubt not, since her sweet face faded from my earthly sight."

The examples of his hysteria about Mary might be multiplied. They will keep on turning up as we go on. But for the moment it will suffice to give some examples from his correspondence in 1837–38. Thus, he wrote to Mrs. Hogarth in October 1837 to tell her about the "sorrowful pleasure" he took in wearing Mary's ring, which he meant to prize till "I am like her." He had never taken it off except to wash.

I have never had her sweetness and excellence absent from my mind so long. I can solemnly say that, waking or sleeping, I have never lost the recollection of our hard trial and sorrow, and I feel that I never shall.

It will be a great relief to my heart when I find you sufficiently calm upon this sad subject to claim the promise I made you when she lay dead in this house, never to shrink from speaking of her, as if her memory must be avoided, but rather to take a melancholy pleasure in recalling the times when we were all so happy—so

happy that increase of fame and prosperity has only widened the
gap in my affections, by causing me to think how she would have
shared and enhanced all our joys, and how proud I should have been
(as God knows I always was) to possess the affections of the
gentlest and purest creature that ever shed a light on earth.

I wish you could know how I weary now for the three rooms in
Furnival's Inn, and how I miss that pleasant smile and those sweet
words which, bestowed upon our evening's work, in our merry
banterings round the fire, were more precious to me than the
applause of a whole world would be. I can recall everything she
said and did in those happy days, and could show you every passage
and line we read together.

If he thought these morbid sentiments would be approved by
the sensible old Scottish woman, Mrs. Hogarth, he was mistaken.
In a diary he kept for a while, he records under the first day of
1838:

I wrote to Mrs. Hogarth yesterday, taking advantage of the
opportunity afforded me by her sending, as a New Year's token, a
pen-wiper of poor Mary's, imploring her, as strongly as I could,
to think of the many remaining claims upon her affection and
exertions, and not to give way to unavailing grief. Her answer came
to-night, and she seems hurt at my doing so—protesting that in all
useful respects she is the same as ever. Meant it for the best, and still
hope I did right.

On the sixth he wrote a few lines about his son's first birthday
but at once wandered off thus:

This day last year, Mary and I wandered up and down Holborn
and the streets about for hours, looking after a little table for Kate's
bedroom, which we bought at last at the very first broker's which
we had looked into, and which we had passed half-a-dozen times
because I didn't like to ask the price. I took her out to Brompton
at night, as we had no place for her to sleep in (the two mothers
being with us); she came back again next day to keep house for me,
and stopped nearly the rest of the month. I shall never be so happy
again as in those chambers three storeys high—never if I roll in
wealth and fame. I would hire them to keep them empty, if I could
afford it.

On the fourteenth he looked at Scott's diary and found
"thoughts which have been mine by day and by night, in good
spirits and bad, since Mary died." Then he cites a passage from
Scott about the beloved in her grave. "She is sentient and conscious of my emotions *somewhere*—where, we cannot tell, how,
we cannot tell; yet would I not at this moment renounce the

mysterious yet certain hope that I shall see her in a better world, for all that this world can give. I have seen her. There is the same symmetry of form, though those limbs are rigid which were once so gracefully elastic. . . . I will not look upon it again." Charles adds, "I know but too well how true all this is."

On February 1st, 1838 he wrote to Kate from Gretna Bridge:

Is it not extraordinary that the same dreams which have constantly visited me since poor Mary died follow me everywhere? After all the change of scene and fatigue, I have dreamt of her ever since I left home, and no doubt shall till I return. I should be sorry to lose such visions, for they are very happy ones, if it be only the seeing her in one's sleep. I would fain believe, too, sometimes, that her spirit may have some influence over them, but their perpetual repetition is extraordinary. Ever, my dear Kate, Your affectionate Husband.

The obsession was genuine; but there is also no doubt that he used it to some extent as a revenge on Kate. He continually made clear to her that she had failed to give him the happiness that Mary had given. (Note the offensive form of the notice in the *Miscellany*, which described Mary as his *chief solace*.) And Kate listened, with that charming lowered head, brooding. And Charles was quite sure that he had impressed her with his sensibility, his goodness. (Five years later he mentioned that the confession of his bed-trysts with the ghost drove the ghost from his dreams. From one angle then this letter, written under the strain of separation from Kate's bed, was an effort to break the ghost spell and come to adult love terms with Kate. But it was not followed up by any full effort to break barriers to intimacy down.)

The shock over Mary permanently warped something in him; and yet when we try to take a full focus of his life and work, it is hard to say if this warping was not also, in his situation, a necessary part of his mechanism of creative release. If that were so, then he would have found something of the same experience with another girl if Mary hadn't been there with her convenient death. Yet, there can be little doubt that no one else could have served so neatly, so efficiently. The sister-relationship which had made her the perfect foil for the child-bearing wife was what made her so terribly potent in death.

The elements of psychotic fixation which her death set up in Charles is inexplicable except on something of the lines already suggested here. Alive, with Kate acquiescent, Mary was the magical restorer of the dream Eden—the sister re-created as an other-half of the wife. But when she died, the whole machinery of taboo-fear was set into action. Her relationship with Charles became the utterly forbidden thing, and she was snatched away by omnipotent authority. At the same time, because her union with Charles had roots deep down in the childhood levels where the wish is omnipotent he had to face the unconscious conviction of himself as her murderer; his death-wish, wanting her irredeemably his and all his, had killed her off. But this dream-act, which removed her jealously from the world and handed her over wholly to himself, upset the psychic balance of his happy relation with her, and made him feel himself vulnerable to attack from the all-powerful authority whose force he had momentarily seized and used. Hence his agony of regret and loss, his uncontrollable desire to possess her grave and mix with her ashes, was based in an extreme guilt-fear, a fear of retribution. His morbid anxiety to keep any form of contact with the dead girl—by holding the grave or seeing her in dreams, by putting his finger through the hole of her ring and keeping it in unbroken contact with his body, by assuring himself that she hadn't been changed into a fury, a source of spiritual danger —all this derived from his fear of being made to confront his sense of guilt.

Hence the way that for years she pervades his work and reaches her apotheosis in Little Nell. Even in *Little Dorrit*, where he makes a decisive effort to break through the beleaguering fears that she represented, she came up again, for the last time, as the child love, the stunted Little Amy Dorrit.

We see, then, that in little more than a year Charles's effort to marry and achieve a fully adult relationship in love had the effect of handing him over to the child-fixation in a more shattering way than ever. The possibility of a real love relation with Kate was ended; but the violent agitation of the deep levels of his spirit drove him forward restless and tormented and rapturous into new dimensions of creative realization.

(It is of interest, by the way, to note how Charles, who is always driven to scatter clues to the thing he is trying to hide, keeps on showing the link between Mary and his suffering heroines by repeating the gravestone formula: "Young, beautiful and good." He repeats it in *Oliver Twist* when stirred by the illness of Rose Maylie; it naturally turns up with the death of Little Nell; and it recurs at the cruel exclusion of Florence Dombey.)

X

It is time now that we paused and had a look round at the world in which Charles had grown up. The years of his childhood and youth were roughly those in which the factory system and the power-machine took stable hold. He was born towards the end of the Napoleonic wars, a time of deep unrest, of vast distress and corruption, when money was becoming a new power in the land and the Luddites were wrecking the machines. The massacre of Peterloo and the general suppressive measures taken against the agitation for reform, the first stages of trade union struggle against the Combination Acts, the desperate and gallant fight of men like Hetherington and R. Carlile for a free working-class press—all this passed over his head. At Chatham, with its fairly steady government employment, only the dim rumour of dangerous men called Radicals troubled his years of play.

Towards the late 1820's, in London, he became more aware of the struggles going on in the political and economic fields, and he rapidly matured into a strong Radical as soon as he had to battle for his own living. The semi-revolutionary situation of 1830–33 found him keenly interested. A mutter of the insurrection that set fire to Bristol finds its way into the verses for Maria Beadnell's album. The year 1830 had seen an economic crisis, with factory unemployment and rapid extension of trade unions, with strong middle-class discontent, and widespread rick-burning and uprisings of the peasantry. Financial threat from the middle class, insurrectionary action by the townsfolk (Bristol) and by the country workers over large areas, forced through the Reform Bill. Throughout this movement, Dickens was faithful to the Radical Left; he deprecated violence but wanted reform at all costs. The basic emotional attitudes generated in him during childhood, which came to their first revolt-focus in an antagonism to dissent, made him link himself without much need for inquiry and argument with the anti-aristocratic demands of radicalism.

His experiences in the law confirmed his belief that the class-system of State control was rotten; and his experiences in the House of Commons convinced him that the political demands of the Radicals were only a mask for increased power to the exploiters of the people. He saw the House as a form devised to hide the truths of exploitation.

None of these convictions were based on a logically constructed political philosophy. The radicalism soon went so far that it ended in a sort of diffused anarchism, which advanced to the point of discrediting all existing State-forms but did not seek further for the forms desirable as supplanters of the present oppressive ones. One way or another this statement is true of all Dickens's life, from the *Sketches* to *Edwin Drood*; and it is easy, and correct enough, to say that he thus represents the lower middle-class Radical, strongly and consistently opposed to all forms of inherited rank and power, and regarding the State as a curse carried on as a feudal or absolutist survival to set barriers and tolls on free enterprise. In order to preserve this attitude he tried to escape from the problems of the industrial proletariat and to see economic activity only in the small forms where the radical illusion could seem justified. Because he had no coherent idea of capitalism, he had no coherent idea of a proletariat. Because he could not see capitalism as a system moving from one stage to another by its own inner necessities, he could not understand the nature of working-class organization; and though he was hostile to big business and factory concentrations in so far as he saw them, he was also hostile to trade unions or other forms giving expression to working-class solidarity. Both big business and trade unions seemed to him excrescences, forces that threatened the world of small units, free enterprise, and good man-to-man relationship which he thought possible and desirable.

These points are indeed highly relevant; and they bring out certain basic limitations of Dickens's thinking from first to last. But if that is all there was to it, then his work would have trifling value. We must go on to ask what artistic use he made of these limitations, and how far that artistic use enabled him to advance (*a*) to a definition of the human condition in terms of his world (*b*) to a definition which grasped the totality of forces operative in his world.

Those questions we shall be able to answer only at the end of our analysis; but we must ask them at the outset, so that we may keep clear what is at stake and that in discussing limitations we are not committing the fallacy of "nothing but."

The first thing that we feel if we look at Dickens's early work is that we are in a pre-reform world, almost a pre-industrialist world (that is, a world of which the attitudes and values are prior to the stage of capitalism represented by the expansion of the factory system and the industrialists' share in Parliament granted by the Reform Bill). In many respects, it is an eighteenth-century world, just as the main literary models that Dickens has before him are eighteenth-century writers, Smollett and Sterne and Fielding.

The early novels (*Pickwick*, *Twist*, *Nickleby*) are set in the pre-reform period. Dickens had known, and still knew, many persons whose lives went well back into the eighteenth century. When he won fame, among the people who wanted to meet him were the Misses Berry who had been dear friends of Horace Walpole (born in 1716); Tibbs in *Boz* recalled when he was in the volunteer corps "in eighteen hundred and six"; and Lilly-vick had heard the French prisoners talk. As late as *Our Mutual Friend* we meet a character Lady Tippins, relic of someone knighted by George III in mistake. ("What, what, what? Who, who, who? Why, why, why?" the king graciously observed.) Cousin Feenix in *Dombey* comes from Pitt's days in Parliament. Turveydrop admired the Prince Regent. In an account of Brighton in the 1860's Dickens talks of the spectres from George IV's days.

Sir Mulberry Hawk is a Mohock; and duelling is still common. Even Dombey accepts the necessity of fighting the seducer, Carker, and would have fought him if Carker hadn't been killed by a train. Hanging was still in the open—a horror that Dickens repeatedly attacked in letters to the press. He remembered the Bow Street Runners with their blue dress and brass buttons. His characters continually dress in eighteenth-century exuberance, Tuckle at the Bath Swarry has a bright crimson coat with long tails, vivid red breeches and a cocked hat. In *Dombey*, Tulking-horne wears black (knee breeches tied with ribbons, and gartered stockings), and Deadlock wears a frilled shirt, a white waistcoat, a blue coat with bright buttons. And so on.

Gas was still a novelty. Tom Grig (in *The Lamplighter*, 1838) had an uncle who hanged himself in disgust at gas; and *Our Watering Place* (1851) told how fiercely debated the issue of gas *v.* oil yet was. The penny post came in in 1840. The electric telegraph was first tried out (between Euston and Camden Town) in 1837, and became an emblem for Dickens as for many others of a strange force uniting men in their own despite, the perfect anti-feudal emblem. ("Few things that I saw, when I was away took my fancy so much as the electric telegraph, piercing like a sunbeam, right through the cruel old heart of the Coliseum at Rome," 1854.)

But it was the railway that most obviously stood out as the

power dividing the ages, cutting Victorian England away from all the past. It is hardly too much to say that with the railway for the first time men did look round and feel that their world was radically different from any past worlds. Significantly, the railway does not appear at all in *Boz*, *Pickwick*, or *Oliver Twist*. In *Nickleby* it figures in the demagogic address of Gregsbury. With *Chuzzlewit* trains appear—in the United States: though Mrs. Gamp, as representative of the British public, blames them for premature births. With *Dombey* the railways come slap in. They play an integral part in the theme. Their minions are smashing up Staggs Garden, Camden (i.e. one of Charles's childhood haunts):

Houses were knocked down; streets broken through . . . buildings that were undermined and shaky, propped up by great beams of wood.

And it is the train that kills off the villain. But even here the pre-machine age insists on thrusting in. Dombey and Bagstock go by rail to Brighton and Leamington Spa, then on to Birmingham by carriage. And we find Charles himself going to Dover in 1845 by coach and proposing return by rail.

The stage-coach and the train. Dickens starts with the one, then across the simple landscape comes roaring the train. At moments he seems to glorify the coach; but continually he stresses the miseries and dangers of the old way of travelling. In an essay he records one of the moments which bring vividly out how the old is swallowed up in the new; he sees a dispirited Post Office guard in a train inside a little box with pistol and blunderbuss, still wearing tarnished gold lace and scarlet cloak, but sootied and robbed of all his importance.

The London with which Dickens begins is pre-reform London, indistinguishable from eighteenth-century London, except that it is dirtier. He sees it furiously spreading, getting dirtier and dirtier, breeding cholera and fevers—with huddled squares in which six months' or a year's excrement is piled up outside the fetid houses—until sheer necessity brings about control despite the screams against interference with private property. This furiously extending London is in one way the basic theme in Dickens; but the changes in their basic significance are grasped imaginatively through their identification with the pangs of change in himself.

He had thrown himself into the exploration of London with the zest which he always felt for a piece of town geography that made the setting of his day-dream dramatizations. He was exploring himself. "I thought I knew something of Town," said one of his fellow clerks at Ellis and Blackmore's, "but after a talk with Dickens I found that I knew nothing." And the itch to explore its windings, its darknesses, never left him. Even when he had come to dislike the place intensely, he went round, sometimes with Wilkie Collins, sometimes alone, driven by an urge he could not fathom. G. A. Sala, after his death, mentioned that he used to meet him striding along "in the oddest places and most inclement weathers."

One more detail which brings out the point of cleavage which runs across Dickens's world, leaving one half back in semi-feudal levels and pushing the other half on into the twentieth century. In *Pickwick*, in the person of Bob Sawyer, we touch the old system of medicine with its deep gap between consultant and practitioner. A consultant was a graduate of Oxford or Cambridge; a practioner the son of tradesman or farmer, who had been apprenticed to an apothecary for five to seven years, cleaning the shop and bleeding less-important customers, and then, after a year in a hospital, passing an examination. Most of Dickens's doctors are of this second class. But there are a few consultants like Dr. Jobling of *Chuzzlewit*, who gets his patients to take policies (to his own profit) in that perfectly-named Victorian business, the Anglo-Bengalee Disinterested Loan and Life Assurance Co.

XI

Charles, then, starts off his work in the 1830's in the comparative lull following the Reform Bill. He had seen through the world of politics, but he was cut off from what was going on in the industrial areas as a result of the new consolidations. Hence, he was at peace to work back over his memories, starting from scenes in the contemporary street and going back to his snug Chatham meanderings. Pickwick and Sam Weller have a faint kinship with Don Quixote and Sancho Panza, but nothing much happens on their quest. Charles hasn't gone far with them before he finds that he has to turn to Chatham and Rochester for firm earth; and so Mr. Pickwick's mildly chivalric effort to right the wrongs of the world turns out to be Charles Dickens's first hurly-burly sortie into his childhood.

As always he makes his sortie back in terms of what he

feels to be the pressures moving forward in his world. But at this moment there is no turbulent stirring of the depths. Despite Charles's contempt for the State machine, he is pretty sure the world is progressing fast, and Charles is a good fellow, with a host of other good fellows, who only have to get together to show an effete aristocracy and a pack of dirty financiers how the world should be run.

He is making his way at a good pace; he has in hand, and soon marries, a lovely girl; and then he has the dream-twin of the lovely girl in hand too. He has broken all sorts of records as a journalist and seen inside all sorts of shams and jobberies; he is being accepted by the literary lions. He wanders back in his work over Chatham; he relives through some of the most painful parts of the family history (John Dickens's imprisonment) and feels quite unshaken. Here is the world, and it can all be turned into a mad joke.

And he does turn it into a fairly mad joke. *Pickwick* has many weaknesses and dullnesses; and except perhaps for Tony Weller there is no character in it able to stand up against Charles's great characters in later books. It is highly derivative and full of imperfectly absorbed influences; but it has gusto, a huge gusto. On the one hand it represents the end of the eighteenth-century picaresque novel, foundering in a tumult of discordant journalistic trends, popular burlesque, satirical reportage, tag-ends of Gothic mystery, overworked types who are both stalely dull and jerking with a new galvanic life. And on the other hand it founds the Victorian novel. It is a paean to a world of blithe hospitalities and comfortable loyalties, and it signalizes the end of that world.

Pickwick in its first five issues, as we have seen, was a failure. "A signal failure," said James Grant. But for Sam Weller's electrifying appearance in the sixth issue the series would probably have been cancelled.

Sam is often held up as an example of cockney humour; but his main speech formula is an old folk formula ("We're all inside, as the bridegroom said when he shut the bride in," Theocritus, XV.) It had been exploited by Samuel Beazley in a farce, *The Boarding House; or, Five Hours in Brighton*, performed in 1811. Simon Spatterdash, a militia man, there keeps on making odd comparisons, such as "Let everyone take care of themselves, as the jackass said when he was dancing among the chickens." An actor named Samuel Vale kept the part alive at the Surrey

Theatre (well known to young Dickens), and made Spatter-dashisms a trick at the disposal of every waggish clerk. Charles can hardly have been unaware of Sam Vale as Spatterdash, and from Sam Vale to Sam Weller is not far. *Vale, Wail, Weller*. Some turn of association brought Charles back to the name that meant so much to his childhood, Mary Weller the tale spinner.

It is an odd point—the kind of odd point always turning up with Dickens—that when Sam appears in the story it is as boots of the White Hart Inn and he is at work with blacking! He achieves "a polish that would have struck envy to the soul of the amiable Mr. Warren (for they used Day and Martin at the White Hart)." After his jokes about the boots and the story of how his father got married through being hustled into buying a licence in Doctors' Commons, there comes the exposure of Jingle, the entanglement of Pickwick with Mrs. Bardell, and the elections; and the story is off.

In the preface he wrote later Dickens commented on the fact, which had been observed, that Pickwick as the story went on became "more good and more sensible." He defended this change by saying that what struck us about a person was first their oddities, and only later we saw under them to the "better part." This was certainly a rationalization, to express the change which had been going on in the author himself as he wrote. The gay bit of journalism turned into a serious novel—with the engulfing of Pickwick by the maw of the law (which here as always in Dickens represented the organized injustice of society). The early rush of the story off to Rochester had been a first weak effort to get down into his own creative sources of memory; with the Fleet scenes he comes closer. The more serious mood was in part induced by the death of Mary, which had occurred shortly before.

But the contact with the depths is never quite established. In some of the interpolated stories the fear motives in those depths spurt up, in crude forms unrelated to the movement of the story, but showing some of the elements which his full expression must incorporate. From this angle there is much interest in the tales of *The Return of the Convict* and of the Madman. *The Return* occurs early (in Chapter VI), between the Rochester visit and the advent of Weller. It tells of a cruel father whose son is condemned to transportation for a felony. The son breaks his mother's heart, but after his sentence returns to the village. No one recognizes him, and he breaks down "in fierce and deadly passion. And such was the return to which he had looked through the weary perspective of many years, and for which he had undergone so much suffering! No face of welcome, no look of forgiveness," etc. At last he encounters his father (now a workhouse inmate) in a field and tries to speak to him; the old man strikes him across the face in terror with a stick. "Father—devil!" mutters the convict and rushes to take him by the throat, but lets go in time. However, the old man ruptures a blood-vessel and drops dead.

A Madman's Manuscript comes in shortly after Sam. It attempts to define a paranoiac who marries a girl in love with someone else. She sees him on the point of murdering her, goes mad and dies. The madman, confronted by the brother of the girl, retorts to him that he, the noble brother, forced the girl into a marriage which he knew she detested, and hurried to profit by her husband's money. He attacks the brother and almost strangles him. "I knelt upon his chest, and clasped his brawny throat firmly with both hands. His face grew purple; his eyes were starting from his head, and with protruded tongue, he seemed to mock me. I squeezed the tighter." But he is pulled off in time and put in an asylum, where he is haunted by the dead wife.

I don't remember forms or faces now, but I know the girl was beautiful. I know she was; for in the bright moonlight nights, when I start from my sleep, and all is quiet about me, I see, standing still and motionless in one corner of this cell, a slight and wasted figure with long black hair, which, streaming down her back, stirs with no earthly wind, and eyes that fix their gaze on me, and never wink or close. Hush! the blood chills at my heart as I write it down— that form is hers; the face is very pale, and the eyes are glassy bright; but I know them well. That figure never moves. . . .

Both stories have the same material: the tragic aspect of the return to childhood. The son who has driven his mother to death and tries to murder his father; the man who drives mad and kills his beloved, and tries to murder her brother. Both are the same man. The madman has been driven mad by "large dusky forms with sly and jeering faces" that crouch in the corners of his room, ancestral horrors, faces from the dark past, voices that tell him he is doomed by the violences of that past, the hag coming out of the box. And in this effort to define paranoic fears we meet the first basic criticism that Dickens makes of the human condition, the men and women round him.

143

Riches became mine, wealth poured in upon me, and I rioted in pleasures enhanced a thousandfold to me by the consciousness of my well-kept secret. I inherited an estate. The law—the eagle-eyed law itself—had been deceived and had handed over disputed thousands to a madman's hands. . . . The madman's cunning had overreached them all. I had money. How I was courted! I spent it profusely. How I was praised!

The girl's family woo him into the marriage they know the girl hates. "I was rich! and when I married the girl, I saw a smile of triumph play upon the faces of her needy relatives, as they thought of their well-planned scheme and their fine prize." Here is a perception that goes deep; that sees under the chicanery of the law and the petty plotting of the respectable citizens the leer of the madman who is really controlling the machinery. The leer by which the socially unjust and the personally egotist are suddenly penetrated and set against a vision of essential evil.

If, now, with the light thrown by these two tales we look back at the sketch on Newgate which caused him so much effort and which George Hogarth specially praised we find an affinity between it and the tales. The sketch ends with a picturing of the condemned felon in his cell. The clock is inexorably striking, and he falls into dazed reverie. He is walking in the fields with his wife:

She is looking—not as she did when he saw her for the last time in that dreadful place, but as she used when he loved her—long, long ago, before misery and ill-treatment had altered her looks, and vice had changed his nature, and she is leaning upon his arm, and looking up into his face with tenderness and affection—and he does *not* strike her now, nor rudely shake her from him. And oh! how glad he is to tell her all he had forgotten in that last hurried interview, and to fall on his knees before her and fervently beseech her pardon for all the unkindness and cruelty that wasted her form and broke her heart!

Then he is back in the court room; then he is madly in flight.

The streets are cleared, the open fields are gained and the broad, wide country lies before him. Onward he dashes in the midst of darkness, over hedge and ditch. . . .

and so on till he sinks to sleep. Then he wakes in his cell again. Here we touch a day-dream that Dickens never outgrew. The emotional substance of the passage about regret, written well before Mary's death, shows how his anguish about her fitted into a predetermined pattern of loss and guilt; it will recur in *Oliver Twist* and elsewhere. The guilt-flight will turn up continually in his nightly dreams and his waking work.

But the moments of horror are insulated in the *Sketches* and *Pickwick*, in these crude insets. Much was to happen before the forces in Dickens which they represented could be fused with the humorous gusto and the power of character-projection which is awakening in *Pickwick*.

XII

In the *Sketches* and *Pickwick* Charles feels no qualms about his audience. He is carelessly one with them, and feels no qualms about himself. Later, he was to think and worry about his public; for the moment he takes it for granted. It is composed of all right-thinking people. Which means that it excludes aristocrats, who are not right-thinking, and Dissenters, who don't read fiction or sketches of any kind.

Aristocrats hover vaguely in the background of the early novels, dim figures like Lord Mutanhed at Bath with his hanger-on in *Pickwick*, or Lord Frederick Verisophy (soft in the brain but embryonically decent) and Sir Mulberry Hawk, the villain of melodrama in *Nickleby*. Such people could not be expected to read *Boz*.

Dissenters classed novels with cards and plays as prime sources of damnation. Their attitude was that of the Rev. Dismal Horror (in Samuel Warren's *Ten Thousand a Year*) who preaches on Miss Snooks: she kept a circulating library, went deeper into sin, visited a theatre on Thursday and died on Sunday. The women in the congregation sob hysterically and vow never to read a novel or see a play. Alton Locke reads Byron in a second-hand bookstall and is caught by his mother with Virgil; she calls in the chapel minister to reprove this sinful behaviour. Mrs. Oliphant, in her picture of the Dissenters of the 1850's, shows them reading nothing but the Bible and their ledgers. Mark Rutherford tells in his autobiography of a minister reading *The Vicar of Wakefield* at a Dorcas meeting; and afterwards Smale, the powerful draper, protests at such stuff being read in mixed company with young ladies present.

What were the dominant literary influences in the 1830's? The decade was one of the flattest and most confused for many a long year. The great romantic tide was in muddy ebb; and the new forces, of which Dickens and Carlyle were to be the spear-head, had not yet clarified. Dickens had absorbed the eighteenth-century novelists from Defoe to Scott, and the essayists from Goldsmith to Washington Irving; but when he looked round at his contemporaries, he could find no clear lead, no creative flow.

On the upper levels of culture a heavy mass of third-rate writing was the best to be detected. Scott's imitators were using all his feeblest tricks without any insight into his greatness. G. P. R. James was the exemplar. The social novel was in the hands of fashionable, faintly cynical observers like Mrs. Gore with her *The Fair of May Fair* (1832), or mediocre romancers like Lady Dacre; the genre had been fixed by Theodore Hook with his effects of upper-class intimacy in *Sayings and Doings* (1824–28). Disraeli had been busy in 1830–33, and produced *Contarini Fleming*; but his work seemed to lead nowhere in particular. Ainsworth and Bulwer, the most vigorous writers in sight, had carried on with the historical novel, but had made a detour round Scott, and had mixed up a brew out of low-life picaresque, melodrama, glorification of bandit and rogue, and Gothic psychological thriller. Ainsworth had romanticized the highwayman; Bulwer (via a Byronic version of the fashionable novel) the highwayman and the murderer.

Among the liveliest work being done were the sea stories of Marryat and several lesser writers, Glasscock and Chamier, Howard and Michael Scott; and the reading of them, plus memories of Chatham, may have helped Charles to his gallery of lovable sea dogs. There were also a number of humorous versifiers, Hood and Barham at the head, who mingled the crepuscular remnants of romanticism with various streaks of popular jesting.

It was, indeed, deep down in the popular levels that one had to look for creatively fertilizing forces. In the thriller and the melodrama, the burlesque and the farce, the puppet show and the broadsheet, powerful new elements were stirring—crude, violent, but rasping with new potentialities. There it was that we must look for the energies which, merging with the eighteenth-century literary models, provided the dynamic new element in Charles's art. Above all, it was his years of haunting the theatre, Covent Garden and the Surrey alike, in his youth, that made possible the great new achievement he was about to bring off in the novel.

The Surrey had something of a democratic revolt

tradition. Back in the days of the Revolution it had staged *The Triumph of Liberty: or, The Fall of the Bastille* (till put down by law as infringement of the rights of Covent Garden and Drury Lane). Here, during the period of Scott's supremacy, the Waverley novels dominated the stage; and Rob Roy led on to the Highland marauder Gilderoy. By 1819 Turpin appeared, and the highwayman came into his own, initiating the popular themes which Ainsworth, Whitehead, and Bulwer exploited. In the 1840's the Report of the Children's Employment Commission stated:

> Several had never heard the name of the Queen nor other names, such as Nelson, Wellington, Bonaparte; but it was noteworthy that those who had never heard even of St. Paul, Moses, or Solomon, were very well instructed as to the life, deeds, and character of Dick Turpin, and especially of Jack Sheppard. . . . According to one of the young factory hands, Christ "was a king of London long ago."

The themes of melodrama fed the thrillers which appeared in cheap mass forms with the 'twenties and 'thirties.

Another trend of the popular drama appeared when a stage version of Pierce Egan's *Life and London* was put on as *Tom and Jerry*. Here contemporary life was dealt with in its various exciting and vicious forms, and the ground prepared for a union of melodrama proper with the contemporary theme. Then the revolt element implicit in the rogue theme changed into a force begetting a critical focus on the material of everyday life. And just as Dickens had begun by drawing strong formative energies out of melodrama, so he now in turn affected melodrama and facilitated its development into a form of critical realism linked with immemorial fantasy themes.

All was now prepared for the pirating of *Oliver Twist* with its ominous figure of Bill Sikes. With his appearance on the stage in 1839 the real business of melodrama was manifest—the fight against evil in its existing shape.

For the understanding of early Victorian drama the critic needs Aristotle's Poetics less than an elementary textbook of political history. He needs to know the contemporary significance of the word "cholera" and the statistics of drunkenness, rather than the proper use of the three unities and the true function of tragedy. But in this study of squalor he need make no original research. One glimpse of social conditions under industrialism will prevent him from laughing at stage exposures that were not funny whatever ignorance may make of them now. Surrey "drink dramas" and factory dramas of the forties are forthright endeavours that shamed the garish entertainments of Drury Lane and Covent Garden. (Willson Disher.)

There was another type of popular literature deriving from the 'twenties, of which Egan's book, mentioned above, was the outstanding example. Deriving from an old genre of rogue literature, it adapted its themes to the corrupt, greedy, brutal, squalid world of the post-Napoleonic period. A world in confused throes of rapid transition, when some people are making a lot of money and many more people are having a hell of a time. The class on the fringe of the money-making are interested in the high jinks that those with a bit more money can enjoy. The scandal themes gain a wider audience, in some ways a grubby and small-fry audience who can't pay much for their reading matter, but are keen to get a look in. In the same way the county world with its jealously fenced preserves of sport is being invaded by new hordes of vulgarians, and some who can laugh at themselves. Others, who don't think themselves vulgar, want to laugh at the invaders. Sporting books sell to new publics; *Bell's Life in London* starts a new sort of journalism; and Surtees cashes in on the situation with his Mr. Jorrocks.

In short, the bank clerk wants to play at being a fast-living buck, and the city gent wants to play at being a huntsman; and all round are others who are amused at reading about them because they feel in such themes the breaking down of old class barriers and the building up of new class formations in which they themselves partake.

Here, then, to a large extent was the public to whom Charles was appealing, and the genres from which he was starting out. Mixed up with the new sort of writings, there had grown up a new sort of drawings, starting off from where the political and social satirists of the eighteenth century, Rowlandson and Gillray, had left off, and tempering their caricature-exuberance with a more careful observation of social event and type. But keeping their fantasy-touch, enough exaggeration to beget a strong impact on the observer, as if a slightly odd focus had brought out the animality and danger lurking under the voluble pretences. Cruikshank is the artist of the transition; and Phiz picks up at Dickens's level (though as an addendum rather than as a free creative force).

Dickens merged elements of the new popular styles and themes with a tougher element drawn partly from Smollett and

Fielding, partly from such contemporary political writers as the rebel Tory, Sydney Smith, and the Radical, Cobbett. He was soon to come to know Smith personally; Cobbett he does not seem to have met, though he must have seen and heard him in the House of Commons. Certain elements of the style of both writers, however, can be detected in his work—the urbane sarcasms of Smith, often with a nice touch of fanciful wit and with a biting balance of phrase; the deeper ironies and direct blows of Cobbett, with his power to make undoctrinaire statements coming straight out of the depths of the suffering people.

At Closer Grips

I

THE notices in the *Miscellany* begot a crop of rumours. *Pickwick* was really the work of a group, which had broken up for some reason. Or Boz was a lad of eighteen who had cracked under the strain and gone to a madhouse. Or he had been sent abroad for some sufficient reason. Or was dead.

In fact his health wasn't good. The effect of Kate's first pregnancy had been to unsettle him. As a child he had so deeply resented his mother's series of pregnancies; and Kate's motherhood did not draw him towards her, but completed the gap. That widening of the gap was bound up in turn with his emotion for Mary, the dream sister-wife free from all such physical unpleasantness. The old attacks, based in some obscure traumatic resistance, began to reappear. "I was seized last night with a violent pain in my head (fortunately just as I had concluded my month's work), and was immediately ordered as much medicine as would confine an ordinary sized horse to his stall for a week." He was thus preparing for a breakdown, and Mary's death following Kate's birth-throes was a signal to his hidden fears that the premonitory symptoms had been justified. This turn into anxiety and spasm was further bound up with his starting on *Oliver Twist*, when he gives himself up to the theme of the unwanted child—the first full-length release of his shrouded fantasy-life in work.

After the lull at North End Charles was reluctantly drawn back into work and money problems; and needing someone on whom to unload the latter he took advantage of Forster's approaches. Besides, Forster had caught him at the moment of extreme weakness, at North End, when the agony of guilt-fears made him feel hopelessly vulnerable and in need of aid. "I look back with unmingled pleasure to every link which each ensuing week has added to the chain of our attachment," he wrote a few weeks later. "It shall go hard, I hope, ere anything but Death impairs the toughness of a bond so firmly riveted."

Though a couple of months younger than Charles, Forster already seemed many years his senior. Son of a northern cattle-dealer, he had determined to become a man of letters, and cultivated S. C. Hall, editor of *The New Monthly*—Hall said later, "I found him a friend when he needed me, but not a friend when I needed him." Fuz had a brusque exterior, and a cabman once called him "the harbitrary gent," but Macready thought him sycophantic of the great. Others thought he had a heart of gold despite a readiness to talk one down in one's own house. Lady Blessington thought him noble minded; Mrs. Lynn Linton pompous, cynical, and jealous. Lady Bulwer Lytton described him as Fuzboz in her *Cheveley* (1839): "Neither tall nor short, but remarkably plebeian-looking, which was the only thing candid about him; he wore white Russian ducks in December, and was not a little proud of being an ugly and noseless likeness of a 'great tragedian,' who he tried to imitate in all things, even to his handwriting . . . a lickspittle . . . having a stock of 'Brummagem' enthusiasm on hand, and being a perfect Borcas at a puff." She depicted him "looking leading articles" when upset and wanting to assert himself. He had all the Victorian virtues and all the opacities and repressions that went with them. But he loved manipulating things behind the scenes, and now for many years he was to control Charles's business destinies. Also, to put a finger in his literary pie, wherever possible. He corrected his proofs from the second part of *Pickwick*, and wasn't backward with suggestions for correction. Dickens used to call him the Lincolnian Mammoth, but did not dare to pillory him till he no longer depended on his good works. Then people who knew recognized him in the pompously complacent Mr. Podsnap.

The first bit of the contract muddle that Charles called on him to solve was a threat from Macrone to issue the *Sketches* in monthly parts, to cash in on the *Pickwick* success. He had full legal right to do so, but Charles felt that the reissue of an old work would "most seriously" injure him as well as bring in no profit. Forster interviewed Macrone and did what he could, but Macrone was firm. Forster then asked if Macrone would sell back the copyright. Yes, said Macrone, on terms. A few hundreds, suggested Forster. Oh, no, said Macrone, a few thousands.

Forster thought this too high, and advised Charles "to keep quiet for a time." But Charles was constitutionally unable to rest under a strain. He took the matter up urgently with Chapman and Hall, who agreed to pay Macrone £2,000 in their own and Charles's name. Forster disagreed in vain. Then in a few months Chapman and Hall reissued the *Sketches* in monthly parts.

Bentley, too, was causing trouble. He wanted to know what was happening about the first of his promised novels—*Gabriel Vardon*. Charles was worried. He went to Forster, who wanted to see the contracts. Charles had only some memoranda.

I fear he has my second novel on the same terms . . . a bad look-out, but we must try to mend it. You will tell me that you are very much surprised at my doing business in this way. So am I, for in most matters of labour and application I am punctuality itself. The truth is . . . that if I had allowed myself to be worried by these things, I could never have done as much as I have. But I much fear, in my desire to avoid present vexations, I have laid up a bitter store for the future.

Forster interviewed Bentley and tried to explain how it would be best for everyone (everyone being Dickens) if Bentley agreed "to more equitable adjustment of their relations." Consequently "some misunderstandings followed."

On June 16th Charles met Macready, the fine character actor of Shakespearean parts with an uncontrollable temper, whom he much admired. *Othello* was being rehearsed, and William IV was ill—would he die and bring about a cancellation of the first night? Macready was worried. Forster opened the green-room door: "Here is Boz!" Macready welcomed Charles with a republican tirade against kings. Bend the knee to Voltaire, yes, but not to "the gold-besotted prurient people for whom nonsensical entertainments like *Semiramide* had to be devised." Charles liked him, and a firm friendship was formed—though Macready managed to ward off all Charles's efforts to involve him in his stage ambitions. Then, while the confusion of Charles's affairs went interminably on, he was carried off by Hablot Browne on a ten-day tour of the Continent. Landing at Calais, they whirled by post-chaise through Ghent, Brussels, Antwerp. At Calais his spirits lightened as he watched the girls dancing heartily in a garden: "in their short petticoats and light caps" they looked "uncommonly agreeable." The bluesurcoated gentleman who acted as guide they found, when ringing for slippers, to be the boots.

Browne had had the right idea in luring Charles off to France and Belgium. A new world was opened up. Charles's eager curiosity was stirred, and henceforth there was increasingly something European about him.

Back in England he continued to go through his affairs with Forster. His high spirits returned, but, as he always protested, the ghost of Mary lurked only one heart-beat away all the while. One minor irritation in the financial situation was the blandly dishonest John Dickens, who was still ostensibly a reporter. All through this year John was trying to turn an unearned penny by pestering Chapman and Hall. In February he had written from a house near Portman Square about a trifling debt to the firm of £4. It just "occurred" to him that at a moment of "some difficulty" C. and H. might extend their "obliging assistance." Herewith his bill for £20, due in April, and please forward the balance at once.

Do not suppose, I ask this on any other footing than that of obligation conferred upon me; and I assure you, though small in amount, its effects to me are matters of grave consideration, because anything that would occasion my absence from the Gallery would be productive of fatal results.

This gloomy hint he followed with an admission that he was intruding, but "recollecting how much your interests are bound up with that of my son . . ."

This kind of thing went on. Late in July the lack of a mere £15 was putting him in a position

of the most peculiar difficulty—as regards home affairs: if it was any matter less urgent than a question of rent, nothing would induce me to intrude my affairs on your notice. Mind, the subject is one of settlement by two o'clock, and unless I can so arrange I am lost.

Only this £15 can get him through "without the appearance of disgrace, and without that annoyance to Mrs. Dickens and my family which would be painful indeed." Blackmail could not be more genteel.

Not long after he writes to explain "my conduct in obtaining, as it were, from you money under false pretences." The debt had mounted to £55; but all he wanted was another £50 to save him from perdition. Would a three-year insurance policy in their favour satisfy them? He nobly admitted that he'd no right to ask their aid.

But when a man is placed in the situation in which I have placed myself, all but subjected himself to the laws of his country, he will snatch at a straw to save himself, not from drowning, but a scarcely milder sentence.

So, £50 "by one o'clock to-morrow," or "the most awful consequences." He is writing "under feelings of the most pregnant and heartrending distress at my own want of common honesty." And he concludes with a homiletic flourish that must have done his heart good. "To what a state of ignominy does one false step lead those who under strong pressure have not the power to resist temptation."

If Charles had known that such letters were going to survive, he would have been more chary about complimenting his father's unfaltering sense of honour. But we can bless the chance that has kept them. They demonstrate the extent to which almost the whole of Charles's wide gallery of parasites have the very accent of John Dickens. Oily Pecksniff may have been based in part on Samuel Carter Hall (and Phiz may have tried to interpret him as Peel), or Skimpole may have taken over many of Leigh Hunt's traits; but here, as in Micawber and Old Dorrit, there is a certain family likeness in the tone and gesture that leads back to John Dickens. Further, the underlying childishness is of much interest for our effort to unravel Charles's own character. These demands, self-pitiful and self-righteous, full of the complacence of the confessing sinner and the good man misunderstood, are extraordinarily Dostoevskian. As we listen we see the large form dwindle to the small child wheedling and lying and protesting, and finally expecting to be patted on the head for telling the "truth" in its own despite. But this childish element, which is a pervasive element of immaturity and "spoiltness" in the father, is only one ingredient in the son's complex make-up, where it works as an unresolved tension preventing him from premature reconciliations with the world.

Dickens was rapidly extending his range of acquaintance. Macready, we saw, was now a friend. Forster had introduced him to Leigh Hunt. George Lewes, book-lover who was to seem charming to George Eliot with the plain, smallpocked face that made Carlyle call him Ape Lewes, called by request at Doughty

Street. But he read a man by his books: "man's library expresses much of his hidden life." And his opinion of Dickens went down when he saw "nothing but three-volume novels and books of travel, all obviously presentation copies from authors or publishers. . . . I did not expect to find a bookworm, not even a student, but nevertheless this collection of books was a shock." When Charles came in, Lewes was "more impressed" with his "fullness of life and energy than with any sense of distinction."

In the spring of this year Talfourd had been working at a Copyright Bill, which he had discussed with Dickens. It aimed to safeguard an author's rights for sixty years—as against the existing state of things where there was little protection against piracy during life and nothing after death. Talfourd hoped to bring it up soon in the House.

About this time Charles, Forster, Macready, and Browne went on a circuit of nearly all the London prisons. As they peered at some prisoners under remand, Macready cried out, "My God! there's Wainewright!"

In the shabby-genteel creature, with sandy, disordered hair and dirty moustache, who had turned quickly round with a defiant stare at our entrance, looking at once mean and fierce, and quite capable of the cowardly murders he had committed, Macready had been horrified to recognize a man familiarly known to him in former years, and at whose table he had dined.

The episode strongly impressed Charles, who had Wainewright in mind when he drew Jonas Chuzzlewit and Rigaud, as well as Julius Slinkton of *Hunted Down*. (Bulwer based Varney of his *Lucretia* on Wainewright, so that the poisoner left no slight trail in Victorian fiction.)

The fascination of jails, orphanages, hospitals, morgues, and lunatic asylums was abiding in Charles's character. His idea of how to get to know a new country or town was to visit such institutions in it. Clearly, a part of him was deeply repelled, and yet he could not control the appeal. It was the appeal of the broken, the rejected, the maimed, the outcast. Such institutions and their inmates fascinated him because he felt that the clue lay there. The clue to the hidden thing and the new life.

II

Charles had good reason to feel himself driven by a devil. He was writing *Pickwick* and *Oliver Twist* together, and soon was to start *Nickleby* before *Pickwick* was finished, and take on the *Memoirs of Grimaldi*; and all the while was editing a monthly magazine and doing odd jobs of writing. His method of recuperation was to rush from work into furious physical exercise. He walked or rode, and Forster found the distances so long that nothing else could be done with the day. At the moment when he was hard pressed by the printers he'd scribble a note to Forster, saying that he must get some rest by going for a fifteen-mile ride out at eleven next morning.

Forster tried to keep the walks down to seven or eight miles a time, and for the moment could hold Dickens down. He got notes like the following ones:

What a brilliant morning for a country walk! . . . Is it possible that you can't, oughtn't, shouldn't, mustn't, *won't* be tempted, this gorgeous day! . . .

I start precisely—precisely mind—at half-past one. Come, come, *come*, and walk in the green lanes. You will work the better for it all the week. COME! I shall expect you. . . .

You don't feel disposed, do you, to muffle yourself up, and start off with me for a good brisk walk over Hampstead-heath? I know a good 'ous there where we can have a red-hot chop for dinner, and a glass of good wine.

The house was Jack Straw's Castle. The rides, however, grew more frequent than the walks. To Richmond and Twicken-ham—Eel-pie House—or Hampstead, Greenwich, Windsor. "WHERE? ? ? ?" He now had a small chaise with a smaller pair of ponies (for Kate); but the ponies had a trick of dashing off up by-streets by day and stopping peremptorily in ditches by night. So, next year, he sold them and bought a proper carriage.

The argument with Bentley was dragging on. At last in September a compromise was reached. The third novel was to be struck out; but the *Vardon* novel (emerging as *Barnaby Rudge*) was to be handed over by November 1838, and Charles agreed to edit the clown Grimaldi's *Memoirs* (then in a manu-script narrative compiled by Egerton Wilks). Forster had his doubts; for now the new historical novel would have to be started before *Oliver* was completed, and then what would happen to the work that Chapman and Hall wanted to follow up *Pickwick*?

On September 9th Macrone died, and his affairs were found in as much confusion as Charles's own. His widow gained very little out of the winding-up of the business.

During the summer the Dickenses had dined with the Smithsons, friends of Tom Mitton who had been on good terms with Charles in his clerk days. At the dinner was a girl (later Mrs. Eleanor Christian) who was charmed by Charles and "the marvellous power of his eyes." Those eyes were "nondescript in colour, though inclining to warm grey in repose." (Most of his friends called them deep blue.)

The collar and lapels of his surtout were very wide, and thrown back so as to give full effect to a vast expanse of white waistcoat. He wore drab-coloured trousers, ditto boots, with patent-leather toes, all most inconsistent with the poetic head and flowing locks.

Forster was there, talking pontifically; but Charles said little and simply looked on. When he did speak, there was a certain thickness in his speech, "as if the tongue was too large for the mouth." Mrs. D. was "a pretty little woman, plump and fresh-coloured, with the large heavy eyes so much admired by men."

The Smithsons, like the Macready and Sala families, loved Broadstairs for the summer seaside. So the Dickenses went there in September, to a modest little house in the High Street with brick front and flint sides; and there again Eleanor met them and thus was enabled to leave us a fine picture of the family and the strange, abstracted demonic state in which Charles now was.

The whole family was there, John and Elizabeth Dickens, as well as Charles and Kate. John she found a slightly pompous and well-preserved old buck. His wife was "very agreeable," ready to enter "into youthful amusements with much enjoyment"—though showing the results of a somewhat hard life.

It was wonderful how the whole family had emancipated themselves from their antecedents, and contrived to fit easily into their improved position. They appeared to be less at ease with Charles than with anyone else, and seemed in fear of offending him. There was a subdued manner, a kind of restraint, in his presence, not merely the result of admiration of his genius, and respect for his opinion, but because his moods were very variable.

In the fine weather everyone sat on the sands under the tall white cliffs and played games; and Kate made puns with an innocent sidelong glance of deprecating fun, and Charles frowned severely, and Kate pouted and giggled. All very loverly.

At the Tivoli Gardens were concerts and quadrilles. Eleanor

danced; but Charles, afraid of being recognized, watched. One evening he was eyeing "a young Marleena Kenwigs," when a man, whom he thought had been following him, stood at his side. Charles lifted his hat, "Are you a native of this place, sir?" The stranger said no. Charles went on, "I beg your pardon, I fancied I could detect *Broad Stares* upon your face." Unfortunately Kate wasn't there to catch the pun.

On the pier they railed off a space with benches, and in this private dance-room ("the family pew") Charles could let go. He loved dancing in the dusk there. Angus Fletcher (Kindheart) whistled and Charles blew on the comb. Then they went to the pier-end to watch the tide come in. One evening Charles, who liked flirting with Eleanor, suddenly threw his arm round her and ran with her right up to the edge of the jetty. There, clinging to a pole, he held her out until the water came up to her knees, talking with melodramatic volubility:

Let your mind dwell on the column in *The Times* wherein will be vividly described the pathetic fate of the lovely E.P., drowned by Dickens in a fit of dementia! Don't struggle, poor little bird; you are powerless in the claws of such a kite as this, child.

Mrs. Dickens had come and protested that he would spoil the girl's dress. Charles went on:

Dress! Talk not to me of dress! When the pall of night is enshrouding us in Cimmerian darkness, when we stand already on the brink of the great mystery, shall our thoughts be of fleshly vanities? Am I not immolating a brand new pair of patent leathers still unpaid for? Perish such lowborn thoughts! In this hour of abandonment to the voice of destiny shall we be held back by the puerilities of silken raiment? shall leather or prunells (whatever that may be) stop the bolt of Fate?

When at last he let the girl go, Kate suggested he should buy her a new dress. He replied:

Never! I have sacrificed her finery and my boots to the infernal gods. Kismet! It is finished! Eureka, etc., etc.; and now I go to tug myself black in the face getting off my pedal covers.

Eleanor may have kept a diary (she did not publish the story till 1887) for she certainly seems to have kept the very intonation of his mock-madness.

Another day the party drove in two landaus to Pegwell Bay. Charles bought some ballad-sheets from a pedlar and shouted

them all the way. Another day he amused everyone during a
sail in a hired boat with his roars: "A reef in your taffrail!
Sheepshank your mizzen! Brail up your capstan bar!" At
evening charades, for Pompadour he wore a wide-brimmed hat
pinned up at one side with a long feather and acted Louis XV.

At a concert a male singer ended *By the Sad Sea Waves* with a
turn-embellished high note. Eleanor asked what it meant.
"That's quite the rule in music," he replied, "as well as in
accordance with proverbial philosophy. When things are at
their worst they always take a turn." One day, talking of
Childe Harold, he said there was too much suggestion of the gin-
and-water that sometimes inspired Byron in "Dazzled and
drunk with beauty, The heart reels in its fullness." Then, as
someone defended the lines, he cried, "Stand back, I am suddenly seized with the divine afflatus! Don't disturb me till I
have given birth to my inspired conceptions." He went to the
window and wrote on the white shutter with a pencil: *Lines to
E.P., after Byron*:

> O maiden of the amber-dropping hair
> May I Byronically thy praises utter?
> Drunk with thy beauty, tell me, may I dare
> To sing thy paeans borne upon a shutter?

He had a habit of sucking his thumb and twisting a lock of
hair round the fingers of his left hand, while in the depths of
thought. Eleanor watched him staring with lack-lustre eye at the
sea and abstracted from everyone round; she became "horribly"
afraid of him, she told him. "Why," he said, "there is nothing
to be afraid of about me." She answered, "Isn't there? You look
like a forest-lion with a shaggy mane on the prowl." And she
cited, "He roared so loud and looked so wondrous grim, His
very shadow dare not follow him." He laughed. "What? do
you play shadow to my lion? Nay then, as Bottom the Weaver
says, I will aggravate my voice so that I will roar you as gently
as any sucking dove."

He was clearly in high spirits; and in such a mood it is hard
to draw the line between gaiety and hysteria. He was forcing the
pace, and the laughter was followed by the exhausted abstrac-
tion. A letter of September shows him recovering from a
moment of breakdown.

I am much better, and hope to begin Pickwick No. 18 to-morrow.
You will imagine how queer I must have been when I tell you that I

have been compelled for four-and-twenty mortal hours to abstain from porter or other malt liquor ! ! ! I done it though—really. . . .

I have discovered that the landlord of the Albion has delicious hollands (but what is that to *you*, for you cannot sympathize with my feelings), and that a cobbler who lives opposite to my bedroom window is a Roman-catholic, and gives an hour and a half to his devotions every morning behind his counter. I have walked upon the sands at low water from this place to Ramsgate, and sat upon the same at high ditto till I have been flayed with the cold. I have seen ladies and gentlemen walking upon the earth in slippers of buff, and pickling themselves in the sea in complete suits of the same. I have seen stout gentlemen looking at nothing through powerful telescopes for hours, and when at last they saw a cloud of smoke, fancying a steamer behind it, and going home comfortable and happy. I have found out that our next neighbour has a wife and something else under the same roof with the rest of the furniture— the wife deaf and blind, and the something else given to drinking.

Once more the observation ends in a surmise of sexual irregularities. Much of his fun reveals a wish to get inside the door, the window, and see what is really going on; to claim an unexpected relationship. Thus, in a prank of these early days, he knocked on a door, lay down on the doorstep, and, when the door was opened, scrambled up and ran away. In much of his behaviour there is the semi-deliberate release of an unconscious pressure along lines to be systematized later by the surrealists.

Consider, too, the fascination of the sea. Charles's ceaseless quest through the convolutions of verbal association is finely expressed in the joke about the high-note turn, the turn of fate, the turn of the tide. By the sad sea waves. The song murmurs already: "What are the wild waves saying?" Charles dreaming from Rochester over the sunset track on the waters; Charles flayed with the cold staring at the waters; Charles scaring Eleanor with something lost and dangerous as he sits staring at the waters. . . . Here is the deep-rooted poet in him; the dreaming child. The death-wish; the path of light to the star; the elemental womb.

In Chapter XVI of *Dombey*, "What the Waves Were Always Saying," where Paul dies, the imagery of rippling light and shadow is blended with the idea of movement through gliding water to a point of final light. Death: the union with the Mother:

Who stood on the bank? . . . "Mamma is like you, Floy. I know her by the face! But tell them that the print upon the stairs at school is not divine enough. The light about the head is shining on me as I go!"

The shining Mother is one with the Star-Sister.

III

Back in London in October Dickens heard that Talfourd's Copyright Bill had been thrown out, and received a letter from an American publisher, who had pirated his works, offering him a bonus. He refused the bonus but offered to enter into an arrangement for sending early proofs of forthcoming novels on contract terms. In dedicating *Pickwick* to Talfourd he paid tribute to his work on behalf of authors.

This month he completed *Pickwick* and went on with *Oliver* (which he had held up during the contract disputes); and paid his first visit to Brighton, where in early November he met a hurricane of wind knocking shutters down and darkened with showers of second-hand black hats (collected by the fishermen). Writing to Forster, he says that he is going to see a play *The Honeymoon*, and that his activities are otherwise "limited to the pavilion, the chain-pier, and the sea. The last is quite enough for me. . . ." He goes on:

I hope to do great things with Nancy. If I can only work out the idea I have formed of her, and of the female who is to contrast with her, I think I may defy Mr. —— and all his works. I have had great difficulty on keeping my hands off Fagin and the rest of them in the evenings; but as I came down for rest, I have resisted the temptation, and steadily applied myself to the labour of being idle. Did you ever read (of course you have though) Defoe's *History of the Devil*? What a capital thing it is! I bought it for a couple of shillings yesterday morning. . . .

Mr. —— was a writer in *The Quarterly Review* who, while praising, cautioned Dickens against exhausting his vein by writing too much and too fast.

Back in London again, he got a letter and silver snuffbox from his old schoolmaster Giles, now running an academy near Manchester. The box was inscribed "To the Inimitable Boz"; and Charles liked the adjective so much that he henceforth often used it as a name for himself.

He was having his portrait drawn by Samuel Laurence and Cruikshank; and was rather carelessly at work on his *Grimaldi* book, dictating bits to John Dickens and perhaps leaving him to muddle along with it. On November 18th a dinner was given to celebrate the end of *Pickwick* at the Prince of Wales Tavern, with a glittering cake surmounted by a figure of Pickwick and a eulogy by Talfourd. Charles got a cheque for £150 before the proceedings, and Chapman and Hall gave him a set of apostle spoons with *Pickwick* characters on them.

He agreed to give them in return another serial, the first number to be delivered by next March. Once more the feeling of intolerable pressure seized him. For one thing, endless piracies and crude imitations of *Pickwick* were appearing, making money for hacks in his despite, bringing him in no return and endangering his reputation. They were liable to make people sick of his themes and characters, and to spoil the market for his genuine work. One pirate-author even called himself "Bos." Beside books, papers, and plays there were Pickwickian songsters, Pickwick comic almanacs, and songbooks, jestbooks and scrapsheets attributed to Sam Weller. *Pickwick* was taken abroad in a tour of France; and even a *Penny Pickwick* was issued.

Amid these glooms the baby, nearly a year old, was christened before the end of 1837 in the "New Pancridge" Church in Euston Square, which architecturally had tried to turn the Erechtheum into a mausoleum. The baby howled during the evening party, and two days later developed measles. The house in Doughty Street was closed to the world, and Charles had nothing to do but get on with *Oliver Twist*.

IV

The new year, as we saw, found Dickens struggling under a weight of spiritual oppression. At Christmas he was pleased to snatch at an offer from Chapman and Hall: £125 for *Sketches of Young Gentlemen* (to follow up *Sketches of Young Ladies*, by Quiz, E. Caswall), to which he did not have to put his name. He worked furiously through January. To Ainsworth he wrote, inviting him to a dinner with Chapman and Hall (with wife):

The illustrious George [Cruikshank] and his stout lady are coming too so that the anti-Bores will be triumphant and keep the Bores in subjection. . . . My month's work has been dreadful, *Grimaldi*, the anonymous book for C. and H., *Oliver* and the *Miscellany*. They are all done, thank God! and I start on my pilgrimage to the cheap schools of Yorkshire (a mighty secret of course) next Monday morning.

John Dickens was also at work. After his pleasant time at Broadstairs he had returned to work and borrowing with renewed vigour; he was also surreptitiously selling pages of his son's manuscripts. "All sorts of annoyances," he wrote to Chapman and Hall, were driving him almost to madness. Would C. and H. renew their last bill once again?

Ignorant that his father was thus almost mad, Charles had determined to rush off with Hablot Browne to Yorkshire in search of material for his new serial. A law case had brought to light some scandalous conditions in schools in the north, and had revived some Chatham memories.

As fellow passenger in the coach they had a Yorkshire schoolmistress who had a long Biblically-larded letter from a father to his son in her school, ordering him to eat boiled meat, and who drank herself out with brandy. Arriving at Gretna Bridge on the last day of January, they moved on next morning to Barnard Castle round which were "all the schools and a dozen old abbeys besides." They stayed at the "King's Head," and went round making inquiries. One of the persons they talked with was a watchmaker named Humphreys, who had a notable long-cased clock inside his shop. They pretended to be *bona fide* searchers for a school, acting for a widowed friend with sons; and called on an attorney, Barnes, with a letter of introduction. He gave them two addresses; then ran after them and said the schools were miserable places.

They went on to William and Bridget Shaw, who kept a school at Bowes with some two hundred pupils and seven assistants. Apparently Shaw snubbed them and sent them off. But someone else handed them over to an usher (who had been dismissed for bad character), and from this man they got all the information they wanted. Much argument has gone on as to Shaw's deserts, and whether he deserved what he got from Dickens. (*Nickleby* made the identification unmistakable by giving Squeers only one eye like Shaw.) Shaw had been charged in court in 1832 with cruelty, and found not guilty of starving the boys, but guilty of neglecting them; and after *Nickleby* he was a ruined man. But whatever the exact merits or demerits of Shaw, there can be no doubt as to the generally bad conditions of the Yorkshire schools, and *Nickleby* did a good job in exposing them.

But as usual with Dickens, the social satire and good work was given its creative force by its fusion with memories drawn from his childhood experiences and dream-life. What mattered was, in the last resort, not the attack on a particular abuse, but the tremendous emotional impact which identified Smike and the other afflicted boys with all the suffering children of Britain at this dark moment of change, with the pangs of growth in Dickens himself. Beyond the sentimentalizing limitations there worked a genuine creative energy, unifying multiple planes of experience and begetting generic images of the human condition.

Rushing back to London, Charles set himself on February 6, 1838, to work on *Nicholas Nickleby*. Now for the next eight months he was to keep on writing instalments of *Nickleby* and *Oliver* turn by turn. During February he wrote the preface for *Grimaldi*, and went on with appeals to Bentley. "Something hanging over him like a hideous nightmare," he begged Bentley to let *Barnaby Rudge* appear as a serial (after *Oliver*) and not at once as a three-volume novel. "The conduct of three different stories at the same time, and the production of a large portion of each, every month, would have been beyond Scott himself." Bentley wasn't agreeable, and another long wrangle began. The nightmare went on. He felt he was turning out a vast amount of work and everyone else but himself was profiting.

In March we find him hard at work on *Oliver* in the midst of the arrival of another baby. Just as he "had fallen on him (*Oliver*) tooth and nail," he was "called away to sit with Kate." This idiom, which treats a book or its chief character as a sort of adversary to be attacked and knocked down, was typical of him always; and it shows often, as here, how his furious attitude to his work was linked on one side with a recoil from things going on around him. The fight with *Oliver* is his inner version of Kate's fight in child-bearing. Three days before he wrote, his second child Mary (Mamie) had been born, and in his impotent distraction he had ridden wildly out some fifteen miles along the Great North Road to dine at Barnet and bring home his horse lamed. Forster, trying to keep up with him, lamed his horse likewise.

On the 13th we see again how he merges his writing activity with Kate's child-bearing. He was, he said, "sitting patiently at home waiting for *Oliver Twist* who has not yet arrived. . . . The comfort is, that all the strange and terrible things come uppermost, and that the good and pleasant things are mixed up with every moment of our existence so plentifully that we scarcely heed them."

On March 30th he gave the toast at a dinner for Macready given by a club to which they both belonged, the Shakespeare Club. Then, as publication day for *Nickleby* was near, he hurried out of town to keep the precedent he had set over the first issue of *Pickwick*, and put up at "The Star and Garter" in Richmond. But he need have had no fear. The sales had rushed up at once to near 50,000.

Almost the whole of the summer was passed at Elm Cottage, Twickenham, where many friends, including Thackeray, visited him. Fanny and Letitia, both now married, came with their husbands, and, of course, John Dickens, smiling, arm-in-arm with his wife, still as interested in living as ever. Fred came lounging, soon to be stowed away in a Treasury clerkship at Charles's request; and Maclise and Beard, hearty chaps, with whom Charles vied in bar-leaping, bowling, quoits, battledore and bagatelle. For the children a balloon club was devised, to which Charley and Mamie were elected as the Snodgering Blee and Popem Jee.

He wrote a farce for Covent Garden, *The Lamplighter*, and in May was elected to the Athenaeum through Talfourd's offices, together with Macready and Charles Darwin. (This was the most astonishing recognition of all. Browning did not get in till 1862; and Macready had been turned down three years before.) Social activities were thickening. Now Dickens was getting into such company as that of Sir Francis Burdett, Samuel Rogers, D'Orsay, Lady Holland and Lady Blessington. His friendship with Angela Coutts (who, in 1837, had inherited two million pounds) was maturing, and he was continually advising her on her schemes of social study and improvement. Partly through her he began to systematize his inquiries into social conditions, read through Dr. Southwood Smith's report on housing in Westminster and Bethnal Green, and met Dr. Smith himself—the indefatigable social worker who originated the first Public Health Act (1848) and who had the clothed and wax-faced skeleton of Bentham in a mahogany case in his house. Then, besides the fashionable dinners, there were the many clubs, including Payne Collier's Shakespeare Club, where many drinks were taken and many speeches given before it broke up through some young barristers jeering at Forster's pomposity.

In the house of Rogers in St. James's Place, in Gore or Holland Houses, Charles found a kind of luxury, a kind of culture about which he had previously known nothing. He perceived, and to some extent understood, the way in which they carried on certain finer elements of eighteenth-century culture; and this perception helped to deepen and enrich his feeling of the contrasts in his world. Gradually he was discovering that the Reform Bill did not merely mean a fraudulent extension of the right to plunder, but that it in some sort represented a parting of the ways. Here, in the fine houses, in the literary talk at Mr. Rogers's breakfasts, in the easy wit in Lady Blessington's salon, in the sense of belonging to the great world at Holland House, he found something he both thirsted for and resented. Something that he admired as part of a graceful past which, whatever its weaknesses and evils, had contributed a positive element to civilization. Something that he hated in so far as it needed to preserve rights and prestiges not based on work and worth; in so far as it was linked with the corruptions and shams that ruled the world. By seeing this rich "society" which both excluded and accepted him, by measuring it against the outer world, by realizing how much of it had roots in a dead way of living, he made his first steps towards a sense of historical change. The unrealized conflict in his early work between pre-industrialist survivals and the forms and forces of an industrialized world now tended to come out, to compel his attention and demand explanation.

In this new sphere of his exploration Kate had no part. The only one of the new great friends who seemed to notice that she existed was Samuel Rogers, who had an eye for a pretty woman but who, even so, didn't ask her to his breakfasts. There was no case here of a socially inferior wife; for Kate had been better bred than Charles. She was simply left behind, relegated to the domestic sphere and then blamed for it; and she was not the woman to assert herself (except weakly and spasmodically) on this or indeed on any issue.

Meanwhile he was sending *Nicholas* on his wanderings and carrying on with *Oliver's* trials.

(*August*) Hard at work still. Nancy is no more. I showed what I had done to Kate last night, who was in an unspeakable "*state*": from which and my own impression I augur well. When I have sent Sikes to the devil, I must have yours.

(*September*) No, no, don't, don't let us ride till to-morrow, not having yet disposed of the Jew, who is such an out and outer that I don't know what to make of him.

As usual, we find the odd physical and generally rough-and-tumble relation to his characters. Especially in killing them off

did he undergo a strong strain which continually made him talk
as if he had murdered them and which was in the end to smash
him up himself. Nancy, in chief, was to have the last word, the
last hug in the death-struggle.

V

Oliver Twist, Dickens's first novel, shows us the starting-
point that emerges out of the welter of past and present influences in the *Sketches* and *Pickwick*. That point is in many ways
of eighteenth-century origin; but the influences of Smollett,
Fielding and Defoe are merged with those of Ainsworth,
Whitehead and Bulwer, and the voices of the Surrey Theatre
are not far behind. Consider Bulwer's *Paul Clifford*, in which a
boy, whose father is unknown, is unjustly jailed on a theft
charge; in jail he learns criminal ways, and later becomes a
bandit-hero. He speaks as an ardent social reformer and rebel
when brought to trial. "When has the law protected me? When
has it ever protected the poor? . . . You leave him to feed himself and then you harry him for doing it, not because he is
guilty but because he is naked and starving." The judge is his
natural father—a situation taken over from Mrs. Inchbald's
Nature and Art, where the judge condemns to death the girl he
started on the road to ruin by seduction. The strong anarchist
emotion was largely derived from Godwin—especially his *Caleb
Williams*.

First, then, we see that Dickens begins with a consolidation of
melodrama and the eighteenth-century low-life novel. The debt
to Smollett, in particular, is obvious. The hero of *Humphrey
Clinker* is a workhouse boy put out as apprentice. In dire
straits, he is taken into Mr. Bramble's service and turns out his
bastard. Oliver, too, is a workhouse boy put out as apprentice.
He falls into dire straits, gets among thieves, is taken up by
Mr. Brownlow, turns out the bastard of one Agnes Fleming,
and is adopted by Mr. Brownlow.

Secondly, there is the attack on social abuses: here directly
on the workhouse system and indirectly on the vast cruelty and
greed that begets the slums and the haunts of crime. There is
even the attack on individual bad characters, like the magistrate
of Hatton Garden (Fang: Laing) into whose court Dickens got
himself smuggled in the quest for material and who was dismissed shortly after *Oliver* appeared.

As part of this social message there is the picture of the dark areas of London, where such things happened—chiefly the section north of what is now Holborn Viaduct, and Jacob's Island in Bermondsey. But at this point the conscious social message begins to merge with the unconscious day-dream of union and guilt. The dark places of London were those which fascinated Dickens when he came to London as a boy and in which he wandered day-dreaming his drama of fear and hope, desertion and discovery. Above all *Oliver* returns to the period when he felt thrown out on to the world and played with fancies of running back to the lost home at Chatham. The novel starts off from childhood sites, with Oliver's workhouse at Chatham, and is one long rationalization of the emotions generated during the Chatham period and translated into the terms of rogue-literature. In the total focus the wandering of the lost child, the rejected child, are one with the demented guilt-progress of Bill Sikes after the murder.

He went through Islington; strode up the hill at Highgate, on which stands the stone in honour of Whittington, turned down Highgate Hill, unsteady of purpose, and uncertain where to go; struck off to the right again, almost as soon as he began to descend it; and taking the footpath across the fields, skirted Caen Wood, and so came out on Hampstead Heath. Traversing the hollow by the Vale of Health, he mounted the opposite bank, and crossing the road which joins the villages of Hampstead and Highgate, made along the remaining portion of the heath to the fields at North End, in one of which he laid himself under a hedge, and slept.

That is, he goes the familiar route of Charles's own walks, the walks deeply interwoven with his fantasies. He goes in the direction Charles went after the death of Mary Hogarth and sinks exhausted at the very spot where Charles went after that death. Sikes's guilt-track after murdering Nancy is the same as that of Charles after he had "killed off" Mary with his all-too-strong death-wish!

The death-wish fantasy appears in several forms in the story. In its brutal guilt-form in the murder of Nancy; in the illness of Rose; in the farewell of Oliver to Little Dick. In introducing the theme of Rose's dangerous illness Charles skirted the image so close to his thoughts, and tried to overcome the pain by denying its moral possibility.

"And consider, ma'am," said Oliver, as the tears forced themselves into his eyes, despite of his efforts to the contrary. "Oh! consider how young and good she is, and what pleasure and comfort she gives to all about her. I am sure—certain—quite certain—that for your sake, who are so good yourself, and for her own; and for the sake of all she makes so happy; she will not die. Heaven will not let her die so young."

And so she doesn't die. And Charles draws the following moral: "There is no remorse so deep as that which is unavailing; if we would be spared its tortures, let us remember this, in time." The logic is that he was to blame for something omitted, something done, which makes Mary's death an unavailing agony to him. What lies behind the statement is the conviction of a throbbing trauma, an unresolved conflict locked round the image of her death and its nexus of hidden fears.

The farewell from the doomed Little Dick is a brief sketch of the other side of the fear to that which is given in the account of Rose's illness. It prepares the way for Paul Dombey and Little Nell.

"I heard the doctor tell them I was dying," replied the child with a faint smile. "I am very glad to see you, dear; but don't stop, don't stop. . . ." "You will be well and happy." "I hope so," replied the child. "After I am dead, but not before. . . . I dream so much of Heaven, and Angels, and kind faces," etc.

This is the moment when Oliver is running off; and Little Dick, hopelessly unreal as a boy, has meaning only as an emblem of the fear from which Oliver runs.

But besides Dick, the fantasy-image of the Lost and Sacrificed Child, and Oliver, the day-dream self, there is Noah Claypole, the horrible example of the warping that the Poor Law system tends in fact to bring about. Dick, Oliver, and Noah all together complete the picture of the human situation here.

There remains the complicated tangle of fantasies round Rose, the lovely good girl with a "blot" on her birth. If we compare the story of the relations between her and the renunciatory Harry Maylie, with whom she is on semi-sisterly terms (acting as the daughter-niece of Mrs. Maylie), with the trio of stories defining Charles's fantasy-relations with his sister Fanny, we find a striking similarity. Here, at the outset, Charles shows basically the same fantasy as in *George Silverman*, written near the end of his life. Rose is surrounded with an atmosphere of the "forbidden," and so Harry gives her up. Then she turns out to be aunt of Oliver, who, however, still wants her as sister.

"Not aunt," cried Oliver, throwing his arms about her neck; "I'll never call her aunt—sister, my own dear sister, that something taught my heart to love so dearly from the first! Rose, dear, darling Rose!"

Remember that Charles had both an aunt and a sister named Fanny, and the aunt had been an important figure in his childhood. In Chapter XXXV, Rose, following her illness, renounces Harry because she must not come between him and his fame, the great place that lies ahead for him in the world—because his union with her would bring a "stain" into his life. The solution is found in the last chapter by Harry renouncing all ambition—a renunciation hardly explained by the story, since Rose is now established with a respectable origin—and going into an obscure position as a country clergyman. ("My hopes, my wishes, prospects, feeling: every thought in life except my love for you: have undergone a change. . . . No mingling with a world of malice and detraction, where the blood is called into honest cheeks by aught but real disgrace and shame; but a home. . . .") He thus acts like George Silverman, but, unlike George, takes a bride into his refuge from the world.

In a confused way Charles has thus edged round to a statement of his desire to get away from the existing relationships of the world, where moral values are inverted, back to "a home," out of the world, where he can satisfy a yearning for union of another kind.

VI

The last word, however, must be given to Dickens's power to draw characters in a method of intense poetic simplification, which makes them simultaneously social emblems, emotional symbols, and visually precise individuals. This is the method of so-called exaggeration or caricature, for which he has been berated by thin-blooded intellectuals, philistine naturalists, and those for whom "psychology" means introspection. The full defence of his method must wait till we come to the end of his career and have seen it in all its subtle diversities. For the moment it is enough to point the emergence here of his full-fledged method in a considerable range of low-life characters, from Bumble and his wife to the Artful Dodger and Fagin.

There are some other minor points, however, worth discussing. First, the odd twist that made him give to the emblem of underground evil, Fagin, the name of the lad who had been so decent to him at the blacking works. He was quite aware of the ingratitude; and we can only say that Fagin had come to stand in his mind for the level of wretched toil into which he had feared himself sinking, the proletarian pit yawning under the petty-bourgeois feet so ominously at this phase of social change —from which, once one was really in it, there seemed no escape. By some queer dialectics of fear Charles changes the good companionship in the pit into the chuckling fellowship of evil. Here is a raw anguish which he hardly dares touch, let alone probe.

Secondly, there was the fact that the book attracted a fair amount of attack as dealing with too dark a theme. The influential upholders of the Poor Law disapproved. Above all, the character of Nancy brought down censure as that of a prostitute treated with sympathy. Dickens replied to these charges in his Preface, and defended himself on the grounds of morality and truth. What the gentlemanly critics were reacting against was at root the tumultuous echoes of the popular tradition that Dickens was importing into serious literature. Bulwer and Ainsworth came in for some of the same abuse, and shortly after Ainsworth was blackballed from a club for having written *Jack Sheppard*. Lord Melbourne put the polite case against *Oliver* when he said, "I don't like that low, debasing style: it's just like the *Beggar's Opera*. I shouldn't think it would tend to raise morals."

Thus for the first time Dickens is compelled to think about the public, his public. Is it everyone? Or is it the moralists? Or is it someone else? He isn't quite sure; but he defends himself and his work sturdily. But the give-and-take between himself and his public has begun. Through writing in monthly parts over a long period, and starting to publish as soon as he started to write, it was possible to gauge the effect of certain trends or characters in the story, and readers had a chance to write in, criticize, suggest.

Thus began one of the strangest collaborations between author and public that literary history can show. By insisting on publishing monthly parts instead of a fully-made three-decker novel, Charles introduced a new relation between writer and public, which did not survive him.

The attacks on *Oliver* had the effect of making him aware of the possibilities in modification of intentions that the monthly parts allowed. (The long period covered by publication also allowed him to put in something of his own growth during that period, and to find his characters going ways he had not charted out when he began.) Now he debated with Forster the fate of the Artful Dodger; and Talfourd stepped in to plead for a second chance for Charley Bates, which was granted.

Later on, Cruikshank claimed that he had originated the story and its characters. He had drawn Dickens's attention to the death of farmed-out children in the parish of St. James's, Westminster, and urged the moral value of a novel on such a theme. He begged Dickens to make Oliver a pretty boy, to win over the ladies, and Dickens agreed. "If anyone will take the trouble to look at my representations of Oliver he will see that the appearance of the boy is altered after the first two illustrations."

More, Cruikshank drew Fagin, Sikes and Nancy before the story was written at all. The originals were models or drinking acquaintances of Cruikshank. "I have often sat in Cruikshank's parlour which numbered among its visitors the burglar Sikes," said a friend of his, R. H. Gooch. "His first name, it seems, was Bill, though his surname has not come down to us." Cruikshank sketched Bill, and Dickens said, "Jaw away, Bill," and took shorthand notes. The originals of Oliver and Nancy also often used to come in.

Probably there is much truth in the story; but, as with the Seymour case, it is largely irrelevant. The emotional and symbolizing power which gives *Oliver Twist* its value is all Dickens's. If we are to look for sources, we must turn to "Peter Grimes" in Crabbe's *The Borough* (1810), certainly known to Dickens, which tells of the fisherman's maltreated apprentices; Marryat's *Snarleyyob, or the Dog Fiend* (1837) with the wretched maltreated cabin-boy, Smallbones, and the prostitute Nancy Corbett, who becomes a good wife; and Bulwer's rebellious *Paul Clifford* (with Godwin behind it).

VII

Charles was feeling exhausted. He was perhaps never to get fully back to the galvanic high spirits of the 1837 summer any more than to the blissful days of Mary's companionship. When Eleanor met him again in London a year or so after Broadstairs she found him quite changed, preoccupied and self-important. Burnett gives a picture of him about this time: his "mind and muscles working (or, if you please, *playing*) in company, as new thoughts were being dropped upon the paper." And he kept muttering to himself as he worked. The process of moving from the actual world to the fantasy-transposition needed more of an effort of will.

By the close of October he was so weary that he could not bear to open letters. He left them a month at a time on his desk. No sooner was *Oliver* finished and a lavish, triumphal dinner consumed, than he rushed off with Browne on the Leamington coach. A dab at Stratford-on-Avon, then a sally to Kenilworth —with a note to Kate to say it was pleasant; they took summer lodgings there in 1839. Warwick Castle, so-so, pictures and view. Then off to North Wales, via Birmingham and Shrewsbury (where he had to take henbane to ease "an ecstasy of pain"). "Through miles of cinder-paths, and blazing furnaces and roaring steam engines, and such a mass of dirt, doom and misery, as I have never before witnessed." Forster at Manchester with letters from Ainsworth to bigwigs, to enable Charles to view a cotton mill.

So Charles met the Grant Brothers of Cheeryble House, who turned into *Nickleby's* Cheeryble Brothers, the employers to whom business is pure benevolence, yet who prosper. Then the three travellers went to give a book apiece to Ainsworth's three little girls in a boarding school, and went to the theatre, where Browne laughed so loudly that he infuriated an old gentleman in the next box.

What he saw of the factories utterly appalled him. He saw the best, he said, and then the worst, and there was no great difference between them. He meant to return next month for three days:

and then into the enemy's camp, and the very headquarters of the Factory System advocates. I fear I shall have little opportunity of looking about me, but I shall be most happy to avail myself of any introduction from Lord Ashley which in the course of an hour or so would enable me to make any fresh observations. . . .

So far as seeing goes, I have seen enough for my purpose, and what I have seen has astonished and disgusted me beyond all measure. I mean to strike the heaviest blow in my power for these unfortunate creatures, but whether I shall do so in *Nickleby* or wait some other opportunity I have not yet determined.

This project to write a novel in support of Ashley's work on behalf of the children in factories did not come to anything, though many years later Dickens was to tackle the factory system in *Hard Times*. What held him back was not any lack of goodwill or fear of annoying people. It was his difficulty of writing an effective novel on matters which he could not fit into his childhood symbolism. He had, in fact, written in *Oliver* a novel which emotionally pleaded the case of the tortured and driven children; but he had done so intuitively. It would have seemed to him an accident that it coincided with Ashley's campaign for the factory children. There was no accident there, however, and in *Oliver* Dickens had chosen the application of the theme which he could make effective.

He went on to North Wales, and Forster joined him at Liverpool. Back in London, he found it difficult to get on with *Nickleby*. To add to his depressions a hack named Stirling had produced at the Adelphi a garbled stage version of the story, inventing his own ending. Pirated and debased forms of *Oliver* were, of course, appearing, *Oliver Twiss* and a *Blue Coat Boy*, and by the end of the year at least eight stage-plays on the theme. In December Forster went with Charles to see the Surrey version, and in the middle of the first scene Charles lay down on the floor and refused to get up till the drop-scene fell.

VIII

In January 1839, he was in Manchester again. A dinner was to be given in honour of Ainsworth, a native of the town, who, to make the occasion more impressive, asked Dickens to go with him. The result was that the dinner seemed to be given in Dickens's honour; and Ainsworth accepted the situation with reasonable grace.

But his entangled contract situation was still galling him; and shortly after the turn of the year he wrote to Forster:

It is not fiction to say that at present I cannot write this tale [*Barnaby*]. The immense profits which *Oliver* has realized to its publisher and is still realizing; the paltry, wretched, miserable sum it brought to me (not equal to what is every day paid for a novel that sells fifteen hundred copies at most); the recollection of this, and the consciousness that I have still the slavery and drudgery of another work on the same journeyman-terms; the consciousness that my books are enriching everybody associated with them but myself; and that I, with such a popularity as I have acquired, am struggling in old toils, and wasting my energies in the very height and freshness of my fame, and the best part of my life, to fill the pockets of others, while for those who are nearest and dearest to me I can realize little more than a genteel subsistence: all this puts me out of heart and spirits; and I cannot—cannot and will not—under such circumstances that keep me down with an iron hand, distress myself by beginning this tale until I have had time to breathe. . . .

I do solemnly declare, that morally before God and man, I hold myself released from such hard bargains as these, after I have done so much for those who drove them.

But whatever God and man thought, Bentley stood more or less on his legal rights. He decided, however, that if Charles was going to plead that editing the *Miscellany* got in the way of his writing novels according to contract, he had better give up editing. Charles himself wanted to get away from Bentley. He hated having to work with or for a man with whom he was on strained terms. "I have burst the Bentleian bonds," he wrote to Talfourd. He also wrote to Ainsworth at seven in the morning, suggesting he should get into touch with Bentley at once and secure the vacant job.

Ainsworth possibly knew more than Charles what was going on. In any event the terrific success of his *Jack Sheppard* in the preceding month made him the very man that Bentley would want. And in fact Ainsworth had no trouble in taking over the *Miscellany*. Out of the taking over, however, arose various misunderstandings that led to a breach between him and Dickens.

John Dickens was now becoming insufferable. Arrests for debt had troubled him and made him in turn trouble Chapman and Hall more and more. And Alf, Charles's brother, had tumbled to the chance of easy money and was trying to bleed the publishers in a modest way: £5, please, to end "a most awkward dilemma." We only get a few glimpses of the way the shiftless of the family tried to batten on Charles; but their efforts went on getting worse until in 1841 his solicitor Mitton had to put a notice in the papers:

Certain persons, having or purporting to have the surname of our said client have put into circulation, with a view of more readily obtaining credit thereon, certain appetences made payable at his private residence or at the office of his business agents.

Henceforth only debts of his own or his wife's contracting would be paid.

So now, in March 1839, Charles decided to get his father away from temptation if possible. On Monday the 4th he went down to Exeter and found a six-roomed thatched cottage on the Plymouth road, at Alpington, with the landlady next door, a fat fresh-looking Devon woman just recovering from an attack "on the nerves." He papered and furnished the house. His mother joined him on Thursday; then his father, brothers and Dash the dog on Saturday. All got safely away, and any hovering creditors with warrants for arrest were thrown off the scent. Forster advanced the pocket-money and Tom Beard bought the coach-tickets and saw the family on to the coach. Everyone liked the cottage, and Charles hoped his father had now gone into permanent retirement. On Monday the 11th he returned to London, where late in the month he attended the dinner given to another retiring figure, Macready, who was leaving Covent Garden. His speech brought tears to the eyes of the listeners. Mrs. Cowden Clarke was much attracted by his "rich wavy locks of hair and his magnificent lustrous eyes." She noted his "remarkably observant faculty . . . perpetually discursive glances at those round him, taking note as it were of every slightest peculiarity in look, or manner or speech or tone."

But even before he gave that speech he knew that John and Elizabeth weren't going to be so easy to get rid of. His mother had written an "unsatisfactory letter." They weren't made for a quiet country life.

In April Charles, Kate and the babes went off to Petersham for four months, and took what was for him a varied literary fare, Swift's works, Leigh Hunt's *Indicator*, English essays, translations of French and German novels. On April 29th his old nautical friend Huffam died.

By June both his parents had begun writing "sneering, hateful letters." Charles complained to Forster of his mother. "I do swear I am sick at heart with both her and father too." By July, however, they were starting to settle down a bit; and after a visit he reported that the place was being well kept.

He himself was deep in a new plan. Hence the many books. In July he wrote all about it to Forster, asking him to sound Chapman and Hall about their intentions after *Nickleby*. He had had offers from publishers who were ready to pay him a percentage of profits, but he declared he would like to stay with C. and H. if they behaved "with liberality." What he would like to do was to issue from March 1840, a new sort of periodical, something like the *Spectator* or *Bee*, but more popular in reach—based on a fiction about some club (reintroducing Pickwick and Sam Weller). Its aim would be:

to write amusing essays on the various foibles of the day as they arise; to take advantage of all passing events; and to vary the form of the papers by throwing them into sketches, essays, tales, adventures, letters from imaginary correspondents, and so forth. . . .

Stories and descriptions of London as it was many years ago, as it is now, and as it will be many years hence, to which I would give some such title as The Relaxations of Gog and Magog. . . satirical papers purporting to be translated from some Savage Chronicles, and to describe the administration of justice in some country that never existed, and record the proceedings of its wise men . . . to keep a special look-out upon the magistrates in town and country, and never leave those worthies alone.

All control was to be in his hands; and he would make visits to places like Ireland and America, to write accounts of them, with tales, legends, etc. He was to be part proprietor and sharer in profits.

Chapman and Hall accorded interest and encouragement. They even agreed to pay him £50 a week and not to ask him to take any of the risk of the publication. Profits to be shared fifty-fifty, and the parts to go on for at least a year.

His mind was being haunted by the image of an old man who had a long-cased clock as his friend, listening to its ticking voice, its cheerful strike in the night, and finding in its very face "something of welcome in its dusty features." This old fellow kept manuscripts in the "old, deep, dark, silent closet where the weights are," and used to take them out to read, "mixing up his enjoyment with some notion of his clock." A club formed round him and "by reason of their punctuality and his regard for his dumb servant," took their name from the clock. So the publication was to be called *Old Humphrey's Clock*, or *Master Humphrey's Clock*, and all the old man's papers were to be "dated From my clock-side."

The immediate origin of this clock-and-man image certainly lay in Humphrey of Castle Barnard; but what had particularly struck Charles about that old man we cannot say. Somehow or other the person of Mr. Humphrey with his clock, encountered during the Yorkshire search for evidence proving true his memory of the maltreated child, had come to emblematize Time for him. Time as human experience, the symbol and person who was to pull together all the scattered material of the periodical, its Gog-and-Magog past and present and future, its satirical and emotional differences in focus.

The Clock-face is a controlling power which the child has to comprehend as one of the first basic efforts of analysis; with the beginning grasp of Time and Death the child's fantasy of the omnipotence of desire breaks down. Paul Dombey on the stairs thinks the clock looks at him; and in a letter written in

1863 to a clock-maker Charles, as in the notes on the periodical project, treats the clock as a person. It has endured "internal agonies of a most distressing nature," and so on. He ends, "if you can send down a confidential person with whom the clock can confer, I think it may have something in its works that it would be glad to make a clean breast of." Just a joke? Yes, but with a man like Dickens his jokes are among the most revealing of his acts; he is then most unguarded, and his rich poetic forces of association pour out without fear.

IX

In September the family went on from Petersham to Broadstairs. Some time during the summer they had been joined by the third Hogarth sister, Georgina. Dickens's publishers, big Chapman and little Hall, came down with Browne's sketches; and the wind blew for three days. "Such a sea! I staggered down to the pier, and, creeping under the lee of a large boat which was high and dry, watched it breaking for nearly an hour. Of course I came back wet through." Eleanor, now at the end of her honeymoon as Mrs. Christian, was also at Broadstairs, and one night she met the Dickenses at the Tivoli Gardens. Charles was dancing with Georgina.

Kate was coming near child-bed again; and another of her sisters was supplanting her. But the simple, blissful union of Charles and Mary could not repeat itself. For one thing Kate was no longer so thoughtlessly acquiescent. Though unable to assert herself, she knew that things weren't right with her marriage, and she couldn't help letting her feelings show at moments.

The decisive moment of break had come at the time of the birth of the second child, Mary. When Charles had ridden wildly out and lamed his horse, he had been riding away from Kate, away from whole nexus of child-birth that he loathed, away from the infant girl, Mary, who could never be Mary. When the marriage later did break up before the world, he looked back and said to Forster, "What is now befalling me I have seen steadily coming, ever since the days you remember when Mary was born." Apparently under the strain of child-birth Kate had said and shown too much.

And so now the second supplanter had arrived, Georgina, a sly purposive shadow in the household. For Charles her presence meant a slackening of tension. He was less alone with

Kate; he had Georgina to cushion all domestic bumps; he had her companionship which, though lacking the rapture of Mary's worship, gave him a certain warmth and ease.

With October the family returned to Doughty Street, which they now felt too small. Charles began to look round. At Macready's advice he thought for a while of Kent Terrace, then decided on 1 Devonshire Terrace near Regent's Park, on which he took a twelve-year lease and started putting in water-closets.

Meanwhile *Nickleby* was completed, and the celebratory dinner was held, at which all manner of cordial things were said. And the third child, Kate, was born. And Barnaby Rudge, too, was born. Charles entered his name among the students of Middle Temple; and exulted in the new house—"a house of great promise (and great premium), 'undeniable' situation and excessive splendour." Thick pile curtains and mahogany doors and carved marble chimney pieces were installed. And at the end of the year the move was made.

X

In *Oliver* Charles had based himself on certain eighteenth-century elements, both in themselves and in their offshoots in contemporary thriller and melodrama; and had used the day-dream of his own childhood-at-bay to give a picture, emotionally true, of the exploited children of his own day. In *Nickleby* he takes certain other eighteenth-century elements, the picaresque of Fielding and Smollett, adds ingredients of burlesque and melodrama from the popular tradition around him, returns to another aspect of his childhood-at-bay, and seeks to give an extended picture of the main forces at work in his world.

Because he is still, to a considerable extent, back emotionally in the pre-reform situation, in eighteenth-century terms, the pattern he evolves is based on the simple opposition of the constructive and destructive aspects in capitalist industrialism. Money still seems a force separable from industry. In the latter sphere men are boldly advancing to a new control of the world, but the contaminations and confusing pressures of money keep breaking in. Money as usury is contrasted with money as a (theoretically) pure medium of exchange.

That is the stage at which he halts for the moment. His picture of the way the two forces work is vague in the extreme; but the general import of his statement is clear enough. On the one hand is Ralph Nickleby, the evil side:

Mr. Ralph Nickleby was not, strictly speaking, what you would call a merchant, neither was he a banker, nor an attorney, nor a special pleader, nor a notary. He was certainly not a tradesman, and still less could he lay any claim to the title of a professional gentleman. . . . Nevertheless . . .

Nevertheless, Charles feels him quite definitely as the evil factor in the situation. The Cheerybles are even vaguer; they have some sort of important business, and they represent the good side of the situation. If one looks at the Grant brothers, from whom they were drawn, one gets a clearer idea of what Charles is trying to say. The Grants, poor sons of a cattle dealer, set out to make their fortune, threw a stick in the air, followed the direction it indicated, thriftily became masters of a little print-works, and in time turned big capitalists and mill owners, at the top of the Lancashire tree. They never got swollen heads, remained charitable, were socially generous. There was no nonsense about them. When Nasmyth, still unknown, went to Manchester, approached William Grant and told him he wanted to start an engineering works, Grant asked what his capital was. He had £63. "Keep your heart up," said Grant, and offered a credit of £500 at 3 per cent with no security.

The Grant-Cheerybles, then, represented the entrepreneur-capitalist at his best, his thriftiest, his kindliest. Charles, with a correct enough intuition, opposes them to Ralph Nickleby and the usurious forces that were so soon to put an end to the entrepreneur Grant type.

Where does the hero, Nicholas, stand in all this? He is finally allied (by marriage) with the Cheerybles and defeats the machinations of Ralph. He regains the heritage (and invests his wife's money with the Cheerybles). But, at this backward-looking moment, that means he regains a landed stake in the country; he gets back to the stage from which his father was ousted by the speculative money-forces. The mechanism of the story is the romantic one of the truth brought to light and the status and inheritance of the hero vindicated.

While the usury side can thus be flatly cut off and opposed to the constructive aspects of the industrial forms, there is little else for a hero to do but to unmask the evil and then retire to a leisured existence on the land. Therein lies, it seems, the good life. But what if the ugly usury side turns out to be implicit in all profit-making activity and permeates what had seemed the Cheeryble innocence and benevolence? Then that innocence becomes the mask of the worst evil of all, the greatest distortion of the human essence; and the venomed forces are present at every point of the constructive energies. Oh, what then?

Dickens's progress is precisely to that point, which lies over the horizon at the moment. Our interest in following his progress lies in watching the new pressures that develop around and inside the romantic formulas of reconciliation, and the new shapes that those formulas take, as he advances deeper into a comprehension of the unity of forces at work in his world.

Dickens is using eighteenth-century forms and methods to get close at the pattern of his own world, in which, indeed, eighteenth-century forms and methods are still vitally involved. In the process he both makes many powerful attacks on particular forms of evil, social and personal, Squeers or the "patriotic" politician, Gregsbury, and creates more of his great generic images of character: Squeers and Mantilini, Miss La Creevy and the Crummles, Mrs. Nickleby and Newman Noggs.

How does he get at the images and the historical pattern via his basic childhood fantasies? By much the same methods as in *Oliver*. Nicholas going up to Dotheboys Hall is Charles going up to Yorkshire to relate childhood fear and contemporary social fact; and through that inroad he rescues Smike, the emblem of himself as the Lost Child. Nicholas and Smike together make up the full self; and so Nicholas, plus Smike, can go off in quest of the heritage, championing distress and righting the wrongs of the world and getting his reward. The death of Smike is then the death-wish robbed of its sting. Smike speaks "of beautiful gardens," in which are "men, women and many children, all with light upon their faces; then, whispered that it was Eden—and so died." Smike, the lost self, dies back into the lost Eden and ensures the contact of Nicholas, the self in the actual world, with those sources of light.

Smike is also the Fool of the folk-formula, the innocent who rebukes the world by his utter ignorance of its values, and who, therefore, somehow becomes the hero of a reversal of values. He is the Tom-all-alone of the Chatham dusk become both the real exploited outcast of the contemporary world and the fantasy image of the lost self.

In the increasing mastery over his material, which Dickens now feels, he can afford to play all round the childhood theme. Thus, while turning Little Dick of *Oliver* into the full-drawn Smike, he also guys the motive of childhood fixation in the humours of the Infant Phenomenon. (In real life, Miss Davenport, pantaletted, with fat legs and florid cheeks, aged about fourteen and looking about nine, who used to be put by her father at the lodgings window with her dolls in the morning and on the stage as Lady Macbeth at night.)

Much of his verve, too, comes from the way in which he is guying his mother in Mrs. Nickleby. About the identification he never made any pretences. "Mrs. Nickleby herself, sitting bodily before me in a solid chair, once asked me whether I really believed there ever was such a woman!" He thus pairs off the return into the luminous Eden of childhood, where all is harmony with the mother, and the rejection of the actual mother as a sort of semi-imbecile, hopeless in the world, ready to listen to the advances of a madman. (The Gentleman in Small-Clothes who woos her must have lived in Byas's Private Lunatic Asylum at Bow, which had a high wall on to which abutted some cottages just as in *Nickleby*.) Writing to Forster at the time he composed this chapter, Dickens remarked that if he kept on getting steam up so strenuously he'd "bust the boiler. I think Mrs. Nickleby's love scene will come out rather unique." The wish to degrade one's parents could hardly go further than this picturing of what his mother's love responses amounted to.

At the same time the ambivalence which appears in Smike's death-bed appears further in the account of the Cheerybles. They end their dinner at home with the toast.

I wish that she could have seen us in our prosperity, and shared it, and had the happiness of knowing how dearly we loved her in it, as we did when we were two poor boys—but that was not to be. My dear brother—The Memory of our Mother.

(It is amusing, by the way, that *Nickleby's* picture of the Cheerybles brought Charles "thousands of letters, from all sorts of people," trying to get "loans, gifts, and offices of profit" out of them.)

The final touches of the Chatham fantasy are added by Kate Nickleby. She is admittedly based on his sister Fanny, but is given the name of his wife—another expression of the wife-sister dream; for so subtly name-conscious a writer as Dickens could not have made this transposition without a deep compulsion, a deep sense of satisfaction. (If there is any truth in the statement that Nicholas to some extent was based consciously on Burnett, we get an even worse tangle; for then Nicholas-Burnett did in fact marry Kate-Fanny. And things are made yet more com-

plicated by the allocation of the magical name Fanny to Miss
Squeers with her amorous attempts on Nicholas.) The conclusion is a sort of family conglomeration:

The first act of Nicholas, when he became a rich and prosperous
merchant, was to buy his father's old house. As time crept on, and
there came gradually about him a group of lovely children, it was
altered and enlarged; but none of the old rooms were ever pulled
down, no old tree was ever rooted up, nothing with which there
was any association of bygone times was ever removed or changed.
Within a stone's throw was another retreat, enlived by children's
pleasant voices, too; and here was Kate . . . the same true, gentle
creature, the same fond sister, the same in the love of all about her,
as in her girlish days.

This passage throws much light on the urge that drove
Charles back to the Chatham area and the buying of Gadshill.
His idea of marriage is one that ensures the return to childhood
and the unbroken union with the sister. In the words omitted
from the passage above we read how Kate among her many
children finds "one so like her own, that to her mother she
seemed a child again." There is all round an entangled return
to something that can never be returned to. Orwell, commenting
on the "incestuous atmosphere" of the passage, cites the ending
of *Hard Cash* by Charles Reade to show how basically Victorian
was the ideal of the enclosed pullulating family:

They all lived together (parents-in-law and daughter and husband)
at Albion Villa, thanks to Alfred. . . . Oh, you happy little villa.
You were as like Paradise as any mortal dwelling can be. A day
came, however, when your walls could no longer hold all the happy
inmates. Julia presented Alfred with a lovely boy: enter nurses, and
the villa showed symptoms of bursting. Two months more, and
Alfred and his wife overflowed into the next villa. It was but twenty
yards off; and there was a double reason for the migration. As often
happens after a long separation, Heaven bestowed on Captain and
Mrs. Dodd another infant to play about their knees, etc., etc., etc.

6

Into History

I

ITH the turn into 1840 the preparations for the new periodical quickened. On January 9th his notes tell us, "At home all day and evening—correcting proofs of *Young Couples*; and considering new work in all possible ways." The Queen's marriage was in the news, and Charles heard from Maclise details about what was going on behind the scenes; for the Queen admired Maclise's work and had commissioned from him pictures which she meant to present to Alfred. Charles worked himself up into a jesting pretence of love for the Queen which ended in something like genuine unbalance.

Maclise and I are raving with love for the Queen. . . . We sallied down to Windsor, prowled about the Castle, saw the corridor, and their private rooms, nay the very bed-chamber lighted up with such a ruddy, homely, brilliant glow bespeaking so much bliss and happiness that I lay down in the mud at the top of the Long Walk and refused all comfort.

He and Maclise, he said, wore marriage medals next to their hearts. The fancy got control of him. For days, weeks, he couldn't work, couldn't sit down quietly, and prowled round the house singing:

My heart is at Windsor, my heart isn't here;
My heart is at Windsor, a-following my dear.

He wrote to Forster:

I saw the Responsibilities this morning, and burst into tears. The presence of my wife aggravates me. I loathe my parents. I detest my house. I begin to have thoughts of the Serpentine, of the

184

Regent's-canal, of the razors upstairs, of the chemist's down the street, of poisoning myself at Mrs. ——'s table, of hanging myself upon the pear-tree in the garden, of abstaining from food and starving myself to death, of being bled for my cold and tearing off the bandages, of falling under the feet of cab-horses in the New-road, of murdering Chapman and Hall and becoming great in story (SHE must hear something of me then—perhaps sign the warrant; or is that a fable?), of turning Chartist, of heading some bloody assault upon the palace and saving Her by my single hand— of being anything but what I have been and doing anything but what I have done. Your distracted friend, C. D.

Forster adds, "The wild derangement of asterisks in every shape and form, with which this incoherence closed, cannot be given." Charles wrote to T. J. Thomson as executor of his will, that there was a bequest he wished to leave the Queen.

I have heard on the Lord Chamberlain's authority, that she reads my books, and is very fond of them. I think she will be sorry when I am gone. I should wish to be embalmed and to be kept (if practicable) on the top of the triumphal arch at Buckingham Palace when she is in town, and on the north-east turrets of the Round Tower when she is at Windsor.

To Walter Savage Landor (known through Forster) at Bath he wrote:

Society is unhinged here by her majesty's marriage, and I am sorry to add that I have fallen hopelessly in love with the Queen, and wander up and down with vague and dismal thoughts of running away to some uninhabited island with a maid of honour, to be entrapped by conspiracy for that purpose. Can you suggest any particular young person, serving in such a capacity, who would suit me? It is too much perhaps to ask you to join the band of noble youths (Forster is in it, and Maclise) who are to assist me in this great enterprise, but a man of your energy would be invaluable. I have my eyes upon Lady ——, principally because she is very beautiful, and has no strong brothers. Upon this, and other points of the scheme, however, we will confer more at length when we meet; and meanwhile burn this document, that no suspicion may arise or rumour get abroad.

No wonder that Landor, who hardly knew him, sent the letter on to Forster with an inquiry, "What does it all mean?" And Charles wasn't only writing like that, he was talking in in the same vein, too, unable to talk about anything else.

Dashing to the Athenaeum, he asked Moncton Milnes if he had heard the National Anthem of Seven Dials being sung in the streets:

> So let 'em say whate'er they may
> Or do whate'er they can,
> Prince Halbert he will always be
> My own dear Fancy Man.

The "daring delusion" of his mad love for the Queen, says Forster, "took the wildest forms of humorous extravagance . . . unflaggingly kept up, to the amazement of bystanders knowing nothing of what it meant and believing he had half lost his senses." In fact the joke was being a little too well carried on, and shows how easy it was for his day-dream mechanism to invade and swallow up normal life.

The move into the new house with a third baby no doubt played its part in increasing the strain; but at root what was tearing him to pieces was his inability to settle to work. He didn't at all know where he was going. The periodical project had kindled his mind in its conception, and nothing had seemed easier than to pour his maturing energies into its mould. But when he came to get at grips with the idea, things weren't the same. The first real pause in the outburst of work that began with the *Dinner in Poplar Walk* sketch had now arrived; and he was finding it very difficult to keep his self-confidence, to concentrate and make the new start. Hence the half-controlled, half-uncontrolled sex fantasy of self-aggrandizement which he focussed on to the Queen, and which, if it did nothing else, hurt and irritated Kate.

On February 10th the Queen was married, and Charles and Kate went to watch the procession from the stand at the Athenaeum. To break Charles from his obsession, Forster arranged a visit to Landor; and near the end of the month, he, Charles and Phiz went off to Bath. Charles enjoyed meeting the old leonine republican; and henceforth he and Forster went every year to visit him on his birthday.

Back in London, he now managed to get down to work, and carefully instructed Cattermole in the drawing of the clock and its setting among antiques. Then, when in April the first issue was near appearance, he dashed away with Kate, after spending the night before at Richmond. Forster joined them the day after his flight at Birmingham with news that

60,000 had been sold and 10,000 more orders to hand. They hurried on to Stratford and Lichfield, and stayed longer than they'd meant; they had to use Alfred Dickens, now a student engineer at Tamworth, to pawn their gold watches at Birmingham.

Back in London Dickens's health was bad after the strain; but a careful diet and exercise restored him. Again he and Forster rode much "in suburban lanes and roads." And about this time he sat as juryman at an inquest on a baby alleged to have been murdered by its mother; largely through him the verdict charged the woman only with concealment of birth. Then either through "the poor baby, or its poor mother, or the coffin, or my fellow-jurymen" he had a violent attack and sat up all night with Kate patient at his side. A raven had now been bought as a pet; and the red-headed groom almost created a law-suit by his too-ingenious devices to control the smoke of the stable chimney. Charles kept an eye on the woman of the inquest, and paid counsel for her defence at the Old Bailey.

Near the end of May they went to Broadstairs. He was still chafing about having any connection with Bentley, who was still without his *Barnaby*. Forster took the matter up for him with Chapman and Hall, who now, in negotiations covering May, June, and July, ended by agreeing to buy all rights in *Oliver Twist* and the unwritten *Barnaby* for £2,250. Now at last Dickens had only one publisher, and gratefully sent Forster a claret jug. But all was not well with *Humphrey's Clock*. The public, disappointed at finding no serial, were ceasing to buy. By devious transitions the complicated project turned into *The Old Curiosity Shop*, the wanderings and death of Little Nell. Sales rose again, and the work was a tremendous success.

Among odd jobs he had agreed to edit for Colburn a collection, *The Pic-Nic Papers*, for the benefit of Macrone's hard-up widow. The work was being more troublesome than he had expected. Colburn kept butting in and doing things without consulting Charles, accepting or rejecting on his own authority. He ignored a contribution from Leigh Hunt and took religious objection to something Landor had sent in.

At the end of June Forster and Maclise had joined Charles for the home journey "by way of his favourite Chatham, Rochester, and Cobham, where we passed two agreeable days in revisiting well-remembered scenes."

In August Macready was at dinner at Devonshire House with

Forster also as guest, and witnessed a scene which he recorded in his diary:

Went to dine with Dickens, and was witness of a most painful scene after dinner. Forster, Maclise, and myself were the guests. Forster got to one of his headlong streams of talk (which he thinks argument), and waxed warm, and at last some sharp observation led to personal retorts between him and Dickens. He displayed his usual want of tact, and Dickens flew into so violent a passion as quite to forget himself, and give Forster to understand that he was in his house which he should be very glad if he would leave.

Forster behaved very foolishly. I stopped him; spoke to both of them, and observed that for an angry instant they were about to destroy a friendship valuable to both. I drew from Dickens the admission that he had spoken in passion and would not have said what he said could he have reflected; but he added that he could not answer for his temper under Forster's provocation, and that he should do just the same again.

Forster behaved very *weakly*; would not accept the repeated acknowledgment communicated to him that Dickens regretted the passion, etc., but stayed skimble-skambling, and at last, finding he could obtain no more, made a sort of speech accepting what he had before declined. He was silent and not recovered—no wonder!—during the whole evening. Mrs. Dickens had gone out in tears. It was a very painful scene.

Indeed, more than claret jugs were needed to cement the relationship of these men, though Dickens had protested that the jug was an urn for his heart, which filled it with its "warmest and truest blood." At times he felt that Forster was too truly drinking his blood out of the formal urn. But he needed him. Not only as a good business adviser, but as the touchstone of his audience. His continual subservience to Forster's opinion was based, not in respect for Forster, but in a wish to keep in well with the public whom he felt Forster expressed. His increasing fret at this relationship was an increasing tension between him and the public. He coquetted to gain Forster's patronizing praise and then made fun of it in his own way. Their devotion to one another became a form of sparring. James Payn used this very term. "I have rarely seen them together without witnessing some sparring between them, sometimes without the gloves." In the brief diary notes Charles kept in 1839 he found time to write on February 7th (his twenty-seventh birthday), "Forster preposterous on the subject of the Drury Lane Theatrical Fund." Dickens would say, as if he couldn't understand why it happened,

" I don't quarrel with my other friends." No other friend represented the great Victorian public.

Early in August Charles hurried off with Kate into Devon on a visit to his parents, taking his work with him, and making one dash at Dawlish, Teignmouth, Torquay. With September he was back in Broadstairs, at Lawn House, between a hill and a cornfield. Rumours got round that he had become a Catholic, and to his astonishment Catholic clergy started writing to him. Angus Fletcher was at Broadstairs and behaving so oddly that visitors took him for Dickens, who, hearing their comments, begged Fletcher to control his "insane gambollings."

By the middle of October he was once more in London, riding in all directions with Forster, rushing to see Maclise at Hampstead, and meeting scores of friends, and yet more scores. The Devonshire Terrace house, fashionably placed, was stocked with a cook, three maids, and a man; and dinners were being given.

He also found time to think about broadsheet songs.

Impelled thereto by specimens recently discovered in his country walks between Broadstairs and Ramsgate, he thoroughly explored the ballad literature of Seven-dials, and would occasionally sing, with an effect that justified his reputation for comic singing in his childhood, not a few of those wonderful productions.

Now he was nearing the time when he would have to kill off Little Nell, and very hard he found it. "The difficulty has been tremendous—the anguish unspeakable," Forster says. "I never knew him wind up any tale with such a sorrowful reluctance as this. He caught at any excuse to hold his hand from it, and stretched to the utmost limit the time left to complete it." Christmas gave him an excuse to delay, and even on Friday, January 7, 1841, he had not done the deed.

Done! done! ! ! Why, bless you, I shall not be done till Wednesday night. I only began yesterday, and this part of the story is not to be galloped over, I can tell you. I think it will come famously—but I am the wretchedest of the wretched. It casts the most horrible shadow upon me, and it is as much as I can do to keep moving at all.

I tremble to approach the place a great deal more than Kit; a great deal more than Mr. Garland; a great deal more than the Single Gentleman. I shan't recover for a long time. Nobody will miss her like I shall. It is such a painful thing to me, that I really cannot express my sorrow. Old wounds bleed afresh when I only think of the way of doing it:

what the actual doing it will be, God knows. I can't preach to myself the schoolmaster's consolation, though I try. Dear Mary died yesterday when I think of this sad story.

He had been refusing invitations, scared of disturbing his state of mind and then having the whole painful process of working himself up afresh to the sticking point. At last he did it.
But still everything connected with the death was a misery. To write to Cattermole the artist broke the wounds open again.

Will you do a little tail-piece for the Curiosity story?—only one figure if you like—giving some notion of the etherealised spirit of the child; something like those little figures in the frontispiece. I am, for the time being, nearly dead with work and grief for the loss of the child.

And again:

You can't imagine (gravely I write and speak) how exhausted I am to-day with yesterday's labours. I went to bed last night utterly dispirited and done up. All the night I have been pursued by the child, and this morning I am unrefreshed and miserable. I don't know what to do with myself.

The act of deciding to kill Nell, and then of killing her, inevitably brought out the guilt-aspects of his relations with Mary. "All night I have been pursued by the child."

II

The Old Curiosity Shop was the least planned of Dickens's books. It simply emerged out of his determination to turn his periodical scheme into a success. The fear that had overwhelmed him at the start of that scheme and that came out in his obsession about the Queen showed itself in his attempt to revive Pickwick and the Wellers. The Gog and Magog formula was beyond his powers; the profound intuition that had stirred him during the first stages proved too much for his intellectual capacity. Willy nilly, he had to let out the ghost which had been haunting him, Mary, giving her the name of Little Nell.
Though he tries to interweave something of the romantic formula, it doesn't work well. Nell dies and can't receive any heritage. As a consolation prize in the romantic unmasking of the mechanism of evil that distorts the share of good things, Dick Swiveller gets a small annuity; but that is all that Dickens can do about it. The legal Brasses are exposed and force-of-evil

Quilp gets drowned; but the full putting to rights is broken by Nell's death. Something seems to have gone radically wrong with the society that lets her be driven to death by the Quilps.

So the picaresque theme is now that of the hounded innocent fleeing from the maniac evil and carrying with her in the tainted old man the perpetual renewer of her distress. We are getting far from the noble Nicholas who can solve his troubles by linking up with the Cheerybles of this world.

In this central theme and the set of generic character-images that circle the innocent we touch the greatness of the book. There is a deep emotional unity despite the haphazard nature of the writing. Dickens hints at a realization of what was happening to himself and his work at the moment when Nell, fleeing from the city of wrath, looks back over the fields and thinks of Bunyan's Pilgrim.

> There had been an old copy of the *Pilgrim's Progress*, with strange plates, upon a shelf at home, over which she had often pored whole evenings, wondering whether it was true in every word, and where those distant countries with the curious names might be. As she looked upon the place they had left, one part of it came back into her mind.

She feels like Christian with the burden fallen away. But as we look at the plate in *Master Humphrey's Clock* we see that Nell is standing where Charles stood as a boy about eleven, looking over from Camden Town at St. Paul's Dome and wondering what strange powers lay in the smoke-wreathed city.

The flight of the Child, with the strange huge figures wavering round. Monstrous grinning figures, Quilp and the Brasses, grotesque smiling figures, Mrs. Jarley and all the riotous performers, Dick Swiveller and Kit. In the dream-haze the Child goes on, deeper and deeper into England, into an earth of black toil and mad laughters, of lovely greenery and fires of hell. Into the hell of industrialism and the brave, mad forms of the folk-merriment that struggles against being blacked out. Into the breaking point, the terrible death flare where life is being transformed incalculably:

> "Don't be afraid. There's nobody here will harm you." . . . echoing to the roof with the beating of hammers and roar of furnaces, mingled with the hissing of red-hot metal plunged in water, and a hundred strange, unearthly noises never heard elsewhere; in this gloomy place, moving like demons among the flame and smoke, dimly and fitfully seen, flushed and tormented by the burning fires

and wielding great weapons, a faulty blow from any one of which must have crushed some workman's skull, a number of men laboured like giants. Others, reposing upon heaps of coals or ashes with their faces turned to the black vault above, slept or rested from their toil.

And there the Child rests, broken, with the workman protecting her while she sleeps. The workman in the strange, hypnotic relation to the dreadful fire.

And so it was towards this that the Child fled from the city. England murdered by the industrial blight: suburban death of man and then again and again the shattering hell and its tortured denizens, ". . . the same interminable perspective of brick towers, never ceasing in their black vomit." And at night the figures moving in the maws of red, and the bands of unemployed with torches, the meetings in the roads, the bursts of rage. "Who shall tell the terrors of the night for that young wandering child?"

After that there is only the slow death in the vault, the churchyard, the church and its paraphernalia of the grave. The odd litter of the curiosity shop has returned, become the very emblems of decay and death. The evil in the old man, akin, despite his love, to the evil in Quilp and the Brasses, has brought the Child down; but her passage through the hell of England into a death of stony peace is also a passage of author and reader into realization of the inescapible flaw in this scheme of things.

There is the rich, positive side of the book. Now let us look at Nell herself, this mere "smear of white" as Mrs. Oliphant called her. She is, of course, Mary Hogarth, plus all the deep experience of sexual fear and guilt behind Charles's emotion for her. But various odd elements went to make up the details of the figure in the book. We are told that the originals of Codlin and Short, the Punch-and-Judy men, were met by Charles and Mark Lemon of *Punch* at Englefield Green, outside Windsor Old Park. Charles asked for a show. "No cutting anything out, mind." Afterwards he gave a sovereign, and played the pipes, while Lemon played the drum, to a curtain of all the characters. Later Charles met the same players at Egham races, and looked on, while a seedy old fellow with a little girl in a stuff dress stood beside him, saying, "May we stay next you, sir, 'cos we're afeard of the gypsies and people." They stayed with the showmen for ten days and then vanished, being thought to have "run away from somebody." If this story is true, we can well understand Charles's fancy being stirred. There is, however, another story, without details, that the idea of Nell arose during his first visit to Landor in Bath, while he was putting up at a house in St. James's Square. Landor admired Nell so much that he used to say of this house, "I would have burned it to the ground, to the end that no meaner association should ever desecrate the birthplace of Nell," and then burst into one of his thundering laughs. Perhaps there was a girl seen in Bath who stirred Charles, or he there told Landor the story of the girl at the races.

One aspect of Nell that must not be missed is the strong sexual emotion expressed for her immature form. Dick Swiveller gets quite worked up thinking of marrying her, and Quilp keeps on treating her lasciviously. When she kisses the old man:

"Ah!" said the dwarf, smacking his lips, "what a nice kiss that was—just upon the rosy part. What a capital kiss."

Nell was none the slower in going away, for this remark. Quilp looked after her with an admiring leer, and when she had closed the door, fell to complimenting the old man on her charm.

"Such a fresh, blooming modest little bud, neighbour," said Quilp, nursing his short leg, and making his eyes twinkle very much; "such a chubby, rosy, cosy, little Nell! . . . She's so," said Quilp, speaking very slowly, and feigning to be quite absorbed in the subject, "so small, so compact, so beautifully modelled, so fair, with such blue veins and such a transparent skin, and such little feet, and such winning ways—but bless me, you're nervous."

It is in fact Dickens who is getting nervous here. Consider Quilp, whose lust for Nell makes him contemplate getting rid of his wife so that he can marry the "child"—who is he? Quilp, whose lust drives the girl to her death?

If the analysis I have been making all along is correct, then Charles in one part of himself is Quilp. Charles "drives" Mary to her death; Quilp drives Nell. And, in fact, many critics have agreed that in the picture of Quilp, his long-suffering wife, and his mother-in-law whom he likes to snub, we have a caricatured version of Charles, Kate, and the in-laws. Dickens here unpacks in a kind of melodramatic burlesque the conflict between himself and Kate, and makes an astonishingly honest statement of his own power to exasperate.

Quilp was, in a sense—in his love for monkey tricks, for instance—Dickens himself as seen by the eyes of Mrs. Hogarth; and the word-conflicts between that comical dwarf and Mrs. Jeniwin, or something like them, certainly took place in real life. (Wright.)

Charles, then, is trying, in his intuitive way, to face out the logic of his entangled guilt and hope.

As so often, he has his foils to the more serious characters. Dick Swiveller also aspired to Nell, but fades out before the superior evil of Quilp and turns into not a bad fellow at all. Having thus escaped the tragic net, he gets his child-love in the person of the Marchioness, a realistic form of Nell, for whom Charles feels that he needs expend no sentiment. Here again we meet an aspect of Charles. Dick is a variation of Potter and Smithers, with emphasis on the frustrated romantic whom Charles made fun of in the early picture of himself. (Dick: Dickens. We often find Dickens signing letters as "Dick.") He puts Dick into the Lant Street where he had stayed during the happier half of his blacking-works days.

And we find the same curious sexual colouration round the Marchioness as round Nell. She is about eleven or twelve and has the stunted form of a child of seven. But Chesterton somehow read the passages about her and Dick as a "happy courtship," and as "a true romance; perhaps the one true romance in Dickens." The text hardly supports him; yet he is responding to something sexually veiled in the whole episode. Something which Charles himself brought out into the open when in the epilogue he tells how Dick had the child educated and several years later married her. And in Hablot Browne's frontispiece to Volume II of *Master Humphrey's Clock* we see Dick on his knees wooing a surprised but delighted child-Marchioness. Lord Dufferin, at the Liverpool banquet given to Dickens near the end of his life, declared, "Under his large-hearted leadership we have come to regard the love affairs of Mr. Swiveller and his Marchioness with greater interest than any elevated ideal of high life."

The final point in the relating of all this skein to Charles is provided by the fact that the Marchioness is based on the little Chatham workhouse girl to whom he used to tell tall stories (in Dick's mood) by London Bridge in his own Lant Street days. Fred, as the Bad Brother, is just another example of the way he couldn't resist using family names in a tell-tale way.

I have already touched on the importance of the sea and the light-track over the waters for Charles. At Broadstairs, while writing this novel, he made the following remark:

I have opened the second volume with Kit; and I saw this morning looking out to the sea, as if a veil had been lifted up, an affecting thing that I can do with him bye and bye. *Nous verrons.*

The suicide fancy that he had been weaving round his hopeless love for the Queen, reappeared at Broadstairs, in a fascination for the sea.

It's now four o'clock, and I have been at work since half-past eight. I have really dried myself up into such a condition which would almost justify me in pitching off the cliff, head first—but I must get richer before I indulge in a crowning luxury.

He wrote that after composing the *Flight from the Town* (cited above). Again later he writes:

I really think the dead mankind a million fathoms deep, the best thing in the sentence. I have a notion of the dreadful silence down there, and of the stars shining through upon their drowned eyes—the fruit, let me tell you, of a solitary walk by starlight on the cliffs. As to the child-image. . . .

And so Quilp, the bad husband who wanted to get rid of his meek wife in order to embrace Mary, is drowned deep. Blotted out under the waters.

Towards the latter part of the book, exalted and agonized, he falls into the blank verse which from now on tended to appear at such points of excitation. Here is a part of the drowning of Quilp broken up into verse:

> But the resistless water bore him down
> before he could give it utterance,
> and driving him under it, carried away a corpse.
> It toyed and sported with its ghastly freight,
> now bruising it against the slimy piles,
> now hiding it in mud or long rank grass,
> now dragging it heavily
> over rough stones and gravel,
> now feigning to yield it up to its own element
> and in the same action luring it away,
> until, tired of the ugly plaything,
> it flung it on a swamp. . . .

Charles is still yielding to Forster's censorship. Thus, Forster objected to a reference to "opera-going senators on Wednesday nights." Charles agreed and altered the passage, but tried to keep his end up by saying:

Of course, I had no intention to delude the many-headed into a false belief concerning opera nights, but merely to specify a class of

senators. I needn't have done it, however, for God knows they're
pretty well all alike.

An odd sidelight on Dickens's choice of themes is given by
Bulwer's *Night and Morning*, published in 1841 and therefore
written at much the same time as *The Old Curiosity Shop*. This
work had a powerful effect on Dickens and needs careful consideration. In it we see the same trends at work as in Dickens's
writing at this time: social realism modified by melodramatic
structure and fantasy-images, and centralized on emotional
symbols from which is drawn the basic critical attitude. Night
and Morning: the darkness and the light, social evil and social
good, but also the deep and dark formative levels of the spirit
and the conscious directions with their welter of distortion and
truth—what Bulwer in the 1845 preface called "new regions
. . . lying far, and rarely trodden, beyond that range of conventional morality in which Novelist after Novelist has entrenched
himself—amongst those subtle recesses in the ethics of human
life in which truth and falsehood dwell undisturbed and
unseparated." Astonishing phrases of deep penetration into the
nature of unconscious polarity!

Night and Morning reveals the Old Man and the Young Girl
who meant so much to Dickens. Here the Old Man has something of the tangle of qualities of the Old Man of *The Old
Curiosity Shop*: he has driven out his son into a life of vice and
crime by his righteousness, but he himself is in the grip of
greed. He is both pathetic and unpleasant; and he is linked
with a grand-daughter who is a child-woman, a thing of
broken and thwarted development, Fanny, who is humiliated
by his actions as Nell by her grandfather's "Don't laugh—it
pains me. . . ." But Fanny is a real character, unlike Nell. She
is, in fact, to some extent the reality of which Nell is a mere
emblem. Her pathetic groping for a stable basis in life, her
fight through from a twilight consciousness, are well expressed.
She thus stands as the link between Nell and Barnaby Rudge.
She is the Idiot, but she breaks through into humanity with a
fullness denied to the "sane." She it is who comes out into the full
Morning. The last words of the story tell of her with her baby:

Fanny saw, from the movement of his lips and the moisture in
his eyes, that he blessed God. He looked upon the mother's face,
he glanced round on the flowers and foliage of the luxurious summer,
and again he blessed God: And without and within, it was Light and
MORNING.

The movement to a new consciousness and acceptance of life has been completed in her.

She is given the typical attitudes of the folk-fool. "There is one thing that always puzzles me—I want you to explain it. Why does everything in life depend upon money?" But she is also used to express the deep movements of new formative forces, which come to fruition in the person whose normal consciousness has been shattered, but which miss out the others.

Though in reality Fanny's intellect was ripening within, yet still the surface often misled the eye as to the depths. It was rather that something yet held back the faculties from their growth than that the faculties themselves were wanting. Her weakness was more of the nature of the infant's than of one afflicted with incurable imbecility. . . .

At other moments there was something so absent and distracted about her, or so fantastic and incoherent, that Vaudemont, with the man's hard, worldly eye, read in it nothing but melancholy confusion. Nevertheless, if the skein of ideas was entangled, each thread in itself was a thread of gold.

The healing of the obstructive pang is done by love.

It can only be an accident that this girl is named Fanny, the name that meant so much to Dickens. But around her we see much of the complex which for him surrounded his Fanny. She is linked with the churchyard, as was Fanny Dickens in Charles's Chatham memories.

"You said you liked the churchyard. See!" And she opened the window and pointed to the church-tower rising dark against the evening sky.

"This is better than all," said Vaudemont: and he looked out from the window in a silent reverie, which Fanny did not disturb.

His mother's grave is the deep link between them. The recognition of love is connected with it in one of the Morning-Night oppositions of the theme:

And there by the GRAVE which had been so memorable a scene in their common history, were murmured those vows in which all this world knows of human happiness is treasured and recorded— love that takes the sting from grief, and faith that gives eternity to love. All silent, yet all serene around them! Above, the heaven—at their feet, the grave.—For the love, the grave!—for the faith, the heaven!

197

Further, the sister-brother relationship is heavily underlined. Fanny calls Vaudemont "brother," and:

"Did you marry your brother, Sarah?" said Fanny, playing with the corner of her apron.

"My brother!" exclaimed the old woman, aghast. "La! miss, you must not talk in that way—it's quite wicked and heathenish. One must not marry one's brother!"

"No!" said Fanny, tremblingly, and turning very pale, even by that light. "No!—are you sure of that?"

"It is the wickedest thing even to talk about, my dear young mistress—but you're like a babby unborn."

Fanny was silent for some moments. At length she said, unconscious that she was speaking aloud, "But he is *not* my brother, after all."

Bulwer (whose own life showed throughout a mother-domination) thus works from a spiritual centre very close to that of Dickens; and the effects of *Night and Morning* on Dickens were immediately strong and lastingly weighty. The novel was much more mature in its critical outlook than anything of Dickens's up to this period, and it importantly determined the direction of his expression. The closeness of its fantasy-basis to the dynamic element in Dickens's own work is remarkable. The emphasis on the lost child, the stolen heritage, the huge cheat of the world, the injustice of the law, the fool's ownership of the clue of love, the brother-sister basis of true love—all this came passionately home to his business and bosom.

III

He earned about £10,000 from the book, thanks to his profit-sharing arrangement. Its popularity, especially in America, was enormous. The tears that Charles himself shed were only precursors of a general flood-burst. Macready pleaded with him to spare Nell's life. ("He blushed," said M., "and men who blush are said to be either proud or cruel; he is not proud and therefore," as C. D. added, "the axiom is false.") When he opened the November number, he "saw one print in it of the dear dead child that gave a dead chill to my blood. I dread to read it, but I must get it over." Later he recorded, "I have read the two numbers. I have never read printed words that gave me such pain. I could not weep for some time." Daniel O'Connell groaned, "He should not have killed her," and threw the book out of the window. A neighbour looked into Lord Jeffrey's library and saw him with head on table; he looked up with tear-filled eyes and she begged to be excused, she hadn't known he had got bad news. Was someone dead? "Yes, indeed. I'm a great goose to have given way so, but I couldn't help it. You'll be sorry to hear that Little Nelly, Boz's Little Nelly, is dead." Edward Fitzgerald was so moved that he extracted and wrote out all the portions about Nell. "It forms a kind of Nelly-ad or Homeric narration, of the child's wandering fortunes, till she reaches, at last, a haven more desirable than any in story."

These were only a few outstanding examples. Almost everyone fell down in admiration. Mary Howitt, Sara Coleridge (who thought Nell a Mignon, but "a lovelier, more English conception"), Washington Irving ("exquisite and sustained pathos"), and the miners of Colorado. On the New York quays crowds collected to shout to ships coming in, "Is Little Nell dead?" Only a few dissented. Lewes found her "maudlin and unreal," and Swinburne later thought her as monstrous as a baby with two heads.

This wide response shows that we must beware of reducing her to the personal neurosis of Dickens. The image evoked something fundamental and general in the contemporary soul. Now there was a bad element in this response, a very bad one —as there was a bad element in the complex of forces which had driven Charles into his morbid attitude to Mary and her death. We cannot simply reduce it to the general sense of guilt over the vileness of industrial conditions, however much that vileness had to do with the image's genesis. No doubt the image relieved the pressure of guilt in the general consciousness, but it also in turn built up something different. Nell in isolation was indeed a mere smear of white and a monster; but in terms of the whole story she was a powerful image of something ghastly in its suffering which men must face if they were to keep their souls alive. She was not a character and not a mere guilt-smear, but she was a symbol of universal suffering, of a spiritual state which the book helped to focus. By bringing to light the hidden horror, the sickness in the blood, the invisible worm, it made possible the counter-movement of the cleansing forces.

Thus, without knowing it, Charles had gone on to write the book in defence of the driven children that he had felt the need at Manchester to write. He had moved from the comparatively remote *Oliver* into the very heart of the pang.

Tears, however, were common. Fanny Kemble, reading

Cooper's *Borderers*, cried so much she half-killed herself and took days to recover. It may not surprise us that Queen Victoria wept at *Home Sweet Home*, but we don't expect Macaulay to confess that Tennyson's *Guenevere* drew his tears and that Florence Dombey "made me cry as if my heart would break." Lady Frederick Cavendish (April 1866) records that she ended Mrs. Gaskell's *Sylvia's Lovers* "in a flood of tears," and regretted getting a headache over a "cruel" work. Even George Eliot, reading *The Crofton Boys* of Harriet Martineau in 1841, had "some delightful crying."

In this way the Victorians were carrying on the sensibility novel of the late eighteenth century; and the hidden allegory of guilt in *The Old Curiosity Shop* has its link with the psychological revelation of such a work as *Caleb Williams*, by Godwin, which deals directly with the problems of the guilt-sense and the terrifying dialectic that inverts the innocent through persecution into the role of the guilty. Dickens, at a violent moment of change, was laying hold of something basic in the universal experience, facilitating the evil pressures, and yet laying the necessary ground for their full defeat.

If we look at the more ephemeral writing of the age we find two trends. One which brutally expresses the guilty circumstance but refuses to accept guilt; one which morbidly extracts guilt from every mishap, especially from the event of death. For the first type take *The Fairchild Family*, a standard book for children with ferocious notions of discipline. When the children quarrel, Mr. Fairchild thrashes them (reciting Watts's "Let dogs delight to bark and bite") and then makes them eat their dinner under a gibbet from which hangs the mouldering corpse of a murderer.

For the second type take the slightly later *Eric, or Little by Little*. Here, the good boy, with two others, is cut off by the tide, and he dies as the result of an unlucky jump. Eric comes under bad influences; his younger brother slips from a cliff and is killed. Eric has a letter from India saying that his mother will probably be dead by the time he reads it.

"O, I have killed her, I have killed my mother!" said Eric, in a hollow voice, when he came to himself. "O God, forgive me; forgive me." They gathered round him: they soothed, and comforted him, and prayed for him; but his soul refused comfort.

He sees the spirits of the others, cries that they'll meet again, and dies of the shock of guilt.

Here, then, we find crudely put forth the brutal facts and the recoil they led to. Charles's problem is to embrace both sides. To show the brutal fact without acquiescence; to define the guilty recoil but to direct the resultant emotion along the right channels.

There had been a strong element of social criticism in the Gothic novel—in such works as Mrs. Inchbald's *Art and Nature,* in the discussion novels of Bage and Holcroft, in the sensibility forms of Godwin. These elements had never quite died out, and they were now flowing into Dickens's work. Direct social criticism appears in such novels as *Michael Armstrong* by Frances Trollope, in which a frontal attack on the system of child-labour is launched. But this well-documented and strongly felt novel had little effect, and is now forgotten, because it simply exposed the brutal fact. Charles, in *Oliver Twist* and the *Old Curiosity Shop,* does not deal in such a documentary way with the fate of the children, but he draws on deep conflicts and tensions which enable him to make his picture of their fate appear of crucial importance. That is, he works from the levels of guilt obsession which are to be found in *Eric,* but he lifts those levels up into a union, artistically, with the socially conscious levels. Hence the enormous dynamic of his work, its great virtues and its many faults. He gives a fruitful direction to the guilt sense, and deepens all the dimensions of life. The elements which he is unable to control artistically appear as the sentimental trends that now irritate us.

But when we understand what he is doing, when we see the way in which he is going down into the depths and welding together violently opposed elements, we can find toleration for the sentiment. We can let it fall back into its minor place and see above and beyond it the triumphant expression of vast new possibilities in life.

IV

The Dickenses now had a large dining-list, from Lord Jeffrey and Sam Rogers, banker-poet, or Miss Burdett Coutts, to artists like Landseer or writers like Bulwer. Sydney Smith, whose satire Charles liked and imitated, had succumbed after Mrs. Nickleby, and became an admirer. The furnishings and food was as showy as possible; the table was loaded with artificial flowers and piles of dessert. And the new method of having servants to hand the dishes round, not merely to place them on the table, was being used. Maclise, bright fellow who could chat, write, or paint with equal facility; Douglas Jerrold, sturdy and satirical humorist in tale and play; Cattermole, artist, who was related by marriage, unsteady and full of fun; genial editor Jerdan; scene-painter Stanfield who knew Turner; unassuming Hablot Browne. All these came and went. Lewes looked in with a sniff to see how Charles's library was getting on. Ah, now there were standard editions of the classics instead of the tripey novels, and Charles was more staid.

He still remained outside philosophy, science, and the higher literature, and was too unaffected a man to pretend to feel any interest in them. But the vivacity and sagacity which gave a charm to intercourse with him had become weighted with a seriousness which from that time forward became more and more prominent in his conversation and writings.

Eleanor Christian looked in with T. J. Thompson, and Charles had to be dragged from his study, distrait and no longer playful. Only when the raven cried "Hullo, old gal," and pecked at her ankles, did he brighten. Fred Dickens, who had come in, said he was going to see a hanging, and Charles told him off sharply for a morbid craving. Thompson said he'd seen a man guillotined. Charles shuddered. "Ugh, that's a messy business, all gore and sawdust. The inverted rope-dance is cleaner though less impressive. I'd keep away from such a hideous spectacle on principle." (But, in fact, he seldom did lose a chance to see such horrors.)

But by far the most important new acquaintance was Carlyle, whom Charles was beginning to revere. He had read *Chartism* and been deeply impressed. At last here was a work of thought which came powerfully home to him. He responded wholeheartedly to the attacks Carlyle made on the classes who monopolized suffrage, land, machinery, Press, religion, communications, travel, paper money, and who had imposed the Poor Law. For the first time he saw the social system in something like a coherent perspective, and discovered that it wasn't an accident that various things he disliked could all be grouped as expressions of class-power. He still continued to think in politico-moral terms rather than socio-economic, and indeed continued to do so till the end of his days, but order was being brought into his thinking, his emotional attitudes. His impulses of revolt, coalescing as they had round the heads of Religion,

Law, Parliament, and State power, were now provided with a philosophic justification.

Chartism (1839) and *The French Revolution* (1837): these were the two books to which he owed a new start. A start which at last had an intellectual structure, however much he still depended on his intuitive radical reactions.

Carlyle purged him of much of his remaining liberal delusions —that is, of a belief in *laissez-faire* with its basis in what Carlyle had called the "cash nexus." He read and assimilated passages like these:

> In these complicated times, with Cash Payment as the sole nexus between man and man, the Toiling Classes of mankind declare, in their confused but most emphatic way, to the Untoiling, that they will be governed; that they must—under penalty of Chartisms, Thuggeries, Rick-burnings, and even blacker things than those.
>
> Vain also is it to think that the misery of one class, of the great universal under class, can be isolated, and kept apart and peculiar, down in that class. By infallible contagion evident even to Political Economy that will reflect, the misery of the lowest spreads upwards and upwards till it reaches the very highest; till all has grown miserable, palpably false and wrong; and poor drudges hungering "on meal-husks and boiled grass" do, by circuitous but sure methods, bring kings' heads to the block!
>
> Cash Payment the sole nexus; and there are so many things which cash will not pay. . . .
>
> Rebellion is the means, but it is not the motive cause. The motive cause, and true secret of the matter, were always this: The necessity there was for rebelling. . . .
>
> Call it not a succession of rebellions; call it rather succession of expansions, of enlightenments, gift of articulate utterance descending ever lower. Class after class acquires faculty of utterance, . . . Necessity reaching and compelling; as the dumb man, seeing the knife at his father's throat, suddenly acquired speech! Consider too how class after class not only acquired faculty of articulating what its might is, but likewise grows in might, acquires might or loses might; so that always, after a space, there is not only new gift of articulating, but there is something new to articulate.

For Carlyle the crisis meant that the governing class had lost the faculty of governing. Charles did not accept this proposition, but the general appeal by Carlyle for *men* appealed strongly to him. What he had gained in essence was a philosophic support for his feeling that something was radically wrong, the feeling that he had put into the symbolism of *The Old Curiosity Shop*, where he abandons the romantic reconciliation for a new working-out of the romantic revolt.

He first saw Carlyle in 1840 at a lecture on great men given at Willis's Rooms. He first met him in November at a dinner of Lord Stanley's, with Guizot and Lord Normanby among the other guests. Carlyle had been reading *The Old Curiosity Shop* and watched Dickens. He was interested in his mobile face, his quiet, observant way of taking people in. Henceforth Dickens made sure of drawing Carlyle into his circle, and reckoned his opinion of the highest importance. Not only anxieties over contracts had held Charles back from getting on with *Barnaby Rudge*. He had certainly drawn the idea for the novel originally from the work of Ainsworth and Bulwer; but when ever he tried to put it down on paper he found that he couldn't feel carried away by their type of ideas, their type of historical approach. Only after the absorption of Carlyle's ideas could he confidently let go.

Now let us look at what had been happening after the first work of the Reform Ministry such as the Poor Law Act of 1834. That Act had been designed to give the poor the choice of going into workhouse or factory. It achieved its effect, and in the late 1830's the Poor Rate fell to between four to four and half million pounds (instead of the seven million of 1831–32). This result was not won without violent resistances, led by Cobbett in the House of Commons in his fight against the Poor Law bastilles. J. R. Stephens, the Methodist minister, cried at Newcastle that sooner than have such barbarous measures in operation, "Newcastle ought to be, and should be, one blaze of fire with only one way to put it out, and that with the blood of all who supported this measure." In some towns the people stormed and burned the workhouses, and clashes between troops and people occurred. In *Oliver* and *The Old Curiosity Shop* Dickens stood unequivocally on the side of those opposed to the Poor Law. These books were his reply to the reformers and the House of Commons.

Meanwhile the 1830's had seen a second wind developing in industrialism through the railway. In 1834–36 some seventy million pounds were raised for rail construction. Heavy industry began, and Britain moved into a temporary position of monopoly in world trade. Ten million tons of coal had been mined in 1800; 1865 saw a hundred million tons. Not only was Britain the first country to build its own railway system; it soon began to build railways over all the world, often financed by London loans. But towards the end of the 1830's things had got into a tangle, and a depression set in. The result was increased agitation among sections of the middle class and the working class for further political and economic reforms. The Anti-Corn Law League and the Chartists struggled for popular support.

In 1839 the first big wave of popular unrest came to a head. Elections for the first Chartist Congress had taken place in October 1838, and in February the Congress met in London, where the Right wing held up Harney's effort to raise the question: What action if the Petition for reform was rejected? In July the Government struck; arrests were made and a brutal police attack launched on the meeting in the Bull Ring, Manchester. For some days the people practically held the town. There were violent clashes in Glasgow, Newcastle, and throughout Lancashire. The Petition was rejected, and the Convention weakly dissolved; but in November Welsh miners made an armed attack to seize Newport.

In 1840 the Whig Government was tottering. The popular resistances, however, had reached a momentary point of arrest.

This was the background of the renewed effort Dickens was making to grasp at an extended artistic method and understanding of his world. The background for his renewed effort to write a consciously historical novel.

V

January 17, 1841, finished off *The Old Curiosity Shop*, and next week was published the first issue of *Barnaby Rudge*, of which a certain amount had been written tentatively at the time of *Oliver Twist*. He wasn't finding it easy to work. On Friday, January 29th, he says, "I didn't stir out yesterday, but sat and *thought* all day; not writing a line; not so much as the cross of a t or the dot of an i." He was seeking to concentrate his forces for the new leap. "I imaged forth a good deal of Barnaby by keeping my mind steadily upon him." (Kate was coming near another childbed.) "Last night," he goes on, "I was unutterably and impossible-to-form-an-idea-of-ably miserable." But now that something of *Barnaby* had come out, he felt released, happy.

The *Pic-Nic Papers* were still causing trouble. Charles was becoming so annoyed with Colburn that he refused to be further implicated in the project which so far had only earned him the widow's blame for the delays. He, however, allowed the book to go ahead with his name as editor.

On February 8th his fourth child, Walter Landor, was born. In March the pet raven died, and Charles wrote a long account of its last hours to Maclise—the castor-oil, the gruel, the muffling of the stable-knocker, the bird's "little property; consisting chiefly of halfpence which he had buried in different parts of the garden," and its last words, "Halloa, old girl." Not long after another raven was found; and a friend remarked that Charles was *ravenmad* (ravingmad).

Since 1838 Charles had known Dr. Elliotson, who had grown so interested in hypnotism that he became suspect at University College Hospital, to which he belonged. He founded a mesmeric hospital, used hypnotism to cure tic, and tried it as an anaesthetic for small operations. Charles was very interested in these unorthodox approaches to disease.

The fall of the Whigs brought him a surprise request to stand as M.P. for Reading. At the end of May he replied that he could not afford to contest an election. Clearly he had been tempted for a moment. Despite his contempt for Parliament, he could not help thinking twice about the chances that the House would give him to put forward his views on public questions. (In April he wrote to the Rev. T. Robinson on the Poor Law, "I will pursue cruelty and oppression, the enemy of all God's creatures of all codes and creeds, so long as I have the energy of thought and the power of giving it utterance.") He seems to have visited Reading to discuss the matter; and in one letter we find his refusing to countenance the suggestion of "support" from the Government. He felt that if he accepted any such support he would compromise his independence. (There can be little doubt that Talfourd, son of a Reading brewer and the sitting Member for the borough, had instigated the approach.)

Jeffrey was in London during April, urging Charles to pay a visit to Edinburgh, where he himself had been driving about with the slogan, "Nothing so good as Nell since Cordelia." Charles liked the idea, put aside a project of going to Ireland, and fixed a visit for June. Meanwhile there was a dinner for the second volume of the *Clock*, with speeches praising everybody and some comic songs.

With Kate he arrived in Edinburgh on June 22nd, and had his magnificent laudatory dinner on Friday the 25th. He was presented with the freedom of the city, and offered another seat in Parliament, this time "for a Scotch county that's going a-begging." He wrote to Forster, "I have declined to be brought in free, gratis and for nothing." After a rush of dinners (and one "supper with all the artists (!!)," theatre-visits, and sightseeing, he dashed into the Highlands with Angus Fletcher for guide, drinking a pint of whisky a day under spouting skies, dizzied by waterfalls and perhaps by negus of sherry-and-nutmeg, and finding Glencoe *terrible*. Kate was doing her best to keep up with him in admiring rocks and getting across swollen streams, till at last, after Stirling, they reached Callendar and he felt an ache for the battledore and shuttlecock of Devonshire Terrace. But they still had many lochs and valleys to see before they got back via Glasgow on July 17th.

On the last day of the month, before going off to Broadstairs, he wrote to Forster about a book by a working-class writer, "I wish we were all in Eden again—for the sake of these toiling creatures." From Broadstairs he wrote:

The sun is sparkling on the water so that I can hardly bear to look at it. The tide is in, and the fishing-boats are dancing like mad. Upon the green-topped cliffs the corn is cut and piled in shocks; and thousands of butterflies are fluttering about, taking the bright little red flags at the mast-heads for flowers, and panting with delight accordingly. (Here the Inimitable, unable to resist the brilliancy out of doors, breaketh off, rusheth to the machines, and plungeth into the sea. Returning, he proceedeth:). . . I had a letter from Napier [of the *Edinburgh Review*] on Saturday, urging the children's labour subject upon me. But, as I hear from Southwood Smith that the report cannot be printed until the new parliament has sat at the least six weeks, it will be impossible to produce it before the January number.

He was feeling politically stirred through the elections and this month printed three satirical poems in *The Examiner*. "By Jove, how radical I am getting," he wrote on August 13th. "I wax stronger and stronger in the true principles every day. I don't know whether it's the sea, or no, but so it is." The poems are as anti-Tory as they could well be, and show how thoroughly he had assimilated the broadsheet tradition of polemical song. *The Quack Doctor's Proclamation* attacks sham-reform in an immemorial folk formula. *Subjects for Painters* picks up from Peter Pindar; and *The Fine Old English Gentleman, New Version* ("To be said or sung at all Conservative Dinners") is a slashing piece of broadsheet sarcasm. It opens with a call for a return to the corrupt old days when:

The good old laws were garnished well with gibbets, whips, and
    chains,
With fine old English penalties, and fine old English pains,
With rebel heads, and seas of blood once not in rebel veins;
For all these things were requisite to guard the rich old gains
Of the fine old English Tory times; soon may they come again!

The brave old code, like Argus, had a hundred watchful eyes,
And ev'ry English peasant had his good old English spies,
To tempt his starving discontent with fine old English lies,
Then call the good old Yeomanry to stop his peevish cries. . . .

The good old times for cutting throats that cried out in their need,
The good old times for hunting men who held their fathers' creed,
The good old times when William Pitt, as all good men agreed
Came down direct from Paradise at more than railroad speed.

In those rare days, the press was seldom known to snarl or bark,
But sweetly sang of men in pow'r, like any tuneful lark;
Grave judges, too, to all their evil deeds were in the dark;
And not a man in twenty score knew how to make his mark.

The days of scarce bread, war, of "shutting men of letters up,
through iron bars to grin." The nation rose up and ended those
days, but the Tory cry runs through the land: "Dear Bread in
England, Sword and Brand in Ireland, and poverty and ignorance everywhere." "So, rally round the rulers with the gentle
iron hand."

So opposed to the dominant political trends did he feel that
he proposed to Forster a departure of "himself and his household goods, like Coriolanus, to a world elsewhere."

One evening this month Charles dined with Dr. Elliotson
and met the Rev. Chauncey Hare Townshend, a wealthy
young clergyman who had seceded from the Church of England and who in his travels had met a German clairvoyant, a
lad named Alexis. In 1839 he had told his experiences in *Facts
in Mesmerism* (with preface dedicated to Elliotson). The
powers of Alexis were exciting Society. He went into a mesmeric sleep and then with bandaged eyes read passages from
books presented to him (which he had not seen before). Once
Kate Dickens put her watch behind his head and he told her
the name of its maker. After such exhibitions Townshend
remarked, "There now, you see that?" One of the audience

once replied, "Yes, I see it, but I don't believe it." Dickens had
seen an exhibition in May this year, and became "a believer in
earnest." He was therefore very interested in meeting Townshend, who considered that mesmerism showed that somnam-
bulism could be brought on, that spirit controlled matter, and
that the mind was the sole source of power. Elliotson and
Townshend had only recently met, and had much to talk about.
And Dickens was so stimulated that he asked Elliotson to
instruct him in animal magnetism.

He learned all that Elliotson could tell him; but for the
moment did not try to put it into practice. Himself, he refused
to be hypnotized.

To spiritualism, which had become a fashionable excitement,
he paid no attention. He refused the grand hostesses who tried
to get him to their table-rappings; but later he did for a while
make some experiments with Buhrer, a man who had invented
a "psychograph" supposed to take down spirit-scripts. Always,
however, he remained sceptical as to any supernatural elements
in spiritualist phenomena.

VI

During September the idea of visiting the United States
grew strong, and not even the fact that Kate wept dismally
whenever he introduced the subject could turn him from it.
Many reasons have been given for this decision of his. L. G.
Clark, an American author and editor (who paid contributors
only with puffs and oyster-stews) had been corresponding with
him since *Pickwick* days. Tony Weller had remarked in *Pickwick*
itself, "Have a passage taken ready for 'Merika and then let
him come back and write a book about the 'Merikans as'll pay
all his expenses and more, if he blows 'em up enough." Charles
had then been thinking of Frances Trollope's book, *Domestic
Manners of the Americans*, which in 1832 had scandalized the
States. He had read that book, as well as Harriet Martineau's
Society in America, which also caused trouble; and Marryat's
Diary in America had interested him. The success of Little Nell
in the States could hardly not have pleased him; and he felt a
certain kinship with Washington Irving as well as a liking for
the work of Fennimore Cooper. It has been suggested that the
flaming lithographs of the Canal and Cairo Company on the
London walls made him want to test out the claims (which
were in fact fraudulent), and that he had invested money in the

company; or that he had been put up by the London publishers to raise the copyright question.

None of these explanations are required. Charles had for some time been thinking of some such visit, as the draft of the *Clock* periodical shows. His extreme restlessness throughout life kept on making him think even of emigration from the days when the Demerara aunt started him off along that line of fancy. In this he was once more echoing a widespread feeling of the 1830's. Railways had stirred people from their old acquiescence in local distress; the Poor Law Commissioners in 1835–36 claimed to have had much success in aiding emigration from East Anglia and the south to the north and Midlands of England, and this increased mobility inside England was linked with an increased movement out of it. By 1840 over 70,000 a year were leaving the country—a number that doubled by the middle 1850's.

But there were still deeper reasons for Charles's desire to travel in general, and to see the States in particular. I have already pointed to the extreme incorrectness of looking on him as a Cockney. His day-dream life (and therefore his work) continued linked with Chatham and London for the simple reason that these were the places of his childhood, and he couldn't be young twice; but his adult mind quickly moved beyond London into the national sphere and proceeded seeking for the clue of historical development in his world. First he turned to the States, and then to Europe. No one could have been less a Little Englander, let alone a Little Londoner.

He wanted to see the States to find out how the American way of life was working out, to understand it in itself before he made any comparisons.

In going to the New World one must for the time being utterly forget and push out of sight the Old one and bring none of its customs or observances into the comparison. (October 12, 1841.)

He wanted to test out if there was any resolution in the States of the darkening conflicts he had penetrated in England.

In October two relatives on the Hogarth side died. Catharine Thomson, Kate's grandmother, who was with Mrs. Hogarth at Brompton; and then, six days after, George Hogarth, aged twenty. Hence arose the agonies already mentioned in connection with Mary's grave. Charles could not bear the idea of it being opened to let the brother in and was in a state of collapse for a month. (The tombstone recorded that George, like Mary, "was taken ill and died in one night.")

The state of prolonged nerves through which Charles had been passing now led to an operation for fistula, which must have helped to intensify his sense of attack.

Fanny and her husband had gone off to Higher Ardwick, Manchester, where they taught music and singing. Burnett had given up the stage for some years; and his mind and his wife's were "chiefly intent on spiritual things." Fanny had come completely under the domination of her husband's ideas. John and Elizabeth Dickens, keen to get away from their white-washed country heaven, came and stayed for months on end with the Burnetts, despite their dislike of evangelical decorum. "Now, Henry," said Fanny, "don't omit family prayer morning and evening during their stay with us. They have never been used to it, but that should not prevent us from continuing our usual habits; it should rather induce us to be firm in maintaining them." Certainly a new Fanny.

Burnett's enthusiasm for the religious leaders [e.g. Rev. J. Griffin] under whose influence he had come and for their teaching irritated Dickens, who became more and more antagonistic towards the Nonconformist ministry. (Wright.)

In the brief notes Charles kept during 1839 he mentions the Burnetts as "Fanny and her husband," not as Fanny and Henry.

VII

With *Barnaby Rudge*, for the first time, Charles tried to plan a book out. *Oliver*, despite its romantic birth-mystery, had simply followed the lines of his runaway day-dream; and *The Old Curiosity Shop* had almost been written in his own despite at the pressure of Mary's ghost. *Barnaby* was an attempt to stand up against Ainsworth and Bulwer on their own ground—to turn from the dangerous reliance on the day-dream which had given such a dynamic to the other two stories, and to become a stable craftsman of the novel. The hope of side-tracking this problem by the *Bee* type of periodical had been ruined; and he had to try the manifest romance.

But he couldn't merely write another Ainsworthian tale. He, the child of the day-dream and the disciple of Carlyle, had to go deeper, find some image or pattern that would truly stimulate

the deep and mysterious sources of his power. The change of
the name from *Gabriel Vardon* to *Barnaby Rudge* was the first
sign that he was getting somewhere. *Vardon* was all too clearly
a superficially romantic idea of the post-Scott epoch; with
Barnaby we approach the level of folk-fantasy in which Dickens
feels at home. But things were still difficult. In the anguish of
concentration he experienced at the turn of 1839–40 we see the
pang of the new form.

He has chosen for his subject a great moment of mass-
upheaval. There we see the pupil of Carlyle differentiating himself from Ainsworth and the post-Scotts. (Bulwer in his own
way, at a less creative level, is going through the same phase,
turning from the author of *Paul Clifford* into the author of
Pompeii and *Rienzi*.) Dickens thus breaks new ground; for in
his work, under the influence of Carlyle, he writes what is the
first novel in which a mass movement is treated in its own
right, as an integral part of the story, not as a mere background
or foreground event through which the characters make their
way. It marks the next stage after that great work *Old Mortality*,
of Scott, where the mass movement is genuinely fused with
event and character but where it does not detach itself as the
sort of over-all force as does the anti-Popery insurrection in
Barnaby. *Barnaby*, indeed, lacks the intellectual cogency and
insight of Scott's work; its method is unstable, but none the
less it breaks fundamentally new ground.

For an intuitive writer such as Dickens, who always worked
one way or another from his own immediate experience, the
books of Carlyle would not provide a creative release unless he
could relate their material and analysis to various stages of his
own life. For *Barnaby* he drew on fairly recent events in which
he had played a part, such as the riotous Kettering elections and
the strike of the reporters he led on *The True Sun*, with the
background of stories about Chartist mass-meetings and the
Bristol insurrection. He also went deeper, to find an image of
the Lost Child, the Fool-Innocent, so that he could organize
the historical material round a centrally evocative theme. When
he had found the Fool Barnaby, he could write the book.

By finding Barnaby, he also found what was for him the key
to Gordon and therefore to the riots. Gordon is the Fool
lifted on to the level of political action, the plaything of forces
which he cannot understand or control, and yet contributing
something of integrity to a mad situation. This is for Charles
the inner tragedy of history, that the Fool-Innocent, symbolic

of the deepest and purest element in the mass-life, is deluded and twisted, is made the tool of the evil scheming forces. Gordon is set between Grueby and Gashford—all Gs—to represent the Fool-power of the people torn between good and evil; he is shown producing through his exertions something that is certainly not what he wanted himself, or what either Grueby or Gashford wanted.

Dickens thus parts company with Carlyle at the moment of uniting with him. Not by intellectual analysis but by the intuitive pressures of his genius. He has listened carefully to the Carlyle who wrote in *Chartism*:

. . . it is a question which cannot be left to the Collective Folly of the Nation! In or out of Parliament, darkness, neglect, hallucination must contrive to cease in regard to it; true insight into it must be had. How inexpressibly useful were true insight into it; a genuine understanding by the upper classes of society what it is that the under classes intrinsically mean; a clear interpretation of the thought which at heart torments these wild, inarticulate souls, struggling there, with inarticulate uproar, like dumb creatures, in pain, unable to speak what is in them!

The latter part of the passage might indeed be taken as a motto for *Barnaby*. But Dickens takes at root a diametrically opposed view to that of Carlyle. He does not believe in the illumination of the upper classes so that heroes and prophets can arise from them and magically reproduce the organic community. With his whole self he turns against such a concept. For him the pang of the inarticulate uproar is the need of the people to illuminate themselves, to become masters of their own souls and lives; and he considers that the upper classes understand only too well, and have always understood, what the tormented Fool is trying to bring forth. They understand and take their counter-measures in time; they manage to twist the direction of the people's energies and make it beget things it has not meant to beget.

This aspect Charles puts forth rather crudely in his characterization of Lord Chesterfield as Chester, the cynical force in the ruling classes which lives by perversion; and round Chester he weaves the romantic theme of guilt, reversal, and evil-masking. With Chester is linked, by the birth-mystery and the guilt-theme, Barnaby. Chester, deliberate evil, and Barnaby, unconscious good. The action of the story goes on at two levels: Barnaby trying to come through the web of madness

213

and deceit at the personal level; Gordon trying to come through the same web at the political level.

For this reason it is necessary in the story to confront Barnaby and Gordon at the outbreak of the uprising.

"It is a bad sign of the wickedness of these times," said Lord Gordon, evading her touch, and colouring deeply, "that those who cling to the truth and support the right cause are set down as mad. Have you the heart to say this of your own son, unnatural mother. . . .

"He has surely no appearance," said Lord George, glancing at Barnaby, and whispering in his secretary's ear, "of being deranged? And even if he had, we must not construe any trifling peculiarity into madness. Which of us"—and here he turned red again—"would be safe, if that were made law."

". . . And you desire to make one of this great body?" asked Lord George, addressing him; "and intended to make one, did you?"

"Yes—yes," said Barnaby with sparkling eyes.

And, indeed, Charles got so carried away by the loon-symbol that he wanted to burlesque it—to introduce as leaders of the rioters three excellent organizers who turn out to have escaped from Bedlam. Forster rightly enough sat on this.

Charles's attitude to Gordon as an historical figure had elements of warm sympathy. Though at this period he usually gave in to Forster's criticisms, he refused to depict Gordon less favourably, and wrote a letter warmly in his defence:

Say what you please of Gordon, he must have been at heart a kind man, and a lover of the despised and rejected, after his own fashion. . . . He always spoke on the people's side, and tried against his muddled brains to expose the profligacy of both parties. He never got anything by his madness, and never sought it. . . .

He protests that to be unfair to him would "lie upon my conscience heavily." With his strong anti-feudal, anti-Catholic sentiments, he could not help to some extent sympathizing with anti-Papist riots—though he could not help remembering that he had heard anti-Papist slogans on the lips of the Tory mob at Kettering.

Many reasons thus conspired to make him depict the people as betrayed from within as well as from without, and yet somehow in the process bringing forth the soul of things good, following the Fool of their own confusions and virtues.

There was also, as always, an important overt social intention. Here, to attack the governmental system as creating by its own impositions and biases the very crimes it took brutal revenge on; to bring out the horrors of hanging. The apprentices' association to which Tappertit belongs was based on the contemporary trade union, which still often carried on much of the masonic methods in initiation ritual and idiom.

From his personal experience Dickens took the theme of the discordant marriage, which he had begun to exploit in *The Old Curiosity Shop*. The humours of the henpecked husband had already appeared plentifully in his work—in Poot, Tony Weller, Nupkins and the two Raddles of *Pickwick*; in Lillyvick, Squeers, and (in the later phase) Mantilini of *Nickleby*; in Sowerby and Bumble of *Oliver*. But it was with Quilp that he took a full grasp of the theme and turned it from an incidental bit of the jokester's stock-in-trade into an important aspect of his definition of society. Marriage henceforth comes close to being included in his objects of hate; it certainly turns into a central butt. All the happy marriages come under the fairy-story formula that rounds off a story; the actually depicted marriages, when they come to life, are shown as scenes of a bitter conflict of wills. Gabriel Varden of *Barnaby* heads a new line of henpecked husbands, which includes Edmund Sparkler, Snagsby, Joe Gargery, and Runty Wilfer.

Dolly Varden is scarcely a character; yet she shows an effort to escape from the Little Nells and the Rose Maylies. She owes the soft flutter of life in her, no doubt, to the fact that Charles now had at arm's length the spectacle of Georgina emerging charmingly from girlhood and coming steadily under his control.

But the great characters are Miggs and Tappertit, Dennis and Hugh, Willett and his circle. And the great quality of this undervalued book comes from the way in which it suggests an elemental force blowing up out of society, out of the people, and shattering the whole structure of things. This force blows the lives of the characters about, and stamps itself on the story as a central formative act of renewal, frustrated and yet holding in its depths a subtle secret.

Barnaby, the folk-fool, with his raven, is not altogether a success; he hovers between the position of a symbol (like Little Nell) and a psychologically-realized person. He is both a poetic folk-image and a study in infantile fixations, and not quite either. Nevertheless, he is at the heart of the book, which could never have come off without him. Here Charles makes a bold effort to find out what the Nell-Smike figure meant artistically and psychologically. He frankly admits the mother-fixation, and tries to follow it out to its conclusions, its origins, which lie in a murder-complex. In the riotous wind that blows Barnaby away from his mother and makes him "reject" her in favour of the role offered by Gordon we see a moment of revolutionary choice, in which the release from the mother-fixation (the birth-trauma as murder-fear) is obtained and the entry into the great purpose beyond oneself is achieved.

But because, as here conceived, the leader of the people, Gordon, is torn by the fool-paradox and can only lead to a disaster, Barnaby himself is going to be cheated of his new status and stature. Dickens is chafing against Carlyle's *Hero Worship*, but he cannot intellectually see beyond the terms of Carlyle's statement of the situation. For him it turns into the proposition that the people are betrayed by their own goodness, which can never realize the depth of evil arrayed against them and which is therefore divided against itself and turns at least in part into the very evil it opposes. Only the Fool can lead against the State; but because the Fool leads, the people will lose. And yet things aren't the same after. The evil is partly defeated, some of the secret is unveiled, the lovers mate, the wicked stumble on their own wickedness, and life gets a new start. Barnaby, the key-figure, the child of murder, is deeply changed.

He recovered by degrees; and although he could never separate his condemnation and escape from the idea of a terrific dream, he became in other respects more rational. Dating from the time of his recovery, he had a better memory and greater steadiness of purpose; but a dark cloud overhung his whole previous existence, and never cleared away.

He was not the less happy for this, for his love of freedom and interest in all that moved or grew, or had its being in the elements, remained to him unimpaired.

He is still tethered to his mother, and works on the land, and fears to set foot in the city streets. But he has gone one essential step towards understanding and articulation of history, the class struggle, the human condition. "A clear interpretation of the thought which at heart torments these wild inarticulate souls," whom Dickens, unlike Carlyle, recognizes as having the clue to the human maze.

The ambivalent relation of the Fool to the dark forces is excellently suggested by the symbolic linking of Barnaby to

his raven, the black bird with its hoarse chuckle "I'm a devil."
In choosing the Gordon riots for the setting Dickens by
intuition, chance, or deliberation picked on the one moment in
English history when his thesis seemed perfectly exemplified;
for these riots came at a moment of obscure transition, when
Wilkite radicalism was at its ebb and the new proletarian forces
were still unstable and incohate. The people in such a situation
turn back to obsolete slogans (the cry once of revolutionary
anti-feudal forces), but these, now archaic, cannot be effectively
directed against the absolutist trends which are dimly appre-
hended as the real enemy. They can only end in frustration. No
other period in our history would so neatly fit Dickens's thesis.

A few small points to end with. Charles was still submitting
to Forster as the censor of the Victorian conscience.

I have shut myself up by myself to-day, and mean to try to go
it . . . Kate being out, and the house peacefully dismal. I don't
remember altering the exact part you object to, but if there's anything
here you object to, knock it out ruthlessly. (March 26th.)

Besides seeing manuscripts, Forster was reading all proofs;
and so, apart from whatever alterations Forster made, Dickens
in writing could not but be aware of this primary audience.
Secondly, there is the strong way in which Dickens, as Barnaby-
Gordon, felt himself the controller of the revolutionary situation.

I have just burnt into Newgate, and am going in the next number
to tear the prisoners out by the hair of their heads. . . . (September 11,
1841.)
I have let all the prisoners out of Newgate, burnt down Lord
Mansfield's, and played the very devil. Another number will finish
the fires, and help us towards the end. I feel quite smoky while I
am at work. I want elbow-room terribly. (A week later.)

On to this point of his work broke the anguish over Mary's
grave and he had to fight to finish the book under conditions
of nervous breakdown. For him it was as though indeed the
seals of the dark were broken, and the ghosts of guilt and
innocence rose up out of the cleft to harry him. It is against this
moment that we must read the passage cited above about
Barnaby reprieved from terror and returning to the Mother, to
the Earth, for a convalescence into clarified memory.

217

7

Choice of Evils

I

CHARLES had made up his mind to go to the States. Kate's tears couldn't turn him aside, nor the cynicism of Lady Holland. ("Why cannot you go down to Bristol and see some of the third and fourth class people there, and they'll do just as well.") At last Kate weakened and gave in. The Macreadies were ready to take the children, and Maclise had painted a little picture of them for the parents to carry along. Charles had enough tie-pins, chains, rings, glowing vests and brocade gowns. He and Kate boarded the *Britannia* at Liverpool with a last-minute present of a pocket Shakespeare from Forster.

On January 4, 1842, they sailed—into terrific storms—and, battered, reached Halifax. Charles was cheered in the streets; and judges, bishops and the rest of them crowded to welcome him. Then the *Britannia* carried him to Boston and the start-off of months of maddening adulation and abuse. There is no need here to follow out the exhausting tour in detail. The endless hand-shaking, the serenades (suddenly realized by Charles with a grin as directed towards the pair of boots outside the hotel-room door), the banquets, the receptions, the visits to prisons and asylums, then the abuse after he had raised the copyright question.

What matters is the shock that Charles experienced. He had meant to come with a perfectly open mind and to judge the new society on its own merits. Politically and socially, he was ready and eager to admire. But he found that he couldn't. "This is not the Republic I came to see," he wrote to Macready. "This is not the Republic of my imagination." It turned out he had a preconception, which he couldn't get rid of, that the States would reveal a society which had overcome the contradictions of English society; that he would find here the way out from the conflict to which he could see no end in the terms posited by the English scene. Certainly the uproar that arose through the copyright speeches contributed to his disillusion. It was hard to believe in the moral superiority of a country where the right to pillage, distort at will, and pirate a foreign author's works was upheld as righteous and even necessary to the national way of life. (Some defenders of the right to piracy argued that it enabled editors and publishers to adapt English writings to the tastes and attitudes of the Americans; others agreed that it made things harder for the native writer, but were so taken by the cleverness of getting something for nothing that they defended the pirating.) But the copyright question alone could not have determined his attitude.

Even less did personal attitudes have anything to do with it. Until he started on copyright, he could hardly have been more praised and fêted; and he never made the mistake of confounding the elements he disliked with other and admirable elements in the national character:

They are friendly, earnest, hospitable, kind, frank, very often accomplished, far less prejudiced than you would suppose, warm-hearted, fervent, and enthusiastic. They are chivalrous in their universal politeness to women, courteous, obliging, disinterested; and, when they conceive a perfect affection for a man (as I may venture to say of myself), entirely devoted to him. I have received thousands of people of all ranks and grades, and have never once been asked an offensive or impolite question—except by Englishmen. . . .

The State is a parent to its people; has a parental care and watch over all poor children, women labouring of child, sick persons, and captives. The common men render you assistance in the street, and would revolt from the offer of a piece of money. The desire to please is universal. . . .

That was not written in the haste of first impressions; it was written after the first copyright speech, and he never modified his opinion that certain free-and-easy aspects of the American situation had bred excellent qualities—qualities that could be imported with benefit into Englishmen. He repeated his tribute in 1862 in an essay, *The Young Man from the Country*. But he could not rest his judgment on this pleasant side of the American character. After stating it, he goes on, "But I don't like the country. I would not live here on any consideration." Why was this? Mere prejudice? Certainly it wasn't the reaction of a man deeply rooted in a sense of the European past, of the Graeco-Roman heritage, of the subtler points of the European art-tradition. Consequently it is all the more significant. If Dickens had simply been a more or less vulgar Radical, he should have been pleased at his American popularity, should have wanted nothing better than to cash in on it. He goes on, "I have a confidence that I must be right, because I have everything, God knows, to lead me to the opposite conclusion; and yet I cannot resist coming to this one."

He is aware of the many reasons why he should fall for the American claims to have found a new way of life, a way that left behind the old European impasses; but he feels even more cogent reasons for resisting. What, then, were those reasons?

To get them clear is essential for the understanding of Dickens and his work; but it is not easy to separate out his key reactions and adduce their full meaning. He is not a systematic political thinker; and he therefore does not arrange his conclusions in a logically worked-out and correlated way. Still, with a little care we can disentangle the crucial points.

They all centre round his feeling that there was no freedom in the States. This was staggering for him; for he had come ready to admire the States as not only more free than England, but also free in a new sort of way.

I believe there is no country, on the face of the earth, where there is less freedom of opinion in reference to which there is broad difference of opinion than in this.

For the form of social and political terrorism which he felt in the States he blamed to a considerable extent the U.S. Press. This opinion, gained first in 1842, he repeated twenty years later without the least modification in *The Young Man*.

When any man, of any grade of desert in intellect or character, can climb to any public distinction, no matter what, in America, without first grovelling down upon the earth, and bending the knee before this monster of depravity . . . when any man in that Free Country has freedom of opinion, and presumes to think for himself, and speak for himself, without humble reference to a censorship which, for its rampant ignorance and base dishonesty, he utterly loathes and despises in his heart; when those who most acutely feel its infamy and the reproach it casts upon the nation, and who most denounce it to each other, dare to set their heels upon and crush it openly, in the sight of all men: then I will believe that its influence is lessening, and men are returning to their manly senses.

But while that Press has its evil eye in every house, and its black hand in every appointment in the State, from a president to a postman, while, with ribald slander for its only stock in trade, it is the standard literature of an enormous class, who must find their reading in a newspaper, or they will not read at all; so long must its odium be upon the country's head, and so long must the evil it works be plainly visible in the Republic.

But how did this terrorism work, and why was it tolerated? It was linked with a corrupt system of government. He describes the House of Representatives in Washington thus:

I saw in them, the wheels that move the meanest perversion of virtuous Political Machinery that the worst tools ever wrought. Despicable trickery at elections; underhanded tamperings with public officers; cowardly attacks upon opponents, with scurrilous news-papers for shields, and hired pens for daggers; shameful truckling to mercenary knaves, whose claim to be considered, is, that every day they sow new crops of ruin with their venal types; aidings and abettings of every bad inclination in the popular mind, and artful suppressions of all its good influences; such things as these, and in a word, Dishonest Faction in its most depraved and most unblushing form, stared out from every corner of the crowded hall.

He sees the American House as the more active realization of the evil forces he has found in the English House. But how is this? How is it that bad elements have been so intensified in the States, where he had thought to find them broken down under a different kind of social movement?

He is forced to the conclusion that the "freedom" of the States is a freedom for the extension of money-power, the power that turns men into things, into instruments for the profit-guided will of other men. There is still the other side which had first attracted him, the throwing-off of feudal fetters, the economic mobilities and the elements of pioneering spirit; but this good side is unable, in the last resort, to affect the money-dominated side.

And so he feels the intense contradictions of the American scene, which are already in many ways worse than those of England. The conflict between the easy-going comradely spirit and the spirit of get rich quick. He feels there a point of ex-treme instability, which, because it is based so powerfully on the illusion of freedom and the fact of money-terrorism, is going to be sometime a world danger. When the contradictions come to their limit of working out, then the terroristic side will be a shattering danger to the earth.

I still reserve my opinion of the national character—just whispering that I tremble for a radical coming here, unless he is a radical on principle, by reason and reflection, and from a sense of right. I fear that if he were anything else, he would return home a tory. . . .

I do fear that the heaviest blow ever dealt at liberty will be dealt by this country, in the failure of its example to the earth.

He has no idea how this "heaviest blow" will come about; for he is no political economist with knowledge of the structural movement of a society. He approaches entirely from the moral side. True, he implicates a vast deal of social and economic aspects in his judgment, but from the viewpoint of their revelation of the moral man. Yet, because his judgment goes deep, he penetrates to the essential conflict, and his words are valid. What he said in 1842 and repeated in 1862 did get at the bedrock of the U.S. situation. It tore away all veils and superficial aspects, and got right down to the basic struggle: between the comradely expansive virtues and the corrupted money ethic. Here, in the States, there was nothing to cushion or divert the continual head-on collision; and with growing economic power the chasm and collision must get worse, until there came the "heaviest blow"—which, in fact, we have seen in our day with the discovery of nuclear fission (largely a European and English discovery in theory) applied by American finance and engineering to become an imperialist terror instrument that threatens the destruction of human society unless the way is found into a new level of world brotherhood, peace, plenty. That Dickens's words have found fulfilment in ways he could not dream of in 1842 does not lessen their significance, their penetration into the core of the American contradiction. There, then, were the main reasons why Dickens found in the States a country essentially lacking in freedom, whatever virtues it might have. His comments are, of course, not always directed by the deep insight which comes out in his key passages of criticism. Having been so unexpectedly disappointed, and meeting such abuse over trying to raise the copyright question in a friendly way, he no doubt felt some of the discomforts and crudities with extra strength. It is unlikely that he would have enjoyed having his coat encrusted with spit even if the States had been the free world of his hopes; but when it turned out the land of unfreedom, he inevitably felt all the more disgusted with the spittle, the lack of perspectives, the conceit, the endless array of unimaginable bores.

The question of slavery he saw as one aspect of the humbug and unfreedom. He refused to have any truck with it in any shape or form. He saw in the attitude to the Negro the final crystallization of the American way of life, its fundamental lie.

They whisper, here (they dare only whisper, you know, and that below their breaths), that on that place [Baltimore], and all through the South, there is a dull gloomy cloud on which the very word seems written. I shall be able to say, one of these days, that I accepted no public mark of respect in any place where slavery was ;—and that's something.

In an argument on the subject, his opponent

was a little taken aback by this, and asked me if I believed in the Bible. Yes, I said, but if any man could prove to me that it sanctioned slavery, I would place no further confidence in it. "Well, then," he said, "by God, sir, the niggers must be kept down, and the whites have put down the coloured people wherever they have found them."
"That's the whole question," said I.

He naturally supported all the anti-slavery movements; but he was the last man to consider that the legal abolition of slavery ended the matter. While the Negro as such was in any way held inferior or penalized, his analysis of the American Lie was untouched; and to the treatment of the Negro in the States in the years following abolition he could have pointed as the perfect illustration of the truth of his argument that the States were the country of unfreedom.

So he passed on from Boston through Pittsburgh to St. Louis, and then north again, into Canada. One effect of Boston was to strengthen his inclination to Unitarianism. He struck up a friendship with Longfellow. The Americans scrutinized the clothes of both Charles and Kate; they wanted to know if his curls were genuine or the result of lotion-fixing; they screwed bits of fur out of his "costly greatcoat" from Regent Street; they were all introduced as "remarkable men"; a Kentucky man found him "flash, like one of the river gamblers."
He got into arguments about Animal Magnetism and at Pittsburgh:

there being present only Mr. Q and the portrait-painter, Kate sat down, laughing, for me to try my hand upon her. I had been holding forth upon the subject rather luminously, and asserting that I had thought I could exercise the influence, but had never tried. In six minutes, I magnetized her into hysterics, and then into the magnetic sleep. I tried again last night, and she fell into the slumber in little more than two minutes. . . .

I can wake her with perfect ease; but I confess (not being prepared for anything so sudden and complete) I was on the first occasion rather alarmed.

Kate, with her feeling of not quite fitting in anywhere, was more than ever helplessly knocking into things.

I say nothing of Kate's troubles—but you recollect her propensity? She falls into, or out of, every coach or boat we enter; scrapes the skin off her legs; brings great sores and swellings on her feet; chips large fragments out of her ankle-bone; and makes herself blue with bruises.

However, she had not screamed "under circumstances that would have fully justified her, even in my eyes," and had never shown any signs of despondency or fatigue despite the unending heavy travel. Her cheerfulness and gameness, he said, had pleased him very much.

When we recall the ghost who haunted his dreams by day and night, and the ghost who haunted the paranoiac of *A Madman's Manuscript*, there is significance in the horror he felt in the Pittsburgh solitary-confinement prison. "What if ghosts be one of the terrors of the jails? I have pondered it often, since then." The thought conjures up precisely the fancy of the tale, though he seems unaware of the connection. "Imagine a prisoner . . . melancholy themes . . . evil conscience . . . some inexplicable silent figure." He came to the conclusion that nightly spectres must haunt the men, and asked a prisoner "if he dreamed much. He gave me a most extraordinary look, and said—under his breath—in a whisper—'No.' "

He himself did not need solitary confinement for the haunting. In the midst of all the noisy triumphs he cannot put "sweet lost Mary" by. "I feel something of the presence and influence of that spirit which directs my life, and through a heavy sorrow, has pointed upward with an unchanging finger for more than four years past." Amid the perpetual thunder of Niagara he thought passionately of her.

At last they escaped to Montreal; and at once, as relaxation, he gave himself up most strenuously to organizing with the garrison an amateur performance of *A Roland for an Oliver*—a farce he had seen C. Mathews perform in in October 1840. Besides acting as stage-manager, he played Mr. Snobbington (in a wig fetched from New York). A second item in the show was *Deaf as a Post*, in which Kate played Amy Templeton to his Gallop. "Only think of Kate playing; and playing devilish well!" It never struck him that why Kate played with him so little in general was because he had allotted her no playing part except that of bed-companion and breeding mother. Here, where he had no other woman of his group available and she was parted from her infants, he had no choice but to give her a further role.

His opinion of her is underlined in *The Cricket on the Hearth* where he developed her propensity to knocks, cuts and bruises in the person of Tilly Slowboy. Tilly was as hopelessly clumsy with babies as with herself. She held the baby upside-down, performed "cow-like gambols round that all-unconscious innocent," and used to "hand it round to everybody in succession as if it were something to drink."

II

In June they were home again, with a shaggy white terrier that at first bore the name of Timber Doddle. Georgina had been looking after the children, and wasn't going to be dislodged from her job. Kate sighed, and was no longer even the mother of her children; she was reduced to the titular lady of the dinner-table, and the inmate of the bed to which, sooner or later, Charles retired. He gave a dinner to chosen friends at Greenwich, and Cruikshank came home in Charles's phaeton on his head, "to the mingled delight and dread of the metropolitan police."

Charles had at once taken up the copyright question, with a letter to the *Athenaeum*, and lost no time in starting on his *American Notes*. A project for a radical sort of newspaper was stimulated by finding that *The Courier*, formerly a Whig and then a Tory paper, was to be incorporated with *The Globe*. He would have liked to have gone on "nailing the true colours to the mast and fighting the battle staunchly and to the death." He asked Lady Holland to sound some of the big politicians on the notion of an evening paper. But no encouragement was given.

In August he was at Broadstairs, reading Tennyson and changing his terrier's name to Snittle Timbery, "as more sonorous and expressive." The children had also acquired strange names. At the moment, Katey, being fiery, was Lucifer Box; Mamey, Mild Glo'ster; Charley was Flaster Floby (Mister

Toby), and high cheek-boned Walter, Young Skull. "Each is pronounced with a peculiar drawl." Both the fascination of the sea and the relation of his associative method of fancy to Gothic romanticism are suggested by the following passage in a letter:

Tennyson all the morning on the seashore. Among other trifling effects, the waters have dried up as they did of old, and show me all the mermaids, at the bottom of the ocean; together with millions of queer creatures, half-fish and half-fungus, looking down into all manner of coral caves and seaweed conservatories; and staring in with their great dull eyes at every open nook and loophole. Who else, too, could conjure up such a close to the extraordinary and as Landor would say, "most wonderful," series of pictures in the "dream of fair women," as—
> Squadrons and squares of men in brazen plates,
> Scaffolds, still sheets of water, divers woes,
> Ranges of glimmering vaults with iron grates,
> And hushed seraglios.

In September he was back in London, and visited the old rebel Hone on his death-bed at Tottenham. Longfellow arrived in England, and Dickens rushed round, showing him England; and Longfellow talked of Dickens's vogue in Germany and of German poetry. *American Notes* had just come out, and Longfellow thought it "goodnatured and severe," and, on the subject of slavery, "grand." Charles introduced him to Tennyson, Browning, Bulwer Lytton; and with Forster took him round Rochester, bursting against regulations into the castle. They also (with tne aid of two prison officials) toured some of the foul night-haunts of London.

By the end of the month Longfellow was gone, and Dickens had rushed off, with Maclise, Stanfield and Forster, to look at Cornwall. He was meditating a new novel and felt inclined to open with a Cornish setting.

Heavens! if you could have seen the necks of bottles, distracting in their immense variety of shape, peering out of the carriage pockets! If you could have witnessed the deep devotion of the postboys, the wild attachment of the hostlers, the maniac glee of the waiters. If you could have followed us into the earthy old churches we visited and into the strange caverns on the gloomy seashore, and down into the depths of mines, and up to the tops of giddy heights where the unspeakably green water was roaring, I don't know how many hundred feet below! If you could have seen but one gleam of the bright fires by which we sat in the big rooms of the ancient inns at night, until long after the small hours had come and gone. . . .

I never laughed in my life as I did on this journey. It would have done you good to hear me. I was choking and gasping and bursting the buckle off the back of my stock, all the way. And Stanfield got into such apoplectic entanglements that we were often obliged to beat him on the back with portmanteaus before we could recover him.

Elsewhere he wrote of Land's End, "with the green sea far under us, lapping into solitary rocky nooks where the mermaids live, who but you only [Forster] had the courage to stretch over, to see those diamond jets of brightness that I swore then, and believe still, were the flappings of their tails."

Back in London he struggled with the new book, changing the name from Sweezleden, Sweezleback, Sweezlewagg, to Chuzzletoe, Chuzzleboy, Chubblewig, Chuzzlewig, and finally, after long thought and discussion, arriving at *Chuzzlewit*. The full title (worked out at the Chuzzlewig stage) was to be: "The Life and Adventures of Martin Chuzzlewig, his family, friends, and enemies. Comprising all his wills and his ways. With an historical record of what he did and what he didn't. The whole forming a complete key to the house of Chuzzlewig." The first notion, as usual, was changed, modified and developed in unforeseen ways as he worked. By the third chapter, however, he had come on the idea of "Old Martin's plot to degrade and punish Pecksniff."

In Cornwall Maclise and Stanfield had made many sketches; and Maclise now went on painting for the Academy *A Girl at the Waterfall*, in which he inserted Georgina into the Cornish scene. Charles determined to get hold of this work and bought it under a pseudonym when it was exhibited. Georgina was now about the same age as Mary had been at her death-apotheosis. She looked enough like Mary to be mistaken for her at a distance, and Charles started seeing "the spirit of Mary shining out" in her sister. He said that with such a sort of Mary rebirth "the past can hardly be separated from the present."

This development is exactly what we would expect from the analysis I have made earlier of the Fanny-fixation and the forms it took in adolescence. Georgina, by her adoring presence, both fixed the obsession more strongly and yet relieved much of the burden of guilt which had come into the open in Little Nell and which had still been fully active in the episode of the graves just before the departure over the waters. The ghost of Mary did not cease to haunt Charles, and was liable to cause him bad twinges yet at moments of anxiety; but an essential alleviation was caused by Georgina's loving attendance. If she had ever left him to marry, it is hard to imagine how he would have been able to carry on, or what torments he would have had to pass through. But he was spared that trial. The bond between him and Georgina soon became too strong for any other man to intrude between him and her soul.

When Hone died early in November, he and Cruikshank with "enormous whiskers . . . like a partially unravelled bird's nest," attended the funeral. In the parlour the Rev. Thomas Binney, a preacher of great fame and author of many hymns (such as *Eternal Light*), asked Cruikshank if he had seen the paragraph about Hone in the papers.

"Oh!" said the clergyman. "Then you will agree with me, Mr. Cruikshank, that it is not only an insult to me, who am the servant of the Almighty, but an insult to the Almighty, whose servant I am."

"How is that, sir?" said Cruikshank.

"It is stated, Mr. Cruikshank, in that paragraph," says the minister, "that when Mr. Hone failed in business as a bookseller he was persuaded by me to try the pulpit; which is false, unchristian, in a manner blasphemous, and in all respects contemptible. Let us pray."

With which . . . he knelt down, as we all did, and began a very miserable jumble of an extemporary prayer. I was really penetrated with sorrow for the family, but when Cruikshank (upon his knees, and sobbing for the loss of an old friend) whispered me "that if he wasn't a clergyman, and it wasn't a funeral, he'd have punched his head," I felt as if nothing but convulsions could possibly relieve me. . . .

Published in 1882, this account caused much scandal and was "denied."

Before the end of the year he had got the new novel under way. He found time, however, to write a verse prologue for *The Patrician's Daughter*, a verse-play by a young author, Westland Marston, which Macready was putting on at Drury Lane on December 10th. In his couplets Dickens championed the right of poetic drama to tackle the contemporary scene, to turn to the present instead of "distant ages out of human view . . . the dead caverns on the shore of Time."

> Is it with Man, as with some meaner things,
> That out of death his single purpose springs? . . .
> Iron is worn, at heart, by many still——
> The tyrant Custom binds the serf-like will;

If the sharp rack, and screw, and chain be gone,
These later days have tortures of their own;
The guiltless writhe, while Guilt is stretch'd in sleep,
And Virtue lies, too often, dungeon deep. . . .
[For] social usage has the pow'r to change
Good thoughts to evil; in its highest range
To cramp the noble soul, and turn to ruth
The kindling impulse of our glorious youth.

The play caused a passing sensation, but did not run long.

III

Charles was full of stirring creative energies. "I feel my power more than ever I did," he said. "I have greater confidence in myself than ever I did." Now at last he could start on a planned novel with a contemporary setting. The theme of *Chuzzlewit* was to be the revelation of "how selfishness propagates itself, and to what a grim giant it may grow from small beginnings." So far he had never had a conscious theme of this sort in his mind before he started work.

And now, trying to work on this new level, he found the network of social relations in which he had tied himself up to be distracting and harassing in the extreme. He even refused to dine with Miss Coutts. "The lapse of every new day only gives me stronger reasons for being perseveringly uncomfortable, that out of my gloom and solitude something comical, or meant to be, may straightway grow up."

He found time, however, to review a pamphlet by Lord Londonderry attacking the Mines and Collieries Bill. Lord Londonderry strongly objected to interference with labour conditions (he was opening up new mines and building Seaham harbour). He was horrified that woodcuts showing the wretched, semi-naked workers in the Report of the Commissioners should pollute the boudoirs of refined ladies. Charles tore the pamphlet up with savage sarcasm; but did not add that when he himself had read the Report, he sobbed with the agony of his pity and anger.

He dashed away in March for Cobley's Farm, Finchley, and then continued with *Chuzzlewit*, coming up to speak for the Press at the Printers' Pension Society dinner—the Press as "the fountain of knowledge and the bulwark of freedom, the founder of free States and their preserver." The printer "is the only product of civilization necessary to the existence of free man."

A May letter to Jerrold in which he mentions his *Child's History* which he is writing to quench any Tory sparks in Charley, and paints the horrors of a hospital dinner he had attended:

There were men there who made such speeches and expressed such sentiments as any moderately intelligent dustman would have blushed through his cindery bloom to have thought of. Sleek, slobbering, bow-paunched, overfed, apoplectic, snorting cattle, and the auditory leaping up in their delight! I never saw such an illustration of the power of purse, or felt so degraded and debased by its contemplation, since I have had eyes and ears. The absurdity of the thing was too horrible to laugh at.

A few days later he was writing to Mrs. Hogarth about Mary:

I trace in many respects a strong resemblance between her mental features and Georgina's—so strange a one at times, that when she and Kate and I are sitting together, I seem to think that what has happened is a melancholy dream from which I am just awakening. The perfect like of what she was, will never be again, but so much of her spirit shines out of her sister, that the old time comes back again at some seasons, and I can hardly separate it from the present. After she died, I dreamed of her every night for many months— I think for the better part of a year—sometimes as a spirit, sometimes as living creature, never with any of the bitterness of my real sorrow but always with a kind of quiet happiness, which became so pleasant to me that I never lay down at night without a hope of the vision coming back in one shape or other. And so it did.

I went down into Yorkshire, and finding it still present to me, in a strange scene and a strange bed, I could not help mentioning the circumstance in a note I wrote home to Kate. From that moment I have never dreamed of her once, though she is so much in my thoughts at all times (especially when I am successful, and have prospered in anything) that the recollection of her is an essential part of my being, and is as inseparable from my existence as the beating of my heart is.

This confession that the bringing out of the truth before Kate, even to the small degree expressed by his letter, had the effect of preventing the dream-tryst, is of much interest. As also the statement that each leap of self-confidence was felt as a warm union with Mary.

Marston had written another play, *Strathmore*, and decided to read it aloud in a hall before trying to get it staged. Marston read monotonously, and at the end Dickens showed him how to do it, impersonating each character in turn.

A Greenwich dinner was given for Black, who had given up editorship of the *Chronicle*; and a Richmond dinner for Macready who was off for America—it was feared that his friendship for Dickens would spoil his tour, and so the latter did not go with the others for the farewell at Liverpool; but he spoke at the dinner and made Macready weep.

In July he and Kate were staying with the Smithsons near Malton in Yorkshire, rejoicing in green woods and friends with an ale-cellar as big as a church. All day long I cantered over such soft moss and turf that the horses' feet scarcely made a sound upon it." Here he wrote for Lady Blessington's *Keepsake* a poem comparing the Moslems, who treat sheets of the Koran as talismans, with the Christians:

> So have I known a country on the earth
> Where darkness sat upon the living waters,
> And brutal ignorance, and toil, and dearth
> Were the hard portion of its sons and daughters;
> And yet, where they who should have oped the door
> Of charity and light, for all men's finding,
> Squabbled for words upon the altar-floor,
> And rent The Book, in struggles for the binding.

Meanwhile the "Christian Pariah"

> Walks through the world, not very much the worse,
> Does all the good he can, and loves his brother.

But things weren't going too well with *Chuzzlewit*, which started off with 20,000 sales and didn't show signs of rising over 23,000. One afternoon in June, Hall spoke of the disappointment and said he hoped they wouldn't have to put into operation the penalty clause of their agreement and make Dickens refund some of his advance. The publishers had the power of deducting £50 from the monthly payments (£150) until their investments were paid back.

Dickens, as usual, rose to the occasion and pulled sales up with the invention of Mrs. Gamp. Still, in July the payment was cut; and Chapman and Hall became "scaly-headed vultures." Dickens wanted another publisher at once. "I am rubbed in the tenderest part of my eyelids with bay salt." Also, "a wrong kind of fire is burning in my head, I don't think I can write." Forster, now literary adviser to C. and H., advised Charles to see how he felt after the seaside.

So the Dickenses went to the sea again, to Broadstairs, for August. But Charles couldn't bear waiting. "Negotiations and delays are worse to me than drawn daggers." In his rage he tried an "insane match" against time by walking eighteen miles on a scorching day in four hours and a half. "I could get no sleep at night, and really began to be afraid I was going to have a fever." Normally he wrote in a bay window from nine to one, bathed, lunched, walked a dozen miles, or lay in the sand reading.

With September he was back in town, rollicking with wine over dinner at Forster's place in Lincoln's Inn Fields or going into the matter of ragged schools with Miss Coutts or the lawyers' clerk, S. R. Starey, who had started a school in stinking Field Lane, Holborn. While strongly approving of the schools, he wanted the religious element as diluted as possible and emphasized the importance of a washing-place "with a good supply of running water, soap and towels."

In October he was sitting on a platform with Disraeli and Cobden in the Manchester Athenaeum, praising popular education; and then rushed round inspecting jails. But as he had looked down at the self-respecting mechanics and factory workers in the Athenaeum and declared, "the more intelligent and reflective society becomes in the mass, the more confidently will writers throw themselves on the feelings of the people," something stirred and sang inside him. And as he walked round the busy city, the idea of a Christmas story came to him, that would get right inside the people.

Within a month the story was written. He had high hopes that it would solve his financial miseries. He tried to get Forster to talk things over with Bradbury and Evans, the printers; but Forster asked him to consult Mitton and wait till after Christmas. Writing the story, says Forster, "he wept over it, and laughed, and wept again, and walked thinking of it fifteen and twenty miles about the back streets of London"; and when it was done, "he let himself loose like a madman."

Mrs. Cowden Clarke had met Charles at the house of Tagart, the Unitarian minister, where Leigh Hunt introduced her. They looked at *Punch* together, and he laughed till he wept, and she was thrilled to see the "limpid, liquid suffusion" in his long, silky-lashed eyes.

At home he sang comic songs to the children who sat on his knees and sang the choruses of "fol de riddy oddy," while Kate sat with bent head, smiling over her ragbag, and then another baby tumbled over and screamed and virginal Georgina slid big-eyed about, already showing signs of a double chin. And this Christmas he gave a party for the Macready children, whose father was still in the States. The elders seem to have enjoyed themselves. Charles did some legerdemain for the children; then after a game of proverbs and a champagne supper with crackers, toasts were drunk and country dances danced. Mrs. Carlyle, who wasn't at home in noisy romps, said that midnight saved the situation, which "was rising into something not unlike the Rape of the Sabines. . . . It was just a little knot of blackguardly literary people who felt themselves above all rules and independent of the universe."

The Christmas story, *The Carol*, came out with illustrations by John Leech; but it earned only £500 instead of the hoped-for £1,000. Charles had had it published as his own venture, taking all profits and paying only a commission to C. and H.; but the method hadn't worked as he'd meant it.

IV

Dickens had tried to keep any animosity out of his *American Notes* and did not mention the copyright questions. The *Notes* bring out his fascination with jails, asylums, homes for the deaf and dumb, etc. The criminal and the madman, the broken and the abnormal, always interest him, and he wants to know all he can, both about the abnormal persons and the method used to help or cure them. He singled out for praise the public institutions for "charity children," which he thought much better than the English institutions with their attempts to produce regimented servility. In his treatment of these institutions he showed that, anarchist though he was in many of his reactions, he stood unreservedly for public action in all such matters as against personal charity.

The *Notes* were not much praised in England, and excited considerable hatred in the States, where the book was consigned to the flames on the New York stage amid applause.

But Dickens did not rest at the offence given by the *Notes*. To pull up the sales of *Chuzzlewit* he diverted his hero to the States and let loose in the novel all the feeling he had tried to restrain in the essays. These chapters, in Carlyle's words, made "all Yankee-doodledum to fizz like one universal sodawater bottle." "Stark raving mad," was Charles's own phrase. He had sought to bring out to the full the contradictions between democratic statements and the actual rule by money values. And in his picture of Edenville, the emblem of the desolation and death caused by the unfettered rule of those money values, he anticipated the historical fact of the miserable Hoovervilles of U.S.A. economy in its matured form.

He clearly started out in *Chuzzlewit* to write a full-length novel of the family chronicle type, with romantic structure and a moral centralization on the themes of hypocrisy and selfishness. Once again he is setting himself to imitate Bulwer and producing something quite different in his own despite. Bulwer's *Night and Morning*, already discussed in connection with Barnaby and Little Nell, set out to attack the hypocritical time-server in the character of Robert Beaufort. Beaufort is a man of decorous phrase and bloodless action, in whom virtue has become a superficial propriety destructive of all truth and warmth. The book is meant as a whole-hearted attack on certain aspects of the Victorian Lie, but Bulwer lacks the penetration, the power to throw up symbolic characterizations which is Charles's saving grace amid his many confusions and sentimentalities. That Bulwer recognized the affinity between *Night and Morning* and *Chuzzlewit* is shown in his preface for an 1845 edition, in which he declares that his aim had been to satirize the hypocrisies of the respectable, as was done by Dickens in the person of Pecksniff.

Chuzzlewit has the romantic mechanisms of the unmasked villain, the regained heritage, the murder flight; and the members of the Chuzzlewit family make up the various aspects of the capitalist situation along the general lines indicated in the discussion of *Nickleby*: Jonas, the dark usurious exploiting murder side, and Young Martin, the adventurously enterprising side, which in the end gets its reward, the accumulated capital of Old Martin. Around Old Martin are collected a family group who between them make up a fairly thorough gallery of the types of scrounger, cheat, and sharp business man. Old Martin himself represents the money-maker become conscious of the polluting nature of the money-ethic and desperately hoping to find some way of purifying his useless hoard. The regeneration of Young Martin from greed, moroseness, bitterness, represents the process whereby his inheritance itself becomes purified, made a possible vehicle for good instead of evil.

Right at the outset of the book we get a magnificent picture of the evil and parasitic Chuzzlewits, among them cousin Pecksniff; and set against them are the suspicious Old Man and the long-suffering Orphan Girl who is sacrificed to his gloom. Gold, declares Old Martin, is the touchstone bringing forth the hidden evil in man.

I have gone, a rich man, among people of all grades and kinds; relatives, friends, and strangers; among people in whom, when I was poor, I had confidence, and justly, for they never once deceived me then, or, to me, wronged one another. But I never found one nature, no, not one, in which, being wealthy and alone, I was not forced to detect the latent corruption that lay hid within it, waiting for such as I to bring it forth. Treachery, deceit, and low design; hatred of competitors real or fancied, for my favour; meanness, falsehood, baseness and servility; or an assumption of honest independence, almost worse than all; these are the beauties which my wealth has brought to light.

Brother against brother, child against parent, friends treading on the faces of friends. . . .

Charles could not have reached this concept of money as the dynamic evil transforming character if he had not had the philosophic support of Carlyle; but in a man so little philosophic in bent, some test of thought in action was necessary, and he had found that test in America. There he could not blame aristocratic and feudal survivals; and he saw the rank evil striking at the root of man in conditions which in so many other ways encouraged comradeship and independence. (Again he owes a certain debt to Bulwer, to his play *Money*, but what is honest, stinging satire in Bulwer fumbling at profundities, becomes a broad vision of the soul of man in Dickens.)

And it is, indeed, the U.S.A. scenes, which Charles found himself switched into writing, that carry the book far beyond a new twist to the romantic formulas. On the one hand we meet Old Martin—the tormented personification of the discovery of money's perverting power—and round him the scurrying mob of perverted competitors, ranging from the active finance-evil of Anthony and Jonas Chuzzlewit to the gigantic figure of Pecksniff, who is much more than a mere hypocrite; who is the very emblem of the evil transformation of values which Victorian capitalism was carrying out. On the other hand is the array of American types culminating in the ghastly picture of the desolation that their ethic wreaks.

The veiled evil, and the open evil: what is there to choose between these two? Dickens's condemnation of America is subtly and justly balanced by his condemnation of Britain. Pecksniff is the incarnation of evil until we turn to the States. The greed of the States is the supreme release of the evil in man until we turn back to Pecksniff. Capitalism matured and capitalism young, usurious finance or the enterprise of the free entrepreneur, the lie at the heart of an old culture and the lie at the heart of a young culture. Both are equally evil. There is no future to this world.

And yet Young Martin is saved. He takes into the new world Mark Tapley, the unbroken spirit of the British common man; and it is in the new world, despite its unbridled money ethic, that he finds his better self. He finds his love of man, through the very hell he enters; and his old bad pride is broken. "He felt and knew the failing of his life, and saw distinctly what an ugly spot it was." Yet even here at the point of self-confrontation the American enters, with the insidious doctrine of unfreedom masquerading as democracy:

He always introduced himself to strangers as a worshipper of freedom; was the consistent advocate of Lynch law, and slavery; and invariably recommended, both in print and speech, the "tarring and feathering" of any unpopular person who differed from himself. He called this "planting the standard of civilization in the wilder gardens of my country."

It should be noted, however, that Dickens does not omit from his American types the genuine freedom lover. That type is given in the man at the boarding-house who admits the charges—who sees the States as divided between a rich isolated "refined" class, and "the great mass" which "asserts a spurious independence, most miserably dependent for its mean existence on the disregard of humanizing conventionalities. . . ." In connection with this man Dickens cites the lines that Tom Moore had written early in the century:

> Oh but for such, Columbia's days were done;
> Rank without ripeness, quickened without sun,
> Crude at the surface, rotten at the core,
> Her fruits would fall before the spring were o'er.

Chuzzlewit thus carries on the new deepening of the romantic themes which *The Old Curiosity Shop* initiated. There is a thoroughly pessimist note as far as existing society and its money-ethic is concerned; but against this are set two factors. One is the great dynamic energy uttered in character projection and the other is the belief that men (and therefore society) can be changed. Martin, brought to the dead end of desolation which is the culmination of American economy, faces death and comes through into a new faith through his relations with Tapley, the unbreakable common man.

On the directly personal side we meet the Fool in the person of Tom Pinch. The folk elements, the pure fantasy, are modified in so far as Pinch is made to some extent a credible figure; the Fool as the socially exploited Innocent unaware of the facts and of his own strength. Only the full unmasking can release him from his enslavement to evil, which, through his misdirected powers of devotion, he has been in fact helping. He is opposed to Old Martin, the paranoiac, who is caught in a net which he recognizes but cannot control. Pinch's passion for Mary, glimpsed in a release-moment of music, is thus the recognition of his fellow slave. The emotion of the pure brother and sister bond (so necessary to Dickens's creative release) is expressed in the relations of Pinch and Ruth. Once more we get the deep, morbid conviction of brother and sister as one flesh—as being one in flesh beyond even the sunderings of marriage. Ruth, in agreeing to marry, cries out:

"I am never to leave him, am I, dear? I could never leave Tom. I am sure you know that."

"Do you think I would ask you?" he returned with a—well never mind with what.

"I am sure you never would," she answered, the bright tears standing in her eyes.

"And I will swear it, Ruth, my darling, if you please. Leave Tom! That would be a strange beginning. Leave Tom, dear! If Tom and we be not inseparable, and Tom (God bless him) have not all honour and all love in our home, my little wife, may that home never be! And that's a strong oath, Ruth!"

Shall it be recorded how she thanked him! etc., etc.

And the note on which the book ends, the note struck by Dickens as most emotionally important for his winding up, is that of Tom at his organ with the children of both Mary and Ruth all round him. "And coming from a garden, Tom, bestrewn with flowers by children's hands, thy sister little Ruth, as light

of foot and heart as of old days, sits down beside thee." The
solution for Charles is that return to the garden of childhood
and the untroubled union with the sister which defeats time.

In Pinch also the motive of love renunciation, which we have
found so prominent in one aspect of Charles's day-dream, is
given full outlet. Through renunciation Pinch gains a fuller
union with his sister.

The long-suffering beloved is given the name of Mary with
Dickens's characteristic inability to control tell-tale names.
Throughout this book we find also his trick of burlesquing his
own deepest emotions and of using himself in a most unashamed
way. It is all part of the child-game, the pretending to be oneself
in order to pretend to be someone else. Showing so much of the
hidden thing, and then snatching it away again. Seeing how
much one can tell without telling anything.

Thus, in the magnificent scene where Pecksniff gets drunk in
the boarding-house (a scene which gives away the extent to
which Pecksniff is based on John Dickens), Charles mocks at his
own deepest feelings. Pecksniff, trying to seduce the landlady,
calls on a "voice from the tomb" to sanctify his sensualities.

"For her sake," said Mr. Pecksniff. "Permit me—in honour of her
memory. For the sake of a voice from the tomb. You are *very* like
her, Mrs. Todgers! What a world this is."

"Ah! Indeed you may say that!" cried Mrs. Todgers. . . .

"Has a voice from the tomb no influence?" said Mr. Pecksniff
with dismal tenderness. "This is irreligious, my dear creature."

When we realize that this was written about the time Charles
was telling Mrs. Hogarth about his emotion for Georgina and
Georgina's likeness to the dead Mary who haunted him, we
get a strange glimpse into both his artistic method and his
personal life. Again, in the relations of Moddle to the two Pecksniff sisters is a self-mock. Moddle, losing to Jonas the sister he
wants, is almost ensnared into marriage with the other one, but
slips off at the last moment to Van Dieman's Land—thus carrying out the emigration to which Charles's own thoughts in
moments of misery turned. (*Mercy* in this relation is *Mary*;
Charity, *Kate*. A slight verbal relation, as usual, weds the names
together.) Taine has been laughed at for taking Moddle seriously
as a gloomy maniac, an English melancholic; but he is not
entirely wrong. Charles is mocking at his own pang, but the
pang is sharp under the mock; and so Taine, in feeling the

reality behind Moddle, is much closer to Dickens than those who see only the joke. Forster mentions that Moddle was a favourite character of Dickens's and cites a letter of April 23, 1844, written as *Chuzzlewit* was finished: "This is the warmest, most genial, most intensely bland, delicious, growing, springy, songster-of-the-grovy, bursting-forth-of-the-buddy, day as ever was, At half-past four I shall expect you, Ever, *Moddle*."

Another aspect of *Chuzzlewit* is the considerable perturbation of sexual emotion that shows up through it. One sign of that perturbation is the Tom–Ruth scene just cited; but its main overflow comes in the character of Mrs. Gamp, whose rumbustious and boozy passage through the book is one long agitation of fancies about procreation and child-birth. Charles could get away with it while the sexual excitement was thus cloaked in humour. Consider these words of the drunken Pecksniff in his nightshirt.

"This is very soothing. Extremely so. Cool and refreshing; particularly to the legs! The legs of the human subject, my friends, are a beautiful production. Compare them with wooden legs, and observe the difference between the anatomy of nature and the anatomy of art. Do you know," said Mr. Pecksniff, leaning over the banisters, with an odd recollection of his familiar manner among new pupils at home, "that I should very much like to see Mrs. Todgers's notion of a wooden leg, if perfectly agreeable to herself."

What a masterly exposure of the whole hidden sex-life of Pecksniff (especially in that touch about the new pupils and the insinuating pedagogic manner); and how brazenly stated in contravention of the prevailing taboos, which denied the right of such words as legs to enter literature at all. Trousers had to be called indescribables, unmentionables, inexpressibles, inexplicables. In *Boz* a lady won't sleep in the room with a man's portrait; another leaves the room at the mention of flannel petticoats. Bumble apologizes to Mrs. Corney for mentioning a man "with hardly a rag upon his back," even though she is a married woman; and in the same novel the butler, speaking of how he dressed in a hurry, says, "Drew on a pair of . . ."; "Ladies present"; "Of *shoes*, sir." In *Chuzzlewit* Mercy is thrown into confusion at being found tying on a doll's petticoat, "really quite a grown-up doll, which made it more confusing;" and Ruth Pinch is so pure that she finds something to blush at in most remarks. Charity Pecksniff is overcome with the "indelicacy" of meeting a male (Tom Pinch) when she is out with

her betrothed Moddle. "I never was so ashamed in my life."
Dickens is continually tilting at this sort of pruriency, though
he long submits to it in his blushing heroines; and in the
Pecksniff scene, and with Mrs. Gamp throughout, he exposes the
inflamed sexuality under the pretty pretences. But in turn the
impetus to such exposures comes in part from his own uneasy
situation at home, contemplating Georgina's placid young
curves and still sensually drawn to Kate. The tensions in his
own sex-life are an essential part of his creative dynamic, and
link with the forces driving him into the social realizations of
his work.

A very different aspect of the way in which he draws on his
dream-life appears in the explicit statement of the death-wish
in Jonas. When old Anthony collapses, Jonas, who thinks he has
poisoned him, is overcome with relief that others were present.
"Someone might have said it was my doing."

"*Your* doing!" cried Mr. Pecksniff.
"I don't know but they might," he replied, wiping the moisture
from his white face. "People say such things. How does he look
now?"
Mr. Pecksniff shook his head.
"I used to joke, you know," said Jonas, "but I—I never wished
him dead."

There the murderer is revealed, and thus Charles has paved
the way from the death-wish and the fantasy-murder to the
actual murder in the wood.
One final point: Tom Pinch at the organ. Pinch as the Fool
or Lost Child image is given the last word in the book, and is
felt by Charles to hold the clue to Time, to the hidden truths of
the human spirit. Inarticulate and hopelessly fooled in his social
relations, he finds a voice in music; he is the unspoiled soul of
the people and the integrity in the artist which looks for an
organic union.

It was then turning dark, and the yellow light that streamed in
through the ancient windows in the choir was mingled with a
murky red. As the grand tones resounded through the church, they
seemed to Tom, to find an echo in the depth of every ancient tomb,
no less than in the deep mystery of his own heart. Great thoughts
and hopes came crowding in his mind as the rich music rolled
upon the air, and yet among them—something more grave and

solemn in their purpose, but the same—were all the images of that day, down to the very lightest recollection of childhood. The feeling that the sounds awakened, in the moment of their existence, seemed to include his whole life and being. . . .

There could hardly be a more precise and profound definition of Charles's own artistic method and outlook. Here the artist in his pang, his gratitude and his sense of loss, is one with the pure sources, the organic depths and the great mass aspiration imaged as the Fool or Scapegoat; he thus grasps at the wholeness of life, and makes one the hidden pattern of childhood and the pattern of renewal in the present, which implicates the future. That is why Mary, the unattainable beauty which is also the immediate dynamic of renewal, appears in the shaft of light and music, to haunt his sense and spirit.

This image of the artist alone with his music in the church of past redemptions is going to reappear at the end of Dickens's life, in very different form.

This church, the heaven of Pinch and the haven of Nell, is going in time to be the hell of Jasper. But we have to traverse much ground before the Gothic image turns into the Rochester reality. Meanwhile it is enough to point out how this image of the sunset church, now seen as the natural home of the Lost Child, the Fool, the Artist, links Charles with the Gothic novel and the sunset poem of the eighteenth century. It is of interest that in the *Mudfrog Papers*, which led on to *Oliver Twist*, the mayoral show is described in terms of gigantesque armour borrowed from *The Castle of Otranto*. This fearsome dream-armour of the municipal powers then turns into the heartless system of Bumbledom crushing the Lost Child.

V

Charles's dreams must have been very strong and clearly remembered. So much of his creative method lies in the infiltration of a dream-sense into scenes of ordinary life. In this method, which he carries to a high intensity of comprehensive definition in the novels and which reveals its bare bones in many of the short stories, he is using something fairly widespread in contemporary writing. Something which goes back to Smollett and has kept vital in popular burlesque and caricature. It can be found at a lesser level of intensity in Douglas Jerrold; and its vindication had been made by Bulwer in 1838,

Q

in his essay *On the Art of Fiction*, which must have been known to Charles:

The greatest masters of the novel of modern life have usually availed themselves of Humour as the illustration of manners; and have, with a deep and true, but perhaps unconscious, knowledge of art, pushed the humour almost to the verge of caricature. For as the Serious Ideal requires a certain exaggeration in the proportions of the Natural, so also does the Ludicrous.

Thus Aristophanes, in painting the humours of his time, resorts to the most poetical extravagance of machinery, and calls the clouds in aid of his ridicule of philosophy, or summons frogs and gods to unite in his satire on Euripides. The Don Quixote of Cervantes never lived, nor, despite the vulgar belief, ever could have lived, in Spain; but the art of the portrait is in the admirable exaltation of the Humorous by means of the Exaggerated.

What quickened "exaggeration" in Charles was the dream-transmutation of actuality. And this activity, which lies at the root of all his creative writing, is most easily detected in the stories, where the compression brings out the lines of force in the fantasy and prevents it from much pretence of being assimilated in normal event.

A passage in a letter from Broadstairs, in September 1843, to an American friend, brings out strongly the relation of the mad element in his humour to his dreams. He starts by saying that he often dreams of America and is then "always endeavouring to get home in disguise," and has "a dreary sense of the distance." Here is the motive of the guilt-flight. He then says how odd it is that an author never dreams of his own characters, and cites a dream of "a night or two ago."

I dreamed that somebody was dead. I don't know who but it's not to the purpose. It was a private gentleman, and a particular friend; and I was greatly overcome when the news was broken to me (very delicately) by a gentleman in a cocked hat, top boots, and a sheet. Nothing else. "Great God," I said, "is he dead?" "He is dead, sir," rejoined the gentleman, "as a door-nail. But we must all die, Mr. Dickens, sooner or later, my dear sir." "Ah," I said. "Yes, to be sure. Very true. But what did he die of?" The gentleman burst into a flood of tears, and said, in a voice broken by emotion: "He christened his youngest child, sir, with a toasting-fork."

I never in my life was so affected as at his having fallen a victim to this complaint. It carried a conviction to my mind that he could never have recovered. I knew that it was the most interesting and fatal malady in the world; and I wrung the gentleman's hand in a convulsion of respectful admiration, for I felt that this explanation did equal honour to his head and heart.

The next words are "What do you think of Mrs. Gamp? And how did you like the undertaker?" and before the anecdote comes a reference to Longfellow's recent marriage and to his wife, "a very beautiful and gentle creature, and a proper love for a poet." So the dream-tale is sandwiched between a marriage event, and Mrs. Gamp's furious aroma of death and birth. We must remember, too, that Kate (who was to bear a child in February) was in September some three or four months advanced in pregnancy. The father christening with the toasting-fork would seem to belong to a set of horror-images of birth and procreation—marriage as an act of cannibalism in Mary Weller's tale; the dead children laid out like pigs' trotters; phrases like this from letters: "after that [dish] two tiny little new-born-baby-looking turkeys, very red and very swollen" (in a letter to Kate, November 1844, while she was nursing an eight-month-old baby); the pie-fancy in *The Holly Tree* (1855) where Mary Weller is somehow merged with Mrs. Pipchin:

My first impressions of an Inn dated from the nursery; consequently I went back to the nursery as starting-point, and found myself at the knee of a sallow woman with a fishy eye, an aquiline nose, and a green gown, whose speciality was a dismal narrative of a landlord by the roadside, whose visitors unaccountably disappeared for many years, until it was discovered that the pursuit of his life had been to convert them into pies.

Christening as the ritual moment of identity in the child seems in the dream merged with the laying on of hands at confirmation. The contact of Father and Child, which should be one of harmonious handing-on of virtue and force, is seen in the dream as a moment of shock, fatal to the father. The three-pronged toasting-fork (giving the image of a pierced child held over the fire) is emotionally merged with both devil-pitchfork and lightning-trident; but instead of successfully murdering the child it recoils with its powers on the father, who is himself destroyed.

My analysis is tentative in detail; but something of this sort of emotional signification must lie within the dream-symbols. What is important and undeniable is the way in which we see the dream method of displacement and symbolization turning an emotion of fear, hate, and horror into a tremendous joke. The fact that Dickens moves straight on to speak of Mrs. Gamp is not accidental.

If now we turn to *The Christmas Carol*, we find the dream method frankly confessed. The hero, Ebenezer Scrooge, is the man of the unadulterated money-ethic. He has been withered and distorted by greed and money-making. On successive nights he is visited by three spirits, the ghosts of Christmas past, present, future. The first takes him back to his childhood, the second to the home of his clerk, Bob Cratchit, the third to a deserted graveyard.

For Charles it is one long visit to the past. To the churchyard of Chatham which was for him the ambivalent symbol of love and loss, garden and desolation. The Cratchit episode is a return to Camden Town days "through several streets familiar to his feet." Here we find the united family; death has snatched away Tiny Tim the cripple, but love overcomes the sense of loss. (Charles had been called to Camden Town because of the death of his young sister.)

The childhood episode is a plain return to Chatham. Scrooge has a little sister Fanny who comes to fetch him from school. She takes him to a nephew's house. "Scrooge's niece played well upon the harp; and played among other tunes, a simple little air (a mere nothing—you might learn to whistle it in two minutes) which had been familiar to the child who fetched Scrooge from the boarding-school—when the strain of music sounded, all the things that the ghost had shown him came upon his mind, and so he softened more and more."

This story is a simple dream-commentary on *Chuzzlewit*. Charles, in the midst of his money worries, has pulled himself up sharply. He who is attacking the money-ethic is himself entangled in the network. What is happening to his soul? He tries to confront his economic anxieties and extract from them the relevant moral. How is the individual, the society, which has come into this state, to escape and find regeneration? His answer is: By a return to the pure sources, to childhood, to the family union where other values than those of money reign. In seeking thus to analyse at length, in dream-terms, the psychology of conversion, of spiritual change, he is drawing on the theme of *Chuzzlewit*, but seeking to give this aspect of that theme a new force.

Once again it is in the rediscovery of the brother and sister relationship, the carrying forward of that relationship into the confused and polluted world of actual events, that he finds salvation.

The dramatization of himself as Scrooge was conscious. In a letter to W. H. Wills from Folkestone in September 1855, he wrote:

Scrooge is delighted to find that Bob Cratchit is enjoying his holiday in such a delightful situation; and he says (with that warmth of nature which has distinguished him since his conversion), "Make the most of it, Bob; make the most of it."

That the idea of the story came to him in Manchester was no chance. He meant *The Carol* to be a blow for the exploited working-class; and its inspiration thus came from an industrial city. To measure the distance he has moved we have only to compare it with *Pickwick's* account of Christmas at Dingley Dell—a pre-industrialist Christmas, a fantasy of hospitable goodwill to all men. The whole point of *The Carol* lies in the handing over of Christmas as a symbol and expression of union to the worker Cratchit, and the cutting of it away from Scrooge the employer. If Scrooge is to be saved, he must go to the Cratchits; and his going (since it transforms him) transforms society. That is, it creates a new relationship between the organizing factors of society and the human beings who are at work.

It is of interest that Hood's *Song of the Shirt* and Elizabeth Barrett's *Cry of the Children* were written and published about the same time as *The Carol*.

VI

But, whatever it had done, *The Carol* had not solved his financial problems. Scrooge had still to meet his commitments; and Lord Jeffrey's maundering wish to see him "rich and independent of all irksome exertions" didn't help. A twopenny weekly had pirated the story as "A Christmas Ghost Story re-originated from the original by Charles Dickens, Esq., and analytically condensed expressly for this work." Charles decided to prosecute this time, and engaged Talfourd as counsel. As a final trouble the Dickenses at Alphington were being increasingly costly nuisances and refusing to stay where they had been put. Still, Charles managed to give a Twelfth Night party, and acted as a black magician with Forster helping in fiery red. When the piracy case came up the Vice-Chancellor considered it one of "such peculiar flagrancy" that he did not even call on

Talfourd to speak—though the pirates claimed to have brightened up the work by giving Tiny Tim a song of sixty lines and "tastefully" remedying "incongruities." Charles was exultant. "The pirates are beaten flat. They are bruised, bloody, battered, smashed, squelched, and utterly undone." He claimed a £1,000 damages at Talfourd's advice.

With February he was inquiring further into the ragged schools; and on the 7th Kate bore yet another son, Francis Jeffrey.

He wrote a miserable letter to Forster on the 10th: his "year's bills, unpaid," were "terrific." Do come soon, as I am very anxious to talk with you. I am not afraid, if I reduce my expenses; but if I do not I shall be ruined past all mortal hope of redemption." He got away from the upset house to speak in Liverpool at a mechanics' institute soirée. With his friend Thompson he encountered the captain of the *Britannia* and had some drinks aboard the old ship, which was in the docks. At seven in the evening he took his chair, pleased that his magpie waistcoat confounded the audience with curiosity. He once more praised universal education and wanted rich and poor to collaborate for this end. But the surprise of the evening was his announcement of a musical item:

I am requested to introduce to you a young lady whom I have some difficulty and tenderness in announcing—Miss Weller—who will play a fantasia on the piano.

Everyone roared with laughter. Charles looked out and saw "the angel face of a girl" shining against the crowd. He could not take his eyes off her. He was introduced and said that he hoped some day she would change her name and be happy, very happy; and asked permission to call on her. He wrote to her next day: "Let me congratulate you with my whole heart on your brilliant achievement last night. Nothing could have been more successful, graceful, charming—triumphant in every particular. I feel a pride in you I cannot express." He burst into verse:

I put in a book, once, by hook and by crook
The whole race (as I thought) of a "feller,"
Who happily pleas'd the town's taste, much diseas'd,
And the name of this person was Weller.
I found to my cost that one Weller I lost,
Cruel Destiny so to arrange it!
I love her dear name, which has won me such fame,
By, Great Heaven! how gladly I'd change it.

246

What he couldn't tell her, what he perhaps couldn't tell himself, was that the primary magic of the name for him was its link with the small nurse-girl of Chatham. But between the associations of Sam and Mary, Christiana Weller had hit him clean in the heart of his richest susceptibilities. She had stepped out of his own mind, out of the childhood garden, into his public life, and he was for the time being beyond self-control.

She came to lunch; and under the glow of his fascination Thompson, too, though a widower and not young, found himself carried away. Charles realized there was something scarcely credible in his own surrender to the girl:

What a madman I should seem if the incredible feeling I have conceived for that girl should be made plain to anyone. Her face will be always in my sight . . . her green fur-trimmed dress must be preserved in lavender.

The "angel's message in her face" was irresistible. An angelic message, because it came from the unpolluted garden. He watched Thompson with keen envy. Lucky dog, his wife had died, and so he was free to take the angel. When at last Thompson confided his emotion, Charles declared that his own lips turned white and the whole current of his blood stopped.

It was like one of his own dream-stories, this return into the past; and there was nothing for him to do but behave like one of his own heroes. He bravely renounced the girl whom he could not get and sent her a two-volume copy of Tennyson's works. He told Thompson not to waver any longer, but, as a man of love and property, to propose forthwith. Away with caution! "Hours with her are like years of common women." Having to depart, he could urge the other man to act—especially as there was no other way of bringing Christiana nearer to himself. Get married, he suggested, "and join us in Italy." A piece of advice which made it seem that he wasn't as resigned as one of his heroes after all. "Do not crucify yourself lest in so doing you crucify her." Thompson was convinced, and won, with Charles's applause, the Noble Prize. But he didn't carry it off to Italy. So Christiana faded out of Charles's life, and with her the light from childhood which she had distractingly fired.

The letters between Charles and Christiana were first published in 1906, to the great scandal of Dickensians. Their publication, indeed, was the first large rent made in the deadly façade of lies which had been built up round Dickens.

It has been suggested that an anecdote, which may be

apocryphal, belongs to this period. One day when Charles sat in dejection at lunch, one of the children whispered to a guest, "Poor papa is in love again."

Two nights after the Liverpool meeting, Charles spoke at a conversatione for the Birmingham Polytechnic. The hall was draped with artificial flowers and behind his chair were hung "immense transparencies" which represented "several fames in the act of crowning several Dicks." Once more he spoke in support of universal education.

Back in London, he faced once more his financial worries and decided he would have to go abroad. He started learning Italian and met Mazzini at Carlyle's. Hearing that Graham, the Home Secretary, had Mazzini's correspondence censored, he took to writing on his envelopes, "It is particularly requested that if Sir James Graham should open this, he will not trouble to seal it." And, while Carlyle wrote to *The Times*, he wrote in protest to the Home Secretary direct. Ardent for the cause of Italian liberty, he offered to compose an appeal for the Italian Relief Committee. In it the English people are urged to welcome these "noble spirits who because of their protest against bigotry and despotism are refugees in an alien land."

His attitude to American and English affairs was no less radical. In March he had written to Forster, as a result of a mild doubting of Macready about slavery in New Orleans:

I believe it is in New Orleans that the man is lying under sentence of death, who, not having the fear of God before his eyes, did not deliver up a captive slave to the torture. The largest gun in that country has not burst yet—*but it will*.

Heaven help us, too, from explosion nearer home! I declare I never go into what is called "society" that I am not weary of it, despise it, hate it, and reject it. The more I see of its extraordinary conceit, and its stupendous ignorance of what is passing out of doors, the more certain I am that it is approaching the period when, being incapable of reforming itself, it will have to submit to be reformed by others off the face of the earth.

Here he prophesies the American Civil War. The importance of the passage for an understanding of his work is seen when we realize it was written as he was nearing the end of *Chuzzlewit*. It helps to bring out the way in which he put into a particular situation (here the unmasking of Pecksniff and the guilt revelation of Jonas) a general and historical significance. For him the end of *Chuzzlewit* symbolically expresses the reforma-

tion off the earth of "society," all the forces of greed and
falsity.

Forster says that about this time he wrote many strong
radical items in the *Morning Chronicle*, which set people talking.
Dickens, being so hard up, was beginning to consider turning
an odd penny through journalism. The editor, however, said
that he could not keep high payments up for regular contributions. Dickens discussed the matter with Forster; and Bradbury
and Evans, the printers with whom he was in negotiation, were
called in. The result was to break off from the *Chronicle*, but
the idea of a new newspaper was mooted.

The copyright case now rebounded on his head. Costs had
been given against the pirates; but they went bankrupt and he
had to pay his own costs, £700. It was no wonder that hereafter
he refused to take action against further piracies.

It is better to suffer a great wrong than to have recourse to the
much greater wrong of the law. I shall not easily forget the expense,
and anxiety, and horrible injustice, of the *Carol* case, wherein, in
asserting the plainest right on earth, I was really treated as if I were
the robber instead of the robbed.

In July *Chuzzlewit* ended, and he decided to move on to
Italy. He had now finally had his way, despite Forster, and
changed over from C. and H. to Bradbury and Evans. They
had to pay C. and H. £1,500, pay Charles £1,500 (they had
already advanced £500); and against this £3,500 he was to
return them £500 when *Chuzzlewit* ended, and in return would
probably ask for another £500 in the spring of 1845. Against
his advances, money would come in from the next Christmas
book and the reissue of the old one, the magazine (or journal)
he had in mind, and "the best workings of the copyrights in
existence."

Having found a tenant, the Dickenses moved out to a
temporary house; and after much argument over the location,
gave a farewell dinner. Then there was a *Chuzzlewit* dinner at
Greenwich to which Stanfield brought Turner who, despite the
hot weather, was wearing a huge belcher-kerchief and wouldn't
take it off. Carlyle pleaded the heat and didn't come. Then off
in July the Dickenses went in a huge, heavy, slow carriage
bought for £45 down.

Before he went, R. H. Horne had brought out *A New Spirit
of the Age*, in which he opened with an essay of his own on

Charles, whom he compared with Hogarth. No one quarrelled with the place allotted to Dickens. In some hurried eight years of work he had broken through and made himself the characteristic voice of his world, the most effective expression of the totality of forces at play in it.

8

Social Crisis

I

THE menagerie or caravan, as he called it, lumbered across France to Lyons, sailed down the river to Aix, then creaked across to Marseilles, and sailed into Genoa on July 16, 1844. The party consisted of himself, Kate, and Georgina; the children, Charley, Mary, Kate, Walter, and the baby Francis (soon known as "Chicken-stalker"); two nurses and the Brave Courier, Louis Roche. He set up in a house at Albaro, on Genoa's edge. "The most perfectly lonely, rusty old stagnant old staggerer of a domain." He had hoped to take Byron's house, but it was too neglected.

The Mediterranean blue astounded him; and he saw colour with a new eye.

I don't know exactly what I have done for my country in coming away from it, but I feel it is something; something great; something virtuous and heroic. Lofty emotions rise within me, when I see the sun set on the blue Mediterranean. I am the limpet on the rock; my father's name is Turner, and my boots are green.

A reference to Turner's picture *War—the Exile and the Rock Limpet*. He felt himself seeing the whole world afresh in the excitement of the strange scene, the strange people. The puppets enraptured him.

. . . too solemnly surprising to dwell upon. They must be seen. They must be seen. The enchanter carrying off the bride is not greater than his men brandishing fiery torches and dropping their lighted spirits of wine at every shake. Also the enchanter himself, when, hunted and overcome, he leaps down into the rolling sea, and finds a watery grave. Also, the second comic man, aged about 55 and like George the Third in the face, when he gives out the play for the next night. They must all be seen.

He frequented the theatre and the opera, though the theatre did not impress him; and later a Russian circus. He kept a keen anti-Papist eye on the religious houses. Then, in late September, he rushed to Marseilles to meet his brother Fred, and they put up at an inn with elephantine fleas. The morning after their arrival at Albaro, Fred would have been drowned if a fishing-boat hadn't picked him up. "A world of horror and anguish crowded into four or five minutes," with Georgina, the nurse, and the children all crying "like mad creatures."

He was dressing to the top of his flamboyant bent and growing moustaches. "Charming, charming. Without them, life would be a blank." Near the end of September they moved right into Genoa, to the Palazzo Peschiere. He wrote another Christmas story, *The Chimes*, and felt that he must try it out on an English audience. He wrote asking Forster to collect the persons. "Shall I confess to you, I particularly want Carlyle above all to see it before the rest of the world?" And again, "Carlyle, indispensable."

On November 6th he set out with his courier, and rushed through Parma, Modena, Bologna, Ferrara, Venice, Verona, Mantua. Venice he found a marvel. "The radiant, unsubstantial magic of the town." Then, via Cremona, he reached Milan on the 20th, to meet Kate and Georgina for a couple of days; then crossed the Simplon and made for London. There he had his audience, and Maclise sketched the company with nimbused Charles confidently reading. "It was worth any travel—anything." He gave a second reading, and then went over to Paris, where Macready was playing Shakespeare.

Carlyle had come, and Forster speaks of his "grave attention," which no doubt satisfied Charles. "I would go at all times farther to see Carlyle than any other man alive." But Carlyle was probably feeling something like the disgust which he later let out when he said, "His theory of life was all wrong. He thought men ought to be buttered up, and the world made soft and accommodating for them, and all sorts of fellows have turkey for their dinner." Though in his recoil there is a healthy dislike of the weak elements in Charles's sentimentality, there is also something bad, the element which later made Carlyle a hero of the Hitlerites. Here was the point where Dickens diverged from him, and translated his belief that the redemption of life must be the work of the common man into stories which are strong in their underlying symbolism but feeble and febrile in their concept of reconciliation; and Carlyle was reacting against the strength as well as the weakness.

But meanwhile, in 1843, Carlyle had followed *Chartism* up with *Past and Present*, in which he matured his criticisms of Victorian society. He reiterates his attack on the atomizing trends, on the cash nexus, on the destruction of human bonds, on the capitalist conception of men as things or instruments. He sees the economic fallacy of capitalism, the flaw at its heart, the way in which the more it increases productivity, the more it increases dearth:

What is the use of your spun shirts? They hang there by the million unsaleable; and here, by the million, are diligent backs that can get no hold of them. Shirts are useful for covering human backs; useless otherwise, an unbearable mockery otherwise. You have fallen terribly behind with that side of the problem.

And, using Jocelin of Brakelond's *Chronicle*, he seeks to draw on medieval days for an idea of the integrated community. Dickens had certainly read this book, with the same keenness as he had read *Chartism* and *The French Revolution*; and his extreme eagerness to gain Carlyle's recognition was based in his conviction that in Carlyle he met the prophetic spokesman of the historical forces at work in their world.

In Paris Charles, on his own, was able to get his first real taste of Continental living, and he liked it. He liked meeting Gautier, Hugo, Dumas, Michelet, Louis Blanc. (He had long past learned French with the ease with which he learned Italian.) He got to know Régnier of the Théâtre Français, and the editor of the *Journal des Debats*, and Delaroche the painter. He met Delacroix, too. And he was able to appreciate the faster tempo, the richer intellectual level of literary and artistic life in Paris. This brief excited visit left a permanent impression upon him, and henceforth he is a good European.

Then, tearing himself away, he coached through mud and water to Marseilles, and after delays sailed through heavy seas in time to spend Christmas with the family. "Their happiness," he wrote to Mrs. Macready, "is more easily conceived than described." He does not mention his own.

The Chimes duly appeared and sold 20,000 at once, earning Charles a profit of £1,500.

II

Before we look at *The Chimes*, it would be as well to consider two events of the Genoese days. First, shortly after going to the Peschiere, Mary returned into his dream-life. He had been lying awake with rheumatism "knotted round my waist like a girdle of pain." Then he dozed off and dreamed.

Observe that throughout I was as real, animated and full of passion as Macready (God bless him) in the last scene of *Macbeth*. In an indistinct place, which was quite sublime in its indistinctness, I was visited by a Spirit. I could not make out the face, nor do I recollect that I desired to do so. It wore a blue drapery, as the Madonna might in a picture by Raphael; and bore no resemblance to any one I have known except in stature.

I think (but I am not sure) that I recognized the voice. Anyway, I knew it was poor Mary's spirit. I was not at all afraid, but in a great delight, so that I wept very much and stretching out my arms to it called it "Dear."

At this I thought it recoiled; and I felt immediately, that not being of my gross nature, I ought not to have addressed it so familiarly. "Forgive me!" I said. "We poor living creatures are only able to express ourselves by looks and words. I have used the word most natural to our affections; and you know my heart."

It was so full of compassion and sorrow for me—which I knew spiritually, for, as I have said, I didn't perceive its emotions by its face—that it cut me to the heart; and I said, sobbing, "Oh! give me some token that you have really visited me!"

"Form a wish," it said.

I thought, reasoning with myself: "If I form a selfish wish, it will vanish." So I hastily discarded such hopes and anxieties of my own as came into my mind, and said, "Mrs. Hogarth is surrounded with great distresses"—observe, I never thought of saying "your mother" as to a mortal creature—"will you extricate her?"

"Yes."

"And her extrication is to be a certainty to me, that this has really happened."

"Yes."

"But answer me one other question!" I said, in an agony of entreaty lest it should leave me. "What is the True religion?" As it paused a moment without replying, I said—Good God, in such an agony of haste, lest it should go away!—"You think, as I do, that the Form of religion does not so greatly matter, if we try to do good?—or," I said, observing that it still hesitated, and was moved with the greatest compassion for me, "perhaps the Roman Catholic is the best? perhaps it makes one think of God oftener, and believe in him more steadily?"

"For *you*," said the Spirit, full of such heavenly tenderness for me, that I felt as if my heart would break; "for *you*, it is the best!"

Then I awoke, with the tears running down my face, and myself in exactly the condition of the dream. It was just dawn.

Of course, he at once shook Kate awake and repeated the dream three or four times: so that he wouldn't falsify it afterwards—and also because this attack on Kate through her sisters was necessary to him. He tries in his letter to Forster to unravel some of the "strings" in the dream. First, he had been thinking of the Hogarths, and Mrs. Hogarth in particular, as he had written in his previous letter; secondly, there was a big altar, once used for family mass, in the bedroom, with a mark on the wall over the sanctuary where a picture used to be, "and I had wondered within myself what the subject might have been, and what the face was like"; thirdly, he had been listening to the convent bells as he lay awake with pain, "and so had thought, no doubt, of Roman Catholic services." But he is still in uncertainty whether what he saw was "a dream, or an actual Vision."

Charles's discussion helps us to understand the dream. He had been in acute pain, in the back and round the loins, and he falls into a releasing sleep. (The association of his pain with a conviction of love-loss is given by a letter of November 1846, in which he says, "I had little pain in my side: excepting that time at Genoa I have hardly had any since poor Mary died.") The analogy with child-birth is obvious; and the altar, the bells, the conjecture about the missing picture lead to the apotheosis of Mary Hogarth as the Virgin Mary, the divine mother with whom he seeks union. This apotheosis gives away the whole background of infantile memories and desires for mother-union which lay behind his frustrated adult loves and which found simplest expression in his emotion for Mary. (That so many potent figures had had the name Mary helps the identification: Mary Weller, Maria Beadnell, Mary Hogarth—and, in work, Mary the bride of Martin.) In Genoa, surrounded by the signs of the Catholicism he detested, he has been stirred against his will by the sounds and sights of mother-worship; and the spirit's suggestion that his true bent lies in Catholicism—a suggestion that runs counter to every moral and intellectual bias of his waking life—comes from his feeling that there is inside him some mysterious force, a deep, unsatisfied yearning for union, which the terms of his waking life cannot meet.

The dream, then, affirms the tension between his conscious mind, its economics and its politics, and the deep creative impulses which look beyond all the compromises for a fully satisfactory compact. In personal terms it repeats that there is something in his emotional life which his actual relations with women can stir but cannot control or satisfy.

This dream came early in his Peschiere residence, which brought him into closer contact with the other English of Genoa. He met Mrs. De la Rue, English wife of a Swiss banker. A flirtation of elective affinities at once began. They found some interesting sympathies drawing them together. Then Mrs. De la Rue confessed her secret sorrow. She was haunted by spirits, the victim of delusions. A phantom wouldn't leave her alone. A mob of bloody things hunted her with hidden faces. What a chance for Charles to use his mesmeric powers—of course, at the anxious request of Mr. De la Rue. And then, once the mesmeric cure started, Charles had to be at the beck and call of the mysterious and charming woman (just an affectionate and excellent little thing, according to him); ready to rush to her spirit-beleaguered side at least once, if not twice, a day.

Here was a liaison to enchant him. It flattered his sense of possessing strange powers; it stirred his emotions of romantic mystery; it kept him on extremely close terms with a nice and interesting woman. For the first time he was really intimate with another person, getting right inside the woman's mind, insisting that she keep nothing away from him. The adventure which he was afraid to take with Kate, the adventure into another's soul, the quest back into the past of that person, he was making under these anomalous conditions with Mrs. De la Rue. The relation was a cross between a love-relation, an exorcism, and a psychoanalytic research.

Between the dream-apotheosis and the living haunted woman, he composed his second Christmas story, *The Chimes*. The direct stimulus was the bells of Genoa, so closely linked with the Mary-advent; and the theme was thus in a sense the offshoot of the Clock symbol. While writing, Charles yearned for London:

Put me down on Waterloo Bridge at eight o'clock in the evening, with leave to roam about as long as I like, and I would come home as you know, panting to go on. I am sadly strange as it is, and can't settle. You will have lots of hasty notes from me while I am at work: but you know your man; and whatever strikes me, I shall let off upon you as if I were in Devonshire-terrace. It's a great thing to have my title, and see my way how to work the bells. Let them clash upon me now from all the churches and convents in Genoa, I see nothing but the old London belfry I have set them in. In my mind's eye, Horatio, I like more and more my notion of making, in this little book, a great blow for the poor.

Now the idea of the Clock as the regulative heart pounding away inside the city of man has become a more active fantasy.

III

The Chimes reveals the whole perturbation of spirit that Dickens was feeling; here his declaration of fellowship for the suffering working-class becomes at last explicit. The story is that of Trotty Veck, a poor old man, who does odd jobs, and whose daughter Meg is going to marry a young chap, Richard. They come in contact with various representatives of the ruling and wealthy classes, who expose a consistent inhumanity, a tyrannous blindness, a murderous desire to "put them down." The old man, who is obsessed with the Bells, thinks that he and the rest of the workers must be somehow bad to have incurred such a fate. He dreams he goes up to the bell-loft, thinks that he has fallen and died. He sees the bell-notes as spirits gushing out on missions among men, directed by the great bell powers; he sees the rich and mighty triumphant in their smugness over the earth, crushing and insulting the workers; and finds (in his freedom from time and space) that their efforts to interfere and spoil the happiness of Meg and Richard have been successful. The lovers drag out an unhappy life, marrying when it is too late; the child Lilian becomes a prostitute; Fern the rebel worker goes to jail again and again, and in the end takes to arson for revenge. Then the old man wakes to find that it has all been a dream; the poor folk are reunited in Christmas happiness, and refuse to accept the keep-them-down counsel of the dehumanized ruling class.

Several points of great interest emerge apart from the clear evangel to the poor. First, we find, as I have said, how powerful in Dickens's mind is the Clock-Bell symbol, the tick or chime of Time. The ascent into the hidden works of the clock-tower, the bell-tower, is repeated from *Master Humphrey*, and emerges directly as the symbol of entry into the hidden meaning of things, the hidden source of life and power. In his account of the spirits pouring out of the bells Dickens writes with great poetic force; and in the draft sent to Forster he brings out cogently what the symbolism means to him:

And the bells themselves, who have a goblin likeness in the midst of their proper shapes, and who shine in a light of their own, will say (the Great Bell being the chief spokesman) Who is he that being of the poor doubts the right of poor men to the inheritance which

Time reserves for them, and echoes an unmeaning cry against his fellows?

Thus, the Chimes represent the great holy moment of human energy, when it breaks through its barriers and opposes itself to the anti-human power of the rich and the mighty. That is why the revelation occurs at the turn of the year. In it the Magnificat is caught and echoed.

This point is brought strongly out by the attack which the bells make on Trotty for having feared that he and his fellows must be bad. The revelation they bring is that the evil does not lie in the self-accusing heart of the broken ones, but in the monstrous complacence of tyranny in the rich and mighty.

In his picturing of the nightmare death-fear out of which Trotty topples into the truth, Dickens reveals manifestly for the first time the great symbolist poet lurking in his melodrama:

Black are the brooding clouds and troubled the deep waters, when the Sea of Thought, first heaving from a calm, gives up its dead. Monsters uncouth and wild, arise in premature imperfect resurrection; the several parts and shapes of different things are joined and mixed by chance; and when and how, and by what wonderful degrees, each separates from each, and every sense and object of the mind resumes its usual form and lives again, no man —though every man is every day the casket of this type of the Great Mystery—can tell. . . .

In the scene where Fern confronts the masters and tells them "the real Truth spoke out for once," we get the plainest statement that Dickens ever made of social cleavage. "We've nowt to do with one another," Fern has already said of the ruling class, and now he accuses them and warns them of the utter gulf between workers and masters:

. . . whether he's a wreck and ruin such as me, or is like one of them that stand here now, his spirit is divided from you at this time. . . . Bring it back, afore the day comes when even his Bible changes in his altered mind, and the words seem to him to read, as they have sometimes read in my own eyes—in Jail: Whither thou goest, I can Not go; where thou lodgest, I do not lodge; thy people are Not my people; Nor thy God my God!

This threat of a final cleavage is given substance later in the vision when Trotty meets Fern and is told that the night of revolutionary fires has come:

There'll be Fires this winter-time, to light the dark nights, East, West, North, and South. When you see the distant sky red, they'll be blazing. When you see the distant sky red, think of me no more; or if you do, remember what a Hell was lighted up inside of me, and think you see its flames reflected in the clouds.

Fern and his child Lilian were later additions to the story. Dickens needed them to make fully explicit his picture of the hell of the poor and the revolt against hell.

The Chimes further brings out the import to Dickens of the Old Man with Girl. When Lilian, the whore, dies broken hearted in the vision, her spirit joins the Old Man, and regains its innocence. "As she died, the spirit of the child returning, innocent and radiant, touched the old man with its hand, and beckoned him away." The final judges of a rotten society are this pair of spirits. They are the driven pair of *The Old Curiosity Shop*, now finally admitted as symbols of a stricken world. The Old Man, looking back on the vast evil, and the Child returned into innocence, into pure union. Charles needs the ghost of Mary-Fanny to hold his hand if he is to stand assured and unfaltering before the alienating world.

Finally, to grasp the working of imagery in Dickens's mind, it is important to note the ending which he originally drafted for the story.

. . . the Truth is trustfulness in them [the poor], not doubt, nor putting down, nor filing them away.

And when at last a great sea rises, and this sea of Time comes sweeping down, bearing the alderman and such mudworms of the earth away to nothing, dashing them to fragments in its fury— Toby [Trotty] will climb a cock and hear the bells (now faded from his sight) pealing out upon the waters. And as he hears them and looks round for help, he will wake up and find himself with the newspaper lying at his foot; and Meg sitting opposite to him at the table, making up the ribbons for her wedding to-morrow; and the window open, that the sound of the bells ringing the old year out and the new year in may enter. They will just have broken out, joyfully; and Richard will dash in to kiss Meg before Toby, and have the first kiss of the new year (he'll get it, too); and the neighbours will crowd round with good wishes; and a band will strike up gaily (Toby knows a Drum in private); and the altered circumstances, and the ringing of the bells, and the jolly musick, will so transport the old fellow that he will lead off a country dance forthwith in an entirely new step, consisting of his old familiar trot.

Then quoth the inimitable—Was this a dream of Toby's after all? Or is Toby but a dream? and Meg a dream? and all a dream? In reference to which, and the realities of which dreams are born, the inimitable will be wiser than he can be now, writing for dear life. . . .

In the draft, then, the threat of the revolt fires is linked with an image of elemental storm and destruction, which merges into that of the bells of renewal, the joyous entry into the inheritance, the festival dance. And which picture is dream, which actual? It is all real, all interpenetrated with dream; and the only ultimate truth in it is that which makes for the renewal of man.

Both Radicals and Tories saw clearly the political point, and either hailed or reviled it. Thus, the Radical Press praised the theme and the method:

It was written purposely to discontent you with what is daily going on around you. Things so terrible that they should exist but in dreams, are here presented in a dream. . . . For ourselves, we will hope that the challenge may be taken . . . in abatement of the long and dire conspiracy that has been carried on against poverty by the world and the world's law.

The Conservative Press hated both theme and method: attacked Dickens as an advocate and exacerbater of the class war and as a writer basing himself on monstrous exaggeration. Instead of preaching love and the Christmas spirit,

he has gone into the very opposite extreme of ranging party against party and class against class; instead of addressing himself to all men, and for the good of all, he has taken upon himself to separate the good from the bad. . . .
There is the same extraordinary combination of decrepit drivelling old men, with fresh young girls. . . .
There is the same association of beauty and superlative excellence with poverty, and of mental dulness and bodily odiousness (if we may coin the word) with wealth . . . the same spirit of exaggeration in expression. (Forster's album of cuttings.)

Brookfield commented that "*The Chimes* was as utter trash as ever was trodden under foot." Lady Blessington tried to argue away "the charge of wishing to degrade the aristocracy." Twenty thousand copies were sold.

The writing of the story had so agitated Dickens that he had wept himself into a disfigured condition. "I was obliged to lock myself in when I finished it yesterday, for my face was swollen for the time to twice its proper size, and was hugely ridiculous."

IV

At midnight of the turn of the year into 1845, he wrote, "The Baby is dressed in thunder, lightning, rain, and wind.

His birth is most portentous here." On January 30th he set off with Kate for Rome. Mrs. De la Rue, who had suffered so sadly during his absence, implored him not to go alone to Trinita dei Monti, as that was where her own infestation by spirits had begun; and she feared that he who had intruded on her spirit-lairs might come in for the same attack. Kate noted that he seemed particularly distrait; she guessed he was worrying about his dear little patient. She discovered after a while that he was concentrating on Mrs. De la Rue and giving her long-distance treatment.

After a detour to Carrara, where Angus Fletcher was staying and where they were serenaded by marble-workers, they passed through Pisa, Leghorn (Smollett's grave), Siena, and at last arrived with due excitement at Rome, which on second glance seemed a pretty dull and degraded place. Only the Coliseum stirred Charles's imagination. But the carnival decorations and maskings delighted him. "Come by the first boat," he wrote to Georgina, now and hereafter his Georgy. "I have been regretting the having left you at home all the way here."

Then he and Kate went off for Naples, where Georgy joined them by boat. Charles was in a fine state of worry about Mrs. De la Rue, and through a telescope watched the mail-bags coming in. After reading the letters of his poor dear little patient he wrote an express letter by return boat asking her husband to bring her on at once to Rome. Meanwhile with Kate and Georgy he dashed round Pompeii, Herculaneum, etc., climbed Vesuvius, explored the slums of Naples, and the pauper graveyards. Then he dashed back to Rome, and waited for Mrs. De la Rue. When she arrived he at once started off his mesmerics. One night Kate woke at one a.m. and found Charles pacing the room till at last he was able to control himself. Another night Mr. De la Rue knocked them up and got Charles out of bed to deal with his wife's seizure. She had rolled herself into an "impossible" hysteric ball. "I only knew where her head was by following her long hair to its source." Charles hypnotized her into unwinding herself.

Between whiles he let himself fail to be impressed by the Pope "carried about like Guy Fawkes," the feet washing, the Good Friday knee-shuffle up the Scala Santa: "Unmeaning degradation." Also he saw ruins, galleries, palaces, catacombs, and a public guillotining. Kate now had Mrs. De la Rue (plus frightened husband) attached to her movements as well as Georgy. When they left Rome, they all left together in the same carriage. Charles gave Mrs. De la Rue treatments all the way, under olive trees, in vineyards, and at wayside inns during the midday halt. As a result she was declared much freer of delusions by the time they arrived back at Genoa, in April.

Kate by this time refused to speak to Mrs. De la Rue. Charles basely covered up his domestic trouble by telling the De la Rues that she was given to nervous breakdowns. Having found this formula, he used it more and more later to cover up Kate's mild and belated rebellions.

They stayed on at Genoa till June, Charles refusing to give up his poor little patient. He had in mind a book of essays on the Italian scene. Though he didn't yet know it, Maria Beadnell had at last got married in February, to a business man named Winter. Charles for his part was thinking of how to import some Italian bad taste into Devonshire Terrace, and wrote home to Mitton to have some imitation wood-graining painted in and ceilings rendered "ornamental." Mitton reported the costs, which so staggered Charles he told Kate about his plans and she at once modified them to a mere wall-cleaning and repainting of windows and doors.

To get away from the packing, Charles made the excuse of work and moved in with the De la Rues, leaving Kate to get on with the hard work though she was now about five months gone with yet another child. Then off they all went to Brussels, where Jerrold, Maclise, Forster met them.

Charles's idea was to get home in order to get out of it again. He threw himself into the organization of theatricals. He was at a loose end. The Christmas stories and the Italian sketches were bringing money; but where they were leading him as an artist, he didn't know. He seemed to have lost touch with his deeper formative powers, which he could agitate into the spasm of a Christmas fantasy but which otherwise seemed to have dried up. No novel that he had attempted so far had come off in the sort of way that could give him confidence as a writer. Unless he was caught up in something bigger than himself, and then set in a magnetic relation to the public, he could not shape out a theme.

In returning to his old love, theatricals, he was perhaps in part impelled by the excitement and pleasure he had got out of reading his *Chimes* twice in the last December; but he was also yielding to a deeper need. Right from childhood on the play of miming and acting had lain at the root of his talent. In theatricals he had found both an outlet for his organizing capacities (as stage-manager) and his miming powers (as actor); more, he was able to exercise these faculties in a group, a small coherent, satisfying group.

Now, with the worsening of relations between himself and Kate, the feeling of lost and scattered creative energies, the growing violence of the whole political situation, he canalized his need for effective group-action into stage work. He was also brooding over the possibility of starting a newspaper which would bring him into vital relation with the political scene. There seemed no other way of getting the close impact which he needed and yet at the same time maintaining himself unsubmerged by the political torrents. Rightly, he feared any political affiliation which would cut him off from his sources of creative stimulus; at the same time he couldn't stay outside politics. In this tug-of-war of impulses he turned to the stage for a renewal of his energies as a writer.

With several friends he got together on the performance of *Every Man in his Humour*, and managed to persuade the touchy Miss Fanny Kelly to let her Soho theatre. He himself was taking the part of Bobadil. With an interval of three weeks at Broadstairs in August, he carried the rehearsals through, and the show was given on September 21st—so successfully that it was repeated for charity before Prince Albert on November 15th at St. James's Theatre. In the interval Lord Melbourne, with his usual aristocratic philistinism, was heard muttering, "I knew this play would be dull, but that it should be so damnedly dull as this I did not suppose."

Georgy was Charles's discreet and charmed companion throughout the autumn—Kate awaiting child-bed. He discussed his plans and other things. What the other things were may perhaps be surmised from the enigmatic remark about Georgy in a letter of his to Mrs. De la Rue: "I have left the matter where it was; trusting to its wearing itself out, on her part, in due course." Georgy, it would seem, had declared her passion. Kate certainly had enough botherations between sly Georgy and spirit-infested Mrs. De la Rue.

On October 28th she bore her sixth child, her fourth son.

During this month Thompson, who had married Christiana Weller and got her with child, decided to go abroad; and Charles recommended Genoa with Mrs. De la Rue as a friend for Christiana.

The second raven died of over-eating putty, and Charles was

at his wit's end about what to write. He had started *The Cricket on the Hearth* but couldn't get on. "Sick, bothered and depressed. Visions of Brighton come upon me." He must get off somewhere else, Brighton or Jack Straw's at Hampstead. "I never was in such bad writing trim as I am this week, in all my life." That was three days after the birth of the son (as yet without a name). He was busy with the newspaper project, but could not still his fears. "Most of all I have, sometimes, that possibility of failing health or fading popularity . . ."

V

All the autumn he was working at his newspaper project. Joseph Paxton, enriched by railways, was ready to support B. and E. on the financial side; and Dickens brought in Sir Joseph Walmsley, rich Liberal organizer, one of the very few persons who had managed to bring amicably together middle-class Radicals and Chartist working-class. Thus unity of Radical and Chartist was, in fact, the basic policy of Dickens in starting off the paper. He wanted to find a common platform on which all men genuinely desiring reform and increased control of the governmental system by the people could co-operate. Where exactly that co-operation would lead he didn't know and didn't care. What mattered was the fact of union against the system. He believed in his bones that the more people had control of their own lives the more a decent system of government must emerge; but his whole emphasis lay on the first half of the syllogism. Otherwise he felt that one would find oneself back at tinkering with the system from above and producing only a different lay-out of abuses. With the political side of the paper he wanted to combine a great deal of scientific and social information.

The idea was good; but in order to realize it Dickens would have had to drop everything else and go wholly into the political arena; and once he had done that he would have found that the union he desired was harder than he had thought, and that he would have to fight in ways he hadn't anticipated.

The motives driving him to the venture were partly economic —a fear that his fictional powers had gone or weakened and that only some sort of journalism could save him from collapse— and partly political, a deep wish to take an active part in the important struggles going on. During the negotiations he showed much vacillation. B. and E. had put his salary down at a thousand pounds; he raised it himself to two. He began to fret at the idea of being tied down to an editorial office and demanded a sub-editor to carry on when he wasn't there. When some city firms failed, he grew scared that his financial backing would be shaken. He went up and down in confidence. Jerrold and Fonblanque were to be leader writers; John Dickens was to be in charge of the reporting staff, and George Hogarth to be musical and dramatic critic; W. J. Fox, Charles Mackay, Mark Lemon, and Forster were to help.

The continued large-scale working-class agitation and trade union organization, with a background which included the Irish famine, had shaken the Tory Government and given new strength to the Anti-Corn Law League. In 1846 the Corn Laws were going to be repealed (with a small tariff till 1849), to the benefit of textile and other exports. For the moment, however, there seemed no easy solution for the rapidly growing popular discontent.

The repression following the upsurge of 1839 had broken Chartism for the moment. But as the leaders came out of jail and organization was reconstructed, another big wave began. The National Chartist Association—illegal, since any national party had been declared unconstitutional—was the first political party in the modern sense: owning an elected executive, grouping in sections, and dues-paying membership. By 1842 it had a membership of 40,000, and was attempting to link with the trade unions; O'Connor had come out of jail in August 1841, and preparations for a new Petition were being made.

The economic crisis which had slackened a bit after the bad year of 1838, suddenly reappeared with wide unemployment and falling wages. Some 3,315,000 people signed the Petition, which Parliament rejected with contumely, in May 1842. A political strike broke out in Yorkshire, Lancashire, the Midlands; but London and the south did not move. Hunger and fierce repression by the Government broke the strike; and trade to some extent brightened between 1843–6, relaxing the tension. It was during this lull that Charles felt the time had come to launch his paper based on a united progressive front.

If now we glance back at his novels, we can summarize the political affiliations. *Pickwick* draws on pre-reform days, but in the midst of its goodwill comes up against the fact of injustices too strong for a joke. *Oliver*, *Nickleby*, and *The Old Curiosity Shop*, step by step, get at grips with the post-reform world in which the Poor Law is the emblem of the renewed drive for exploitation of the people, and the lot of the Child expresses a key moral problem of industrialism. In *The Old Curiosity Shop* the industrial background and the agitated state of the people loom up to play an essential part in the symbolic progress of the Child tied to the crazed Old Man. In *Barnaby* Dickens tries to achieve full historical focus for the frustrated outbreaks of 1839.

Then comes the break. He goes to the States to get a world view of what is happening and what is at stake; since, if there is any solution from within the system, it should be apparent, even if only in rough form, in the Republic. He wrote *Chuzzlewit* during the period following the suppression of the popular outbreak of 1842. In it he states his belief in the bankruptcy of the system and in the possibility of human renewal. Then, in the lull, he wrote his Christmas stories, in which he stated that the forces of renewal lay with the common people and that capitalist economics led to a new kind of hell. But, in his desperate effort to relate this sharpened sense of his world's pattern to his methods of fantasy (out of which alone he could draw the energies for creative advance), he feels distracted, exhausted. He can no longer let his fantasy go in the simple way of his first group of works; he has got to find a more decisive and active relation to the historical movement around him. And for the moment it is too much. Dickens, like the Chartists, is temporarily exhausted, maturing new lines of advance.

The key, then, to his state of mind, its deadlock and its new potentialities, must be sought in *The Carol* and *The Chimes*. And when we grasp what those stories are doing, the profound fantasy-effort to grasp the fundamentals of struggle which underlie their structure, we grasp something of the way in which he is steadily moving deeper into himself and into his world. Into people.

VI

One of Charles's ideas for raising money had been a three-halfpenny magazine with a name like *The Cricket*. Forster argued against it, and wanted a Christmas story. So the magazine turned into *The Cricket on the Hearth: A Fairy Tale of Home*. "I wrote this story," said Charles, "to awaken some loving and forbearing thoughts never out of place in a Christian land." It was savagely attacked as cheap and offensive. *The Times* denounced it; and Forster was very worried. His remonstrances with Dickens had no effect, and all that he could see in Dickens's resistances to his advice was self-admiration. He recorded his fear that "this partial passion would grow on him till it became an incurable evil." It was his first facing of the fact that there was something in Dickens implacably opposed to the Victorian values which he, Forster, incarnated.

The theme of *The Cricket on the Hearth* is that love and fellowship belong to the working-class and that the master cannot buy himself into them; he must rediscover his common humanity before he can share in the forces of delight. The tale thus repeats, at a less dynamic level, the moral lesson of the two preceding tales.

VII

At last all the problems connected with the newspaper seemed lavishly solved—though worries over foreign correspondents must have got mixed up with rehearsals of *Every Man in His Humour* in the office on the second floor of 90 Fleet Street. John Henry Barrow, his uncle, whom he tried in vain to get sent out to India, was made sub-editor; and on January 17, 1846, the machines were christened. After a trial dummy, the first issue came out on the 21st, at fivepence. In less than three weeks Dickens had resigned.

Hardly had the paper started off than he wrote to Forster that he had been thinking his plans over for "going abroad to write a new book in shilling numbers." The decision which he had been unable to take when he had no political burden on his shoulders he took as soon as the burden descended. He wanted to get out at all costs. He felt "tired to death and quite worn out."

This decision was no doubt speeded up by internal friction. He chafed at the interferences of Bradbury, who controlled general expenditure; he did not like adverse criticism; and so on. But at root it was the admission of having come up against a blank wall, against the dead resistance in the whole economic and political set-up to his notion of how things should be done, the admission to himself that his allies were not quite the allies he had taken them for.

The recoil forced him abruptly into himself, and at long last released again his capacity to work on a full-length novel.

In the first issue of the paper he had started off a series of travelling letters, which came out in book form as *Pictures from Italy* in May. He also managed in his short editorship to raise the question of public hangings; and shortly after he had resigned and Forster had taken over, he contributed his *Hymn of the Wiltshire Labourers* and *The British Lion*, which show how close his liking was for the broadsheet type of poem of popular protest, pathetic or satirical. *The Lion* was signed Catnach, the name of a famous ballad singer, and has as chorus:

> Right toor rol, loor rol, fee faw fum,
> The British Lion bold!
> That was always a-going for to do great things,
> And was always being "sold."

The *Hymn* was inspired by a speech given by a Wiltshire working woman at Bremhill, which asked, "Don't you all think that we have a great need to Cry to our God to put it in the hearts of our greassous Queen and her Members of Parlerment to grant us free bread."

His latest son was now christened Alfred d'Orsay Tennyson, which gave rise to many witticisms. "Alfred is common to both the godfather and the devil-father," said Browning and the conjunction gave you "a curious notion of the man, I fancy." Dickens was feeling restless again, rushing round. "Vague thoughts of a new book are rife within me just now; and I go wandering about at night into the strangest places, according to my usual propensity at such a time, seeking rest, and finding none. As an addition to my composure, I ran over a little dog in the Regent's Park yesterday (killing him on the spot), and giving his little mistress, a girl of thirteen or fourteen, such exquisite distress as I never saw the like of."

His general agitation was much increased by the Dilke episode mentioned above, which dragged out his past in the blacking works. Reluctantly he told Forster, though he managed otherwise to keep the matter secret. Still, the fact of having to speak even to one person of such a matter, so dreadfully entwined with his deepest anxieties, could not but have agitated his whole being and increased his state of spiritual unbalance.

He wanted to get away from England altogether, preferably to some place near Mrs. De la Rue. Writing to her about his walking out of the newspaper, he said that he wanted to get on with a new story in twenty parts, "and I think I could write it more comfortably and easily abroad, than at home." But Kate

had some will of her own, if not much, and she wasn't going
near Mrs. De la Rue again if she could help it.

I need not tell *you* that *I* want to go to Genoa? But Mrs. Dickens,
who was never very well there, cannot be got to contemplate the
Peschiere though I have beset her in all kinds of ways. Therefore
I think I should take the middle course for the present, and coming
as near you as I could, pitch my tent somewhere on the Lake of
Geneva, say at Lausanne, whence I could run over to Genoa
immediately.

My Diary of March the 19th, 1845, is lying open on my desk,
and looking at it I see this entry—*Madame D. L. R. very ill in the
night. Up till four* . . . what a miserable devil I seem to be cooped
up here, bothered by printers and stock-jobbers, when there are
bright Genoas (with bright patients in them) and ruined coliseums
in the world!

He let Devonshire Terrace, and took the chair at the General
Theatrical Fund Association (for old or ill actors). Never, he said,
had he been to a play without gaining "some pleasant association, some favourable impression." Then he drew up for
Miss Coutts a scheme for dealing with "lost girls," and told her
he would go thoroughly into methods used in Paris.

The family departed down the Rhine, via Ostend, and at
Mainz Charles discovered how extensive his influence was in
Germany. (Marx had acclaimed him in the *Rheinische Zeitung*;
and Engels considered him one "of a great spiritual family
united in all lands.") Then, by train from Strasbourg, they reached
Basle and went on by road to Lausanne, where before long they
found a rose-embowered doll's house of a villa, with a room
overlooking Lake Leman for his study. Opening *Tristram
Shandy* for a word of "guidance," he came on, "What a work
it is likely to turn out! Let us begin it!" So next morning he
began *Dombey and Son*.

He found the work difficult. "You can hardly imagine what
infinite pains I take or what extraordinary difficulty I find in
getting on fast." He was inclined to blame the lack of a crowded
city in which to lose himself at the right moment.

I suppose this is partly the effect of two years' ease and partly of
the absence of streets and numbers of figures. I can't express how
much I want these. It seems as if it supplied something to my brain,
which I cannot bear, when busy, to lose. For a week or a fortnight
I can write prodigiously in a retired place (as at Broadstairs) and a
day in London sets me up again and starts me. But the toil and

labour of writing, day after day, without that magic lantern is
IMMENSE! ! . .

My figures seem disposed to stagnate without crowds about
them. . . .

The fact was that in London he lost himself in contacts, in
solitude he lost himself in frittering anxieties. Both attitudes
were based in the same fears and doubts, the extreme dis-
equilibrium out of which alone his creative work could proceed.
In London he tended to become the mere journalist; alone he
tended to dissolve in day-dream. Only when the social recoil
and the day-dream came vitally together could he create. But
that bringing together of the opposed elements was getting
more difficult every year and making him pay an increased
price. He was at the mercy of "an extraordinary nervousness
almost impossible to describe." To get past that anxiety he had
to let himself get totally mastered by his theme. Hence the
demonic element in his work was liable to get mixed up with
his actual living.

I hold my inventive faculty on the stern condition that it must
master my whole life, often have complete possession of me, make
its own demands on me and sometimes for months put everything
else away from me.

He finished off his de-theologized New Testament for his
children; wrote on ragged schools; and worked out the idea
for the next Christmas book. He visited Chillon. "Great God,
the greatest mystery in all the earth, to me, is how or why the
world was tolerated by its Creator through the good old times,
and wasn't dashed to fragments." He gathered a small circle of
English residents and read his work to them. The need of a more
direct contact with his public was becoming an ache with him.
Visitors kept coming, the Talfourds, or Hallam being tremendous; and one day Tennyson heard *The Queen of the May* being
sung and walked in. But Charles was worrying all the while.
"I was thinking the other day that in these days of lecturing and
readings a great deal of money might possibly be made (if it
were not *infra dig*) by one's having readings of one's own books.
It would be an *odd* thing. I think it would take immensely."

In October *Dombey* started appearing in print, and a local
revolution broke out. Dickens's account of it gives so clearly
his political outlook—and the episode itself is so similar in
many ways to the sort of thing happening in a larger way in the

new democracies of post-1945 Europe—that his words deserve to be cited in full.

There were stories of plots against the Government when I was there (Geneva), but I didn't believe them. For all sorts of lies are always afloat against the radicals, and wherever there is a consul from a Catholic Power the most monstrous fictions are in perpetual circulation against them: as in this very place, where the Sardinian consul was gravely whispering the other day that a society called the Homicides had been formed, whereof the president of the council of state, the O'Connell of Switzerland and a clever fellow, was a member; who were sworn on skulls and crossbones to exterminate men of property and so forth.

There was a great stir here in Lausanne, on the day of the fight in Geneva. We heard the guns (they shook this house) all day; and seven hundred men marched out of the town to go and help the radical party—arriving at Geneva just after it was all over. . . .

The Government was afraid; having no confidence whatever, I dare say, in its own soldiers; and the cannon were fired everywhere except at the opposite party, who (I mean the revolutionists) had barricaded a bridge with an omnibus only, and certainly in the beginning might have been turned with ease. The precision of the common men with the rifle was especially shown by a small party of *five*, who waited on the ramparts near one of the gates of the town, to turn a body of soldiery who were coming in to the Government assistance. They picked out every officer and struck him down instantly, the moment the party appeared; there were three or four of them; upon which the soldiers gravely turned round and walked off. . . .

It is a horribly ungentlemanly thing to say here, though I do say it without the least reserve—that my sympathy is all with the radicals. I don't know any subject on which this indomitable people have so good a right to a strong feeling as Catholicity—if not as a religion, clearly as a means of social degradation. They know what it is. They live close to it. They have Italy beyond their mountains. They can compare the effect of the two systems at any time in their own valleys; and their dread of it, and their horror of the introduction of Catholic priests and emissaries into their towns, seem to me the most rational feeling in the world.

Dickens, then, unreservedly supports the use of revolutionary force against the threat of reaction—and he classes the introduction of Catholicism as an acute threat to liberty.

Apart from this, you have no conception of the preposterous, insolent little aristocracy of Geneva: the most ridiculous caricature the fancy can suggest of what we know in England. I was talking to two famous gentlemen (very intelligent men) of that place, not long ago, who came over to invite me to a sort of reception there —which I declined. Really their talk about "the people" and "the masses," and the necessity they would shortly be under of shooting a few of them as an example for the rest, was a kind of monstrosity one might have heard at Genoa.

The audacious insolence and contempt of the people by their newspapers, too, is quite absurd. It is difficult to believe that men of sense can be such donkeys politically. It was precisely such a state of things that brought about the change in Lausanne. There was a most respectful petition presented on the Jesuit question, signed by its tens of thousands of small farmers; the regular peasants of the canton, all splendidly taught in public schools, and intellectually as well as physically a most remarkable body of labouring men.

This document is treated by the gentlemanly party with the most sublime contempt, and the signatures are said to be the signatures of "the rabble." Upon which, each man of the rabble shoulders his rifle, and walks in upon a given day agreed upon among them to Lausanne; and the gentlemanly party walk out without striking a blow.

VIII

But the isolation was becoming too much for him. On the one hand, "I like this place better and better . . ." and on the other

The absence of any accessible streets continues to worry me, now that I have so much to do, in a most singular manner. It is quite a little mental phenomenon. I should not walk in them in the day time, if they were here, I dare say; but at night I want them beyond description. I don't seem able to get rid of my spectres unless I can lose them in crowds.

However, as you say, there are streets in Paris, and good suggestive streets, too; and trips to London will be nothing then.

So Paris it was, and an "eligible mansion" found the next day—"something between a baby house, a shades, a haunted castle, and a mad kind of clock." And a colossal walk that Saturday night in the streets, and again all Sunday. He also began to think again of a periodical, a weekly one.

He went to London a week before Christmas, to fix up an edition of his works with new prefaces and to look in on a dramatization of his Christmas *Battle of Life* by Albert Smith: "The densest and most insufferable nonsense." But he waited for the ovation of the first night. Fred, his brother, he found wanted to marry the sister of Christiana Weller. Charles objected strongly; and so did the Wellers. But the marriage came off.

Back in Paris he tried to write, but parties snared him, and he couldn't resist the opera. The new year 1847 brought with it the need to kill off Paul Dombey; and such passages of writing he always felt like a murder. Fanny had become very ill; and the thought of her rose powerfully into his mind from the shrouded depths after a long subsidence. Dr. Elliotson had already examined her for lung trouble, and she cried for joy when he declared her unaffected. Then in November she collapsed during a song at Manchester. "I am deeply worried about her," Charles said; and he put into the death of Paul his revived emotions about the lost sister. He built Paul consciously on the poor little deformed child she had borne, Henry. The Rev. J. Griffin wrote of this Henry that he was always happy, and yet "meditative and quaint in a remarkable degree." Fanny was especially worried about her lack of ability to look after him. Like Paul he was taken to Brighton, and lay for hours on the beach with his books.

The Battle of Life lacked the fantasy-verve of the first two Christmas books. It is drawn directly from Dickens's brooding over Georgy and her future, and tells of a young girl who nobly surrenders her sweetheart to her sister. "That he should be my brother, and your husband, if the course I took could bring that happy end to pass; but that I never could (Grace, I then loved him dearly, dearly!) be his wife!" Georgy's relations to Kate are thus idealized; and we feel that the story has been written to console her and himself for being unable to marry. Under the pleasant orchard earth lie the corpses of forgotten battles; and life is an invisible web of failure, sacrifice, and undefeated love. But the immediate personal pressures have worked too strongly the statement of this theme, and symbolic depth is lacking.

Incidentally, in the one amusing character, Clemency Newcome, we find a variation of Dickens's fantasy-love of the secrets involved in the convolutions of words. A love reaching back to the child's interest in the strange adult signs that hold unapprehended clues:

. . . the formation of certain cabalistic characters, which required a deal of ink, and imaginary counterparts whereof she executed at the same time with her tongue. Having once tasted ink, she became thirsty in that regard . . . and wanted to sign everything.

Twenty-three thousand copies were sold at publication; but there was dislike among the gentlemanly party. *The Times* once more attacked. "I see that 'the good old Times' are again at issue with the Inimitable B.," Dickens wrote. "Another touch of a blunt razor on B.'s nervous system—Friday morning. Inimitable, very mouldy and dull. Hardly able to work. Dreamed of *Timeses* all night. Disposed to go to New Zealand and start a magazine." Usually he managed to evade looking at reviews. Ever since about 1838 he had taken a resolution not to upset himself by reading the stupidities and abuse that make up criticism.

The way in which *The Battle of Life* had revealed the cleft stick in which he found himself between Kate and Georgy was shown by the dreams he had while writing it.

I dreamt all last week that the Battle of Life was a series of chambers impossible to be got to rights or got out of, through which I wandered all night! . . .
The mental distress, quite horrible.

IX

Dickens was now getting used to Paris and its people. He was impressed by Hugo and his "vast gloomy old theatre" of an apartment. He liked to hear the chat about Hugo having the actress Julie Drouet as mistress while Madame Hugo seemed satisfactorily set up with Sainte-Beuve. Kate was once more laid up with child and so Georgy had a perfect excuse for going everywhere with Dickens and taking trips into the environs of Paris.

Paul was killed off on January 14th. Chirpily he had written, "Paul I shall slaughter at the end of number five": but when the time came it broke him up. "Between ourselves, Paul is dead," he wrote to Miss Coutts. "He died on Friday night about ten o'clock, and as I had no hope of getting to sleep afterwards I went out and walked about Paris until breakfast next morning." The effect on the public was only equalled by Nell's death. "Oh, my dear, dear Dickens! . . ." cried Jeffrey, "I have so cried and sobbed over it last night, and again this morning." Hallam, one of the few untouched, wrote to Mrs. Brookfield, "Milnes, Thackeray, and your uncle own to tears."

Forster arrived in Paris on top of Paul's death and gave Charles the pretext for a fortnight of rushing round, seeing Lamartine, Chateaubriand, Dumas, Gautier, Sue, Régnier. . . . Then Charley became ill at school in London, and so the

Dickenses decided to return home ahead of plans. Devonshire Terrace was still let, so they rented a house in Chester Place, where the fifth son, Sydney Smith Haldimand, was born in April.

Charles went off helping Miss Coutts about lost girls, and a rescue home, Urania Cottage, was set up at Shepherd's Bush.

He went on dining out and giving dinners, and dashed with eagerness into theatricals for the benefit of Leigh Hunt. The Government spoiled things a bit by awarding Hunt a pension of £200 a year; and the London performance was dropped. But *Every Man in His Humour* was given once more in July, this time in Manchester and Liverpool, earning £400 profit. In August he sat on the committee drawing up a plan for the buying of Shakespeare's house at Stratford for a national monument.

He met Hans Andersen, and dashed off to Broadstairs, returning in October to take up residence again at Devonshire Terrace. While at the seaside he had started the Christmas book *The Haunted Man*; but being unable to finish it off in time he put it aside, and there was no book for this Christmas. On December 1st he spoke at the Leeds Mechanics' Institute, with a bad cold, on popular education; and after Christmas at home went up to Glasgow with Kate to open the new Athenaeum. Writing to Georgy, he described how "the Inimitable did wonders" (praising the initiative of working-men in self-education), and mentioned casually that Kate had been taken ill in the train between Edinburgh and Glasgow. She had in fact had another miscarriage. He adds that she was ashamed of having missed the celebrations and wanted to hush her absence up. "But I say that, like murder, it will out, and that to hope to veil such a tremendous disgrace from the general intelligence is out of the question."

The last day of the old year and the first of the next were spent at Edinburgh, where Kate had collapsed again. Charles rushed off sightseeing and had a talk with Jeffrey, in which he heard that the dramatist Sheridan Knowles had gone bankrupt. He discussed the chances of getting Knowles made curator at Stratford, despite the fact he had become a Baptist minister.

X

Back in London he went on, in the new year of 1848, with the problem of collecting money for the Stratford curatorship (the local borough council had bought the house); and of

couse took the opportunity of once more starting theatricals.
The end of *Dombey* was near, and he felt easier in mind.

When the February Revolution broke out in France he
hailed it with joy, and wrote an ecstatic letter to Forster, whom
he knew would not approve:

Mon ami, je trouve que j'aime tant la République, qu'il me faut
renoncer ma langue et ecrire seulement le langage de la République
de France—langage des Dieux et des Anges—langage, en un mot,
des Français! . . .

Vive la gloire de France! Vive la République! Vive le Peuple!
Plus de Royauté! Plus de Bourbons! Plus de Guizot! Mort aux
traitres! Faisons couler le sang pour la liberté, la justice, la cause
populaire!

Jusqu'a conq heures et demie, adieu, mon brave! Recevez de
ma consideration distinguée, et croyez-moi, CONCITOYEN! votre
tout devoué, CITOYEN CHARLES DICKENS.

That could hardly be more clear; but it is very hard to trace
the way in which his sympathies held or fell off during the rest
of the year. In early March he wrote to Macready:

I think Lamartine, so far, one of the best fellows in the world;
and I have lively hopes of that great people establishing a noble
republic. Our court had best be careful not to overdo it in respect of
sympathy with ex-royalty and ex-nobility. These are not times for
such displays, as, it strikes me, the people in some of our great towns
would be apt to express pretty plainly.

The last sentence can refer only to the Chartist working-class
of the industrial towns, who were making their voices heard at
the moment on many topics; and the tone of the reference shows
his sympathy with them at least on one point. How far he continued to understand and support the French revolutionaries
when Lamartine proved incapable of carrying forward his
Republic we do not know. Probably he viewed the June
Revolution with confused and divided emotions.

As to his reactions to the situation in England, with the great
Chartist demonstrations and the Petition of April, we have no
word. The completion of *Dombey* seems to have left him for a
while devoid of the power to grasp out and enter purposively
into events. He had managed to say, with very great expense of
spiritual and nervous energy, what he felt about the world at
this phase of its movement; and he had to leave it at that. April
saw the last instalment of *Dombey* and the plunging into the
play projects. But he was also worried about Fanny, who in
May was brought to London to be near the doctor, Sir James

Clark. She was entirely wrapped up in Christian conviction and often begged her friends to read out the fourteenth chapter of John. Charles asked her if she had any care or anxiety in the world; and she answered, "No, none." She did not want to die at her age, but she was quite without fear. "Burnett had always been very good to her," he told Forster, "they had never quarrelled; she was sorry to think of his going back to such a lonely home; and she was distressed about her children. . . . I need hardly tell you how it moved me." And he ended, "I don't know why I write this before going to bed. I only know that in the very pity and grief of my heart, I feel as if it were doing something."

The sight of dying Fanny was affecting Charles more than he knew. It drove him back on his past in a painful way, coinciding as it did with a turning point in his work and a turning point in history. He found himself driven more and more to try to get out the truth of himself in a gush of memories to the only man who had penetrated into his hidden self, Forster. "I hardly know why I write this. . . . I am more at rest for having opened my heart and mind to you. . . . This day eleven years, poor Mary died." He hardly knows what he is or what is happening to him, but he feels the upheaval in the depths. And this personal pang holds also the essence of his reaction to the events of the year. Fanny is dying, Mary is dying again, the world is in the judgment scales.

Emerson had been in England since October of the preceding year (except for a visit to Paris to see what the revolution meant); but Dickens only now, on May 4th, met him, with Carlyle, at Forster's rooms. The conversation got on to the theme of the open lewdery of the London streets, and Carlyle held forth on whoredom in general. Male chastity was a thing of the past, he declared. Dickens agreed. Emerson protested that men of the better level went virgins to their marriage couch. Dickens retorted that incontinence was taken for granted in England—so much so that if his own son were particularly chaste he would be as worried about it as if he were in poor health.

This conversation shows us a Dickens not at all mealymouthed, a Dickens who keeps on trying to break through the Victorian conventions. A Sternean Dickens, who pops up in that boarding-house sketch by Boz and who has difficulty in not getting excited every time a young girl comes into the room of his story. Who lets himself go when the sex can be smothered up in a joking atmosphere or a mild tilt at contemporary taboos. Who finds pleasure in writing like this to Lady Blessington:

I am told that in Devonshire there are young ladies innumerable, who read crabbed manuscripts with the palms of their hands, and newspapers with their ankles, and so forth; and who are, so to speak, literary all over. I begin to understand what a blue-stocking means, and have not the slightest doubt that Lady —— (for instance) could write as entertaining a book with the sole of her foot as ever she did with her head.

Who writes of a Burns Festival:

Robertson told me also that Wilson's allusions to, or I should rather say expatiation upon, the "vices" of Burns, excited but one sentiment: and added, very sensibly, "By God, I want to know *what Burns did*! I never heard of his doing anything that need be strange or unaccountable to the Professor's mind."

Who jokes of two lads brought up in Switzerland in "such perfect purity and innocence, that they were hardly to know their own sex."

Accordingly, they were sent to no school or college, but had masters of all sorts at home, and thus reached eighteen years or so, in what Falstaff calls a kind of male green-sickness. At this crisis of their innocent existence, our ogre friend encountered these lambs at dinner, with their father, at Cerjat's house; and, as if possessed by a devil, launched out into such frightful and appalling impropriety that years of education in Newgate would have been as nothing compared with their experience of that one afternoon. After turning paler and paler, and more and more stony, the baronet, with a half-suppressed cry, rose and fled. But the sons—intent on the ogre—remained instead of following. . . . Isn't it a good story? I can SEE our friend and his pupils now.

Who retails scandal about the British abroad without a murmur of disapprobation. "Lady Walpole bye the bye is living alone (or with some Austrian lover) at Florence," or "Young Brinsley Norton, two and twenty years old and living on £2 a week . . . has married . . . a bare-footed girl off the Beach, with whom he had previously fulfilled all matrimonial connections except the ceremony."

The play-acting went on, with Charles in his glory, taking charge of everything, stage-managing and acting. He loved the sense of controlled group activity; he loved the unconventional contacts with young women. Rehearsing at the Dean

Street theatre, in May they gave two shows at the Haymarket—
the *Merry Wives of Windsor* and the farce *Love, Law, and Physic*
on May 15th, and the same farce with *Every Man* on the 17th, for
the Queen and Prince Albert. Then off they toured: Manchester,
Liverpool, Birmingham. Back in London, he planned a return
to Birmingham with the *Merry Wives*, the farce, and an after-piece
Past Two O'clock in the Morning. Then in July they were all off
to Scotland, with the addition of *Used Up* for the second show in
Glasgow.

Mrs. Cowden Clarke, who was one of the company, gives us
some idea of his enjoyment:

> In *Love, Law and Physic* he used to tuck me under his arm with
> the free-and-easy familiarity of a lawyer patronizing an actress whom
> he chances to find his fellow-traveller in a stage coach. . . . It is some-
> thing to remember, having been tucked under the arm by Charles
> Dickens, and had one's hand hugged against his side! One thinks
> better of one's hand ever after.

Back in London he felt deflated, lost. A letter to Mrs. C.
C., in which he conjured up parts they had played, gives
away his deep-seated discontent despite its gay tone.

> I have no energy whatever, I am very miserable. I loathe domestic
> hearths. I yearn to be a vagabond. Why can't I marry Mary? Why
> have I seven children—not engaged at sixpence a night apiece, and
> dismissable for ever, if they tumble down, not taken on for an
> indefinite time at a vast expense, and never—no, never, never—
> wearing lighted candles round their heads. I am deeply miserable.
> A real house like this is insupportable, after that canvas farm wherein
> I was so happy. . . .
>
> You had a sister once when we were young and happy—I think
> they called her Emma. If she remember a bright being who once
> flitted like a vision before her, entreat her to bestow a thought upon
> the "Gas" of departed joys. I can write no more.
>
> Y[oung] G[as] THE (DARKENED) G[as] L[ight] B[oy].
> P.S.—"I am so completely blasé—literally used up. I am dying for
> excitement. Is it possible that nobody can suggest anything to
> make my heart beat violently, my hair stand on end—but no!"
>
> Where did I hear those words (so truly applicable to my forlorn
> condition) pronounced by some delightful creature? In a previous
> state of existence, I believe.
>
> Oh, Memory, Memory!
>
> Ever yours faithfully
> Y—no C. G.—no D. C. D. I think it is—but I don't know—"there's
> nothing in it."

He wants to be anyone but himself.

Fanny was lingering on, without hope. They went to Broadstairs and Kate had a bad carriage accident, but was unhurt. Charles kept going out to get wet through in the rain and find all sorts of great things among the rocks on the beach. He was trying to write *The Haunted Man*. Then Fanny died, and the funeral at Highgate was on September 8th. The Rev. J. Griffin said, "Mr. Dickens appeared to feel it very deeply." (The deformed child, Henry-Paul, died soon after.) In the same month he replied to a gift from Mrs. C. C. of an embroidered blotting case with a letter signed: R. *Shallow Cust-alorum*, *Abraham Slender*, *Robert Flexible*, *Charles Coldstream*, *Doctor Blank*, *Young Gas*, *Bobadil P. Snobbington*, *and Charles Dickens The Mild Manager*. And, meeting Forster at Paddock Wood station, he visited Rochester and Chatham yet once again.

Then, after some more of London, he made a dash for Brighton in November, with both Kate and Georgy. Writing to Stone about a drawing for the Christmas book, he said, "You will really, pictorially, make the little woman whom I love." Brighton, he said, was "a gay place for a week or so; and when one laughs and cries, and suffers the agitation that some men experience over their books, it's a bright change to look out of window, and see the gilt little toys on horseback going up and down before the mighty sea, and thinking nothing of it." Kate was once more nearing child-bed.

His personal feelings about marriage and babies appear in the character of Johnny Tetterby in *The Haunted Man*, whose whole life is daily offered on the "insatiate altar" of the Baby. The fantasy about Fanny in this story has already been considered; in it he entirely displaces Henry Burnett by himself. Under the stress of his own breaking-down marriage and Fanny's death, he penetrates through the complex emotions about Maria, Mary, Kate, and Georgy which had veiled and extended the original love pattern built up round Fanny. He gets back to the simple basis, and to some extent feels relief at being able to restate his position in clarified terms.

XI

It is now time to consider what Charles had done in *Dombey*. Written in recoil from the failure of his attempt to become a political editor directing the people of Britain, it shows a great leap from *Chuzzlewit* in its social comprehensions and its intellectual organization. It breaks from the romantic unmasking theme, and turns instead to the theme of decay and renewal, which had come up in *Chuzzlewit* and been sharply grappled with in *The Carol* and *The Chimes*.

It is the story of Dombey, the capitalist, who destroys all human relations by his pride, his coldness, his pure reliance on the ethic of money, the story of the nemesis he brings on himself, his break up, his regeneration. All his humanity, such as it is, is canalized into his passion for the son who is to carry on his name; and the son dies. He marries a beautiful woman, whose aristocratic pride is perverted into an arctic hate through the knowledge that she has been bought and sold like a thing. Through her comes the blow that shatters him, when she leaves him for Carker.

On the other hand, his neglected daughter Florence finds love, shelter, and union with the common folk whose attitudes have not been distorted through the money-ethic; and when he is broken, he has nobody but her to turn to.

Dickens is thus taking boldly as his theme the development of capitalism since 1830. Dombey symbolizes the new money-power which can break into the aristocratic preserves. His marriage with Edith expresses this new strength of the capitalist. (As with *Oliver* and *Chuzzlewit*, Dickens is probably starting off from a point defined by Bulwer Lytton. *The Disowned* deals with an egoist, Vavasour, who twines all his hopes round a son who turns out quite unlike him; but Dickens soon makes his treatment of the theme centrally significant in a way all his own.)

Dickens's greatness as a novelist lies in the way in which he can define general tendencies in terms of personal relations and create his over life-size figures who are simultaneously fantasy projections, social emblems, and intensely individualized entities. We are therefore justified in looking inside the story of *Dombey* for its social allegory as long as we do not try to reduce the story to that allegory alone.

If we compare the treatment here with that of *Chuzzlewit* we find an enormous advance. The allegorical aspects are incomparably better incarnated in figures who are both social types and distinct individuals. But the allegory is none the less there. Dombey stands for the new social dignity and power of the capitalist with his blinkered outlook; but there is no simple cankering of greed in his spirit. His very pride has certain justifications; he has achieved something new and significant.

The cankering is expressed through Carker, the manager, who is a lesser man and whose egoism has become centrally perverted with resentment and meanness. He draws Dombey on to his ruin. He represents the side of capitalism which is necessarily there as part of the blindness of Dombey and which is necessarily destructive.

Edith represents the reluctant union of the landed aristocracy with the new capitalist force. She preserves, despite her aloofness and bitterness, an element of pre-capitalist humanity, a demand for love; and so she joins forces with Carker to wreck Dombey.

Florence represents the element of humanity and love inside Dombey, which he has driven out by the chill money-ethic. Through Walter and Captain Cuttle, the despised common folk, she finds happiness and union, as Edith, doomed by her own inner discord, cannot hope to find them.

A point of strain in the story gives away the point where the human working out chafes against the allegorical structure. Dickens has to use the coming together of Edith and Carker as the basis for the destruction of Dombey; nothing else can fully reveal the inner crisis of Dombey and all that Dombey represents. Carker and Edith are impelled demonically towards self-destruction, which does not matter as long as Dombey is brought down in the process. But this structural need of the theme cannot be quite translated into personal terms, since Edith cannot possibly love Carker. "Of course she hates Carker in the most deadly degree. I have not elaborated that, because . . . I have relied on it very much for the effect of her death." Jeffrey, however, wrote refusing to believe that Edith was Carker's mistress; and Charles, who up to then had apparently meant her to give herself out of sheer hatred of both Dombey and Carker, changed his mind. "What do you think of a kind of inverted *Maid's Tragedy*, and a tremendous scene of her undeceiving Carker and giving him to know that she never meant that?"

The result is to give an air of unreality to the whole Carker–Edith theme. But it would be a mistake to think Dickens was here succumbing to fear of Victorian morals. He made Oliver a bastard, he gave Lady Dedlock a lover, and he had Little Em'ly seduced. He would not have shrunk from putting Edith into Carker's bed if he had felt the need to do it. He lost conviction on this point because the action concerned was allegorical rather than human.

The greatness of the book resides, as usual, in the magnificent characters who give inner life the social allegory, Susan Nipper or Captain Cuttle, Mrs. Pitchin or Major Bagstock, Mrs. Skewton or Miss Tox, down to minor people like Mrs. Macstinger, or the Chicken, or Cousin Feenix.

It is worth pointing out that, with his extension of social knowledge, Dickens has given up simply guying the aristocracy. The amiably helpless Feenix is drawn with all kindness; and more important still, Edith Skewton is given a strength and an integrity which he had never managed before to give a woman character. Here Dickens breaks through the simpler, petty-bourgeois outlook with which he began, and expresses his acceptance of the whole cultural tradition—the upper levels with all their subtleties and complications as well as the immediately popular levels. His disillusion over middle-class objectives plays a part in this extension of sympathies, but also his experience of French and Italian cultures has much broadened his outlook.

The Lost Child fantasy is divided between Paul and Florence. Paul gets the death halo; Florence the neglect and the cruel exclusion.

Into the person of Carker Dickens puts something of his own inner discord. Carker seems at moments genuinely in love; at other times he is driven solely by hate and envy.

She gave him the gloved hand she had maimed last night. He took it in one of his, and kissed it and withdrew. And when he had closed the door, he waved the hand with which he had taken hers and thrust it into his breast.

That is a lover's gesture, and cannot be meant as other. Charles had given much thought to this sort of thing. Thus he writes in a criticism of some acting:

I am much mistaken if any man . . . would crush a letter written by the hand of the woman he loved. Hold it to his heart unconsciously and look about for it the while, he might; or he might do anything with it that expressed a habit of tenderness and affection in association with the idea of her; but he would never crush it under any circumstances. He would as soon crush his heart.

In fact, Dickens puts into Carker, almost against his will, some of his own growing desire to break through the marriage bond; and in the fine image of the flashing teeth he communicates a sense of the face as a tightening mask, a thing suddenly vulnerable as well as a thing of triumphant lust—his own face suddenly strange, frightening, getting outside his control in its revelation of rebellious emotion.

Carker is run over by a train as he flees from the pursuit of the wronged husband. The place where he is run over seems certainly Paddock Wood station (where we saw Dickens meeting Forster for the fresh visit to his childhood locations). This train image is profoundly important for Dickens, and indeed is in the end to kill him, as the imagined train killed Carker. Carker as the guilt-self of Dickens is run over, crushed; and if we think back we shall recall that when Dickens revisits the key places of his childhood, he finds the ravaging train has smashed things up. He goes back to Chatham, and the playing grounds are ruined and turned into smutty deserts, and the tunnel maw gapes for its victim. He goes back to Camden Town, and finds that Euston has smashed up the haunts from which he first looked fascinatedly over towards London. He goes back to his school, and finds that the Birmingham railway has driven right across and shorn an end off the school house. When the frontispiece of *Dombey* was drawn, there appeared in it a monster train with demon eyes; and this was in very truth the nightmare train which ran the guilt-self down in the lifelong pursuit.

Beyond these personal implications of the train there stands the sober fact that the railway was the prime force wrecking the old England with all its vices and its virtues, ruthlessly driving through into a new era. As publicist, Dickens generally hails rail and telegraph as forces of unadulterated good, creating networks of anti-feudal communication and drawing the nation together in a goodwill that must exile all wars. As artist, he feels differently and his attitude is strongly ambivalent. The railway becomes the emblem of the heartless forces of exploitation. When Carker falls under the train, he falls under the very force of which Dombey himself is only the instrument.

9

The Bleak House

HENRY Fielding Dickens was born on January 6th, 1849. The theme of *Copperfield* was coming into Charles's mind. Ever since the episode of Dilke had ripped away the veil from his workshop days, he had been unable to keep his mind off the past. He could no longer let his emotions overflow into his work out of that past as in *Oliver Twist*; he felt the need to go back and examine, to understand exactly what had happened and what it meant. Under the shock he made an effort to start an auto-biography; but though he wrote a section on his workshop days, he could not bring himself to go further or do anything with it. He shrank from the public statement of those lowly times; but, more deeply, he himself shrank from the effort to make a direct statement of them, because he rightly felt that the analytic methods at his disposal could not grasp the full truth of what had happened. He had no choice but to turn back to fiction in order to get at the truth.

That did not mean that the attempt at an autobiography was useless. On the contrary, it stirred up the depths in a peculiarly fruitful way; it was a necessary act in his development. But it must be seen as one aspect of his whole movement during the years 1847–49. That movement included his frustrated attempt to find a close direct contact with political events through the *Daily*, his discovery of the European revolutionary movement and of French culture, his desperate effort begun by the Christmas books to find a conscious relation between his fantasy-formations and the social patterns of his world in all their full-ness, his deepening entanglement between Kate and Georgy, and the profound shock of Fanny's death. All this coming to a head in his thoughts and feelings during the crucial year of 1848, so that the political revolutions are mixed up with the deep pivotal changes in his life and work.

He felt 1848 thus as a pivotal point in his development, the final loss of his reliance on the intuitional flow of his work. *Dombey* had expressed intellectual maturity; and now he had to get a basically new grip on himself and his world. Hence the effort at last to write a directly autobiographical novel.

On New Year's Eve 1848 he dashed down to Norwich with Leech and Lemon, looked at a murder spot and a murderer in jail and the hanging place; went on to Yarmouth, walked to Lowestoft and was back in London by January 10th, 1849. Then, in recoil from the child-bed flight, he began writing and ignored the upset in the house, going out with Georgy when he wanted company. "Deepest despondency, as usual, in commencing, besets me." At the month's end he and Forster went to Bath for Landor's birthday.

In February he went to Brighton where he was joined by the Leeches. The landlord and his daughter both went raving mad, and Charles with Leech helped the doctors to overpower the lunatics. "You would have said it was [a scene] quite worthy of me, and quite in keeping with my usual proceedings." Charles went on thinking: "A sea fog to-day, but yesterday inexpressibly delicious. My mind running, like a high sea, on names—not satisfied yet, though." In May the first issue of *Copperfield* appeared.

In June he was walking fourteen miles in a day, and going to Vauxhall to see the representation of the Battle of Waterloo. Then in July he went to Broadstairs, and after a while on to the Isle of Wight, where he hired a villa at Bonchurch for six months. At first he liked the place a lot; and a bright-haired lad who played with his sons was Swinburne. Leech had an accident bathing, and Charles hypnotized him out of his pain. But he himself was getting into a bad way and blamed Bonchurch. He described his state half jestingly:

... feeling of sickness ... so that his legs tremble under him ... an extraordinary disposition to sleep (except at night, when his rest, in the event of his having any, is broken by incessant dreams) ... lying down in bed in the fitful intervals [of thought]. Extreme depression of mind, and a disposition to shed tears from morning to night. ...

They moved on to Broadstairs again.

Meanwhile in September had been published an appeal for the Italian refugees, which Dickens wrote. This document is of great importance as proving that he had not altered one jot from the revolutionary attitudes expressed in 1847.

They are the good citizens who, when Rome was abandoned by her Monarch and Executives, answered to the general voice, and arose to give her law, tranquillity and order; who built upon the ruins of a monstrous system which had fallen of its own rottenness and corruption, one of moderation and truth. . . .

They are the soldiers who defended that Government against the united arms of bigotry and despotism, and defended it successfully.

The French reaction which had sent an army to save the Pope he accused of an "act of such stupendous baseness that it will remain an ineffaceable stain upon the honour and name of France."

"How well I remember his arched eyebrows and laughing eyes," wrote T. A. Trollope, "when I told him of Garibaldi's proposal that all priests should be summarily executed."

Nearing the end of *Copperfield* in October, he wrote to Forster, "If I were to say half of what *Copperfield* makes me feel to-night, how strangely, even to you, I should be turned inside out!"

Back in London in November he went to see the crowds assembling the night before the execution of the murderer, Mrs. Manning, and once more tried to stir public feeling against public hangings. (In vain : not till 1868 were they stopped.) Mrs. Manning herself left a deep impression on his mind—leading to Hortense in *Bleak House* and Jaggers's housekeeper in *Great Expectations*. Then the Dickenses went to visit the Watsons, whom they had met in Switzerland and who lived at Rockingham Castle, Northamptonshire. Here Charles saw something of feudal pomp, and the memory of it went into the picture of Chesney Wold in *Bleak House*. Here, too, he met Miss Mary Boyle, with whom he did some scenes from the *School for Scandal* in the great hall, followed by conjuring tricks.

On the day of his return to London he wrote one of his serious mock letters to Mrs. Watson with a drawing of a pierced heart in it. At ten o'clock he had drunk wine and "I felt distinctly that it 'was changing these thoughts to madness.' On the way here I was a terror to my companions, and I am at present a blight and mildew on the house. . . . P.S. I am in such an incapable state, that after executing the foregoing usual flourish I swooned, and remained for some time insensible, Ha, ha, ha! Why was I ever restored to consciousness! P.P.S. 'Changing' these thoughts ought to be 'driving.' But my recollection is incoherent and my mind wanders."

He tried to throw himself again into a magazine project. *The Robin* or *Mankind* or *The Household Voice*. At last he fixed on the name *Household Words*, and went ahead with the plan. He felt that he could not get along without some steady money-earner which also insured contact with his audience.

II

Because in *Copperfield* Charles is trying on the whole to follow out (underneath superficial veils) a fairly direct autobiographical line of narrative, he comes closest to writing an ordinary novel and discarding the deep emotional and philosophical tensions that emerge when he builds on the conflict of day-dream and actuality. (In speaking of such a conflict I mean the tensions that come from a basic day-dream theme interpreted in terms of realistically defined action, not of the flittering point-to-point movement between the inner fantasy of self and the continual small shocks of the outer world. The latter method, which logically followed out leads to introspective analysis, is rather the method of *Copperfield*.) It is then via *Copperfield* that, generally speaking, Dickens links on with the tradition of critical realism in the Victorian novel from Mrs. Gaskell to George Eliot and Trollope. But though in its way a highly important work, and one which Dickens had to write at this point if he were to advance, it lacks the tenacious creative vitality of his other novels.

Only in the relations of Steerforth and David do we touch on the deep tensions out of which Dickens's creativity comes. From one angle Steerforth is the strong, handsome, assured gentleman that one part of Dickens would have liked so much to be; he is thus the day-dream of noble virility, admired of all. But here the realism gets at grips with the fantasy, and from another angle Steerforth is the pure cad, all the worse a cad because of the qualities that enable him to get away with his insolence. Dickens takes revenge on Steerforth for being the easy gentleman that he himself can't be.

Thus, *Copperfield* becomes in many ways the simplest of Charles's novels in its view of society. The gentlemanly party (mainly typified by the Steerforths, though also by some connections of Mrs. Strong) are either sterilely aloof or heartlessly bad. The bourgeoisie are worse because more varied in their evil, which ranges from the villainies of Murdstone or Heap to the lies and cheats of Spenlow or the weakness of Wickfield. The lower middle-class or working-class, from Micawber to the Peggotties, are the repositories of human values.

The class conflict of the Steerforths and the Peggotties is stated explicitly. Steerforth sees the Peggotties as creatures of another species. "They may be thankful that, like their coarse, rough skins, they are not easily wounded." The seduction of Little Em'ly and her moral murder is Steerforth's carrying out of this proposition, and is Charles's disproof of it. Also, Charles begins in this book his outright campaign against toadyism, the middle-class vice that he grew to hate more and more. The conversation at Mrs. Waterbrook's dinner table is the first full blast in the campaign. And this, it has rightly been pointed out, is a post-1848 symptom, as Charles begins to feel in his bones that the middle-classes all over Europe have somehow funked a great moral and social chance.

But the tension between David and Steerforth is never worked out with full drama, because the day-dream is not at the heart of the book's conception. Though the story gives us a number of very valuable points of revelation about Charles's life, it gives us no central focus of discovery. The works before it, though less mature in many ways, had a dynamic it lacks. Still, there are a number of characters in which his full verve gets loose, Betsy Trotwood and the Micawbers, Heep and Peggotty, with many fine lesser characters, Mr. Dick or Mrs. Gummidge.

The Micawbers are, of course, John and Elizabeth Dickens. Micawber, with his parody of moral and economic optimism, had a dual effect on readers; some took his catchwords at their face value and used them to encourage; some took him as a horrible example, as Mary Kingsley did in her resolve to stay solvent; others, like James Smetham, were filled with "wholesome terror" in contemplating him.

Certain aspects of the *Oliver Twist* fantasy appear in *Copperfield* in more rationalized form. David runs away from his menial job and escapes the Murdstones, the parents in their lowering form. And his flight takes him to Chatham—though, partly to disguise the facts, partly to have a longer distance to traverse, he then goes off down the Dover Road that Charles as a child had often in part traversed.

The child-wife appears in two forms, as David's mother and as his first wife Dora. The immaturity and helplessness of Mrs. Copperfield is emphasized. Betsy Trotwood calls her a "poor child," a "baby," and on this point Miss Murdstone agrees. Dora is throughout a "child-wife," and even calls herself such. Though, to depict her, Charles called on memories of Maria

Beadnell's small frail charms, and used some of Maria's properties such as her dog, Dora is a dream compound of Fanny, Maria, Mary. . . . And Agnes ("my child-wife's old companion") is simply the dream reduced to flesh, Kate instead of Maria, Georgy instead of Mary. Dickens's dream-predilection for the child-wife appears even in Little Em'ly. As for Dora, apparently she dies of a miscarriage, having the grace to perish before becoming the fecund wife of Dickens's fears.

In the account of Mrs. Copperfield Dickens has set out a pure dream-picture of the child-wife whose husband dies off so early that he ceases to have any significance in the mother and child relation. Child and mother are blissfully united. Then the dark shadow of Murdstone falls across. The father returns in his evil shape to break the union. It is no accident that in his fantasy reconstruction Charles builds the intrusive father on the basis of the authority which we have seen as first clouding his life with a sense of repressive interference, that of religion. Murdstone incarnates the evangelism we have discussed as Dickens's first emblem of threatening authority, which shadows the home life. The name is characteristically made up of "murder" and "stone" (and Dickens cannot stop himself from making the "murderer" collation through the mouth of Betsy Trotwood).

The death-wish fantasy which inevitably is bound up with the infantile levels of mother-union appears outright in the passage cited far back about David's return from school when he finds his mother suckling the baby, and, after a twinge of jealousy, wants to die upon her breasts. It comes out further in the way the mother dies off when he leaves her; and the grave-fantasies associated with her death have the same basis as those begotten by Mary's grave, in which Charles so earnestly wanted to lie.

"On the last night, in the evening, she kissed me, and said: If my baby should die, Peggotty, please let them lay him in my arm and bury us together. (It was done, for the poor lamb lived but a day beyond her.) Let my dearest boy go with us to our resting-place, she said, and tell him that his mother, when she lay here, blessed him, not once, but a thousand times. . . ."

I remembered her from that instant, only as the young mother of my earliest impressions, who had been used to wind her bright curls round and round her finger, and to dance with me at twilight in the parlour. . . .

The mother who lay in the grave, was the mother of my infancy; the little creature in her arms was myself, as I had once been, hushed for ever on her bosom.

Mrs. Micawber, on the other hand, is the fertile Elizabeth Dickens (strengthened with the image of fertile Kate). "I may remark here that I hardly ever, in all my experience of the family, saw both the twins detached from Mrs. Micawber at the same time. One of them was always taking nourishment."

In the usual way that Dickens mixed himself up with his characters we find him signing a gloomy letter, "Yours Despondently, and Disgustedly, Wilkins Micawber." In making the Micawbers emigrate he carried out in their person one of the projects with which he had continually toyed.

In Mr. Dick, Dickens makes an extremely percipient statement about his method of work, which also shows much insight into the process of neurosis-formation as later unveiled by Freud. Mr. Dick has his obsession, King Charles's Head. Betsy Trotwood says that Mr. Dick had a shock (his "favourite sister . . . took a husband" and was made wretched):

"It had such an effect upon the mind of Mr. Dick (*that's* not madness, I hope!) that, combined with his fear of his brother, and his sense of his unkindness, it threw him into a fever. That was before he came to me, but the recollection of it is oppressive to him even now. Did he say anything to you about King Charles the First, child?"
"Yes, aunt."
"Ah!" said my aunt, rubbing her nose as if she were a little vexed. "That's his allegorical way of expressing it. He connects his illness with great disturbance and agitation, naturally, and that's the figure, or the simile, or whatever it's called, which he chooses to use. And why shouldn't he, if he thinks proper?"

That passage is a first-rate example of the subtleties which Dickens often masks in a joke.

In Mr. Spenlow (as later in Mr. Casby) Dickens got his own back on Mr. Beadnell; but the portrait also shows the shift in his attitudes over the years. The man of business who in 1832 had seemed the noble defender of reform is now seen as a mean and lying cheat.

In the later parts of *Copperfield* Dickens, through default of a dominating theme, falls back patchily on various oddments of romantic motive (birth-mystery and regained heritage); but these motives are not integrated as they had been in *Oliver* or *Chuzzlewit*, or as they were to be in *Bleak House* or *Our Mutual Friend*. Still, by reason of the lessened pressure this book develops more coherently than any other of Dickens's work a method of writing everyday naturalistic narrative, of showing an individual moving through his social career step by step, and of dealing with small passing tensions of character and environment. Hence its cooler tone, and the unsentimental treatment of such matters as David's hearing of his mother's death at school.

From the viewpoint of Dickens's own development *Copperfield* is a pivotal work as he shifts his main balances. From the viewpoint of the Victorian novel in general it is the work of basic influence through which Dickens enters in the main stream of lesser contemporary work, transforms that stream, and leaves in it a large number of new potentialities. But he himself could only develop at this level of lessened energy if he slackened from his main creative task. Out of *Copperfield* he found the power to return to the higher level; and he returned.

III

The originating idea of the new magazine was close to that of *Master Humphrey's Clock*. In the latter case Dickens had been dominated by the image of Time, the Clock, the regulative principle of society, intruding intimately into personal life and yet providing the general point of coherence. Now he had been stirred by an image of a similar pervasive force, "a certain SHADOW which may go into any place, by sunlight, moonlight, starlight, firelight, candlelight, and be in all homes, and all nooks and corners, and be supposed to be cognisant of everything, and go everywhere, without the least difficulty. . . . It will concentrate into one focus all that is done in the paper."

Once again the idea proved too big, but it helps to give us insight into Dickens's creative process, which merged the child's desire to listen behind doors and to read the hieroglyphs of adult secrecy with a social conscience wanting to ferret out all evil. "A sort of previously unthought-of Power going about."

This idea of a haunting Thing was given up as the project got down to earth; but the final result was still something new in popular journalism, which offered good fiction, verse, essays informative on historical and topical subjects, all generally based on the Radical progressive outlook which Dickens had hammered out for himself. Among the first whom he asked to contribute was Mrs. Gaskell, whom he had recently met and whose *Mary Barton* he had been reading—"a book that most profoundly affected and impressed me."

Offices were taken in Wellington Street, Strand, and W. H.

Wills (who had worked on *Chambers's Journal* for three years) was taken on as assistant editor. The first issue came out late in March 1850, calling itself "the gentle mouthpiece of reform." To buck up the emotional appeal Dickens put his *A Child's Story of a Star* into the second issue; and the third issue provided a job for John Dickens through a *Narrative of Events*, intended as a truthful record of important social, cultural, economic events. With the next issue Dickens started off a series of *Supposing*, ironically pointing to social reforms. On June 7th he attacked the different legal treatment given to "a gentleman of good family" and "a Socialist or Chartist."

Now till the end of his life this sort of journalism was to continue; and if we examine it we find that he consistently upholds the Radical cause and presses for reforms in most spheres of life. Despite his anarchist emotion on such matters as law and Parliament, we find that he always supports governmental action on behalf of the poor or oppressed. But though a lengthy account of his ideas on social and economic reform might be compiled from his editorial policy and his own contributions in *Household Words* and its successor, the key concept is always moral. He believes that every man or woman or child has full right to equal opportunities for development and enjoyment. During the later thirties and the forties he had had the same ideas, but in the extremely unsettled conditions he did not know exactly how to put them into action without destroying his literary career. Now, in the period 1850-70, which, despite its many conflicts, was one of consolidation and expansion, he finds his platform and knows how to use it.

In view of the importance of the theme of coach and railway in his work, there is interest in the following passage from an article *Lungs for London* (which may be by Wills but certainly expresses Charles's own outlook):

Bricklayers spread webs and meshes of houses with powerful rapidity in every direction, suburban open spaces being entombed in brick and mortar mausoleums, the Lungs of London are undergoing congestion. Finsbury and Islington have suffered most. Within my recollection Clerkenwell Green was the right colour. Moorfields, Spafields, and the East India Company's fields were adorned with grass, and he must be young indeed who cannot remember cricket playing in White Conduit, Canonbury, Shepherd and Shepherdess, Rhodes and Laycock. Thanks to the window tax and the bricklayer fresh air will be thoroughly bricked out. A bath for Finsbury is too urgent a demand for the dense population to allow of much time being wasted in knocking at the door of the Treasury. The public must bestir *themselves*.

Henry Morley (who founded Morley College) wrote articles attacking industrialists for not giving adequate protection for machine workers. Harriet Martineau wrote in as stoodge for the National Association of Manufacturers, and Morley had a strong word against the printing of her "misstatements" in the magazine. Dickens commented, "I do not suppose there was ever such a wrong-headed woman born—such a vain one and such a humbug."

His method of work has been described by one of his amenuenses:

Dickens would arrive at his office, No. 16 Wellington Street, at about eight o'clock in the morning and begin dictating. He would walk up and down the floor several times after delivering himself of a sentence or paragraph. He was generally tired out by eleven o'clock and would then go to his club. Dickens had a very odd habit of combing his hair. He would go through the performance a hundred times a day, and, in fact, never seemed to tire of it. It was invariably the first thing he did on entering the office.

Soon after the magazine was launched, Dickens hurried off to Knebworth with Kate (and Georgy) to discuss Bulwer Lytton's scheme for helping hard up writers and artists. In June he dashed for Paris with Maclise to see pictures and hit a heatwave; in two days he was anxious and dashed home again, and paid his friend Egg to paint Georgina. He sent the household down to Broadstairs and waited for Kate to bring forth yet another baby. When it was born he hurried for Broadstairs and set up with his "little housekeeper Miss Hogarth." Kate, who for years had been displaced from control of her own house in most matters, was now well out of the picture. At Broadstairs the Dickenses stayed in Fort House (also called Bleak House) on the top of the cliff.

In November *David Copperfield* ended; and Dickens rushed into play activities. In aid of the Guild scheme of Bulwer Lytton, *Every Man in his Humour* was given at Knebworth, and also Mrs. Inchbald's farce *Animal Magnetism*. Kate had been going to take a part in the latter; but with her ill-at-ease body she sprained an ankle, and so Georgy took her place on the stage as well as at home.

For Christmas Charles thought up the idea of a special

number of his magazine, and this proved a highly successful idea, which was repeated yearly for some time.

The year 1851 opened with more play-acting. In January Charles and the village carpenter knocked up a stage at the castle of Rockingham. *Used Up* and *Animal Magnetism* were given, with Georgy and Miss Boyle (become Charles's devoted "Meery") taking parts. In February Kate's grandfather, George Thomson, died and was buried near Mary Hogarth; and Charles shivered through a visit to the half-finished glass building for the Great Exhibition. In March, Kate, still ill after child-bed, was taken down to Great Malvern by Georgy and Charles, who had written to a local doctor that the case was a "nervous one"— of "a peculiar kind."

The Duke of Devonshire had agreed to lend his house for a performance of Bulwer Lytton's specially written play, *Not so Bad as we Seem*; and a stage was being laboriously built there. Charles asked Egg to ask a young writer, Wilkie Collins, to take a part, and Collins agreed. Collins had turned to literature from commerce and law; he had written a life of his artist father and an historical novel, *Antonina* (1850) imitating Bulwer. Dwarfish, bulgy-browed, bespectacled, with dainty hands and feet, he had a love of the mystery maze in story-telling, which he was later to develop with much power. Charles, with his flair for spotting talent, had picked him out, and soon the two men became close friends. Steadily Collins supplanted Forster. With his red ties and blue-striped shirts, and his Bohemian habits, he was well suited to fit into Charles's new moods. At present he was clean-shaved, but like Charles himself was to grow bushier in the next few years.

Charles, on a visit to Malvern, was recalled to be present at his father's death-bed. John Dickens had been operated on (without chloroform) for his old complaint; and the effects killed him. Rehearsals were held up. Then Charles spoke at the yearly dinner of the General Theatrical Fund; and on arrival home found his girl Dora had died of convulsions. Forster went down to Malvern to tell Kate.

With May the exhibition opened; and on the 10th Charles gave an important speech at Gore House on sanitary reform. He insisted that "searching sanitary" measures were a primary necessity and that to think of putting religion or education in their place was nonsense. And finally the acting began with Bulwer's play before the Queen, Albert, and Lord Macaulay. At the second performance, as after-piece, *Mr. Nightingale's Diary*, by Dickens and Lemon, was given, with Dickens as Gabblewig. In later performances he acted several parts in succession.

After London came a tour which took in Derby, Sheffield, Nottingham, Sunderland, Newcastle, Manchester, Liverpool. "I sincerely believe that we have the ball at our feet," he wrote in excitement from Liverpool, "and may throw it up to the very Heaven of Heavens." At Manchester, "We carry the fiery cross! I have been so happy I could have cried." Kate (with Georgy) travelled with the company: £4,000 was raised for the Guild, and in 1854 Bulwer Lytton carried a Bill in Parliament for the Guild's incorporation.

While this acting had been going on the family had summered at Broadstairs; a Copperfield Dinner was held, and work with Miss Coutts for the rescue of prostitutes was continued. Charles at Charley's insistence, got tickets for the Duke of Wellington's funeral and reported the public interest as something mad, "a grievous thing, a lapse into barbarous practices . . . a pernicious corruption of the popular mind just beginning to awaken from the long dream of inconsistencies, horrors and ruinous expenses" of death ritual. (Throughout, he detested Victorian funerals as ugly, ludicrous, and commercialized; and put his sentiments into his will.) In his magazine he now wrote *Trading in Death*.

November saw the ending of *Bleak House*; and he moved from Devonshire Terrace to Tavistock Square where a large studio could be converted into a theatre. He saw to the furnishing of the house, and fixed between study and dining-room a door painted with dummy books, *The Quarrelly Review* (4 vols.), *Lady Godiva on the Horse*, *Five Minutes in China* (3 vols.), *Hansard's Guide to Refreshing Sleep*, *Malthus's Nursery Songs* (2 vols.), *Socrates on Wedlock*, *Kant's Eminent Humbugs* (10 vols.), *Adam's Predecessors*, *Was Shakespeare's Mother Fair?* (4 vols.).

This year saw Kate's one publication, a cookery-book, *What shall we have for Dinner?* written by "Lady Maria Clutterbuck." The book shows the heavy eating that went on still in well-off Victorian houses and ruined the health of these indefatigable guzzlers. It also gives support to Charley's statement, "I wonder how many dinners were begun with a glass of Chichester milk-punch; how many were finished with a dish of toasted cheese." These artery-hardening diets could not be kept at bay indefinitely with all the violent exercise that Dickens took.

An American wrote that Dickens told him he was abstinent from breakfast till about half an hour before dinner. Four hours of work and then four hours afield (on foot or horse); brandy and seltzer before dinner, sherry at dinner and port with cigar with dessert, finally more smoking and brandy and water before going to bed.

IV

At home Georgy was acting as secretary as well as other things, and he dictated his *Child's History* to her. In January 1852, it began as a serial in his magazine. For the rest, the tour was going on with its fiery crosses and balls kicked to heaven. In March, again, child-birth and the starting of a new story coincided; a son, Edward Bulwer Lytton, was born and *Bleak House* began publication.

Throughout his married life Charles took an attitude of jesting or irritated blame to Kate for her fertility. His phrases always assume that she is solely responsible for thrusting children on him. When a woman about this time asked to be allowed to stand as godmother to a child of his, he answered, "May I never have the opportunity to give you one." He wrote to Lemon, "I don't congratulate you on the Baby, because I can't bear to be congratulated on my own babies." To someone else, "My wife has presented me with No. 10. I think I could have dispensed with the compliment." He suggested asking the Bishop of London "to have a little service in St. Paul's beeseeching that I may be considered to have done enough towards my country's population." When Kate was pregnant, he described her as being in an "uninteresting condition." He referred to his "tons of children," and wrote enviously to Wilkie Collins, "I am so undoubtedly one of the sons of Toil—and father of children—that I expect to be presently presented with a smock-frock, a pair of leather breeches, and a pewter watch, for having brought up the largest family ever known with the smallest disposition to do anything for themselves." In *Chuzzlewit* much fun had been made of Mr. Harris—"dreadful timid . . . stopped his ears in a dog-kennel" when his first child is being born; when the ninth comes he hurts his wife's feelings by suggesting it is one or two too many. Years later, Dickens, writing to Yates, refers to the time "when Mr. Harris went into an empty dog-kennel to spare his sensitive nature the anguish of over-hearing Mrs. Harris's exclamations on the occasion of the birth of her first child." It would be hard to beat the complacence of these attitudes. (Bulwer in 1832, when his wife was nearing child-bed, wrote to a woman friend about his wife's figure and swore to limit his activities to one babe only. Nothing was "so ludicrously uninteresting as an author with a large family, at least of legitimates." So here, too, was an attitude which Bulwer and Dickens shared.)

As for the children themselves, he liked playing with them and giving them parties when they were small. But when they started growing up, especially if they were boys, he lost interest in them and wanted to get rid of them. Charley remarked that the dream-children were closer to his father's heart than the living children ever were.

In May he was touring again, at Birmingham; in August, at Sunderland; in September, at Liverpool. From July to September he rented a house at Dover for the family, but Kate (with Georgy) went on his travels; and when the children could be packed back to London he went with Kate (and Georgy) to Boulogne, and liked the ramparts and the fishermen. He cheered up. Back in London, he worked on *Bleak House*, and edited *Household Words*, with much high spirits among his pals. But the deaths of friends—Mrs. Macready, Watson, d'Orsay—sent a chill over him. "The tremendous sickle certainly does cut deep into the surrounding corn, when one's own small blade has ripened. But *this* is all a Dream, may be, and death will wake us."

The year 1853 opened with a dinner at Birmingham. Dickens declared that the age of patronage and venality was over. He ridiculed the idea that writing for the people meant writing down. Literature, he said, "cannot be too faithful to the people—can not too ardently advocate the cause of their advancements, happiness and prosperity." He declared his unbounded admiration for the working-class, "their fortitude, patience, gentleness, the reasonableness of their nature, so accessible to persuasion, and their extraordinary goodness one towards another," and said that he had tried to communicate this sentiment.

Household Words carried an article making a fierce attack on workhouse administration.

At the end of April he spoke at the Royal Academy banquet. The Vice-Chancellor (in the absence of the Lord Chancellor) tried to defend the Court of Chancery—clearly against the attacks of *Bleak House*. Dickens ironically welcomed the claim that an increase in the number of judges was ending all the troubles. Mrs. Beecher Stowe saw Kate there and described her as "large, tall, well-developed and high-coloured with an air of frankness, cheerfulness and reliability."

In May he wrote to Mrs. Gaskell about her *Ruth*, "I called those two women [in it] my dear friends! Why, if I told you the fiftieth part of what I have thought about them you would write me the most suspicious of notes, refusing to receive the fiftieth part of that." He was still giving Miss Coutts advice on her social schemes; and was arranging yet another play-acting when he suddenly could stand it no longer.

He was amusing himself with a trial at spiritualist table-turning when the pains rushed on him, his old kidney pains (which at Genoa had been connected with the Mary Advent). His head began to ache, and he rushed for Boulogne with Kate (and Georgy). On the way he read delightedly the manuscript of Wilkie Collins's *Anne Rodway*, and spent the summer in a château where (to his joy) the hall was almost all of glass and the rooms were thick with mirrors and clocks. Mary Boyle came on a visit up "an avenue of hollyhocks," and Wilkie Collins stayed in a near pavilion.

On August 27th *Bleak House* was done, and a dinner given at Boulogne. (It is astonishing how readily these Victorian artists and writers dashed round to such events, saw each other off at Liverpool, and went off in groups on wild holidays.)

October and November were spent in a hurrying holiday of this sort, Charles and Wilkie Collins and Egg with his sad face and dry humour. Of course, Charles went to Genoa to see the De la Rues and the Thompsons; and the disillusion that overtook his returns (except that to Chatham) came up here as usual. Mrs. De la Rue, still haunted, refused to be taken into his mesmeric power, and wondered at his black vest and black cravat. Christiana was slipshod, absorbed in playing about with paints, while her husband taught arithmetic to the two little girls (later to be the battle painter Lady Butler and the poetess Alice Meynell). The Peschiere house had become a school for girls. However, at Naples Charles met Henry Layard, a keen and fearless Radical, whose talk was finely invigorating, who had become famous through his work on Nineveh, and who was now tracing Italian pictures.

From Turin Charles wrote to Kate asking her to make things up with Mrs. De la Rue, telling her that her position "beside these people is not a good one, is not an amiable one, or a generous one—is not worthy of you at all." He said that now she must see the events of nine years ago in proper perspective.

You know my life and character, and what has had its part in making them successful; and the more you see of me, the better perhaps you may understand that the intense pursuit of any idea that takes complete possession of me is one of the qualities that make me different, sometimes for good; sometimes, I dare say, for evil, from other men.

About this time he felt a passing recrudescence of affection for Kate and his letters were full of warmth. Kate, glad to oblige, wrote to Mrs. De la Rue in friendly vein.

Back in London in December, he went off to Birmingham to read his Christmas stories as he had promised early in the year. Kate was given a silver flower-stand. To a second reading, only working-men and their wives were admitted; and in his address Charles declared that it was necessary and right for workers to take a share in the management of industry. Somehow by co-operation there would be made an end of exploitation. The Mechanics' Institute was a model structure for the whole of England.

If we turn from these hopeful words to his novels, we get a glimpse of the deep contradictions in his attitude.

V

Bleak House is the first attempt to devise a novel on the ground cleared by *Copperfield*. Its very title gives away the mood of dark anger in which it is conceived. Looking at the post-1848 world, Dickens feels none of the joyous belief in painless progress that the bougeoisie now felt. Rather, what he felt was the human check. The dark forces preying on men have been given more power, and what he sees is a desolation, the Bleak House of Man. The house-image was derived, as we have seen, from the childhood memory of Tom-all-Alone's at Chatham where houses were wantonly blown up, and the dusk inhabitant was a wailing Bedlamite ghost.

The central nature of the house-image, the image of the ruined and desecrated house, is to be seen if we glance at the various titles that were originally devised for the novel.

1: Tom-All Alone's. The Ruined House. 2: Tom-All-Alone's. The Solitary House that was always shut up. 3: Bleak House

Academy. 4: The East Wind. 5: Tom-All-Alone's. The Ruined
(House, Building, Factory, Mill) that got into Chancery and never
got out. 6: Tom-All-Alone's. The Solitary House where the Grass
Grew. 7: Tom-All-Alone's. The Solitary House that was always
Shut up and never Lighted. 8: Tom-All-Alone's. The Ruined Mill
that got into Chancery and never Got Out. 9: Tom-All-Alone's.
The Solitary House where the Wind howled. 10: Tom-All-Alone's.
The Ruined House that Got into Chancery and never got out.
11: Bleak House and the East Wind. How they both got into
Chancery and never got out. 12: Bleak House.

Forster tells us, "The first intention was to have made Jo
more prominent in the story." We see, then, that Dickens's
originating emotion was much concerned with childhood
images of loss and desolation and that Jo links the blacking
factory with the Chatham waste.

A potent element in quickening the sense of childhood
desolation had been the death of Fanny. I have already discussed
the important revelation of *A Child's Story of a Star* and *The
Haunted Man*. To that we may add *The Child's Story* of 1852, in
which the series of losses and partings that make up life are
recorded in fairy-story form, and the lost beloved is Fanny:

So, he went away with that young man, and presently they came
to one of the prettiest girls that ever was seen—just like Fanny in
the corner there—and she had eyes like Fanny, and hair like Fanny
and dimples like Fanny's, and she laughed and coloured just as
Fanny does when I am talking about her. So, the young man fell in
love directly—just as Somebody I won't mention, the first time he
came here, did with Fanny. Well! he was teased sometimes—just as
Somebody used to be by Fanny; and they quarrelled sometimes—
just as Somebody and Fanny used to quarrel; and they made it up and
sat in the dark, and wrote letters every day, and never were happy
asunder, and were always looking out for one another, and pretending not to, and were engaged at Christmas time, and sat close to one
another by the fire, and were going to be married very soon—all
exactly like Somebody I won't mention, and Fanny!

Here, partly through the coy style and partly through the
splitting of character in the dream-method, it is difficult to
make out exactly what he is talking about; but the excited,
evasive stimulus of the name Fanny is not in doubt. He cannot
bear to use any other name to express the lost love, the lost
relationship which constituted happiness.

The sense of personal loss is fused with a conviction that the
world has taken a wrong turning. Beginning from the image of

Tom-All-Alone and the Lost Child, the desolated place of a union once Eden, he moves into the heart of the contemporary situation. The London slum becomes the immediate festering location of the wrong done to life. But to depict the misery without relating it to the cause, the malformed and malforming structure of society, is impossible for Dickens. Therefore he fuses the two ideas of the foul slum and the governing law, using for his purpose the juxtaposition of the Law Courts and the ghastly slums round Chancery Lane.

No doubt he was helped in his decision by receiving a pamphlet about a Chancery case (in which the costs amounted to three times the amount of the debated legacy) and by recalling the notorious Jennings case over the property of an old miser of Acton. But he needed little stimulus to pick on the law as the emblem of all that was wrong with the State. From first to last he saw the law as the organization set up to protect exploitation and injustice, and to work hand in glove with that committee of exploitation, Parliament. (His last work, *Edwin Drood*, has his best joke on the subject. "It is not enough," says Mr. Sapsea, "that Justice should be morally certain; she must be immorally certain—legally, that is.")

So he worked out his complicated story, which all revolves round the emblem of the law as the force of injustice and evils at work inside society, the coercive expression of the tyrannical State. The direct satire is powerful, and might well move Lord Denham, Chief Justice, to protest; but so effectively had Dickens done his work that the Lord did not dare to raise the issue of the law, and merely objected in the name of Mrs. Jellaby, the philanthropical monster of the book. (So did Harriet Martineau; but she might well do so, since Mrs. Jellaby was largely based upon her.)

In *Dombey* Dickens had covered a fair stretch of the social scene, and had placed Dombey in his world of money-power. But now he attempts something much more comprehensive. Not only is the law and all its works depicted, with various legal types, but around the legal structure are arranged the other groupings which express aspects of State power, the aristocrat Sir Leicester and the parliamentary exponents, the Boodles and the Buffers, with the ideologues whose support is needed for the State, to bemuse or crush the common people— the religious Chadband and the reformist Jellaby.

Against these groupings stand the ordinary decent folk whom they oppress or deceive, ranging from the wretched Jo to the sturdy George, from the boisterous Boythorn to the indomitable Mrs. Bagnet.

The story depends largely on the romantic themes of lost heritages and mysterious births. The interest centres round Lady Dedlock; but though ostensibly it derives from romantic concepts of guilt and persecution, the moral and intellectual force of the artistic symbols transforms Lady Dedlock's story into the main expression of a revolt against ruling values. A guilty society pillories her for love and its misfortunes, and finally drives her to destruction. Thus she is set against the legal mechanism, the State, as the suffering individual on whom the burden of guilt descends socially and psychologically. With her guilt that a false code of social ethics creates, there is bound up the real guilt of her submission, her fear, her failure to cleave to lover and child; and her tormented pride, torn by this double pressure, makes her tragic death an inevitable aspect of the break in secrecies and hates which the revelation of the truth implies.

Edith Dombey had been the first attempt made by Dickens at this sort of portrait—the woman who has an essential nobility, quickened by her contempt for the values to which she submits. Having once given in, she relentlessly takes revenge on those who have brought her down or concentrates on herself the scorn she feels for the world. Having once made the wrong concession, she cannot find the right basis of rebellion, and can only bring misery on herself and those with whom she is associated. Dickens felt intensely sympathetic to this moral dilemma; and indeed through Edith Dombey and Lady Dedlock he attained a quality of tragic purity which was necessary for his work and for the fuller explication of the charge against society.

Lady Dedlock's fate thus raises the full human dilemma posited by the existence of the law or State. The obvious conflicts precipitated by the law have relevance to the issue; but they would be incomplete without this revelation of the full complexity of the problems of guilt, nemesis, purification, recognition. Dickens in his allegorical way indicates this point with the woman's name. Her husband may represent the obstructive feudal forces, which desire deadlock in social conflict; she herself concentrates the main psychological issues implicit in the human condition under these circumstances, the spiritual deadlock.

On the political side Dickens brings one issue right out into the open: that of the new industrialist against the feudal land-owner. He gives Sir Leicester all possible credit; he is a good feudal landlord and preserves decency and dignity under the most trying domestic circumstances. But he is drawn unmis-takably as the representative of decadent social forces, and against him is set the hardy northern industrialist who stands for a totally different set of social values. Dickens puts Sir Leicester in the best possible light, but with his limitations made evident; while the ironmaster, member of a rising class, has his own native sense of dignity to oppose to the feudal concepts. He in no way represents the money-forces, the Dombeys or the Merdles; rather he represents a phase of industrialism when the hard-working entrepreneur (often a worker with specially inventive vein) has little dependence yet on banks or capital outside his own small reserves. The type does not recur in Dickens's work; for the phase was already, after 1850, nearing its end, doomed by the vast extension of the credit-mechanism and of world commerce.

The book is rich in minor characters of much vitality: Con-versation Kenge, Vholes, Guppy, Jobling, Tulkinghorne, the Smallweeds, Gridley, Miss Flite, the Snagsbies, Chadband, the Jellabies and Mrs. Pardiggles, the rumbustious Boythorn (based on Landor) and the parasitic Skimpole (based on Leigh Hunt).

Much argument has gone on over the morality of basing characters on actual people, especially on friends. Georgina Hogarth tried to defend Dickens by saying that all his characters were in fact composites of various people, and that anyhow all were "types and not actual people." Clearly there was a certain truth in saying that Dickens at times consciously amalgamated traits from different people in one character; but no writer of any value could work simply and consistently on such a method, and to claim that his people are merely types is to assert that they have no creative virtue. To a friend Dickens admitted that his creations were "real likenesses" though not tamely based on the copying of all external details.

There is yet one more point of symbolism which has been missed by commentators, though it stands boldly at the core of the story: the "spontaneous combustion" of Krook, the so-called Lord Chancellor, the unpleasant rag-and-bones merchant with his many underhand dealings. Krook is a deliberate doubling of the part of the Chancellor, meant to represent the filth and darkness which is the other side of the law's respected dignitaries and deeds. His blowing up is a symbolic statement of revolution.

The importance of the symbolism to Dickens is shown by his determined effort to vindicate the physical possibility of such a blowing up. His preface attempts to give evidence and cite authorities in support of the fantastic event. He never wrote better than in the passages where he piles up the suspense and sense of evil round the greasy death of Krook; and he finishes off the account with words which leave beyond any doubt the import of the symbolism for him.

Help, help, help! come into this house for Heaven's sake!

Plenty will come in, but none can help. The Lord Chancellor of that Court, true to his title in his last act, has died the death of all Lord Chancellors in all Courts, and of all authorities in all places under all names soever, where false pretences are made, and where injustice is done. Call the death by any name Your Highness will, attribute it to whom you will, or say it might have been prevented how you will, it is the same death eternally—inborn, inbred, engendered in the corrupted humours of the vicious body itself, and that only—Spontaneous Corruption, and none other of all the deaths that can be died.

By using basic romantic themes and by projecting characters of great dynamic force, Dickens had shown his power, from *The Old Curiosity Shop* onwards, of making the crisis of his story seem the crisis of all men, of a whole society. But now he goes deeper and finds symbols to express basic moments of change, revolution, world collapse and renewal. Krook stands for the "rotten rags" of a doomed society; and his destruction is an essential part of the whole scheme of human renovation.

It is worth while noting also the way in which the central duality of Krook-Chancellor and the symbolic explosion of inner corruptions are reinforced by the theme of the fog with which the book opens. The material fact of the fog is used to communicate the sense of a spiritual darkness, a socially pervasive veil of untruth. This ubiquitous darkness, with the spider's web of the law operating at its core, is linked with the horrible night of decay and foulness when Krook explodes, and with the ceaseless drip of pitting rain that rots the home of the Dedlocks.

VI

The year 1854 opened with Fielding's *Tom Thumb* for the children in the large room in Tavistock House. Then Dickens went off to Preston to see what a strike looked like. He wanted at long last to write the directly industrial novel that had haunted his plans ever since Little Nell. In *Bleak House* he had shown the new man, the industrialist in his positive aspects, set against the semi-feudal world of Chesney Wold. Now he wanted to show the other side, the dehumanizing forces and the lot of the workers. Arriving in Preston on a Saturday he found everything quiet and the skies clean of smoke. "A nasty place (I thought it was a model town)." He saw a bad production of *Hamlet*, and next day attended a meeting of the delegates in the Cockpit, impressed by their strength, calmness, common sense. On Monday he watched strike-pay being given out, and then went to an open-air meeting where the workers sang:

> Awake, ye sons of toil! nor sleep
> While millions starve, while millions weep
> Demand your rights; let tyrants see
> You are resolved that you'll be free.

Back in London he talked with Layard, who wanted to get into Parliament and fight there. Dickens promised to help with all possible support. He wrote in defence of Layard and his ideas. He told his public that unless they rebuilt the houses of the poor they were murderers. He told the workers not to be taken in by men calling themselves reformers and only wanting a seat in the House. Instead, let them get ahead with organizing trade unions. There lay hope. But as for Parliament, it "is become just the dreariest failure and nuisance that ever bothered this much bothered world."

Then came the Crimean War. "I feel as if the world had been pushed back five hundred years." He saw that war was a diversion from a forward movement at home. The people, cheated once more, were to be tricked in war passions; they were to be lured to sing "their own deathsong in *Rule Britannia* and allow their own wrongs and sufferings to be obscured by cannon-smoke and blood-mists!" All his acquaintances were pouring money into the patriotic fund without a thought for the ravages of cholera, "of which in London alone an infinitely larger number of English people than are likely to be slain in

the whole Russian war have miserably and needlessly died."
From Boulogne he wrote later (1856) after the war: "Nobody
at home has yet an adequate idea, I am deplorably sure, of what
the Barnacles and the Circumlocution Office have done for us."
And optimistically added, "But whenever we get into war
again, the people will begin to find out." (A passage of value,
also, in showing succinctly how he used the term "Circumlocution," not for any civil service in the abstract, but for
governmental organization in general under the parliamentary
system.)

In April *Hard Times* started publication. Georgy was now in
good control of the household. When Edmund Yates called, a
footman showed him into the drawing-room and Georgy came
to say that Mr. Dickens was busy, but if the visitor was the son
of the actor Frederick Yates he would be received at two on
Sunday.

In June he was at Boulogne again, and stayed till well into
October. "I am three parts mad, and the fourth delirious, with
perpetual rushing at *Hard Times*. I have done what I hope is a
good thing with Stephen, taking his story as a whole. . . . I have
been looking forward through so many weeks and sides of
paper to this Stephen business, that now—as usual—it being
over, I feel as if nothing in the world, in the way of intense and
violent rushings hither and thither, could quite restore my
balance." That was in mid-July. The book was dedicated to
Carlyle.

In September the magazine followed on with Mrs. Gaskell's
North and South, another novel of the industrial scene.

Back in London, Dickens spoke at a dinner of the London
Commercial Travellers' Schools, and attacked war as the
paralysis of trade, enterprise and the peaceful arts, but admitted
that it was justifiable against a despotism. Thus, he moved
round to an acceptance of the Crimean War: an example of the
confusion resulting from his lack of any fundamental political
and economic theory to supplement his moral convictions. The
war had, however, deepened, if that were possible, his anti-
Parliament creed; and he revived his old skit on Hawsa Kummauns.

He gave readings of *The Carol* at Bradford, Reading, Sher-
borne, and arranged a show of *Fortunio and his Seven Gifted
Servants* for the children.

VII

We can now glance at the general background of the works written since Dickens had made an effort of revaluation with *David Copperfield*. That novel he had been driven into by his feeling that he must return directly to the sources of his inspiration and gain a new start. Mixed with this feeling had been the decisive turn in the life of the British people marked by the years 1848–49. The first great phase of industrialism had closed, and with it the vast massings of revolt under the banner of the Charter. The revolutionary upheavals all over Europe in 1848 had shaken up, if not broken down, the various feudal survivals in the political and economic spheres; and the result was a tremendous expansion of industrial method and railway communications. Between 1850–60 the face of Europe changed, and the decisive momentum into the modern world showed itself.

England had led the way in this development, and it now reaped the benefits of the rapidly expanding world trade. Among the working class the old militant unionism fell away. The Grand National with its fighting schemes had crashed in 1842; it was followed (1845–50) by the National Association of United Trades, a federal body to which local unions affiliated, which kept to a cautious policy. After 1848 the hope of using the unions for political triumphs faded out; and the unions in general took up a sectional conservative policy, averse from strikes, and seeking only to bargain for a superior position for their own members. They aimed at gaining this position largely through the restriction of apprenticeships, discouraging overtime, and, at times, subsidizing emigration. "The scarcity of labour," said the flint glass makers in 1849, "was one of the fundamental principles . . . it was simply a question of supply and demand."

At the same time there were gains. Solid organization was beginning to be built up in the industries requiring technical skill, such as the engineers; and staying power was a result. For the long fight ahead this was the main point; but at the moment the socialist vision and fighting spirit was quenched to a considerable degree. Ernest Jones went on trying to rebuild Chartism, but the mass movement had ebbed.

The 'forties had seen a deep change in the novel, derived from the impact of Chartism. In the 'thirties the limit of social consciousness was fairly well represented by Mrs. Trollope's attack on child-labour in *Michael Armstrong* and Dickens's attack on the Poor Law in *Oliver*. The great contribution of the 'forties was to enlarge comprehension, so that specific issues such as child-labour or the Poor Law were seen as parts of the larger moving whole. *Night and Morning* and *Chuzzlewit* tackled broad themes; *Sybil* brought the mass-movement of the workers right into the forefront; and 1848 saw the release of a series of important novels on the basic social question—novels by Mrs. Gaskell, Charles Kingsley, Charlotte Brontë, Dickens. These works were directly the result of Chartism whether they overtly dealt with the Chartist theme or merely drew on the new clarified atmosphere of struggle.

Mrs. Gaskell was a key figure in this development. She had lived in Manchester sixteen years and knew what working-class conditions were. Suffering from a deep personal pang, she tried to objectify her sorrow by seeing it as only part of a vast mass of misery—"to give utterance to the agony which, from time to time, convulses this dumb people." She began *Mary Barton* in 1845, but did not publish it till October 1848. Her heroine is a factory girl; and all the political issues of the day, agitation and strikes, make up the material of the story.

I had always felt a deep sympathy with the careworn men, who looked as if doomed to struggle through their lives in strange alternations between work and want: tossed to and fro by circumstances apparently in even a greater degree than other men. . . .

The Manchester Guardian savagely called this attitude a "morbid sensibility to the condition of operatives."

Charlotte Brontë began *Shirley* in 1848 and published it in October 1849. She had grown up in an industrial area, and knew the events she described; for Haworth, inhabited by workers in worsted mills, had long been a centre of riot and agitation. Kingsley reacted powerfully to the struggle of 1848, and his efforts to depict the sweated worker and the ground-down country labourer followed from it.

The influence of Carlyle, so crucial for Dickens, can be detected throughout these novelists born from Chartist storm and stress. Mrs. Gaskell had been so affected that in *North and South* she even picks up his theme of Germanic blood, and her ruthless industrialist foreshadows the Nazi.

Dickens had at once recognized the import of Mrs. Gaskell's work and claimed her as a contributor to *Household Words*. The influence of *Mary Barton* was strong in *Hard Times*; and in 1853 he had been much affected by her *Ruth*. (In turn he influenced her.) *Hard Times* was followed in *Household Words* by *North and South*.

VIII

Hard Times is a short novel for Dickens; and its shortness is the expression of the intractibility he felt in the material. He wanted to go deep into the heart of the suffering people; but he could not manage to find the dream-image which would provide him with that dynamic of union necessary for the full deploying of his creative virtues. The result is that he approaches the theme "objectively" and only partially succeeds in getting right inside it. His full self is not implicated, though morally and intellectually he feels the utmost loathing of the Manchester School of economics and emotionally he feels a deep sympathy with the workers. The petty-bourgeois fear of organization intrudes to prevent him from a full identification of himself with the strikers; and no powerful symbols develop which can intuitively cement the material as in his other novels. There is no centralizing dynamic image.

Hence the comparative hardness and thinness of the book. His struggle to grasp the theme appears, as usual, in the titles chosen and discarded:

According to Cocker. Prove it. Stubborn Things. Mr. Gradgrind's Facts. The Grindstone. Hard Times. Two and Two are Four. Something Tangible. Our Hard-headed Friend. Rust and Dust. Simple Arithmetic. A Matter of Calculation. A Mere Question of Figures. The Gradgrind Philosophy.

He was quite clear in his mind that he wanted to oppose the notion of men and women as things, instruments of exploitation. His emotional attitudes on this point had been given philosophical force through Carlyle; but he could not accept Carlyle's solutions with their religious tinge, their backward look at medievalism, their glorification of the strong man. He wanted a change of heart, but he was too much a realist to think that such a change could happen without struggle, without a ceaseless attack on actual conditions.

T. A. Jackson comments:

If in *Bleak House* he represents Mr. Rouncewell as fighting strenuously and competently against the rule of Sir Leicester Deadlock and his class, while in *Hard Times* he shows Rouncewellism militant emerged in Bounderbyism triumphant, he gives no hint or whisper of anything so supremely foolish as a wish for the return to the past. On the contrary, the aristocratic Mrs. Sparsit, who lives as a decorative parasite upon the vulgarly brutal exploiter, Bounderby, makes us, in moments, almost pity Bounderby—except for the fact that he deserves all and more than he gets. The aristocratic James Harthouse, equally a parasite upon the Bounderby-Gradgrind class, completes, in his dandaical boredom, and unprincipled heartlessness, the scornful repudiation of everything aristocratic which Mrs. Sparsit begins.

And he rightly urges that Dickens is feeling out for a way of expressing his sense of the need for "a completion of the revolutionary process of emancipation." But he is hardly right in saying that Dickens saw only a demagogic parasitism in trade union agitators. Here, as in so many matters, Dickens reveals an ambivalent attitude; he wants the workers to unite and insists that the people will have to take for themselves the rights that will never be given to them by Parliament, but at the same time he feels something frightening in the fact of mass organization. He advocates trade unionism and shrinks from its results.

That is why he sets up Stephen Blackpool as the ideal sort of worker, opposed both to the strike and to the economics of Gradgrind. The result is that no effective conclusion, emotional or artistic, is developed in the novel. Dickens's ambivalence is never resolved. He does not set Stephen up flatly as an enemy of strike methods. Stephen refuses to join in merely because he has given his word to Rachel; and when the boss assumes that he is anti-union, Stephen defends the strikers and says that they believe they are doing their duty by one another in uniting for protection. The conflict thus remains up in the air, and the conversion of Gradgrind has no force or meaning.

Only at one point does the book seem likely to kindle into genuine Dickensian symbolism—when the members of Sleary's Circus come in, at the start and the end of the book. Here we feel the breath of life, and it is the opposition of the fantasy-life of the circus to the grinding round of toil which gives *Hard Times* its hint of a true revolutionary quality. The circus stands for the release, the fullness of life, which the workers are cheated out of. Painfully and weakly carrying on the festival liberations which were once integrated with labour and art, it yet stands for the day of the fullness of things, the dream of the happiness of freedom.

The circus thus suggests how Dickens could have used the material of *Hard Times* for a great work of art; but he did not quite screw himself up to the point of adventuring into the heart of the theme, and the book remains a sketch.

Still enough comes out to make the tale a worthy plea for the underdog, a downright condemnation of the lot of the industrial workers. For Macaulay the book was one of "sullen Socialism"; and Ruskin read it eagerly and was much affected. Ruskin lacked the temperament to enter whole-heartedly into Dickens's artistic method and its inner meanings, but he still gained much from the story:

Let us not lose the use of Dickens's wit and insight, because he chooses to speak in a circle of stage fire. He is entirely right in his main drift and purpose in every book he has written; and all of them, but especially *Hard Times*, should be studied with close and earnest care by persons interested in social questions. They will find much that is partial, and, because partial, apparently unjust; but if they examine the evidence on the other side, which Dickens seems to overlook, it will appear, after all their trouble, that his view was finally the right one, grossly and sharply told. (*Unto this Last*, 1860.)

Dickens's personal problems appear in the predicament he involves Stephen in. Deserted by a drunken wife, Stephen wants to marry Rachel, whom he loves and who could make a good home for him; but the prohibitive costs of the divorce courts prevent him. This incident, together with others that crop up, are used to build the thesis that the law is the prerogative of the rich and always works against the poor. A sort of footnote to the integrated anti-law theme of *Bleak House*. The loveless marriage of Louisa (based on the cash-nexus) is the counterpart on the upper levels of Stephen's love-frustration.

It has not been noticed that Dickens drew the culminating episode of *Hard Times* from a paper, *A Tale of the Forest of Dean* (in *Household Words*, August 9, 1851). This paper tells of an anti-enclosure rising in the forest; and the hero, who wants resistance by force, is falsely accused by an enemy of being an *agent provacateur*. The rough woodmen lower him down a disused coal pit and leave him there, but his girl Mary is worried and gets a hint as to what has happened. She persuades a farmer to go out with her in the rainy dark and lower her down the pit. She finds her lover there, gives him a drink of brandy and a kiss, and rescues him.

That Dickens drew on this tale for *Hard Times* there can be no doubt. Stephen, who has been accused of robbery, is anxious to clear himself; in his haste he falls into a disused coal pit; Rachel worries about him and finally locates him in the pit.

Dickens has thus taken up a story of militant revolt and used its material to express his theme of the "lost" proletarian. *A Tale* described the foresters failing through their fear of one another, which leads them into the very betrayal they want to avoid; *Hard Times* showed the man who has tried to escape the responsibilities of struggle falling into the pit of his own death. Dickens labours the point that the pit represents the dilemma of loss that besets the worker, whichever way he chooses. "I ha' fell into a pit that ha' been wi' th' Fire-damp crueller than battle." Cruel in work, cruel in stoppage of work. "See how we die and no need, one way or another—in a muddle—every day."

Stephen then picks up the theme of Dickens's Chatham Childhood, the Star that represents union with the beloved sister. He has watched it shining as he lay in the deep dark, and now he draws Rachel to look at it together with him (exactly as Dickens has described himself and Fanny looking up at the Star of promise and union). "I ha' seen more clear, and ha' made it my dying prayer that all the world may on'y come toogether more." He dies, in the moment of the Star.

And so the Childhood Star of united brother and sister has become the symbol of a united world, in which the dilemma of Stephen no longer exists. The star-sister image of edenic union has been earlier prepared for (Book I, Chap. XIII) where Stephen cries, ". . . th' time, when thou and me at last shall walk together far awa', beyond the deep gulf, in th' country where thy little sister is." Then "he kissed the border of her shawl again, and let her go. . . . He stood bareheaded in the road, watching her quick disappearance. As the shining stars were to the heavy candle in the window, so was Rachel, in the rugged fancy of this man, to the common experiences of his life."

The Full Picture

I

EIGHTEEN FIFTY-FIVE opened with the elaborately produced play for the children, reviving stage hunger. Paris, too, was calling with a kind of life that seemed enormously more satisfying than anything England could offer. Charles wrote to Régnier that he and Wilkie would soon be off to enter into the "diableries of that delightful city." His birthday was celebrated by a Gravesend dinner; and he began, as a token of growing method in work and fear of failing energy, to adopt an idea of Collins's, a book of memoranda, hints for work.

Then, as he was about to run for Paris, Maria Beadnell, now Mrs. Winter, broke in on his life again. Idly glancing at some letters by the fire, he put them aside and went on reading. "But I found my mind curiously disturbed, and wandering away through so many years to such early times of my life, that I was quite perplexed to account for it. There was nothing in what I had been reading, or immediately thinking about, to awaken such a train of thought." He looked again at the letters and suddenly recognized her hand. "Three or four and twenty years vanished like a dream, and I opened it with the touch of my young friend David Copperfield when he was in love."

He read on with "perfect delight" till he struck the mention of Maria's two daughters. "In the unsettled state of my thoughts, the existence of these dear children appeared such a prodigious phenomenon, that I was inclined to suspect myself of being out of my mind, until it occurred to me, that perhaps I had nine children of my own! Then the three or four and twenty years began to rearrange themselves in a long procession between me and the changeless Past, and I could not help considering what strange stuff all our little stories are made of." That processional tension between present and past was indeed the stuff of which his large stories were made.

He told Maria in his reply that he hardly ever went into the City still without walking up "an odd little court at the back of the Mansion House" and coming out by the corner of Lombard Street:

Hundreds of times as I have passed the church there—on the way to and from the sea, the Continent and where not—I invariably associate it with somebody (God knows who) having told me that poor Anne was buried there. If you would like to examine me in the name of a good-looking Cornish servant you used to have (I suppose she has twenty-nine great grandchildren now, and walks with a stick), you will find my knowledge on the point, correct, though it was a monstrous name, too. I forget nothing of those times. They are just as still and plain and clear as if I had never been in a crowd since, and had never seen or heard my own name out of my own house. What should I be worth, or what would labour and success be worth, if it were otherwise!

He declared that he would be charmed to meet her again and have a long talk, but he was off to Paris next morning for a fortnight. As soon as he was back, Mrs. Dickens would call and fix a dinner. As if they were still in danger of carrying on the old tiff, he mentioned that they had met Mary Anne Leigh at Broadstairs "about fifty years ago," and he had been sarcastic when "Mrs. Dickens and her sister, who read all the marriages in the papers," read about Miss Leigh's. In a rush of gossip he mentioned that his mother "has a strong objection to being considered in the least old, and usually appears here on Christmas day in a juvenile cap which takes an immense time in the putting on." And he recalled a meeting with Mrs. Beadnell and the girls in Cornhill,

going to St. Mary Axe to order mysterious dresses—which afterwards turned out to be wedding garments. That was in the remote period when you all wore green cloaks, cut (in my remembrance) very round, and which I am resolved to believe were made of Merino. I escorted you with native gallantry to the Dress Maker's door, and your mother, seized with an apprehension—groundless upon my honour—that I might come in, said emphatically: "And now, Mr. Dickin"—which she always used to call me—"we'll wish *you* good morning."

Then he recalled how the word Paris once meant the loss of the beloved—when "my whole existence was once entirely uprooted and my whole being blighted by the angel of my soul being sent there to finish her education!" He ended with a burst of emotion and an attempt to say what it meant to meet again "in the strife and struggle of this great world where most of us lose each other so strangely."

In Paris, now, he did not escape from London; for he could not forget the return of the old love into his life. He wrote a long letter from the Hotel Meurice, speaking outright about his great passion. He hopes she will tell her elder girl some day:

> I loved her mother with the most extraordinary earnestness when I was a boy.
>
> I have believed since, and always shall to the last, that there never was such a faithful and devoted poor fellow as I was. Whatever of fancy, romance, energy, passion, aspiration, and determination belong to me, I never have separated and never shall separate from the hard-hearted little woman—you—whom it is nothing to say I would have died for, with the greatest alacrity! I never can think, and I never seem to observe, that other young people are in such desperate earnest or set so much, so long, upon one absorbing hope.
>
> It is a matter of perfect certainty to me that I began to fight my way out of poverty and obscurity, with one perpetual idea of you. This is so fixed in my knowledge that to the hour when I opened your letter last Friday night I have never heard anyone addressed by your name, or spoken of by your name, without a start. The sound of it has always filled me with a kind of pity and respect for the deep truth that I had, in my silly hobbledehoyhood, to bestow upon one creature who represented the whole world to me. I have never been so good a man since, as I was when you made me wretchedly happy. I shall never be half so good a fellow any more.

He spoke of those young days as a dream which changed him, and asked if she had recognized herself in Dora.

As soon as he was home again, he wrote a third letter. Maria's return into his life had now begun to mingle with the day-dream, and he hoped for a confidence which "may be between ourselves alone."

He wrote more directly as the lost lover.

> My entire devotion to you and the wasted tenderness of those hard years which I have ever since half-loved, half-dreaded to recall made so deep an impression on me, that I refer to it a habit of suppression, which now belongs to me, which I know is no part of my original nature, but which makes me chary of showing any affections even to my children except when they are very young.

316

He told her that she was "always the same in my remembrance," and laughed at her statement that she was "toothless, fat, old, and ugly." He summoned up memory after memory of his devotion, and carefully prepared the way for some kind of liaison. She had suggested a meeting in Paternoster Row.

I am a dangerous man to be seen with, for so many people know me. At St. Paul's the Dean and the whole chapter know me. In Paternoster Row of all places, the very tiles and chimney pots know me. At first, I a little hesitated whether or no to advise you to forego that interview or suggest another—principally because what would be very natural and probable a fortnight hence seems scarcely so probable now.

Still, I should very much like to see you before we meet when others are by—I feel it, as it were, so necessary to our being at ease— and unless I hear from you to the contrary, you may expect to encounter a stranger whom you may suspect to be the right person if he wears a moustache.

You would not like better to call here on Sunday asking first for Catherine and then for me? It is almost a positive certainty that there will be none here but I, between 3 and 4. I make this suggestion, knowing what odd coincidences take place in streets when they are not wanted to happen; though I know them to be so unlikely that I should not think of such a thing if anyone but you were concerned. If you think you would not like to come here make no change. I will come there.

But Maria's heart failed her, and no secret meeting took place. Kate, who knew nothing of what had been going on in the letters, called on Mrs. Winter and asked her and her husband to dinner.

The shock of Maria's middle-aged presence was devastating; but Charles got through the dinner and even called once on the Winters, where he saw the little dog Jip, stuffed, in the hall and confirmed his impression that Maria liked something strong in her tea. Then he did his best to wriggle out of her desires for the promised intimacy. The remarks he made about the demands of his work were true enough in general; but directed towards her at this moment they were the merest evasion. If he was retreating wildly into writing it was to get away from her and the blow of her bitterly disillusioning return.

In the ghostly unrest of going to begin a new book my time is like one of the Spirits in Macbeth, and "will not be commanded"— even by me. . . . (*March.*)

317

. . . the restlessness or waywardness of an author's mind. You have never seen it before you, or lived with it or had occasion to think or care about it, and you cannot have the necessary consideration for it. . . .

The mere consciousness of an engagement will sometimes worry a whole day. These are the penalties paid for writing books. Whoever is devoted to an Art must be content to deliver himself wholly up to it, and find his recompense in it. I am grieved if you suspect me of not wanting to see you, but I can't help it; I must go my way, whether or no. . . .

I am going off, I don't know where or how far, to ponder about I don't know what. Sometimes I am half in the mood to set off for France, sometimes I think I will go and walk about on the seashore for three or four months. . . . I agreed to go to Constantinople when Parliament rises. To-morrow I shall probably discuss with someone else, the idea of going to Greenland or the North Pole. The end of all this most likely will be that I shall shut myself up in some out of the way place I have never yet thought of, and go desperately to work there.

Once upon a time I didn't do such things, you say. No, but I have done them through a good many years now, and they have become myself and my life. (*April.*)

She offered to come on a Sunday; he said that he'd be away for many Sundays. He tried to take an interest in her small girl, and to reduce their relationship to that. In June the child died, and he wrote a pious letter of consolation, adding "It is better that I should not come to see you."

But the encounter had stirred more in him than even his large words could utter. He protested in the letters before he saw Maria Winter, that the name "Maria," or even a glimpse of almost joined eyebrows, anywhere, in the States or Italy, on "the stateliest occasions" and the most unceremonious, had carried him clean away to the pang of the past. When she coyly hinted that he exaggerated, he was deeply hurt.

I have positively stood amazed at myself ever since! And so I suffered, and so worked, and so beat and hammered away at the maddest romances that ever got into a boy's head and stayed there, that to see the mere cause of it all, now, loosens my hold upon myself. . . .

No one can imagine in the most distant degree what pain the recollection gave me in *Copperfield*. And, just as I can never open that book as I open any other book, I cannot see the face (even at four-and-twenty) or hear the voice without going wandering over the ashes of all that youth and hope in the wildest manner.

And now the "mere cause" had turned out to be a silly, kindly, fat woman. Where did truth lie?

He didn't know the answer, but he did know that he wasn't any better reconciled to a quiet, kindly, fattening woman, Kate, to whom for no ascertainable reason he found himself married.

The irruption of Maria had coincided with a return to childhood's home. He had been told that "Gadshill" (surprisingly inherited by Eliza Lynn, a contributor to his magazine) was in the market; and on the way to Paris he broke his journey at Chatham to inspect the property, a fair-sized house and 120-odd acres.

In Paris he thought for a while of definitely abandoning domicile in England and becoming a Parisian. Then, on his long walks by the Seine, he got the key-word *Circumlocution* and knew what his book was to be. He had found the basic image for his attack on the Parliamentary State of England.

Back in England, in the recoil from Maria, he pushed on with the schemes for settling in Chatham, with the new book, *Nobody's Fault* (*Little Dorrit*), and with more furious play-acting. He put on Wilkie Collins's play *The Lighthouse* at Tavistock House, acting the lighthouse-keeper and giving banquets after the shows. His prologue emphasized his sense of unreality, of grasping at art as the sole stability in a shadowy broken world:

> They are but shadows, as the rower grim
> Took none but shadows in the boat with him.
> So be *ye* shades, and, for a little space,
> The real world a dream without a trace.
> Return is easy.

And in a song he wrote for the play he told of some wrecked sailors. One of them carried a child on through the jungle and mire, till the captain told him to leave the child or himself be lost. The man said he'd wait till the fire burnt out; and when it was ashes, the child was dead.

All these years Charles had been trying to save the child in man; but the wreck of the world was making it more and more difficult.

This image stuck. Next year he wrote, as a Christmas story, *The Wreck of the Golden Mary*, in which he revived the memory of the little golden girl of childhood love and drowned her at sea despite the devotion of a brave sailor.

II

At the same time he was fighting at Layard's side against the State system, He spoke at a meeting at Drury Lane on June 27, 1855. He claimed that "in my sphere of action I have tried to understand the heavier social grievances and to help to set them right." The country "is silent, gloomy. England has never found an enemy one-twentieth part so potent to effect the misery and ruin of her noble defenders as she had been herself." Discord was piled up "on the heaving basis of ignorance, poverty, crime." There was "no understanding of the general mind in Parliament," and so "the machinery of government goes round and round and the people stand aloof." He had joined the Society for Administrative Reform, he said, because men must get together for good citizenship, but he had little hope of anything worth while coming out of Parliament itself.

Then he rushed to Folkestone to get on with *Nobody's Fault*; went back to London to preside at a Thackeray dinner; and then hurried off for Paris. This time he discarded Kate altogether, and he and Georgy had the pleasure of being alone on the journey and in the search for rooms. They found an apartment looking on the Champs Elysées, and settled in on their own. He wrote and told Kate that Georgy hadn't been able to sleep the first night on account of the smell in her room; but next day he forced the porter and his family to clean up. Kate, after having received this assurance of purity, came over with the children.

Nobody's Fault now became *Little Dorrit* and started appearing in print; and Charles (except for a December dash to read at the Mechanics' Institute in Peterborough and Sheffield) settled in to Parisian life. Ary Scheffer painted him, and he got to know Dumas, Scribe, Sand, and others. The incomparably more highly developed art-life of Paris fascinated him, and he felt London to be provincial as well as foul. In February of the new year Taine wrote on him in the *Revue des Deux Mondes*; and though the essay saw only certain aspects of his work, it was the first piece of serious criticism he had had. He could now feel that he really belonged to the central stream of European development.

That Dickens did in fact belong to that stream and that he had in his way as great an effect on European trends as had Scott and Byron is a point often missed. He was the only English writer after Byron who did so.

Taine missed much of the humour and could not grasp the

unfolding pattern of historically changing man in Dickens's work, the deep spring of creative renewal in that pattern. But he did see many of the social correlations, the emergence of Dickens from the English romantic movement, and something of his suffering passion. He saw also something of his strange visual associative power which operates in terms of a centralizing spiritual principle. "The eye, partaking of the quickness of the flashing light, saw in its every gleam a multitude of objects which it could not see at steady noon in fifty times that period." Rightly, he links this deep new associative energy with the scientific focus and tempo of the age, comparing Dickens's lidless eye to the daguerreotype view.

The way that eye worked is well shown by an episode of November, when Charles had hurried back to England for a funeral. He strode out on one of his long, aimless night walks, and suddenly, near Whitechapel workhouse, saw through the dim light of the rain seven "dumb wet silent horrors, sphinxes set up against that dead wall, and no one likely to be at pains of solving them until the General Overthrow." They were girls, for whom the casual ward had no room. He gave them each a shilling. "Look at me," said one young girl, without a word of thanks, and went off. A silent ring of sodden wrecks gathered round to watch, but did not intervene to beg money for themselves; then silently parted to let him go striding on into his hurrying darkness.

For such moments he walked in the night or strolled through the streets of noon or sat in a crowded room. To catch the revealing moment, to meet the sphinx of his own pang. To answer and pass on, ever forwards, into the past.

III

The suggestions he had made in a panic to Maria did not turn out so improbable after all. He felt the need of some decisive break; he wanted to get away from people. Already in 1854 he had been writing to Forster about his uncontrollable restlessness and a project of six months in the Pyrenees. "A floating idea of going up above the skyline in Switzerland, and living in some astonishing convent, hovers about me." Later he was still drawn by a plan of going high up in the Pyrenees. The sense of irrevocable loss—the sense of an "unhappy loss

or want of something" which he had stressed in *Copperfield*—
was getting worse and worse.

. . . the so happy and yet so unhappy existence which seeks its
realities in unrealities, and finds its dangerous comfort in a perpetual
escape from the disappointment of the heart round it.

Naturally he tended to blame Kate for this void.

Am altogether in a dishevelled state of mind—motes of new books
in the dirty air, miseries of older growth threatening to close upon
me. Why is it, that as with poor David, a sense comes always crushing
on me now, when I fall into low spirits, as of one happiness I have
missed in life, and one friend and consolation I have never made?

The discovery that Maria even less than Kate could have
filled the void increased his instability. In January 1856 he
once more wanted to get away.

Again I am beset by my former notions of a book whereof the
whole story shall be set upon the top of the Great St. Bernard. As I
accept and reject ideas for *Little Dorrit*, it perpetually comes back
to me. Two or three years hence, perhaps you'll find me living with
the Monks and the Dogs a whole winter. I have a serious idea that
I shall do it, if I live.

He had to make monthly visits to London from Paris, to see
the magazine was all right; and in February he stopped at Gadshill to complete arrangements for the purchase. In March he
spoke at the annual general meeting of the Literary Fund and
told the committee they would have to decide whether they
existed to help authors or to carry out "a course of expensive
toadying" and their "own puffing." And he learned to his
amusement that Forster had become engaged to the well-off
widow of the publisher Colburn.

In April he visited Macready, and wondered if he would
emigrate to Australia after finishing *Little Dorrit*.

I have always felt of myself that I must, please God, die in harness.
. . . However strange it is to be never at rest, and never satisfied,
and ever trying after something that is never reached, and to be
always laden with plot and plan and care and worry, how clear it is
that it must be, and that one is driven by an irresistible might until
the journey is worked out! It is much better to go on and fret,
than to stop and fret.

Wilkie Collins was staying only a few doors away on the
Champs Elysées, and in talk they conceived the idea of the

play *The Frozen Deep*, which Collins wrote and Dickens largely rewrote. Into this play went a number of Dickens's main ideas: clairvoyance and love, shipwreck, the saving of the weaker by the stronger, love renunciation—all tangled in a drama of love rivalry. Virtually a collaboration throughout, the work held something drawn from the essential relationship of these two men. It told how an older man, the strong one, loves the same woman as a weaker man, but gives way to him and is broken. Not that Charles and Wilkie were competing in love for any particular woman; but Charles was already beginning to feel a sort of jealousy towards the young man who had his future before him and seemed inhibited by none of the suppressions and voids he lamented in himself. It was not a jealousy with any personal bitterness in it; and the two men seem to have remained on good terms till the end. It was rather an impersonal sense of displacement by the younger generation, a keen but not altogether unpleasant feeling of regret for not being able to take life and love so easily. In his strength he gives way, but he also hopes to regain something of his lost youth by companionship with the young man. In Wilkie's company Charles can take a different attitude to women, a lighter and warmer attitude; and he can treat women differently.

It is hard to know exactly how far Dickens was drawn into the careless hedonism of Collins. Even in the censored state of their correspondence we find him writing in a much looser way. Thus, "the gentle Glyn, on being called for, heaved her snowy bosom straight at me" (March 1855). He describes some of his movements in Paris:

Some pretty faces, but all of two classes—wicked and coldly calculating, or haggard and wretched in their worn beauty.
Among the latter was a woman of thirty or so, in an Indian shawl, who never stirred from a seat in a corner all the time I was there. Handsome, regardless, brooding, yet with some nobler quality in her forehead. I mean to walk about to-night and look for her. I didn't speak to her then, but I have a fancy that I should like to know more about her. Never shall, I suppose. (*April* 1856.)

They certainly went round together and picked up the light wenches they called "periwinkles."

If you should be disposed to revel in the glories of the eccentric British Drayma, on Saturday evening, I am the man to join in so great a movement. (*Jan.* 18, 1853.)
Any mad proposal you please will find a wildly insane response in your ever, C. D. (*May* 11, 1857.)

On Wednesday if the mind can devise anything sufficiently in the style of sybarite Rome in the days of its culminating voluptuousness, I am your man. (*May 22, 1857.*)

But how far Dickens let these encounters carry him, we can only guess. Certainly, as the 1856 passage cited above suggests, under pretence of nosing out material he was on the look-out for some tragic engrossing woman. His attitude was serious, however much he may have let himself go in Collins's easy cynical company.

The image of shipwreck went on haunting him. He had read his kinsman, Sir John Barrow's, *Voyages of Arctic Discovery* (1846), and also Rae's report on Sir John Franklin's last Arctic expedition with its story of hardship and starvation, and the definite statement that the campers had resorted to cannibalism. He refused to accept this statement and wrote against it; and went on to read all the tales of shipwrecks (the *Bounty*, *Peggy*, *Juno*, *Pandora*, *Medusa*) that he could get hold of.

For the summer the family had gone on to Boulogne, Collins coming too. Charles couldn't bear to go back to London for any long stay.

I have never taken to it kindly since I lived abroad. When ever I come back from the country now and see that great heavy canopy lowering over the housetops, I wonder what on earth I do there except of obligation.

So he put on a French worker's blouse and loitered on the piers to spite the damnable English trippers. Sore throats in late August compelled a return to London. The Hogarths had been left in charge of Tavistock House, but he had them bundled out. He could not bear their "imbecility."

In September Wilkie Collins was made assistant editor of *Household Words*. Dickens took up afresh the idea of public readings from his books; Forster sternly objected, but his counsels were growing of less importance. Charles went on rehearsing his part for *The Frozen Deep* on his walks, to the "great terror" of Finchley and its environs. By the end of October the script was finished and Forster made some suggestions which Dickens didn't approve; and November opened with discussions and alterations. The Tavistock stage was reconstructed and the stink of size pervaded the house. Miss Meery Boyle appeared to exchange a few flirting words with her great man; and *The Wreck of the Golden Mary* appeared in the Christmas number of *Household Words*. In *The Frozen Deep*, Mary Dickens, Charles's eldest daughter, was playing the part of Clara, the debated heroine of the play.

IV

The year 1857 opened with a performance. Dickens's prologue in verse brought out the extent to which he looked on the icy, unchanging north as a symbol of the inner landscape, the archetypal forms of Jung, the fundamental psychic patterns: what he had called "the Unchanging Past" in his letter to Maria. The words are spoken through "mists and darkness; soft music through-out":

> ... not all the winds that stir the mighty sea
> Can ever ruffle in the memory. ...
> To that white region where the Lost lie low,
> Wrapt in their mantles of eternal snow,
> Unvisited by change, nothing to mock
> Those statues sculptured in the icy rock,
> We pray your company. ...
> Not only yet that on our little glass
> A faint reflection of those wilds may pass,
> But that the secrets of the vast Profound
> Within us, an exploring hand may sound,
> Testing the region of the ice-bound soul,
> Seeking the passage at its northern pole,
> Softening the horrors of its wintry sleep,
> Melting the surface of that Frozen Deep.

In the play, Wardour (Charles) and his rival Aldersley (Collins) are both wrecked on the same arctic rocks. Clara, through her clairvoyance, can see the rivals at death-grips. Wardour, however, gives up his murderous intentions, and protects and nurses Aldersley back to life. Clara turns up with the rescue ship. Wardour gives her and Aldersley his blessing, and dies.

Charles threw himself into his part with such intensity that his son Charley recorded his behaviour as "positively alarming —not to say painful. In his demented condition in the last act when he had to rush off the stage, he went at it with such a will that the others had to attack him like prize-fighters." Charley was "tossed in all directions" and was "black and blue two or three times" before the play even opened. It was hardly acting; rather it was a form of demonic possession.

In February Charles got possession of Gadshill and went off

with Kate to a hotel at Gravesend where the food was good, to superintend alterations and water-boring.

On April 13th Talfourd's play *Atalanta* was staged at the Haymarket. A young actress, Ellen Lawless Ternan, made her first appearance in it, taking the part of Hippomenes. The facetious playbill describes Hippomenes as "specially retained in Court for the prosecution of his studies, which are ultimately acquitted on the grounds of insanity." Charles possibly knew her a little, as she belonged to a well-known acting family; for he went to her dressing-room before she made her entrance on the stage, and found her tearful at having to show so much leg in her male part. He consoled her and talked her out of her moral doubts, and thought her a "most attractive and sweet little thing." The critic of the *Era* thought her a "débutante with a pretty face and well-developed figure, who when she had gained more confidence would become an acquisition."

Her tears and her legs remained in Charles's thoughts, and when the question of doing *The Frozen Deep* with professional actresses came up, he suggested her. Her mother, Fanny Jarman, had been a famous actress in her day. Christopher North, comparing her with Fanny Kemble and Fanny Kelly, said she was "equal to either in power and pathos, and superior to both in grace, elegance and beauty." Oddly, there was a tradition of clairvoyance in the family and an uncle of Ellen claimed to have seen his grandmother at the instant she lay dying some miles off. She had two other sisters, Frances Eleanor (Fanny) and Maria; and all three went on the stage.

Little Dorrit has a full account of Charles's prying behind the scenes in the account of Fanny Dorrit, and there we can read his liking for the labyrinthine confusions of the stage world and its groups of chorus-girls. Fanny Dorrit, who takes to a musical career, can hardly have been developed without something of Fanny Dickens in her; and in her determined careerism we get an echo of Charles's resentment when the real Fanny moved off into her world of exciting prestige while he was doomed to drudge. In this part of the story Little Dorrit represents his own humble status in the old days, but not his bitterness. Into Fanny Dorrit, however, have also gone elements observed from girls recently met in the stage world, who probably include the Ternans.

Hans Andersen had come to stay with Dickens; and in the

innocence of his soul was charmed with the beautiful domestic atmosphere, and with Kate Dickens in particular ("so gentle, so motherly . . . pretty . . . a certain soft, womanly repose . . . such a light into her large eyes, such a smile upon her lips . . . Agnes"). Kate liked his archaic gallantry and the little posies he plucked with his own hands; and took him round to such things as *The Messiah* at the Crystal Palace or Ristori as Lady Macbeth.

Meanwhile Charles had seized the chance of Douglas Jerrold's death to start off in June and July a series of benefit shows of *The Frozen Deep*, to one of which the Queen came. Georgy was keeping touch with Maria Winter; she could not have feared her rivalry very much, but she was taking no chances.

While acting in *The Frozen Deep*, Charles was suddenly seized with the idea of *A Tale of Two Cities*.

A strong desire was upon me then to embody it in my own person. Throughout its execution, it has had complete possession of me; I have so far verified what is done and suffered in these pages, as that I have certainly done and suffered it all myself.

Somehow the retreat into the symbolic ice, the naked struggle, the clairvoyance of love, the ultimate renunciation, coalesced in his spirit into the image of revolution, the achievement and the loss of love in the depths of the people's struggle to break out of oppression.

In July he gave three readings of *The Carol* for Mrs. Jerrold —though the Jerrolds were not at all pleased at being made so prominent a charity cause. Of the audience he said, "Their enthusiasm was something awful." More and more he was feeling impelled to seek this direct contact with people.

In the same month he sent off his son Walter to take up a cadetship in India (gained through Miss Coutts); and from now on with a great display of paternal self-control he did his best to despatch his sons off into as distant a part of the globe as possible. Georgina ably abetted him. Walter had been discouraged from trying to write, and had no wish whatever to take up a military life. "A sad trial," said Charles, "thank God it is over." In a couple of days he had pushed it out of his conscience. (Walter didn't fare well in India, and, after being posted to hill country, he died of haemorrhage at Calcutta on his way home in 1863.)

Charles had turned back to more productions of *The Frozen Deeps*. But before we go on with the important effect that decision had on his life, we had better look at *Little Dorrit*, which had come out in its last instalment in June.

V

Little Dorrit, which, with *Our Mutual Friend*, represents Dickens's mature and epical presentation of Victorian society, grew up gradually out of a number of key ideas. At first it was called *Nobody's Fault*, and was to show the progress of a man who causes calamity after calamity, and always says after each fresh mischief, "Well, it's a mercy, however, nobody was to blame, you know." Indeed four numbers were written with this theme in mind before the name (on the eve of publication) was changed.

But new ideas kept breaking in. No sooner had Dickens started than he wrote, "The story is breaking out all round me, and I am going down the railroad to humour it." He felt dissatisfied and wanted to start all over again. He felt that it would have been better to keep the travellers, with whom the novel opens, unknown to one another and later to make their life-threads criss-cross in unexpected ways. Then, after he had started on the Marshalsea setting, he felt the possibilities of bringing Old Dorrit into a fortune. "I am not quite resolved, but I have a great idea of overwhelming that family with wealth." Then the first idea of showing up individual self-deception gave way to the idea of showing the whole ruling system as one meant to deceive everyone with a maddening method for the evasion of responsibility, which worked out as masking all the evils in society and government. Late in January 1856, he wrote from Paris, "I have a grim pleasure upon me to-night in thinking that the Circumlocution Office sees the light, and in wondering what effect it will make. But my head really stings with the visions of the book, and I am going, as we French say, to disembarrass it by plunging it into some of the strange places I glide into of nights in these latitudes." Through the Circumlocution Office he found the way to the society scenes, the Hampton Court dowager sketches, and Gowan, the artist who fails the responsibility of his calling; and had the link between the satire on the State and on finance—Dorrit in his new wealth naturally finding his place in high society. Then came the financial scandal of the Sadlier affair, which gave the final stimulus needed for the exposure of the alliance between high society, government, and finance.

I had the general idea of the Society business before the Sadleir affair, but I shaped Mr. Merdle himself out of that precious rascality. Society, the Circumlocution Office and Mr. Gowan, are of course three parts of one idea and design. Mr. Merdle's complaint, which you will find in the end to be fraud and forgery, came into my mind as the last drop in the silver cream-jug on Hampstead Heath. I shall beg, when you have read the present number, to enquire whether you consider Bar an instance, in reference to K. F., of a suggested likeness in many touches.

The book, then, built itself up almost by its own momentum out of the original idea of deception and self-deception. As he worked, Dickens felt himself bubbling over with new concepts of social and personal relationship, which turned into new artistic methods. "In Miss Wade I had an idea, which I thought a new one, of making the introduced story so fit into surroundings impossible of separation from the main story, as to make the blood of the book circulate through both."

As usual, the advance into the realization of the actual implicated a return to origins, a reliving through old day-dreams on a new level. He went back to have a look at the Marshalsea and found a portion of it remaining, including "the rooms that have been in my mind's eye." He even meditated taking them. In Old Dorrit he penetrated to the depths of his father, and defined also his own deep fear—the fear of exposure which he felt as a fear of social degradation, but which had its roots in the fear of facing up to all that his childhood sense of loss and rejection involved. Old Dorrit thus becomes a symbol of the Victorian bourgeoisie, living on a lie, afraid above all of having to face up to origins, afraid of the reality behind the fine words. Old Dorrit, remorselessly impelled towards the moment of self-exposure, is a symbol of his society impelled towards the dreaded reckoning day.

Dickens's ambivalence towards his sister Fanny appears in the two girls, Fanny and Amy, who stand for different aspects of the real Fanny: the good sister, who sacrifices herself and thinks only of love; the bad sister, who heartlessly considers only her own career. (And this theme of the contrasted sisters links also with the Kate–Georgy conflict.)

The dynamic of the book comes from the desire to strip away all masks. Old Dorrit is exposed as a jail-bird, Merdle exposed as a swindler, Mrs. Clennam with all her tormented religion exposed as a creature of greed and hate. There is, too, the rowdy exposure of Casby, whose patriarchal exterior is merely a veil for money ruthlessness. The Circumlocution Office itself cannot be exposed, as it stands for the very fabric of the class State; but the exposures of the dominant individuals in the story combine to give the effect of stripping bare the whole basis of lying, hate, fear and exploitation without which there could be no Circumlocution Office, because there would then be nothing to hide.

"We all know how to deceive ourselves—that is to say, how people in general deceive themselves—as to motives of action," Dickens writes. This theme—which had been given broad symbolic value and social reference in Mrs. Clennam, Old Dorrit, and Merdle—appears in more restricted and humorous lines in the episode of Flora—the stripping of illusion from youthful idealism in love. As we have seen, Flora was Dora re-met, Maria Beadnell in her fat forties; and in thus mercilessly depicting her Dickens is doing more than commit a rudeness and outrage all etiquette. In laughing at the love illusions which had fabricated a Dora he is laughing at one of the potent forces which keep people blind to the pervasive Lie. Arthur Clennam, in awakening from a rosy illusion and turning to the plain, devoted Amy, is turning to the truth and its sources in the common people.

This point is brought out by the mechanism of the story which makes the union of Amy and Arthur arrive out of the mingled disasters of Merdle and Old Dorrit.

At the same time the degree to which Dickens's fantasy-dynamic is here dependent on childhood attachments is shown by his insistence in making Amy a sort of child-monster.

The story is built on the usual romantic ingredients of lost heritages, sudden fortunes, hidden bastardies and unknown wills. And as usual in Dickens the romantic resolution by revelation is given artistic validity by its merging with the action of the socially symbolic themes. In *Little Dorrit* with its huge canvas there is a tremendous spilling over of invention in minor characters, who elaborate or emphasize the meaning of the protagonists. Pancks, Casby and Flintwinch, Gowan and all the denizens of Society, fill out the dark side of the picture: while the poor folk of Bleeding Heart Yard, Dorrit's mild old brother, Doyce, stand for the other side. The Meagleses stand betwixt and between, good-hearted but succumbing to the worship of success and prestige. They are pushed about by the pressures they do not understand, bringing Clennam and Doyce together, but also encouraging Gowan because of his aristocratic connections. Their qualities are subtly expressed in their relation to Harriet (Tattycoram); they feel a genuine kindness towards the girl, yet hurt with their smug patronage. Thus comes the link between their behaviour and the deeper evils: Tattycoram runs off with Miss Wade, whose hatred plays its part in aiding Mrs. Clennam's schemes.

Mrs. Clennam stands for the full creed of Calvinist and capitalist fear and hate of life, in which theological arguments are used to support the basest acts of greed and revenge. (Dickens here gets in a strong attack on the Nonconformist Sunday.) Her money-lust is closely entangled with sexual bitterness and repression; and this is the point where Miss Wade comes in. She represents the twist of sexual perversion and hatred which Dickens emphatically insists is a consequence of the dissociative evil of capitalism. He here (in *The History of a Self-Tormentor*) makes an astonishing study of perversion, as documented as a psychoanalytic case-book, which shows how effectively he could have probed if he had wanted to concentrate on psychological niceties and analytic nuances.

If in Miss Wade he seems writing in the post-Freudian epoch, in his treatment of Flora he unlocks his powers of word-play and anticipates Joyce. Again, he shows what he could have done in exploiting a particular vein if he had chosen to concentrate on it. Flora's chatter, devised to show her semi-drunken release of a free flow of association, strikes out a new method of character revelation.

I declare I never was so cut up since your mama and my papa not Doyce and Clennam for this once but give the precious little thing a cup of tea and make her put it to her lips at least pray Arthur do, not even Mr. F's last illness for that was of another kind and gout is not a child's affection though very painful for all parties and Mr. F a martyr with his leg upon a rest and the wine trade in itself inflammatory for they will do it among themselves and who can wonder it seems like a dream I am sure to think of nothing at all this morning and now Mines of money is it really, but you must you know my darling Love because if you never will be strong enough to tell him all about it upon teaspoons, mightn't it be even best to try the directions of my own medical man for though the flavour is anything but agreeable still I force myself to do it as a prescription and find the benefit, you'd rather not why no my dear I'd rather not but still I do it as a duty, everybody will congratulate you some in earnest and some not and many will congratulate you with all their hearts but none more so I do assure you than from the bottom of my own I do myself though sensible of blundering and being stupid and will be judged by Arthur not Doyce and Clennam. . . .

(Indeed, Dickens with his sense of word-play at times experiments with isolated word-combinations, such as "hobbledehoyhood" for clumsy adolescence or "floricultural cauliflower." Naturally, he never went very far with this experimentation, but he obviously enjoyed it.) This extraordinary intuitive sense further appears in coupling Flora with the odd person, Mr. F's Aunt, in which a condition of completely blank consciousness is startled by momentary bursts from the unconscious. One might almost say that while Flora stands for the free release of association Mr. F's Aunt stands for the surrealist clap of the absurd; and that both these techniques (revealed here in seminal force) are linked with the violences of dissociation, with the distractions of love-loss, in this novel which penetrated so deeply into the human condition under capitalism.

It was perhaps characteristic of Thackeray that he spoke of *Little Dorrit* as "damned stupid." He was not the only person affronted by its gigantic force and penetrating vision. For instance, the *Globe* attacked it as "twaddle." Dickens, who protected himself by never reading criticisms of any kind, chanced on this. "I was ludicrously foiled here the other night in a resolution I have kept for twenty years not to know of any attack upon myself. . . . I was sufficiently put out by it to be angry with myself for being such a fool, and then pleased with myself for having so long been constant to a good resolution."

On the other hand, Bernard Shaw has declared that it was *Little Dorrit* which made him a revolutionary.

The political point of the attack on the State as the Circumlocution Office is emphasized if we look at the germ of the idea in a story, *A Poor Man's Tale of a Patent*, written early for *Household Words*. There, with the noise of the Chartist movement still loud in his ears, Dickens tells about a worker who invents something and is wrecked by his efforts to bring it before the authorities. But this preliminary sketch of Doyce and his troubles is noteworthy in showing the political idea that accompanies the theme from its first moment.

A Poor Man's Tale tells how the inventor, though a poor smith, is no Chartist. It emphasizes this point:

I am not a Chartist, and I never was. I don't mean to say but what I see a good many public points to complain of, but still I don't think that the way to set them right. If I did think so, I should be a Chartist. But I don't think so, and I am not a Chartist. I read the paper, and hear discussion, at what we call "a parlour," in Birmingham, and I know many good men and workmen who are Chartists. Note. Not Physical Force.

But the smith has a friend who *is* a Chartist. "Moderate. He is a good speaker. He is a good speaker." This Chartist, Butcher, delivers speeches on the impediments in the way of reform and the burdens that fall heaviest on the working-class. The smith is unconverted. But at the end of his sad experience with the invention, he is forced to change his tune. "Further. In William Butcher's delivering 'that the whole gang of Hanapers and Chaff-waxers must be done away with, and that England has been chaffed and waxed sufficient,' I agree." Though the political point is not pressed any further, the whole moral is that the Chartist has been right in his contention about the State and the mild smith-inventor has been wrong. One is justified then in seeing the whole concept of the Circumlocution Office as linked in Dickens's mind with the Chartist effort to transform the nature of the State.

Incidentally, one sees again Dickens's anticipation of later tricks of style. In this story he writes throughout in a broken staccato rhythm. "What I had to tell, I have told. I have wrote it down. I hope it's plain." The method of using an almost inarticulate idiom to express the pangs of a simple character wrenched into new experiences, new discoveries, is here clearly set out.

II

Separation

I

HAVING decided to produce *The Frozen Deep* at Manchester, Charles wrote to Wilkie on August 2, 1857, "It is an immense place and we shall be obliged to get the best who *have been* on the stage." The best, of course, turned out to be Ellen Lawless Ternan, Maria Ternan and Mrs. Ternan. It looks very likely that he had decided on the Manchester performance in order to have an excuse for supplanting the Dickens amateurs with the Ternan professionals; and on August 17th he wrote saying he was off to give "three days' drill" to "the professional ladies who are to succeed the Tavistock girls."

Ellen as Lucy had a short part, but if it had been written to upset Kate it could scarcely have been more apt.

Lucy (addressing Clara): Perhaps my own experience might one day help me in guiding you. You have once or twice wondered why I was still a single woman. My dear, I shall always remain what I am now, because the man I love with all my heart is . . .
Clara: Dead?
Lucy: Dead to me. Married. . . . I don't think he ever suspected how dearly I loved him.

Nor can Kate have been much more pleased with the casting of a farce, *Uncle John*, to be given with *The Frozen Deep*. Here elderly Uncle John was Charles, and was going to marry young Eliza (Ellen); but his niece (Maria Ternan) and her husband (Wilkie Collins) managed to get Eliza compromised with her drawing-master, and the usual set of complications ensued.

In this farce Uncle John gave Eliza "wonderful presents—a pearl necklace, diamond ear-rings." So one day during the rehearsals Charles tried to give Ellen a bracelet. Somehow the present fell into Kate's hands, who asked for explanations. Charles retorted by demanding her confidence and insisting that she call on Mrs. Ternan. He didn't like to think his daughters might misjudge his morals. Katie, however, knew what was going on and was no fool; she

took her mother's part in so far as it was possible for her to do so. But the situation was a difficult one, since Dickens had sternly impressed upon them (all the children) that "their father's name was their best possession—which they knew to be true—and he expected them to act accordingly. . . ."

One afternoon at the commencement of this affair, Katie happened to be passing her parents' bedroom (which stood ajar) when she heard somebody crying. Entering the room, she found her mother seated at the dressing-table in the act of putting on her bonnet, with tears rolling down her cheeks. Inquiring the cause of her distress, Mrs. Dickens—between her sobs—replied:

"Your father has asked me to go and see Ellen Ternan."

"You shall not go!" exclaimed Katie, angrily stamping her foot. But she went. (Miss Storey.)

And so Ellen got her bracelet and stayed in the company. Charles went defiantly off to Manchester. In his desperation he threw himself more madly than ever into the part of Wardour. "He literally electrified the audience," said Wilkie Collins. Charles himself wrote to Miss Coutts that when the curtain fell "we were all crying together," and Mrs. Ternan and Ellen had to come and put Maria "in a chair and comfort her, before taking her away to be dressed for the Farce." He mentions incidentally that he had long known the Ternans on the boards. "I remember her (Maria) on the stage, a little child, and I daresay she was born in a country theatre."

To Forster he made no pretences, and wrote saying that he had married too young, and now "it is too late to say put the curb on." He said that he asked for no "immunity from blame," and had been guilty of "a thousand uncertainties, caprices, and difficulties of disposition." But he sought honestly to put his full moral problem:

You are not so tolerant as perhaps you might be of the wayward and unsettled feeling which is part (I suppose) of the tenure on which one holds the imaginative life, and which I have, as you ought to know well, often kept down by riding over it like a dragoon—but let that go by, I make no maudlin complaint. I am always deeply sensible of the wonderful exercise I have of life and its highest sensations and have said to myself for years, and have honestly and truly felt, this is a drawback to such a career and is not to be complained of.

335

But he couldn't sustain such a philosophical attitude for long. "My misery is amazing." On August 29th he wrote to Collins from Gadshill, "Partly in the grim despair and restlessness of this subsidence from excitement, and partly for the sake of *Household Words* I want to cast about whether you and I can go anywhere." He added: "I want to escape from myself." He told Stone he was suffering from "low pulse, low voice, low spirits, intense reaction."

Early in September he and Collins went north, to Carlisle and the fells. Collins sprained his ankle in a fall, and Charles had to act the part of Wardour in fact, taking Collins "melodramatically" on his back and carrying him up to bed. They went on to Doncaster, and Charles felt that the races and the betting were loathsome beyond words.

They wrote an account of the trip for *Household Words*, in which (changing the pseudonyms to the real names) Charles says to Wilkie, "It's no trouble to fall in love."

"It's trouble enough to fall out of it, once you're in it," says Wilkie. "So I keep out of it altogether. It would be better for you, if you did the same."

This is a bowdlerized version of the advice that Wilkie must have given throughout the tour. Take her to bed, but don't lose your head about her. That would have been more truly in the key of Wilkie's attitude. But Charles couldn't act like that; he wanted a great love, a renewing fire. And so he took the step of ceasing to sleep with Kate. We have the letter to Kate's maid, Anne, telling her to have the door between dressing-room and bedroom closed up and a small iron bedstead provided for his own use. "The sooner it is done the better."

In November he spoke in support of schools for orphans and necessitous children; and on December 1st read at a party his story, *The Perils of Certain English Prisoners* (partly written by Collins). Christmas itself and Twelfth Night were naturally without any high spirits. Luckily, some of the boys were at school at Boulogne.

Charles had set his face against any moralizing advice from Forster or others; he was going on with his determination to wreck his marriage, and yet he had at the same time to keep a grip on his public. The strain was terrific; and from now on till the end it was seldom going to relax. But he had his faithful Georgy to help him along. Without the least hesitation she betrayed her sister and provided the sole bulwark which could

have enabled Charles to weather socially the storm he was
raising.

II

In February 1858 he gave a moving speech in support of the
Hospital for Sick Children. More and more he kept turning to
the project of reading his works as the only way of feeling sure
about his hold on people. His misery at home grew more acute.
"I can't write and (waking) can't rest one minute. I have never
known a moment's peace or content since the last night of *The
Frozen Deep*. I don't suppose that there was a man so seized and
rended by one spirit."

But he could escape that rending while he read in public.
And if he couldn't yet take the plunge to read for his own
profit, he could do it for charity. He rushed to Edinburgh in
March and read *The Carol* there, and in April he read it in London for the sick children. Between the readings he spoke at
the 13th Anniversary of the General Theatrical Fund:

Every writer of fiction, although he may not adopt the dramatic
form, writes in effect for the stage. He may never write plays, but
the truth and passion which are in him must be more or less reflected
in the great mirror which he holds up to Nature.

Kate, meanwhile, unable to contain her misery, told her story
to her parents. Charles made various proposals for separate
maintenance, which were rejected. Mrs. Hogarth and her
daughter Helen started talking about Ellen; and Charles, hearing of it, refused to make any settlement on Kate unless the
Hogarths signed a paper agreeing that the separation had not
been due to any immorality on his part. This they refused to do.

Georgy's equivocal behaviour was worrying the Hogarths.
"We had thought her disinterested." Only the rage against
Ellen stopped them turning more emphatically on her. But
negotiations dragged on. Forster at last intervened and took
charge, arranging a legal separation. Mrs. Hogarth bore Kate
off to Brighton, and while Forster acted for Charles, Mark
Lemon chose a solicitor for Kate.

The terms agreed on were £600 a year for Kate; and on her
return to London she went into a small house of her own in
Gloucester Crescent, Camden Town. The Hogarths reluctantly
signed a declaration against the statements they had themselves
helped to circulate. Charles wrote a long explanatory letter,
explaining nothing, to Miss Coutts, who had tried to come in
on Kate's side.

In his main worry—how the public would take the matter—
he published a personal statement in *Household Words*, June 12,
1858. Here he assumed a tone of intimacy and denounced the
whispering as "abominably false." He had already canvassed
the possibility of getting the statement into *The Times*, and he
wanted it in *Punch*. *Punch's* publishers, Bradbury and Evans,
however, declined to use their influence, and he became savagely
bitter against them and against Lemon, the editor, who had
been one of his best friends. He also drew up a longer statement in which he emphasized incompatibility of temperament
and declared that but for Georgina the parting would have
come much sooner. Georgina had sacrificed youth and life to
his family; for years Mrs. Dickens had wanted to go away;
two wicked persons (the Hogarths) had aspersed a "virtuous
and spotless creature. I know her to be innocent and pure and
as good as my own dear daughters"; Mrs. Dickens now believed
all that.

This statement he gave to his readings' manager, Arthur
Smith, for discretionary use. A copy of it reached America, was
printed in the *New York Tribune* in August and reprinted in
English papers. Dickens was much upset and referred to it as his
"violated letter." Throughout these months he behaved like one
possessed. "My father was like a madman when my mother left
home," said Katie. "This affair brought out all that was weakest
in him. He did not care a damn what happened to any of us.
Nothing could surpass the misery and unhappiness of our home."

More unfairly, he also made remarks about a "mental disorder" which had made Kate think she would be better away.
This disorder seems to have had no more reality than the nerves
which had kept her away from Mrs. De la Rue; but it has led
to unfair surmizes that she was a secret drinker.

She felt the separation badly. A friend tells how she burst
into tears one night in a theatre box when Charles came into
the opposite one; and had to be taken home. "I thought I
should never be able to leave her." Later, in 1870, shortly after
Charles's death, a caller found her "looking well, being calm,
and speaking of matters with a certain becoming dignity. She is
resolved not to allow Forster, or any other biographer, to
allege that she did not make Dickens a happy husband, having
letters after the birth of her ninth child, in which Dickens
writes like a lover."

But now, from 1858 on, she was nothing but a dull ache of
remorse in the back of his mind.

Georgy held the household together, smoothed over the questions and anxieties of the children, turned a smiling face to the world, and diverted gossip from Ellen. She at last had her way and had driven Kate out of the house; but she hadn't managed to get Charles for herself. Her triumph came on terms that made it a defeat; but she clung to it.

She remains the most hidden of all the persons closely associated with Dickens's life, even harder to get at than Ellen Ternan. For long it was taken for granted that she was Charles's mistress though these beliefs never found their way into print, for the main support of the great Dickens Lie lay in the pretence of her moral behaviour. But with the full disclosure by Wright and Miss Storey of Dickens's connection with Ellen, the problem of her exact relations to her brother-in-law is rendered shadowy once more. How odd that this eminently deceitful and hypocritical person has been treated with such tenderness by practically every biographer.

She hated Kate whom she had wronged, as she showed by coldly cutting out of Charles's letters all the loving references to his wife. She kept Mamie, who was dominated by her, from visiting Kate. She made no bones whatever about accepting Charles's mistress into the house, but she fought with all her strength to hide the truth from the world. When Thomas Wright started sniffing out that truth as far back as 1893 she wrote to him and tried to stop any disclosures; and G. A. Sala wrote a letter to the *Manchester Evening News*:

Everybody who was intimate with Dickens is aware that Mr. Forster's Life is almost an exhaustive one. I say almost, because there are circumstances connected with the later years of the illustrious novelist which should not and must not be revealed for fifty years to come at the very least.

(The same sanctifying attitude appears in Langton's book on Dickens's childhood, where the author defends his inquiries by saying that he has found nothing discreditable to Dickens—inferring that if he had, he would have refused to publish.)

Georgy took charge of the children—Edward (6), Henry (8), Sydney (10), Alfred (12), Francis (13), and the two girls (18 and 19). Walter was in India, and Charley at twenty could be considered capable of looking after himself. Her mendacious tactics can be read in a letter she sent to Maria Winter, where she says that Kate had always been quite incapable of looking after her own children, who had been thrown on others all along. Kate had often wanted to go away, but Charles had stopped her. Now by mutual consent and for no other reason they had parted. And so all true friends like Maria would rally round and start "quietly silencing with the real solemn truth any foolish or wicked person."

Then, having used Maria, she dropped her; and later on wrote about her with calculated contempt in order to discredit any attempts to resurrect Charles's early love for her.

Charley was allowed to live with his mother after his father had extracted from him a letter declaring that he did so out of no preference for her. This letter Charles showed round. Perhaps he didn't know that Charley rather liked going to his mother's house, since it suited him to keep in with Bradbury and Evans—having fallen in love with Bessie Evans. "Dear Charley is so kind and gentle," said Kate.

III

On July 12, 1858, in the midst of these troubles, Landor, in flight from the law at Bath, came bursting with a niece into Dickens's house in search of Forster. A dinner-party was on, with the Lord Chief Justice present; and Dickens went out to pacify the old man, who, to his surprise, did not start denouncing the law but sat on a bed and chatted about the Latin love-poets. Dickens's domestic upset, we see, thanks to Georgy's presiding over the table, wasn't stopping entertainments.

Nine days later Dickens gave a rousing speech at the meeting, presided over by Charles Kean, which was the means of founding the Royal Dramatic College. With August he started off on a provincial tour, hurrying from Clifton to Exeter and Plymouth, back to London and then off to Manchester, Wolverhampton, and so on. He said he wanted quiet, but "perhaps it is best for me not to have it just now and to wear and toss my storm away." Maria Winter tried to lure him into a visit at Liverpool, sending him her sister Anne's pathetic death-verses; but he wept and evaded her. Later in August he went off to Ireland. Throughout these tours, as also his later ones, his letters anxiously and exultantly record the tremendous effect his readings had on the audiences. Especially with the working-class sections he is deeply aware of an electric sort of solidarity, which now became the most precious thing in his life—except perhaps the body of Ellen.

When exactly he first possessed that body, we do not know. Certainly we may take it that at the time of the public statements he hadn't seduced her and though intending to do so was still in a sort of high lyrical ecstasy which enabled him to carry off the fine sentiments. As certainly we may take it that the emotion driving him off on his tours, though linked with the emotion making him desire the girl, was in some ways a flight from the dread moment when the seduction would take place.

He was back in Gadshill on September 6th; but almost at once he dashed off on another exhausting tour of readings, from York to Scarborough, then up by steps to Dundee and Aberdeen, and back via Derby to London on November 5th. That month Maria's husband went bankrupt and she appealed to Dickens, who wrote a very guarded letter of sympathy, pointing out that her father was quite a rich man.

In December, Ellen, of whose acting abilities Charles had a high but perhaps biased opinion, appeared as Alice in a comedy *The Tide of Time* by B. Bernard at the Haymarket. Charles was being painted by Frith, and cutting up the scenery of *The Frozen Deep* to be framed as pictures.

He was now preparing to retire to Gadshill, back to the location of his childhood from which so much of his thoughts and feelings had never strayed. In April the first instalment of *A Tale of Two Cities* began, and he managed to break from Bradbury and Evans, whom he could not forgive for their keeping his statement out of *Punch*. With methods more high-handed than strictly contractual, he wound up *Household Words* and began *All the Year Round*, which he controlled till his death.

In midsummer he wrote the story *Hunted Down*, based on the poisoner Wainewright, but expressing his own inner disquiet. It is a tale of a murderer who, living on the proceeds of his female victims' insurance policies, is exposed by the lover of one of the girls.

By the autumn his resolve to get out of London became final though Forster argued that it would damage his reputation not to have a town house for his marriageable girls. The furniture was taken from Tavistock Square to Gadshill, except for enough to furnish a sitting-room and two bedrooms at his magazine's offices. Now the dislike of London which had been growing on him became fully articulate. He loathed the stinking river. "London is a vile place."

In this survey it has been necessary to treat the earlier events in Dickens's life with more detail than the later ones. Though he remained throughout his life subtly responsive to the social currents around him, and each work must be seen as emerging from a powerful tension between the movement of history and the fantasy-patterns of his inner life, the small matters of daily life grow ever less significant for him. They matter only in so far as they impact on the deep patterns. To record at length the endless odd details of social intercourse in these years is to confuse the issues and to lose the rich creative purpose of his movement in the superficial ebb and flow.

Especially in the years between 1860 and 1870 there is little point in heaping up minutiae. His course is finally set, and he goes doggedly along it. On the one hand he has Gadshill and the entertainments there; on the other hand he has the magazine keeping him in direct contact with the literary world, and under his tutelage a new kind of reportage, exploited by clever young men of whom Sala is the most outstanding, has appeared.

At home he has Georgy and his two young nubile daughters, though Katie, who had a will of her own (unlike Mamie), soon got away by marrying C. A. Collins, brother of Wilkie. (Charles sobbed with his head in the girl's wedding-gown in her bedroom, "But for me Katie would not have left home.") Outside, he has Ellen.

He had his writing, though that was even more than before a laborious job. He wrote *A Tale of Two Cities*, *Great Expectations*, *Our Mutual Friend*, and the unfinished *Edwin Drood*— some of his greatest work. And he had his readings, which claimed more and more of his energies. The searing break with Victorian values which the rupture of his marriage had signalized made this ceaseless reassurance of union with his public a necessity for him.

Each of these interests deserves some separate attention.

IV

First Ellen. Katie described her as a small, fair-haired, rather pretty actress, with no special attraction save her youth. "She flattered him—he was ever appreciative of praise—and though she was not a good actress she had brains, which she used to educate herself, to bring her mind more on a level with his own. Who could blame her? He had the world at his feet. She was a young girl of eighteen, elated and proud to be noticed by him." Her sister Fanny married T. A. Trollope.

On March 12th, 1859, Ellen was still acting: in *The World and the Stage* by P. Simpson.

Then she seems to fade off the stage into Dickens's arms. He took for her a house at 2 Houghton Place, Ampthill Square, near his boyhood homes of Johnson Street and the Polygon, in Mrs. Ternan's name, from 1861 to 1865. Here he used to call on her two or three times a week. Berger, the musician who had written music for *The Frozen Deep*, sometimes went along and played cards with Charles, Ellen, and Mrs. Ternan on Sunday evenings, or played the piano for the duets of the lovers. He thus describes Charles about this time:

He might have been taken for a well-to-do country gentleman . . . walking with almost military precision. His complexion was ruddy. . . . He was always very well-dressed, frequently wearing a black velvet waistcoat, which looked very smart with the long gold watch-chain that depended from his neck. His voice was remarkably mellow and capable of great modulation. His laughter was most hearty and sonorous, quite infectious to the hearer. His handgrip made your fingers tingle long after he had released them. . . .

He was an agile dancer, light on his feet and graceful in his movements. I have played Sir Roger to his dancing until I was exhausted while he showed no sign of fatigue.

The house at Houghton Place was empty from 1866 to 1868, though in the will of 1869 (with 1870 codicil) Ellen is described as of that address. Katie speaks of "an establishment of her own at Peckham." This was Windsor Lodge, a garden house with country view, no doubt chosen because it lay between Wellington Street and Gadshill, which was rented in 1867 by "Frances Turnham," and from 1868 to 1870 by "Charles Tringham." Thomas Wright, who found out these facts, found also that a local charwomen and jobmaster knew of Charles Tringham as an author writing a mystery story, and still in 1935 there was a sumach tree and a quince under which Charles T. was remembered to have sat.

Charles used to visit Ellen here two or three nights a week as at Houghton Place. Notes are known in which he instructs his manservant to take presents to Miss Ellen.

Take Miss Ellen a little basket of fresh fruit, a jar of clotted cream from Tucker's and a chicken, a pair of pigeons or some nice little bird. Also on Wednesday and Friday morning, a little variety each day.

Ellen now managed to visit Gadshill, under Georgy's complaisant eye. Miss Storey mentions that in the later 1860's:

Ellen Ternan came to stay, followed by Katie, who, when she heard of the visit of Nelly (as her father called Miss Ternan—pronounced Tern*an*) and that she had taken a hand at cricket, observed: "I am afraid she did not play the game."

But Katie had spirit and refused to be controlled by kind aunt Georgy. From the outset she had been on her mother's side, and even wrote at the time a life of her father in which she put the case for Kate; but this was unfortunately burned.

Charles took Ellen to Paris. We know this because she was with him when in 1865 on his way home he was involved in the bad railway accident at Staplehurst. Eight carriages fell into the river, and many people were killed or injured. Both Ellen and Charles were unhurt; and Charles at once set to work helping the injured—somewhat surprised that the brandy he administered had the effect of killing a lot of them off at once. Though he thus rose to the occasion and seemed none the worse for the shock, in fact it had gone deep and played a decisive effect in hastening his death. He who had planned the death of the amorously guilty Carker under the charging engine had been caught in a railway disaster while travelling with the girl of his guilt.

But that point I shall consider later. For the moment let us look at the effect which Ellen had on his work, and in particular on the girls in it; for that, in default of the letters which passed between the two, is our only way of reconstructing her character.

We see at once that Dickens, with his inability to hide trails which one deep part of him wants to blazon defiantly before the world, keeps linking Ellen Landless Ternan with his heroines through their names. Estella Provis of *Great Expectations* is a sort of anagram of "Ell-la-ess-te." Bella Wilfer carries on something of a jingle with Estella, with Wilfer added to bring out a touch of wilful capriciousness; and Helena Landless is Ellen Landless without any disguise. Rosa Budd lacks this verbal link, but has a name clearly devised to express desirable young womanhood. There is only a slight verbal link between Ellen Ternan and Lucie Manette, the first heroine conceived by Charles after the liaison began; but the identification of Charles Dickens and Charles Darney is obvious.

344

Lucie was depicted in the early stages of the affair, and seems to hold Charles's simple idealization of Ellen as a serious and charming young woman. Immediately afterwards there is a sharp change, which must be linked with some sort of growing disillusionment. Estella, Bella, Rosa, Helena, in varying ways are determined girls who haven't much nonsense about them. The element which Charles had put without much sympathy into Fanny Dorrit here comes out into his central conception of femininity. The shock of his discovery that Ellen wasn't hopelessly in love with him and was indeed using him for her own ends is certainly to be traced in the portrait of Estella. In Pip he utters his sense of exclusion, of beating with useless devotion against some impenetrable core of coldness and calculation.

I loved her simply because I found her irresistible. . . . I knew to my sorrow, often and often, if not always, that I loved her against reason, against promise, against peace, against hope, against happiness, against all discouragement that could be.

Estella marries the unpleasant Drummle for money and position. That she is broken into a more human response and takes her Pip after all, was not an integral part of the story, and was stuck on the end because Bulwer Lytton couldn't bear an unhappy ending. The moral of *Great Expectations* was meant to be one of exclusion, and so it remains in the total effect of the book.

There was a link between Estella and Edith Dombey (and to a lesser extent Lady Dedlock). In inventing the fable of the evil education that has killed all love in Estella, he was salving his hurt by finding an impersonal reason for his failure to penetrate into the spirit of Ellen and unloose there the springs of warmth and joy. At the same time he was generalizing his pang and saying that it was an evil set-up in society which made these hard hearts. For the first time he was trying to face up fully to the problem of evil. Till now he had created many figures of evil, from Bill Sykes to Squeers, from Quilp to Jonas Chuzzlewit, from Murdstone to Blandois; but they had been sharply drawn enemies environing the devoted ones, devils in a bad dream which was ultimately the dream of the man who invented the good and the faithful, yet cut apart. He had made a slight lunge at the problem of transforming evil into good in the individual when he showed Martin Chuzzlewit breaking away from his bad heritage; and in the fable of Nell and her half-mad grandfather he had for a moment caught a deeper symbolism. But

345

now he was facing a sterner question: How can Pip be so made as to desire as his ultimate good a girl with a heart of stone?

Thus he breaks through any too simple thesis that "environment" has created Estella. On the one hand he makes her the child of a murderess, and raises (rightly, without trying to answer) the question: What are the full facts of inheritance in all their organic and social complexity? He takes the mad dream of love-revenge which has moulded Estella without her own consent, and links it with the wider theme of an evil murderous strain running through society. Why, the story asks, and how, do these two elements come together? The pang of loss, the murderous power. One of the greatest scenes in Dickens's work is that where Jaggers takes the murderess by the wrist and shows her hands to Pip, who is quite unaware of the connection with Estella.

Further, there is the link between the evil distortion of Estella, which through a perverted sense of loss turns all desire into the desire of money-power, and the day-dream of Pip, who wants (in apparent innocence) to embrace the beautiful perverted thing and who moves in the direction of the same perversion.

Thus Charles's desire for Ellen, which operated first by driving him to a work on revolution, at the next phase drives him to tackle with deepened insight the problem of evil.

Bella Wilfer shows him tackling the problem at a lower level of intensity. He has got over the first overwhelming shock of discovering the cold and mercenary element in Ellen, and tries to consider her as a human being. He sees that she has had a hard life, and finds excuses for the cry, "I love money, and want money—want it dreadfully. I hate to be poor, offensively poor, miserably poor." And because he is seeing her with sympathy he feels that there is hope of her redemption. Give her a chance, and her goodness, her capacity for love, will come out. Hence the elaborate scheme of the Boffins to force her into facing herself and accepting love.

By the time he came to write *Edwin Drood* he could use, with more detachment, the material given by his love relations. Into Rosa he puts Ellen's girlish charm, her wilfulness without malice, her spoilt reliance on love. Into Helena he puts the stronger aspects of her character. Helena is "half shy, half defiant, fierce of look; an indefinable kind of pause coming and going in the whole expression, both of face and form,

which might be likened to the pause before a crouch or a bound."
In all these girls, Estella, Bella, Rosa, and Helena he puts his
new sense of something unpredictable in women, a tension of
anger and love, which hovers between an agonized bitterness
and an amused tolerance.

Through Ellen, then, Dickens has come to take women
seriously, to treat them as human beings in their own right.
Previously, with two exceptions, he had treated them as symbols,
as jokes, as lyrical images of love without character, or will-less
appendages for the provision of comfort. The two exceptions
had been the aristocratic Edith and Lady Dedlock. His access
to the great world and its dinner-tables had made him recognize
that women with strength of character and intelligence could
exist; but they remained on the other side of a social fence. The
recognition of their existence was extremely important for him;
but he could not come to close terms with their reality. Ellen
brought him sharp up against that reality, not indeed in an
aristocratic form (which would have been impossible: the
social gulf had in the last resort been only a gulf in experience),
but in simple terms of a man entangled with a woman whom he
could not wholly subdue.

This in itself would have been important, and would have
had effects in his work; but under the circumstances it had a
crucial effect. For the coming to terms with the difficult Ellen
involved a breakdown of the Victorian respectabilities. In his
daily life he might fight to preserve the pretence of those
respectabilities; but their last real hold on his inner man had
gone. That was why his pact with Ellen involved as first step
the turning to a directly revolutionary theme, as next step the
radical revaluation of his youthful illusions and hopes, and as
third step the creation of a completely critical and creatively
valid vision of his world, *Our Mutual Friend*.

Ellen thus liberated him from the final effects of the Fanny-Mary
complex, the sense of guilt derived from the death-wish and its
mother-attachment. By breaking through the taboos and
accepting a socially guilty situation, he decisively shook off
the old day-dream patterns of guilt and fear, and achieved a
fully creative balance in his perception of the relations of
individual and society at a moment of shattering change—his
perception of the entanglement of responsibilities. This girl
whom he called Nelly liberated him from the ghost of Little Nell.

As usual we find that Dickens's personal development has
kept close pace with developments in the general social sphere.

347

The 1860's, during which he discovered in Ellen the claim of a woman to consideration in her own right, were the decade which saw the advent of the New Woman. Throughout the 1850's the tide had been slowly rising with the active emergence of outstanding women like Florence Nightingale, Octavia Hill, Sophia Jex-Blake, and Emily Davies, who took part in social work, education, even political reform. A signal of the change had occurred in 1851 with the visit of Miss Lydia Bloomer from the States. Greeted at first with incredulous ridicule, the feminist movement began to seem serious towards the end of the 1850's. It was in 1860 that Queen Victoria wanted to check "this mad, wicked folly of Women's Rights, with all its attendant horrors, on which her poor, mad sex is bent." Clough in his *Bothie* advocates work for women and records that such views were considered at Oxford "indecent and profane, immoral and communistic." In 1865 Mill as M.P. introduced, vainly, the first Bill for women's votes.

Elizabeth Lynn (from whom Dickens had got Gadshill) was one of the women who attacked the movement. In 1868 in *The Saturday Review* she wrote on the girl of the period, accusing her of bold talk, unseemly jokes, slang, love of pleasure, indifference to duty, love of money and horror of useful (i.e. domestic) work.

Thus, through Ellen, Dickens was able to embody in his novels the change in relations between the sexes which the advance of industrialism in the post-1848 situation was bringing about.

V

Ellen, in releasing Charles from the guilt-complex represented by Lost Child (Nell, Olive, Joe, Pinch, Paul, etc.), was bringing to a head a resistance against various aspects of Victorian morals, which had been chafing him for some time. Roughly, the guilt-complex was one with his sentimentality and its death-bed scenes, its funking of the issues of sex. Previously, that complex had been a necessary part of his creative development. Without it he would never have found his unity with the mass of the public. Through it he struck home to the innermost heart of the period's pang, and got under the defences as nothing else could have done. True, the effect was inevitably ambivalent. It stimulated and dissipated the guilt-sense of men who were engaged in the primary processes of industrialization—whether they were on the exploiting or the exploited side of the fence.

That is the first essential thing to grasp. To see the sentimentality merely as an escape, a palliation, a bourgeois lie, is to misunderstand everything. The lie was there, but deeper still was the terrible utterance of the pang. That was why the people recognized in his work the incomparable statement of what they were passing through.

The "perversions" in Dickens's outlook are distortions due to the refractions of the historical situation in a creatively unifying view which simultaneously rejects and accepts what is going on. Rejects it because it is cruel and tends to deny human values; accepts it because there is no other way forward. All creative expression has this kind of ambivalence—acceptance and rejection—secreted somewhere at its heart; but the particular balances inside the unifying intuition will be determined by the historical pressures. The age of Dickens was eminently perilous and difficult; and he took the only course which ensured at one and the same time a maximum of contact with the human condition and the best possible artistic resolution of the problems posited by that contact.

He had begun, as we saw in looking at the *Sketches*, with a light-hearted attitude to sex, which quickly fell away under the increasingly refined demands of the new middle-class public and his own intensifying inner conflicts. "We must go with the times, my lord," says Disraeli's Tadpole. "A virtuous middle-class shrinks with horror from the French actresses; and the Wesleyans, the Wesleyans must be considered."

Dickens accepted this need to compromise at first without any second thoughts. In the preface to the first edition of *Pickwick* he plumes himself on bringing no blushes to young cheeks—though he was ready enough elsewhere to laugh at the phrase. Dr. Marygold reads the poster, "Schools admitted by private arrangement. Nothing to raise a blush on the cheek of youth or shock the most fastidious."

Then, before he knew what was happening, he was being hailed as the champion of noble and refined sentiment. At Harvard in 1842 he heard the Professor talking about his uniformly moral page which could be always shown to "the most delicate female," and that kind of praise thickened with the years. At the same time, from quite early, he found himself attacked as vulgar and offensive, beginning with objections to Pickwick's milieu and to the low company of Bill Sykes and Nancy.

When he introduced the theme of seduction, he was careful to involve it in disastrous consequences. Steerforth is drowned, and Lady Dedlock, after a life of remorse, is persecuted and dies miserably. Now and then, however, Dickens hungered for a franker treatment; he toyed with the idea of sending Walter Gay to the dogs, and consulted Forster: "Do you think it can be done without making people angry?" He had a deep contempt for namby-pamby writing. The bricklayer tells Mrs. Pardiggle:

No, I ain't read the little book what you left. There ain't nobody here as knows how to read it; and if there wos, it wouldn't be suitable to me. It's a book fit for a babby, and I'm not a babby. If you wos to leave me a doll, I shouldn't muss it. How have I been conducting of myself? Why, I've been drunk for three days; and I'd a been drunk four, if I'd a had the money.

In the States, after listening to the moral praise, he said, "Too much of the old Puritan spirit exists in these parts." Mrs. Hominy in *Chuzzlewit* is horrified at the mention of the naked eye, philosopher and author though she be.

Bulwer Lytton put the position excellently when he complained of Tennyson as the perfect writer for an audience of schoolgirls and Oxford dons. Rosina Bulwer, years before, in *Cheveley*, had pointed to the censoring effects of the young girl:

Miss Tymmons was, in spite of her *ponçeau* coloured hair, considered by her parents, and indeed by every one in Blickingly except the Simmonses, a very *genteel* (!) girl; for she sat very upright on her chair, never had a crease upon any of her clothes, scarcely ever spoke, and never laughed at anything that she heard or read, for fear it should not be proper, and had forbidden her brothers (with whom she was an oracle) to read the *Pickwick Papers* because, as she said, they were so "very low and ungenteel," and for her part she could not conceive why people thought them so clever.

A contributor to *The Mirror of the Time* commented on an essay in *The Family Herald*:

The writer says that a year ago he took two little girls to see *Othello*, and that he was disgusted. He did not find it "morally beautiful." The little girls "felt uncomfortable." Perhaps they did, at his running commentary; and we must observe that, judging from this article alone, we for one should not like to entrust our little girl, or any other little girl, to his care. This play-going "Quilp" should certainly not take out our little "Nelly." (A. B. Richards, 1851.)

This *Family Herald* spirit was what created Bowdler's castrating rape on the classics, and made Shakespeare, in particular, a dangerous force.

Douglas Jerrold, a good humorist, in his story *Jack Runnymede*, satirizes the general bowdlerizing fervour. A theatrical company discuss the emasculation of *The Beggar's Opera* ("a family edition of John Gay"), cut out everything suggestive even remotely of sex, and then go "to get themselves measured for silk flesh-coloured legs and blue satin slips for a piece of mythology." (The kind of costume which enabled Charles to console Ellen about her legs.) Jerrold comments:

Immortal John Gay! He did not snip life as young ladies were wont to snip watch-papers, after what pattern they would; he simpered away nothing of its reality into conventional no-meaning, etc.

That states exactly the attitude Dickens developed and stated most powerfully in his scathing pictures of Mrs. General and Podsnap. Mrs. General, a horrid creature, declares that "a truly refined mind will seem to be ignorant of the existence of anything that is not perfectly proper, placid and pleasant." She wages a stern war against passion.

She had a little circular set of mental grooves or rails, on which she started little trains of other people's opinions, which never overtook one another, and never got anywhere. Even her propriety could not dispute that there was impropriety in the world; but Mrs. General's way of getting rid of it was to put it out of sight, and make believe that there was no such thing. This was another of her ways of forming a mind—to cram all articles of difficulty into cupboards, lock them up, and say they had no existence. It was the easiest way, and, beyond all comparison, the properest.

Mrs. General was not to be told of anything shocking. Accidents, miseries, and offences, were never to be mentioned before her. Passion was to go to sleep in the presence of Mrs. General, and blood was to change to milk and water. The little that was left in the world, when all these deductions were made, it was Mrs. General's province to varnish. In that formation process of hers, she dipped the smallest of brushes into the largest of pots, and varnished the surface of every object that came under consideration. The more cracked it was, the more Mrs. General varnished it.

And in the person of Podsnap (his old mentor Forster) Dickens launches a fierce attack on Victorian shams:

A certain institution in Mr. Podsnap's mind which he called "the young person" may be considered to have been embodied in Miss

Podsnap, his daughter. It was an inconvenient and exacting institution, as requiring everything in the universe to be filed down and fitted to suit. The question about everything was, would it bring a blush to the cheek of the young person? And the inconvenience of this young person was, that, according to Mr. Podsnap, she seemed always liable to burst into blushes when there was no need at all.

In such a scene as that showing Miss Podsnap at lunch with the Lammles, Dickens in masterly way attacks the hypocrisy, and exposes the sex preoccupations of the so-innocent young person. In *Edwin Drood* he makes an amusing attack on Miss Twinkleton's method of censoring and morally reconstructing novels for young girls as she reads them aloud.

It is in the later books that Charles's sense of extreme discomfort at the moral burden of the blushing maiden comes right out into the open; and his strong attitudes on this matter are bound up with the forces driving him to Ellen's arms. (Note also, however, that the protests against the "young person's" castrating powers grow as the Miss Dickenses show up as obviously nubile.) In *Our Mutual Friend* he dares to bring in a girl, Lavinia Wilfer, who simply refuses to blush and who insists on speaking about under-petticoats in male company. The New Woman is arriving.

The system of moral taboos, which Charles had begun by accepting as a sort of sanitary measure aimed against the brutal behaviour of the Regency days, is gradually discovered to have turned into a system of life-denying values.

Undoubtedly the new idea of literature as a "family" commodity, which involved the reading aloud of books to large or small groups, played an important part in the emasculating trend. Thus, P. H. Wickstead (born 1844) says, "For many years, Scott, read by my father as few could read him, was part of the life of the household." Both novels and sermons were still read aloud after dinner by one of the parents, often the father; and we find husbands often reading to their wives. T. A. Trollope records of his father, "He was extremely fond of reading aloud to assembled family in the evening; and there was not one individual of those who heard him who would not have escaped from doing so, at almost any cost. Of course it was our duty to conceal this extreme reluctance to endure what to him was a pleasure. . . . I remember—oh, how well!—the nightly readings during one winter of *Sir Charles Grandison*, and the lasting disgust for that production which they occasioned." Ann

Taylor says, "From my mother's habit of reading aloud at breakfast and at tea, we were always learning something." The habit was not only middle-class. Thomas Burt, a coal-heaver's son in Northumberland, testifies that *"Uncle Tom's Cabin* was read aloud in our little family circle, and gave us many hours of happy, thrilling, and not unwholesome excitement." And it was by such readings that much of Dickens's work was made known among the working-class. In 1847 Mrs. Hogarth's elderly charwoman exclaimed, "Lawks, ma'am, is that young gentleman upstairs the son of the man that put *Dombey* together?" (Young Charley was in the house, sick with scarlet fever.) She explained that she never thought there was a man who could have put *Dombey* together. She lodged at a snuff shop, and on the first Monday of every month the landlord gave a tea and read out an instalment of *Dombey*—only those of the lodgers who had subscribed getting any tea, but all being allowed to hear the reading. "Lawks, ma'am," said the woman, "I thought that three or four men must have put together *Dombey*."

This method of group reading had many advantages. It encouraged the lively, the dramatic, the dialogue with living intonation. It filled the written words with resonances of a new sort; it made the unseen audience more palpable, and set up new bonds between reader and writer. Therein we touch one of the main reasons for Dickens's insistence on periodical publication, which made this popular participation more easy; and for his need to read his work aloud to his own groups (ultimately to everyone, the whole world) in order to test out the responses, the give and take.

This peculiar participation of the novel readers in the work of the novel writer is found only in this period, and it reaches its full effect only in Dickens himself. To some extent other writers of his day, from Bulwer to Wilkie Collins, were affected; but not in the powerful way that Dickens was. Another aspect of the close entanglement of writer and reader appears in the general assumption of the reality of the novel characters. The way in which the audience kept in interfering, demanding or begging that certain developments should or should not take place, was remarkable.

This interference reached its height in the case of Little Nell, which demonstrates the enormous importance of that figure for the grip Dickens got on his readers. But it never ceased altogether. It is bound up with the intense emotionality which

I have already touched upon. There was something very raw in all these people; and in their deep spiritual starvation they entered into the lives of novel characters with an extraordinary and anxious eagerness. "We were intimate," said Lilian Faithful of C. Yonge's tales, "with every detail of their lives as with the lives of our sisters, cousins and aunts." Girls did really draw their idea of a desirable mate from their books; and letters are thick with remarks about novel characters as about real people. In the creator himself, in Dickens, we have found the trick of continually identifying himself with one or other of his people, signing letters in their names and miming their nature. Figures like Mrs. Gamp or Mr. Micawber lived in the mind of the Victorians in a way hard to recapture; and we find as strong an individual as William Morris taking on the mime of himself as Joe Gargery and Mr. Boffin as an essential part of his self-expression.

Though it was mainly Dickens who attracted these attentions, a writer like Wilkie Collins was able to stir the imagination and emotions, though to a lesser extent. Miss Elizabeth Chambers says that her twin sister was so worked up about *The Woman in White* that she wrote to Collins saying that she simply must know the fate of Laura, and Collins wrote a courteously jesting reply. Cloaks and bonnets, waltzes and quadrilles were called after the "woman in white."

The group reading, especially in the family circle, led to the sort of censorship and mutilation that Dickens satirizes in Miss Twinkleton. Lucy Lyttleton (under April 1859) records, "Granny began yesterday to spout to us the new novel about which the world raves, *Adam Bede*, to be duly bowdlerized for our young minds."

The result was that under this circumspect regime a new attitude to frankness arose. Dickens might satirize it, but he dared not go too far in transgressing it or he would have lost his hold on his readers. The trouble over *Oliver Twist* and Bulwer's or Ainsworth's low-life crime stories was the first sign of the clash. The writers protested but gave way; for the low-life stories were rather a hang-over from the last century than an expression that their artistic conscience need defend. What had been valid and important in those stories had been the sense of pity and horror for the lot of the poor; and that could be expressed in more effective forms.

Both Dickens and Bulwer went on protesting and fighting in their own ways. Bulwer was a much lesser writer; but there was a genuine streak of artistic and human honesty and under-standing mixed up with all his decorative flamboyances; a keen sense of new potentialities. Lacking Dickens's deep sense of creative patterns which at once put him in both strong accord and discord with his world, he floundered about, confused but striking sincerely out, and then getting somewhat scared of the results because he was guided by no certain principle of dis-sidence. In the mid-forties he tried satire in *The New Timon*; a melodramatic fantasy, *Lucretia*, meant to show money as the force ruling the world and distorting human emotion; and a reply to the attacks on *Lucretia*, *A Word to the Public*. He had a troubled sense of dark subterranean creative powers striving to find outlet in a deadened and perverting world; but when he tried to formulate his theories in the face of moral attack he tended to fall away into a conventional moral defence—vice unmasked and virtue rescued; yet he continually returned to the attack and in his allegories (*Zanoni*, *A Strange Story*, *The Coming Race*) he revealed elements of profundity as well as romantic bombast. His career is of interest in showing how tangled up and easily diverted an author was likely to be in that world unless he knew exactly what he was doing.

Dickens escaped this sort of confusion by a superficial con-formity and a bitter working out of essential conflict in masked symbolic terms, coming out into the open of satire and direct attack only when he could count on a modicum of common ground between himself and his lower-class readers. The latter points of outlet are of great importance in his work; he would have stifled without them. But the basic fight goes on at very deep levels.

Mrs. Trollope to a slight extent, and then Mrs. Gaskell, had taken up the fight on the overtly social level; and in 1847 Charlotte Brontë, writing from the industrialized area of York-shire, broke in with *Jane Eyre*, a work of great importance in letting fresh air into the Victorian drawing-room. The review of Miss Rigby (later Lady Eastlake) in the *Quarterly Review*, expressed the conventional attitude, "We have no remembrance of another [book] containing such undoubted power with such horrid taste"—in tone of mind and thought identical with the forces which had "overthrown authority and violated every code, human and divine, abroad, and fostered Chartism and rebellion at home." If its author was a woman, "she must be one who for some sufficient reason has long forfeited the society of her sex." For many years no young lady could admit that she had read such a wicked book. Mrs. Gaskell's *Ruth* (1853) started another storm, because the unmarried mother in it was looked after by a Nonconformist minister who agreed to let her represent herself as a widow. Matthew Arnold found *Vilette* "hideous, undelightful, convulsed, restricted," thus showing himself one of the most philistine of the Victorians.

To make an extensive and stable breach in Victorian smugness was impossible; but these and similar blows by the novelists, which include the tremendous attacks levelled by Dickens in *Little Dorrit* and *Our Mutual Friend*, did shake more of the foundations than was apparent at once, and kept some of the doors open to the future.

The new sort of lending library, with Mr. Mudie as the emblem of righteousness, had come to the head during the 'fifties. In 1860 Mudie enlarged his premises and in 1864 was a limited company. He soon began to exercise a veiled but strong censorship, refusing to handle Meredith's *Richard Feverel* in 1859 and Charles Reade's *Cream* (with its *Autobiography of a Thief*). Mudie was Nonconformist; and W. H. Smith, who during the 'forties started off with the idea of railway bookstalls, had been reared in strict Methodist principles. His influence stimulated cheap editions and strengthened the moral controls.

When Dickens began as magazine editor, he had to think out his moral policy clearly, or he was liable to wreck everything. On one hand he had been much attracted by certain freedoms in the French literary situation; which confirmed elements of revolt in himself. On the other hand he had at all costs to maintain his hold on the public. There was opportunism in all this, but nothing fundamentally insincere. Dickens was the sort of writer who, lacking in intellectual strength, could only work effectively through formulating his deepest elements of conflict in fantasy terms. When he tried to make the conflict wholly overt, he could only write a *Hard Times*. And the situation was such that only Dickens's sort of fantasy-formulation could get inside people. In protecting himself against premature rebellions on isolated issues, Dickens was ultimately protecting his more integral powers of revolt.

Thus he wrote to Forster about a French play which he liked as true and courageous:

... one of the best melodramas I have ever read. Situations, admirable. ... I am very curious indeed to go and see it; and it is an instance to me of the powerful emotions from which art is shut out in England by the conventionalities. . . . The authors have really taken the French dramatic bull by the horns, and put the adulterer in the right position.

And, though not highly sensitive to paintings, he felt something vital in art at Paris, which was quite absent in England. He found, says Forster, that English art showed up as "small, shrunken, insignificant, niggling." He declared of the English:

Somehow or other they don't tell. Even Leslie's Sancho wants go, and Stanny is too much like a set-scene. It's no use disguising the fact that what we know to be wanting in the men is wanting in their works—character, fire, purpose, and the power of using the vehicle and the model as mere means to an end. There is a horrid respectability about most of the best of them—a little, finite, systematic routine in them, strangely expressive to me of the state of England itself.

Mere form and conventionalities usurp in English art, as in English government and social relations, the place of living force and truth.

Profound words. But Dickens could not sustain them or work out their full conclusions. Still, he shows the way that the question nags at him; even when he makes a joke of French obsessions with adultery and with psychological suggestion:

Likewise about dark shades coming over our wedded Emmeline's face at parties; and about F handing her to her carriage, and saying, "May I come in, for a lift homeward?" and she bending over him out of the window, and saying in a low voice, I DARE NOT! And then of the carriage driving away like lightning leaving F more philosophical than ever on the pavement.

As editor he tended to be a little querulous about women writers trying to be French. Elizabeth Lynn he thought liable to imitations of Balzac; he paid for her tale *Sentiment and Action*, but held it up as not quite wholesome; her *Marie's Fever* he thought an "imitation" of the French. (Holm Lee's story, *Gilbert Messenger*, about an unhappy marriage upset him so much that he sent it back in fear of waking "too painful emotions.")

His ideas on what could be got over to the Victorian audience are clarified by remarks to Wilkie Collins. In 1866 he wrote against a dramatization of *Armadale*:

Danger. Almost every situation in it is dangerous. I do not think any English audience would accept the scene in which Miss Gwilt

357

in that widow's dress renounces Midwinter, and if you got so far, you would never get through the last act in the Sanatorium. You could only carry those situations on a real hard, wooden stage, and wrought out (very indifferently) by real live people face to face with real live people judging them—you could only carry those situations *by the help of interest in some innocent person whom they placed in peril, and that person a young woman.*

There is no one to be interested in here. Let who will play Midwinter, the saving interest cannot be got out of him. There is no relief from the wickedness of the rest; and in exact proportion to the skilful heaping up of it the danger accumulates.

Here the moral issue is fused with an artistic one. The statement is not very clear, but Dickens seems to say that you can beat the moral resistances and achieve artistic success, only if you oppose to evil a pure young woman. This at least throws some light on the function of the "pure young woman" as an image of self-identification in his work.

In February 1867 he wrote about the case of Reade's *Griffith Gaunt*, which had roused furious attack in both England and in the States. Reade had just instituted a libel suit against an American paper (in which he finally gained damages of six cents). Dickens first declared, "Say everything that is brotherly in art for me to Reade"; then, having read the novel, he made many reservations. After praising the work as one with brilliant fancy and tender imagination, and speaking scathingly of the critics who could call such writing pornographic, he added:

Cross-examined, I should feel myself in danger of being put on unsafe ground, and should try to set my wits against the cross-examiner, to keep well off it. But if I were reminded . . . that I was the Editor of a periodical of large circulation in which the Plaintiff himself had written, and if I had read to me in court the passages about Gaunt's going up to his wife's bed drunk and the child's being conceived, and was asked whether, as Editor, I should have passed those passages . . . I should be obliged to reply No.

Asked why? I should say that what was pure to an artist might be impurely suggestive to inferior minds (of which there must necessarily be many among a large mass of readers), and that I should have called the writer's attention to the likelihood of those passages being perverted in such quarters.

Asked whether I should have passed the passages where Kate and Mary have the illegitimate child upon their laps and look over its little points together? I should be again obliged to reply No, for the same reason.

Asked whether, as author or Editor, I should have passed Neville's marriage to Mercy, and should have placed those four people, Gaunt, his wife, in those relative situations towards one another, I should again be obliged to reply No. Hard pressed upon this point, I must infallibly say that I consider those relative situations extremely coarse and disagreeable.

Throughout this letter he shows himself afraid of being brought into court on such an issue; and the warmly praising terms in which he begins end in the rather vicious last sentence. We meet here the limitations in the attitude he had set up, with its surface agreements with Victorian morality, its deep dissents, and the confused border-line between surface and depth, where he was liable to turn into the very thing he most deeply disliked, the smug father of the family, the Podsnappian averter of the eyes.

VI

He tells us that it was in the very midst of acting and producing *The Frozen Deep* that the idea of *A Tale of Two Cities* came to him. His wish to emphasize this point brings out the way in which the sharp turn back to the historical tale arrived through the deep perturbation of spirit he was undergoing at that time. What, then, was the relation of this tale to his emotions of rage, defiance, fear and desire as he felt himself impelled to the point of breaking with his past?

On the one hand, the deep nature of the breach with all his customary acceptances is driving him to make a comprehensive effort to grasp history in a new way—in direct as well as symbolic form. Nothing less will give him safety. And the fact of history he feels the need to grasp is the fact of revolutionary change, of basic conflict and resolution. Thus, the hidden dynamic of his previous work comes out into the open, inevitably expressing itself in terms drawn from the master, Carlyle. He looks to the French Revolution, partly because it is the great event of convulsive change from which his own world has come, and partly because Carlyle, his guide in matters of basic historical theory, has dealt with it. *The French Revolution*, we know, was a book which he had read and re-read till its story was indelibly imprinted on his mind; and now he wrote to Carlyle asking for a loan of the cited authorities. The story runs that Carlyle jokingly sent him all his reference books, "about two cartloads." And in his preface to the novel Dickens wrote:

It has been one of my hopes to add something to the popular and picturesque means of understanding that terrible time (the French

Revolution), though no one can hope to add anything to the philosophy of Mr. Carlyle's wonderful book.

But though this need to make a fundamental reconsideration of the nature of history was certainly central in the impulse that Dickens felt, it had to fuse with a more immediately personal nexus of emotions and images before it could take full grip of him. In the midst of his domestic troubles and play-acting he did not feel simply an intellectual need to revalue history. The desire to break through obstructions and mate with Ellen turned into a desire to write about the French Revolution because some image or symbol made Dickens feel a basic coincidence between his own experience and the Revolution. What was this image?

It was that of the Imprisoned Man in the Bastille.* The Lost Man who has been jailed so long that he has become an automaton of oppressed misery; who has forgotten even the source of his wrong, the cause of his misery; who needs to break out of the Bastille in order to become human again.

Here is the core of the novel. *A Tale of Two Cities* is built up from the story of Dr. Manette unjustly imprisoned, and its whole working out is concerned with the effects of that unjust imprisonment, which tangle all round the doctor and recoil back on him in unpredictable ways. The fate of the doctor is thus for Dickens both a symbol of the Revolution, its deeds, causes and consequences, and of himself, immured in a bastille of lies and cruelties, and seeking to break through into the truth, into a full and happy relationship with his fellows—to discover the trauma of the past which keeps distorting all aims and hopes. It was the frenzied sense of environing pressures, of an unjust, inescapable mechanism, which caught Dickens up in his wild play-acting and gave him a sense of release when he determined to write the novel. The writing, then, was part of the whole nexus of will and desire, revolt and fear, which carried him successfully into the arms of Ellen.

The title which Dickens originally intended to give the novel was *Recalled to Life*. Though he dropped this for the novel itself, he kept it for the first part, and it expresses the originating emotion of the story. Another proposed title, *Memory Carton*, shows the same idea from another angle—that

* It is perhaps not altogether irrelevant that in the years 1800–50 the common term of hatred for workhouses was "bastilles." The bastille prisoner was still the wronged and deserted child.

of the need to break through the layers of memory to the basic cause of the pang in order to achieve release, regeneration.

It has been pointed out (by T. A. Jackson) that there is a close underlying similarity between the plot of *A Tale* and that of *Little Dorrit*. Dorrit and Manette are both imprisoned for a score of years. Both are released by forces outside their own control, and continue tormented by their jail experiences. Dorrit is haunted by the fear of social exposure, which comes finally in the collapse of Merdle. He thus embodies Dickens's own fear of the past, his fear of being exposed; he also embodies the bad conscience of a whole society which dare not contemplate truly its origins (and his jailing is paired off with the self-imposed immolation of Mrs. Clennam in the puritanic house of greed). But in Manette the symbolism goes deeper still. The experience of oppressed misery has not merely twisted him, as it twisted Dorrit; it has broken down the whole system of memory. He is kept going by a blind exercise of the craft learned in the cell of oppression, and only the intrusion of events from the Revolution can bring him back to full consciousness and release him from the obsession. Then he finds that the bitterness engendered by his sufferings as an innocent wronged man has caught him up in a complex net, inside a larger reference of social action and reaction, from which escape is possible only after a great sacrifice has been made—in the person of Sidney Carton, who finds regeneration in death.

In this dire tangle of moral consequences we see Dickens facing up to his own confused situation and trying to equate his own moment of painful choice with the revolutionary moment in history when so high a price must be paid by both guilty and innocent for the rebirth of life, the renewal of love.

The lacerated and divided state of Dickens's emotions at this moment of choice is also revealed by the device of having two heroes who are practically twins in appearance and who love the same girl. Both Carton and Darnay are generous fellows, but one is morally well-organized, the other is fecklessly a misfit. Carton, however, by his devoted death reaches the same level of heroic generosity as his rival; his gesture of renunciation completes the ravages of the Revolution with its ruthless justice and transforms them into the act of purification and redemption, without which the life of renewed love would not be possible.

Thus, in the story, Dickens gets the satisfaction of nobly giving up the girl and yet mating with her. He splits himself in the moment of choice, dies, and yet lives to marry the beloved, from whom the curse born out of a tainted society is at last removed.

There is consequently a number of ambivalences in the story; and Dickens shows himself divided in his attitude to the Revolution. His petty-bourgeois fear of mass movements is still alive; but the fascination of such movements, which stirred so strongly in *Barnaby*, is even keener than his fear. On the one hand he clings to the moral thesis to defend the Revolution: the old regime was vilely cruel and bestialized people; it could not help provoking excesses in return as the bonds slipped. But this thesis, to which Carlyle had sought to give a grandiose religious tang, now merges for Dickens with a deeper acceptance.

Crush humanity out of shape once more under similar hammers and it will twist itself into the same tortured forms. Sow the same seed of rapacious license and oppression over again and it will surely yield the same fruit according to its kind.

Six tumbrils roll along the streets. Change these back again to what they were, thou powerful enchanter Time, and they shall be seen to be the carriages of absolute monarchs, the equipages of feudal nobles, the toilets of flaring Jezebels, the churches that are not my Father's house but dens of thieves, the huts of millions of starving peasants.

This passage begins with the simple moral statement; but then the tumbrils, conjured up as mere counterpoises to the feudal carriages, become emblems of a great purification sweeping away the reign of the old iniquity. They express a ruthless transformation of society; they are far more than an allegory of cruel tit-for-tat; they appear as forces of triumphant righteousness, changing line at the root.

Throughout the book there runs this ambivalent attitude towards the Revolution, shuddering, yet inclining to a deep and thorough acceptance. And the personal story, the symbolization of the whole crisis in Manette and his fortunes, makes a serious effort to work out the dialectics of give and take in the Revolution, the involved forces, the ultimate acceptance and resolution in death and love, in the renewal of life.

The working out of the clash of forces is, in fact, more carefully and effectively done than in any previous work. The weakness does not lie on this side, but lies in the comparative thinness of the characterization. The strain of grasping and holding intact the complex skein of the story is too much for Dickens at this difficult moment of growth. But his instinct, as usual, is right. He needed this stenuous intellectual effort to get outside himself, to master the difficult moment, to rebuild his foundations. After it he could return to the attack on his contemporary world with a new sureness, with new thews of drama, with new breadths of comprehension.

It is probable that the working on and acting in *The Frozen Deep* (the most serious effort at a tragic drama with which he was connected) had had its effect on helping to discipline his novel form. But in order to gauge that effect we must see the strenuous attempt at stage expression going on as part of his whole personal crisis, absorbing tensions from that crisis and returning them in modified shapes. The give and take between him (as writer, as man, as actor) and Wilkie was bound up with this whole phase of conflict in which *The Frozen Deep* played a key part. From now on he was aware of Wilkie's skill as plot organizer and set out to beat him, though it was not till *Edwin Drood* that the rivalry came into the open.

There is a statement of his which brings out clearly the way in which he linked the emergence from a state of imprisonment with revolutionary action. He declared that the two most dramatic descriptions in all literature that he could recall were, first, that "of the Woman in White appearing in the Hampstead Road after her escape from an asylum in Wilkie Collins's famous book," and second, "the stirring account of the march of the women to Versailles in Carlyle's *French Revolution*." The link between these two images (one of individual escape, the other of communal break-through) cannot be accidental; they stirred him so strongly because they touched a basic response. We may note further the nexus of ideas which equates the existing world with madness, dream, and sees the revolutionary moment as the break into a liberating consciousness, a new kind of group action. We are helped to grasp the reason for the extreme potency in Dickens's mind of the image of Dr. Manette and the way in which it raised for him the whole complex problem of the relationship of past and present, conscious and unconscious, repetition-compulsion and freedom. And the fact that it is the image of Woman (alone or in collective act) that stirs the deep response helps us to see how the issues of liberation were now more than ever also sexual issues.

What militated against the initial popularity of *A Tale* was the comparative thinness of characterization and the elements of revolutionary acceptance. Though many of the descriptive passages own a new power, there is little release of character-fantasy. Such persons as Manette, however, show a new persistence in Dickens of psychological analysis, and the Defarges show what untapped sources of dramatic force he could draw on.

The final evasion of the book's meaning came about through the successful melodrama based on its material, in which all emphasis was falsely put on Carton and the revolutionary truths sentimentalized away. This fake popularization is of importance, since it reveals very clearly the way in which the impact of Dickens's social criticism was deadened in England and the emphasis in his work industriously shifted by critics and readers to the superficial aspects of his work.

Lucie is meant to represent Ellen; but at this stage Dickens knows very little about the real Ellen, and Lucie is therefore a stock figure of heroine. Himself he has divided among Manette, Darnay, and Carton. Manette breaks out of the jail of the past, snared in a net of good and evil; Carton, aware only of wasted energies, goes into supreme renunciation, which is also the final working out of revolutionary justice; Darnay, after his goodness of heart has brought him to the edge of ruin in the revolutionary reversal of values, comes out into happy union.

Charles Darnay has the revealing initials C. D.

Once again we find that Dickens is in some sort following in Bulwer Lytton's tracks. The way in which his personal problem is split up among Manette, Darnay, and Carton suggests something of the method of *Zanoni*, in which all the characters are externalizations of one .or other dominant aspects of the creative struggle. (This semi-allegorical splitting up of the self is quite different from the relating of all characters to a total dynamic concept, which gives them a symbolic value as well as an individual reality. In Dickens both ways of unifying a work of art are present, the dramatic realization and the lyrical projection.) But though *Zanoni*, which, published in 1842, must have been well known to Dickens, doubtless exerted a certain general influence on the latter's method, its effect on *A Tale of Two Cities* can be traced in more precise ways.

Both novels deal with the French Revolution. Bulwer's attitude is far from that of Carlyle. With his odd type of Tory anarchism he abhors the Revolution politically, and tries to reduce it largely to a demented terrorism. But in the working out of his allegory he cannot help giving it further values, which in the end achieve something like a full acceptance of its action at deeper levels than that of intellectual judgment. Zanoni, the idealizing and integrating art activity, is opposed to old Mejnour, the contemplative and analytic mind. And both these figures are opposed to Glyndon, the emblem of art-science which strives to rise above convention and stereotype, but is stricken down by the fear that lurks below the threshold of all adventures into the unknown (the human future, the unconscious). Both Glyndon and Zanoni compete for possession of Viola (love, the affective life, union). The spiritual drama of their conflict is linked throughout with the convulsions of the Revolution. So Bulwer, despite his hectic denunciations of the terror, is in fact identifying the innermost struggle of human and artistic values with the struggle of revolutionary social forces.

In his story Viola is arrested in Paris at the height of the terror (through the jealous hauntings of Nicot and Fillide). Glyndon, whose contact with her was the direct cause of her danger, has fled; but Zanoni steps in and substitutes himself for her on the guillotine.

The derivation of *A Tale of Two Cities* from *Zanoni* is thus obvious. In the years between 1842 and 1859 Dickens's mind had transmuted the tensions and forms of *Zanoni* into something very different, but the umbilical cord remained. Whereas the story of *Zanoni* is frankly and wildly symbolic, *A Tale* has rationalized and psychologized the ingredients. Dickens, like Bulwer, wants to define the moments of personal pang and growth in terms of the revolutionary situation and to find thereby the clue to human and artistic renewal. In Bulwer the emblem of new life is the Child; in Dickens it is the United Lovers. For Bulwer, Zanoni must sacrifice himself to save the new life, because the idealizing activity has gone too far and has lost full human sympathy; and Glyndon must flee, because he is the artist who cannot break through fear into the new life. The book ends with the people breaking into the prison and coming upon the young mother and her babe.

Even in the riot of their joy, they drew back in astonishment and awe. Never had they seen life so beautiful; and as they crept nearer, and with noiseless feet, they saw that the lips breathed not, that the repose was of marble, that the beauty and the ecstasy were of death. They gathered round in silence; and lo! at her feet there was a young infant, who, wakened by their tread, looked at them steadfastly, and with its rosy fingers played with its dead mother's robe. . . .

Thus, the whole machinery of struggle has fallen away, but is destined to reappear in the new life as it develops—and because the new life is in fact *new*, the emotion it begets is hope of an enlarged happiness. At the same time its orphaned condition expresses the fact that the tremendous drama of Love, Creation, Revolution exists inside the framework of human continuity and must come back for its working out to "normal life."

In *A Tale*, with its less obvious allegory and its more direct acceptance of the Revolution, the romantic formulas of "lovers restored to one another" and the defeated curse are used; and it is the misfit, the man of wasted talents, who must make the sacrificial gesture. The restoration of love, being the defeat of the curse, is also the purification of memory, the conclusion of the Manette quest into evil and repetition-compulsion.

But though there are thus wide-reaching differences between the two books, *Zanoni* underlies *A Tale*; and by grasping its symbolism we can better understand both the impulse driving Dickens to his story and the wider significances of its theme.

Yet again a sharp light is thrown on Dickens's intentions by noting a contemporary work which has strongly influenced his conception. Behind *A Tale of Two Cities* stands *Zanoni* and Carlyle's *History*; but more immediately is entangled a less-known work, the play *The Dead Heart* by Watts Phillips, a minor playwright and artist of the day. Watts Phillips had been trained by Cruikshank at the time when that artist was illustrating *Oliver Twist*; he studied in Paris and was present during the February Revolution of 1848, when, though his political understanding was slight, he felt considerable sympathy for the insurgents; he also knew Carlyle's *History* well. His play in part derived from an episode in that *History* which certainly lay also behind *A Tale*.

I have a knowledge (from my long residence) of the French *people*, and know the literature of the revolution *well*. My only borrowing was from an incident related in Carlyle's history (concluding chapter of third volume) in which an old man, the Marquis de something, answers to the roll call in place of his son (who is asleep) and takes *his place in the tumbril*.

But memories of 1848 certainly gave the vivifying touch:

Glorious things are expected. Liberty *has* dawned on France. Hurrah! . . .

I came home last evening over the Pont Neuf, and stopped for some minutes to look at the crowd of buildings (the Cité) which formed the gloomy masses that stretched along the river's banks—the faint and flickering lights that shone on the dark waters—the tall towers of the various edifices, all so quiet and yet so grand in their indistinctness—when I was roughly disturbed in my meditations by crowds of fellows marching (from some banquet, I imagine) over the bridge, and roaring the revolutionary songs. No sooner were they passed than a body of the Garde Mobile succeeded, their bayonets glistening in the moonlight.

The *Ça ira* still ringing in my ears, I walked on, musing upon the scene, which might have been an extract from the drama of the First Republic; and when I looked up—standing in the old Place de la Révolution—I almost expected to see the tall, gaunt form of the guillotine, showing black against the sky, and blasting, like the upas, with its hideous aspect the passers by.

So he wrote in letters from Paris in 1848. He composed *The Dead Hand* some years before *A Tale*, though it was not produced till the year of the novel's publication, 1859, Boucicault had made an adaptation of Dumas's *Chevalier de la Maison Rouge*, in which the Bastille and the revolutionary crowd had appeared; and this was the probable reason for the delay in staging Watts Phillips's play. In April 1859 *A Tale* began its instalments, and Watts Phillips was at once dismayed.

Of course they will make a play of Dickens's new tale, *The Two Cities*, and (if you have read it) you will see how the character of the man "dug out" of the Bastille will clash with the man in *The Dead Heart* written more than three years ago. . . . The tone of the resurrection from the Bastille ought to have been *fresh* in my play, not in his story. It's very heartbreaking. (June 2nd.)

As a result, a speedy effort was made to produce the play, which was first acted on November 10, 1859. Then the later instalments of the novel turned out to have used the same *dénouement* as *The Dead Heart*—the substitution of one man for another at the guillotine, in an act of self-sacrifice.

A single theme may be used accidentally by novelists or playwrights; but when two main themes coincide and entwine (the resurrection from the living death of the Bastille and the sacrificial death), it seems likely that there is some direct contact. The death-substitution motive was certainly floating about. Dickens had *Zanoni* in mind, and something of the sort had occurred in Dumas's play, as also in *All for Her* by Palgrave

Simpson and Merivale. It is the combination of this motive with that of return to life which is surprising.

But there seems little doubt that Dickens had read or heard *The Dead Heart* long before beginning *A Tale*. The biographer of Watts Phillips says:

> The author, indeed, went so far as to say that the piece was "seen by Dickens long ago." It seems that when he first sent the piece to [the manager] Webster, the latter took it down to Brighton, and there read it to two or three friends, one of whom was the novelist.

This statement was never contradicted; and we may therefore assume that Dickens knew Watts Phillips's play and had been much moved by its conception, which he revived in his own form to express the crisis of change he felt in breaking with Kate.

What, then, had he got from *The Dead Heart*? The name itself gives a clue to the debt. The Bastille is in some sort the Dead Heart, which must break open with new life; and Dickens could not but feel much of his own plight in the romantically rent hero, Robert Landry, who begins as a hopeful young artist, is horribly changed by the hell of twenty years' imprisonment, returns to life, becomes a resolved revolutionary leader, and then finds release from his inner contradictions by a redeeming death. Here we meet a fully worked out theme, which Dickens breaks up and then recombines. Landry is Manette, Charles Darnay and Sydney Carton all in one: the sufferer, the reborn, the accuser of social evil, the revolutionary leader, the rent lover, the hopelessly divided romantic. Also, through the direct way in which for Watts Phillips the two Revolutions are merged, we get the contemporary link in a much more direct way than in *A Tale*.

This play, taken with *Zanoni*, thus gives us the full commentary on Dickens's intentions: his desire to find a pattern which would express both his own pang and the revolutionary conflicts of history.

And through it we can underline the extent to which Manette, Darnay, and Carton are all Dickens, all one person. Here, as in *Zanoni*, the emphasis is on the giving way of the old before the claims of the new. The revolutionary moment breaks open, the struggle which has been perpetuating against its own will an outworn conflict is abruptly ended, and only the new life remains. In *Zanoni* that theme was revealed in the symbol of the babe. Here it comes out in the fact that Landry dies to restore to Catherine Duval her son; the play ends with Catherine embracing the son and learning the truth about Landry by looking through the window to see him mount the guillotine. (By a stage device the prison walls slid away and the guillotine appeared: thus the two aspects, death and renewal, were brought together.)

The romantic hero, at the end of his tether, gives way to the youth who regains his mother. The hero is barred away and must go to death. (Note how the lost wife-mother chances to be a Kate.) In the play the *Zanoni* theme is redefined in a more rationally mature way, which is more assimilable to Dickens's own inner conflict. We see that the Manette-Darnay-Carton complex holds a father-son conflict, which is later to come out clearly in *Edwin Drood*. The romantic artist, perverted by suffering and yet turned into a strong revolutionary agent, finds his completion by making way for the young Baptiste. Dickens feels himself confronted by the younger generation, Wilkie Collins and Sala, who go easily into issues that are still baffling for him; and by the young girls, his daughters and their friends, and Ellen Lawless Ternan, who turn easily to the loves and laughters he has lost or never had. But he refuses to accept the *Zanoni* solution, the babe coming out of the prison-stone or Baptiste finding his mother's breast again in safety. He wants to share in the new life. So he splits up the Zanoni-Landry figure; and gives to Manette the horror and rebirth, the rigid accusation and the revolutionary conscience, and to Darnay and Carton the entangled conflict of love. So one half can lose, because then the other half wins. Carton-Dickens goes down and renounces; but Darnay-Dickens takes the girl and finds his place in society.

A Tale was dramatized, as Watts Phillips had feared, and the public saw the connection of the two stories:

The two plays caught on, and their resemblance to each other attracted universal attention, society divided itself into two factions —the Celestites and Dickensites, the Websterites and Phillipsites. Then came accusations and recriminations as to coincidences and plagiarisms, and bad blood arose on both sides. (Coleman.)

VII

A Tale of Two Cities had appeared in *All the Year Round* from April to November, 1859. Next year in December *Great Expectations* began, and ran on to August, 1861. The latter novel showed the result of the effort of concentration made in *A Tale*; its theme was worked out with a new economy and a new precision in the definition of entangled relationships. Dickens clearly felt at this point, after the overstrain of *A Tale*, the need to make another direct revaluation of his own experience, his childhood fancies; and so once more he returned openly to the Chatham-Rochester area. More, to help himself in his return to the personal theme after the epical canvas of *A Tale*, and to ensure that he kept to the point, he wrote in the first person as in *David Copperfield*. But his power of dramatic translation of the day-dream had greatly increased since 1849, and the personal material is much more surely controlled, related in a masterly way throughout to the social issue and the artistic problem.

I have already touched on the way in which Ellen appears in this book and by changing Dickens's attitude to women changes his art. From one angle the book records the sharp turn into disillusion that the great expectations of his love for Ellen have taken. "Is this cold and scheming creature the love which has haunted me all my life?" he asks. But in asking that question he inevitably asks a lot more questions. If the principle of love has deceived him, his whole attitude to himself and to society has been based on untenable conclusions. His whole life has been based on an illusion.

Hence the book becomes a thorough attempt at self-examination. "All other swindlers upon earth," says Pip, "are nothing to the self-swindlers, and with such pretences did I cheat myself." The pretences were the day-dream that the lovely girl haunting the house of mysteriously accursed wealth was destined for him and that he was chosen out of the ruck by the mistress of the house for the inheritance of higher things. In attacking these pretences, in revealing their falsehood, their basis in a distorted view of reality, he is attacking the heart of the day-dream which had carried him through his early years and had persisted to some extent right up to *A Tale*. In *Nickleby* he had assumed the romantic right of the hero to a life of unearned leisure; in *Chuzzlewit* the crisis of Martin was in some sort a crisis in the notion of the heritage. *Bleak House* showed in Richard Carstone the effects of living on hope to get an unearned place in life; and in *Little Dorrit* the sudden accession to unearned wealth devastates Amy's hopes, till the Merdle collapse releases her. A new type of hero slowly appears: the worried hard-working Arthur Clennam.

But now Dickens sharply turns back and confronts fully the basis of the romantic solution, the gaining of wealth and position by some chance event which reveals the "true heir." He declares it false from every aspect. The romantic heroine is, in fact, in his world a vicious careerist, and the romantic hero is a good fellow vitiated by his unjustified claims on life. He is a man who seeks to deny his origins in common life.

Once again Dickens, who in his own life was so deeply agitated by desire and fear of the past, desires to relive the Edenic day-dream and to show up the fear of exposure as unworthy and contaminated; one again he attempts to evalue the agitating thing. The shame of Dorrit, the deep terror of Manette, here becomes the day-dream evasion of Pip, who builds his life on a set of false assumptions which, if persisted in, mean the loss of manhood and honour, despair and perversion.

Thus, beginning as an image of Dickens himself, Pip becomes the emblem of his age. Once again Dickens fuses his inner conflict with the conflict of the world around him. Pip turns into an emblem of the deep and hopeless falsity of the Victorian world, the Great Expectations that throve so loudly after the Great Exhibition. Behind all the hopes of rising in the world, Dickens insists, there lies a murder of love, a degradation of human relationships. The term *Great Expectations*, indeed, has a dual reference—to the lie-based hopes of the post-1850 situation and to the defeated hopes of the 'forties. Dickens must have known some of the many variations of the song *There's a grand time coming, lads . . . Wait a wee bit longer*, of which his friend Charles Mackay wrote a version—the song that proclaimed the coming rule of freedom and plenty.

Unfortunately Bulwer Lytton argued Dickens out of the "unhappy ending" which he had intended; and Dickens imposed the romantic solution in modified form on a book which throughout was based on an unrelenting attack on such solutions. But this deformation of the end cannot effect the creative impact of the novel as a whole. Dickens in concise, uncompromising terms sets out the moral that has kept growing ever stronger since the flight of Little Nell with the Old Gambler: The system of capitalist society is based on the denial and distortion of human values. True, human beings are not everywhere broken down into money values, into things of the market; that is because the system cannot swallow everything. But the individual, in so far as he is a member of such a society, is distorted and internally rotted.

Here lies Dickens's greatness, in his capacity to grasp and understand this fact in all its fullness. Only Shakespeare before him had been able to live at this intense heart of the struggle of values. *Dickens maintains an unbroken faith in people with an entire pessimism as to capitalist society.*

Just as *A Tale of Two Cities*, when carefully examined, turns out to be in many ways the story of *Little Dorrit* translated into a revolutionary setting, so we find in *Great Expectations* many symbols carried over from *A Tale*. Manette, haunted into madness by the injustice of the past, is close to Miss Havisham, haunted into madness by the injustice of the past. Both are closed away from the world; one into the Bastille through an impotent attempt to redress a wrong, the other into self-imposed darkness through a broken heart. Both are driven into the creation of a curse that they end by fearing and wishing to end, in vain.

The curse of Manette, which, by its working out, symbolizes the contradictions of the Revolution, is thus one with the curse of Miss Havisham, which, by its working out, symbolizes the contradictions of capitalist society. In that society the primal curse of unlove works in a complex way, breaking some, partially distorting others, strengthening those who rebel or dissent. The struggle of Manette or Miss Havisham to break through the benumbing curse with its repetition-compulsions is one aspect of the whole struggle of life to renew itself despite the hell of capitalist relations. It conditions, it is an integral part of, the struggle of Darnay or Pip for love and self-respect. And this symbolism in turn reaches back to that of *Little Dorrit*, where the guilt-curse works through the self-imprisonment of Mrs. Clennam in the dark house of greed, which is doomed to fall; and that of *Bleak House* with its relation to the Tom-all-Alone of Dickens's childhood.

The fact that the inheritance turns out to be the gift of a ferocious criminal is an ironic twist; the discovery of the fact is a spasmic moment in the drive to self-consciousness. But there is a deeper irony in the fact that Pip the gentleman had been quite content to inherit, as he thought, from the crazed woman of the curse, and it is only when the contaminated money takes on an obviously reprobated social tint that he is driven into realization of the curse's effect upon him. His passion for Estella is thus revealed as the sexual form of the deep, evil, perverting society; and his masochistic self-immolation on her disdain becomes the expression both of his fall from human dignity and of his desire to save the suffering soul of humanity at whatever personal cost. For the person whose power of love has been murdered is the worst sufferer of all, has endured the worst wrong; and the impulse to accept pain from him or her is at least in part based in a wish to atone—to bring the sufferer to the point of awakening from the evil spell, the point of self-knowledge where the cruel act is confronted and acknowledged.

The wronged and suffering soul in the beautiful desired body —there seems the deepest possible contradiction, the most potent image of both the evil thing and the thing to be saved.

That is why Dickens in his relations with Ellen is forced to a sharpness of realization absent in his work before *A Tale*. She helps him to bring together with a new strength of awareness the elements which he had more intuitively assembled in *Little Dorrit*.

That, too, is why in the novel he gives Estella as mother a murderess. From no other womb could have been born the girl whose suffering soul seems to hold the fiercest contradictions of the contemporary world. And as a final touch of allegory he makes Magwitch, Pip's convict benefactor, her father. She is the child of murder and rapacious greed. Yet, in the story, her mother is shown as a woman whom we feel to have great depths of suffering, pride, and strength; and her father owns elements of good nature and gratitude which make him in the long run a more sympathetic character than the law-abiding citizens who wish to hound him down. In the tensions between the allegorical meaning of the characters in the story and their complexities as real people there develops a full dialectical sense of the process of transformation continually going on in society.

It is also worth noting that the imprisonment theme appears not only in Miss Havisham, but also in the convict and in the enslaved mother of Estella. The convict's effort to break the exclusion edict is what precipitates the revelation of real relationships.

One small detail, not without interest. When we bear in mind the magical nature of name associations for Dickens, we can hardly doubt that in Miss Havisham, the dispensing goddess of fortune in small Pip's eyes, there must be some connection with Mrs. Navisham, who had lived at 5 Ordnance Terrace, Chatham, and who was the Old Lady of Our Parish in Boz's *Sketches*. "She had a great number of pensioners"; on Saturday a levee of old men and women waited in the passage for their weekly gratuity; she contributed (lavishly by local standards) to charities; and when she entered church there was a "little bustle in the side aisle, occasioned by a general rise among the poor people." Mrs. Navisham thus seems the outstanding example in Dickens's childhood memories of a person liable to distribute valuable patronage, an elderly woman invested with a golden aura of unpredictable largesse.

We know that she took a special fancy to Charles's little sister Letitia, who was a very pretty child; and we have only to imagine some Micawber-like remark by John Dickens ("Whom would the old lady leave her money to? Letitia, her favourite?" or some such idea rising of its own accord in the mind of a small boy jealous of the attentions paid to his sisters, to find the origins of the Havisham fantasy.

The point is worth making, since it shows once more the obstinate lingering of Dickens's theme around childish hopes and fears, loves and losses, and the important part played by his sisters in his day-dream life. This glimpse of jealousy about the favoured Letitia helps us to understand the boy's relations to the gifted Fanny, and makes Estella at one level a sister-image.

Though *Great Expectations* carries on with the concentrated method of *A Tale of Two Cities*, it regains fullness. Once more the tumult of minor characters breaks in, slightly chastened, but owning all its old imagic energy. From Miss Havisham and Magwitch to Joe Gargery or Bill Barley, they have that extraordinary sense of inhabiting their own private worlds and yet impacting as units of society, which only Dickens can create. Outstanding are Jaggers and his man Wemmick; as usual, Dickens is at home in using the law and its henchmen as a microcosm of society, its forces and its constrictions. The skill with which he shows the conflict between their public selves, hard as nails, and their private selves full of sentiment, helps to give depth to the general critique of the novel: the revelation of the chasm between day-dream and reality, between aspiration and actuality, between the vision of love and beauty and the fact of spiritual crucifixion.

12

Final Judgment

I

IN July 1860, young Kate Dickens had married Charles, the brother of Wilkie Collins. Mrs. Dickens was not asked to the ceremony. Later in the month Dickens lost his brother Alfred, and took on the charge of the widow and her children. Old Mrs. Dickens had been weakening for some time. She was better, he said, on one of his visits; for "the instant she saw me she plucked up a spirit and asked me for 'a pound'!" A letter of August gives us a last exasperated glimpse of her decline.

My mother, who was also left to me when my father died (I never had anything left to me but my relations), is in the strangest state of mind from senile decay, and the impossibility of getting her to understand what is the matter, combined with her desire to be got up in sables like a female Hamlet, illumines the ghastly absurdity that is the chief relief I can find in it. Well, Life is a fight, and must be fought out.

He goes on with a reference to Wilkie Collins's mistress:

Wilkie has finished his *White Woman* (if he has done with his flesh-coloured one, I should mention that too) and is in great force.

In *Great Expectations* Wemmick says, "It's a good rule never to leave documentary evidence if you can help it, because you don't know when it may be put in." Dickens acted up to that principle this year by burning all the private letters in his possession "in a great holocaust" and crying, "Would to God every letter I had ever written was on that pile."

In March 1861, he began his second series of public readings, starting with six in St. James's Hall. As they went on, he slept "horribly" and found "his head dazed and worn out by gas and heat." The readings were a great success. Both as reader and actor, Dickens had the power of throwing himself into the parts with entire abandon, with an irresistible magnetic energy. For these six readings he cleared £500.

His interest in odd characters, especially those demented and solitary, was unabated. While staying at Lytton's house with Georgy and young Mary Dickens, he went to call on a rich recluse near Stevenage, who lived in filth with a "blanket and a skewer," crouching with staring eyes in a dirty kitchen.

His son Charley, sent to China, had returned, determined to marry Bessie Evans. Dickens strongly objected, but at last gave in, though he refused ever to enter the house of the young couple. He did not attend the wedding.

His very satisfactory tour manager fell ill, but another was found, who proved highly inefficient. Dickens went on a long tour which included East Anglian and Kent towns, Newcastle, Edinburgh, Liverpool, Torquay. His new Christmas story, which made use of the recluse he had visited, *Tom Tiddler's Ground*, sold some 300,000 copies. Then with the turn of the year he rushed off touring again: "perfectly astonishing" audiences.

In the spring he spoke at a banquet for the Artists' General Benevolent Institute, making a plea for the artist who must "win the battle of life with his own hands, and with his own eyes," using himself up in the process. To the newsvendors he spoke of the function of the newsman in preserving freedom. In July Georgina was ill. Dickens found rooms in Paris, and stayed there with her and Mamey. But even in Paris he found it hard to be happy. His old friends seemed all dead or exiled. Now "Victor Hugo is an old photograph in the shops with a quenched eye." Still, he read from his books at the British Embassy. Back in England, he spent Christmas at Gadshill, unable to work through the noise of the boys. "They boil over the house. By the end of January he dashed back to Paris and was happier, reading again at the Embassy and dreaming at Arras on his birthday about the "amiable seagreen Robespierre." He wept at the theatre and was taken "disfigured as he was by crying" into an actress's dressing-room. Then he made her weep copiously through his readings at Ary Scheffer's.

Then he is back in London, driven by the girls' excitement about the "season." Egg died, his mother died, his mother-in-law died. Thackeray died. Dickens sent another son out to India. And so on. These external events of the later years have little importance. His course is set. Old friends die off, and those who haven't died come on a visit. The children are a nuisance, though he likes the young girls. However, at parties he can still be the magnificent and charming entertainer of the young; and he likes to act the part of the Squire of Gadshill, arranging cricket matches and playing around with the many pets. He packs off yet another son to Australia; and sets up a Swiss chalet, gift of the actor Fechter, in the grounds of his house, so that he can write in a seclusion of green leaves, clouds, birds. He dashes off to Paris and his feet swell; he visits Bulwer Lytton, and they carry on with their scheme of benevolent houses for hard-up writers, which no writers ever want to inhabit. And so on.

At Gadshill he brings into a dance a friend disguised as a broken-down wandering musician, and himself dances with "simply immense" energy; and chases a bat out with a hip-bath in his hand. Strolls in the garden after breakfast with a cigar; writes till 3.30; then takes a long walk to Cobham Park or the marshes—sometimes with Georgy; makes gin-punch before bed. Aunt Letitia ("Betsy Trotwood all over") puts her foot through a floor being repaired, and two stable-men have to haul her out. Charley starts a *Gadshill Gazette*; but when he sends a poem into *All the Year Round*, his father rejects it. And so on.

Only three things still mattered. Ellen, and readings, and work. Ellen and the readings had the more nagging hold; for between August 1861 and his death he wrote only one completed novel, *Our Mutual Friend*. To a large extent the readings had become a substitute both for living and working; they turned into a sheer drug, a stimulus that led nowhere except to a greater need of itself. Throughout his career we have seen the desire for direct use of the mimetic faculty, a direct contact with audiences. But though this desire clearly came out with special strength at moments of discontent and unbalance, and accentuated them, it did not become a dominant and continuously unsettling element in his life till after the break with Kate.

There were many factors conspiring to produce this state of mind. From early in his career we can detect a fear that his writing vein will dry up and a wish to have acting to fall back on. This fear grew stronger at moments throughout the fifties, and became urgent after the break with his wife. He had the feeling of a whole herd of relatives and children battening on him, using up his money; and this feeling was one factor in turning him against the fertile Kate. A sense of maddening economic pressure never left him.

The document he published after the break shows how intimate he felt the relation between himself and the public. The break, which was as much a break with Victorian values as with Kate, made him terrified that he was going to lose his hold on his public. For, apart from the direct shock of the break on that public, he knew, deep inside himself, that he could only write when passionately moved by a theme, a symbol, and that the task of keeping true to his themes and symbols, while at the same time holding his public, was going to be tougher than ever. Simultaneously he felt a fear of completely drying up and of finding himself isolated from his public. This fear, reaching deep down into the creative depths, coincided with the economic fear.

Hence the tremendous !satisfaction gained by the readings. Not only did they bring in good sums of money without any further need of writing; they also gave him direct proof of his unslackening hold on the people. The response that he got to every fine point of humour or emotion was the living proof of his unity with the people; and now that he had faced more and more up to his total rejection of the ruling values in his society, the more and more he felt the need of this response from the people themselves. It gave him a sense of safety without which he could not have continued his work, and yet it got in the way of his work by directing his energies along new channels, setting up a give and take which became an end in itself as well as a stimulus and reassurance. The mechanism set up to protect him from fear had to keep on working all the while, instead of being able to do its job and then give way to his creative work.

This development in one way is a logical result from the peculiarly dynamic relation that Dickens had reached with his public; it represents a one-sided emphasis in that relation. The by-product of the creative energies, so to speak, has taken over the place of those energies themselves. As soon as he stops the direct contact, he finds, not a clear space for renewed creative work, but a need to go on with the contacts.

Behind this urgency lay his guilty conscience over Ellen; but behind his connection with Ellen lay his whole need to break with existing social relationships. Hence his dilemma. He has broken away; and yet if he is to continue his work he must find some new line of contact, some ceaseless reassurance of love from the people.

II

Much of his life was now concealed from the eyes of all but a small group of close friends. His habit of wandering round in strange places at strange times of the day or night went on; and he had a secret retreat in an apartment close to the "Five Bells" at the corner of Hatcham Park Road and New Cross Road. Nearby was a deaf and dumb establishment which inevitably caught his interest (and appeared in *Dr. Marigold's Prescriptions*, 1865). He had now, in 1864, started a new novel, *Our Mutual Friend*, and set a number of its scenes in this locality.

Among his nieces was Emily Barrow, a pretty young girl with a pretty young friend, Charlotte Elizabeth Lane. Both girls went to a school in Lewisham High Street where they were taught French, music and dancing. Somehow Emily found out that Dickens had his apartment near the "Five Bells," and, taking Charlotte with her, called on him. Dickens liked her; he liked them both. He asked them to call at Gadshill. He took them round, and among other entertainments carried them into the Bank of England to see "the gold being shovelled up with shovels." Emily, Charlotte and Emily's sister became frequent visitors at Gadshill; and Charlotte, after rejecting Emily's brother, ran off with a young Deptford schoolmaster.

This renewed contact with young girls certainly helped Dickens to regain his balance after the sexual bitterness of *Great Expectations*. Emily and Charlotte mingled something of their gay selves with the image of Ellen in order to beget Bella Wilfer (and later the mixture reappeared, in lighter measures, in Rosa Budd). Emily had no doubt chattered excitedly at the spectacle of the endless gold in the Bank; Ellen, Dickens knew, had a way of getting the gold into her fingers. So Bella in the novel "thought, as she glanced at the mighty Bank, how agreeable it would be to have an hour's gardening there with a bright copper shovel, among the money." The schools that Dickens described in the novel were obviously set in the "Five Bells" area; and the chatter of Miss Peecher and Mary Anne seems to derive from the babble of Emily and Charlotte about their school lives.

When the girls were at Gadshill they watched reverently the moods of the great man.

He would sit at the table oblivious of all seated near him and it was difficult at such times to get him to enter into any conversation. It would almost appear as though he were in a temper if anyone spoke to him. Then he would suddenly push back his chair; leave the table while in the middle of a meal, hurry off to his writing, and sit for an hour or two.

III

Our Mutual Friend, to which Dickens at last nerved himself, is in many ways his supreme work. It lacks the concision and dramatic close texture of *Great Expectations*; but instead it owns a spacious breadth of definition. Even the elements of turbid confusion contribute to the total effect, in which a complete judgment on the life of Dickens's world is delivered. Nothing less than the conjuring up of the whole of society, its tangled cross-currents and involved patterning, will suffice for such a definitive vision. At moments he seems tiring; but always he pulls himself together in time. The result is one of the greatest works of prose ever written. A work which finally vindicates Dickens's right to stand, as no other English writer can stand, at the side of Shakespeare.

Dombey, Bleak House, and *Little Dorrit* had been mature works before this, in which he attempted a broadly based picture of the human condition and Victorian society. The first had shown the withering effects of the money-ethic on human values; the second, taking the law as the symbol of the State and all its powers, had uttered a basic rejection of the existing State form; the third had dealt with the lie, the rottenness of guilt and fear, at the social core. In *Our Mutual Friend* Dickens resumes all these judgments in a huge involved novel, in which he carries his forms, artistically and emotionally, to their limit of significant expansion. The fundamental contrast in all his writings, between the vileness of all existing forms of State organization and the indomitable powers of renewal in man, is here carried to breaking point.

The central idea of *Our Mutual Friend* is the struggle for a dust-heap. Rubbish in the mid-Victorian period was a valuable product for contractors, but a curse for Londoners. Such removals as went on were the work of private agents who collected the dust and rubbish in dumps in North London (roughly in the area now filled by King's Cross and St. Pancras stations). These dumps were sifted for rags, cinders and fine dust—for paper-making, for fuel to smelters, for concrete-making. No doubt the idea for the novel came through a paragraph in the newspapers which told of a very large fortune left by one of the dust contractors. But the reason why a chance jest was felt by Dickens to provide the main theme for his most serious novel was because the notion of wealth as a foul dust-heap, over-which men spent their time struggling, stirred his deepest ironies. The equation of money and filth or dung goes far down in the psyche, as dream-analysis has shown. In using the dust-heap as the emblem of the great prize for which men were fighting, Dickens starts off with a fantasy-image which fitly utters his contempt and hatred. (At the same time his own increasing obsession with the readings as a money source means an element of self-contempt driving him on into the attack.)

But there is a further point in the choice. Since the early days of his reporting, Dickens had used the term "dust-heap" to express his contempt and hatred of Parliament, of the whole State system. And indeed, William Morris, who was soaked in Dickens's imagery, carries on the image; in his lecture *Communism* he speaks of England as "a counting-house on the top of a cinder-heap, with Podsnap's drawing-room in the offing." The citation of Podsnap shows how definitely he was drawing on the Dickensian myth. In *Hard Times* it appears in a variation: "He [Gradgrind] then returned with promptitude to the national cinder-heap, and resumed his sifting for the odds and ends he wanted, and his throwing dust into the eyes of other people who wanted other odds and other ends—in fact, resumed his parliamentary duties."

The fight for the dust-heap, the intrigue over the inheritance of the dust-heap, is thus in one sense an allegory of the struggle for control of the State. Clearly, this is a point which must not be pressed too far. There is no carefully worked out allegorical scheme; but at the same time there can be no doubt that much of the originating dynamic of the theme comes from these hidden significances of the dust-heap for Dickens. It draws its sources from a deep imagery-cluster from which come also the *"merde"* of Merdle and the rags and bones of Krook, the symbolic Lord Chancellor of *Bleak House*, on the one hand, and, on the other, the paternal grave of *Copperfield*—". . . and the light upon the window of our room shone out upon the earthly bourne of all such travellers, and the mound above the ashes and the dust that once was he, without whom I had never been."

IV

The plot of *Our Mutual Friend* deals with the confusions resulting from the misanthropic behaviour of the owner of the dust-heap, who disinherited his son, then apparently relented. The relenting is, however, only a mask for a further expression of hatred. The son, John Harmon, is to inherit part of the property only if he marries a girl whom his father is sure will harry him in a married hell. This son seems to have been drowned; in fact, he is alive but remains hidden because he wants to find out about the girl without her knowledge. The faithful worker, Boffin, thus seems the sole inheritor; and the coming into fortune perverts his whole character. (The perversion turns out only to be an assumption; but at this point we fail to believe the story. Through its allegorical necessities Boffin has to pretend hard-heartedness in order to bring about the salvation of the wilful Bella; and his return to good nature is bound up with the return of the lost son to his proper status, his return into life and identity. But the picture of the perversion through wealth has been too true, too effectively done. In point of fact we feel two Boffins. One the worker perverted into greed and cruelty through partaking of money-values; and the other the worker who carries intact through the pressures of circumstance his good heart, his love, and who emerges as *deus ex machina* at the crucial moment of human change.)

The Change of Heart, or Reversal of Values, is the theme that lies at the root of the tale of the fight for the dust-heap. Mixed with the larger issues is Dickens's hope that Ellen will be redeemed into a creature of love and devotion. But what gives force to this central theme are various outlying themes that move in and merge with the general issue. These include the blackmail schemes of Wegg, who shows the hopelessly perverted underdog; the domestic miseries of the Wilfer household, pivoted on the constricting effects of poverty; Betty Higden's horror of the workhouse; Jenny Wren's crippled dilemma born out of poverty and drunkenness; the tangle of blackmail and murder on the waterside; the anguish of Bradley Headstone, whose love-frustration is only one aspect of the whole false turn taken by society, which has pushed him into a distorting situation. All these sub-plots or accretions are derived from the main theme, the effects of the money-ethic on human beings; they show the various reactions from poverty, and the crippled body of the devoted Jenny is balanced by the crippled mind of the schoolmaster Bradley.

The latter is specially important for the working out of the theme. On him weighs the main burden of murderous distortion, driving him into violence; and he shows how far Dickens had advanced in criticism of his society and its methods. The boy who has risen in the world and educated himself is no longer a figure of admiration. What Dickens now sees in him is the distortion of the human essence, which might have had a better chance of salvation if he had remained at the level of Jenny and Betty. By bettering himself he has destroyed himself; he has become a frenzied cog in a mechanistic universe of phoney knowledge and money-values. Dickens, in his picture of this frustrated man, makes a decisive rejection of Victorian educational methods, the whole outlook which imagined progress as mechanistic reduplication and which wanted education to further a false concept of man.

Hence the pathos of the devotion of the poor to an ideal of education which can only distort their outlook on life. Old Hexam hates education, but his girl Lizzie scrapes and contrives in order to get her brother educated to the level of pupil teacher. The nemesis is that she thus becomes drawn into the orbit of Bradley Headstone's frustration, and his murderous passion encircles her. The fight for Lizzie thus becomes the human aspect of the dehumanizing fight for the dust-heap. Bradstone is entangled in his own net of evil; and Lizzie comes through into happiness. Her triumph is another aspect of the "coming back to life" of the lost son who has the rightful claim to the dust-heap. It therefore involves further consequences: the drawing of Eugene Wreyburn into faith, love, energy.

Here again we see the change in Dickens's attitude. At first glance Eugene is the type that Dickens has most pilloried in the past, the aristocratic idler who can't find anything worth doing. But how can Dickens, in his gnawing hatred of all the ways out that the world can offer, now turn to make fun of such a man as Eugene? On the contrary, he finds a deep sympathy with his attitude. But he is too profound an artist to remain at passive sympathy for the misfit, the person who finds all social activity absurd and worthless. What interests him is the process whereby Eugene, the rebel misfit, can be brought into acceptance of life and love.

Eugene falls in love with Lizzie, the poor and illiterate girl. Dickens is in deadly earnest, and he sees nothing to satirize in Lizzie. Here he comes down to bed-rock. In Lizzie he touches on the fundamental element of aspiring and accepting love in human nature, which the working-class basis preserves and develops. Through her Eugene regains his self-respect and finds a purpose in life.

Thus the romantic themes of the lost heir and recovered identity are given a new direction by being merged with the complementary themes of Bella's redemption from the money-ethic and Eugene's redemption from loss of purpose by union with the working-class girl.

As usual, Dickens has distributed his divided emotions among various characters. On the one hand he is the declassed Eugene who finds regeneration by mixing with the great stream of common life. He is the man who comes up out of the dead in order to mate with the redeemed beloved. (The theme of the drowned man who turns out to be alive is thus a version of the previous series of imprisoned people who break through, or escape only by an apocalyptic death, from a life become murderously constrictive. And as usual there is doubling of the motive. As in *A Tale of Two Cities*, the resurrection of life is expressed both in the psychological theme of Manette and in the physical theme of body-snatching by resurrection men, so in *Our Mutual Friend* the return to life is expressed both in the theme of the Rokesmith guising and in the physical theme of Riderhood body-trade.) Against this movement upwards there is the movement down of Riderhood and Headstone, who go down into the waters of death, from which the hero has arrived. Dickens is Headstone, the frustrated lover, whose rising in the world has only led to an impasse and who cannot break through. The image of Quilp emerges from the dark waters to merge with Headstone and drag him down.

Against the images of poverty and its effects of good and evil there is set the class of the impenetrably smug Veneerings, with the adventurer Lammles and the dim aristocrat Twemlow among the trimmings, and with Podsnap as the supreme expression of their bland brutality and dehumanized values. Here Dickens completes the picture he had drawn in *Little Dorrit* of the ruling sections of Victorian society as irredeemably damned. Here the final mastery of his method shows itself, his power to use a fantasy-invention of character to depict class-types and to set the "human beings" over against this background as against the essential forces at play on their struggling lives as they love, fear, and yet love.

The conscious political attitude to which he had come in these years is plainly stated in a paper of 1867 in which he praises co-operative activity among the workers and makes a furious onslaught on patronage. "Whatever is done for the comfort and advancement of the working man must be so far done by himself as that it is maintained by himself." And in the last public speech he gave before his death he reiterated his illimitable faith in the people and his total lack of any sort of faith in the governing classes.

V

Under the strain of his revolt and his anxious love for Ellen, Dickens's health worsened. While writing *Great Expectations* he suffered from sleeplessness and "distressing pains in the face." In the midst of writing *Our Mutual Friend* his train accident occurred, which had a bad effect in deepening his anxiety. He had gone to France with Ellen and her mother and on the way back they were in the train that toppled into the river at Staplehurst, near Maidstone. The Folkestone train passed by accident over a bridge where the line was under repair: eight of fourteen carriages plunged into the stream. Dickens's carriage "was caught upon the turn by some ruin of the bridge, and hung suspended and balanced in an apparently impossible manner. Two ladies (Mrs. Ternan and Ellen) were my fellow-passengers, an old one and a young one." Mrs. Ternan called, "My God." Ellen screamed. "I caught hold of both of them" and begged them to compose themselves. They were huddled down in a corner of the inclined carriage. Dickens climbed out with great caution and stood on the step, looking down into the sheer drop. People were jumping through windows into the swamp. Dickens at last caught the attention of one of the guards, who were running wildly about, and got him to unlock the door. They got out and Dickens went round with brandy trying to restore the injured. He gave brandy to a cut-about man, who died.

Then I stumbled over a lady lying on her back against a little pollard tree, with the blood streaming over her face (which was lead-colour) in a number of distinct little streams from the head. I asked her if she could swallow a little brandy and she just nodded, and I gave her some and left her for somebody else. The next time I passed her she was dead. Then a man . . . came running up to me and implored me to help him find his wife, who was afterwards found dead. No imagination can conceive the ruin of the carriages or the extraordinary weights under which people were lying, or the complications into which they were twisted up among iron and wood, and mud and water.

Dickens behaved with much presence of mind—though doubtless it would have been better for the injured if he had known the probable effects of brandy on cases of bad shock. In his postscript to *Our Mutual Friend* he mentions that Mr. and Mrs. Boffin were involved in the accident, but came through undamaged.

The after-effects were acute. The experience, wrote his son Henry, "left a shock upon his nervous system from which he never quite recovered. I have seen him sometimes in a railway carriage when there was a slight jolt. When this happened he was in a state of panic and gripped the seat with both hands." Yet, through his readings, he had continually to travel about by train, all the while fighting down his fear.

Finally, when he died in 1870, he died on the anniversary of the railway accident. He did not die of anything in particular; he collapsed and died. He died of some sort of internal shock. He died by living through the railway accident again. Why?

Earlier in this book I pointed out how strong in Dickens was the image of the train as a revenging force, a nemesis, a monster coming up behind him and ravaging all the green of the past. It was not by chance that he threw the seducer Carker under a train. Now he himself was the seducer, in the very train with the girl he had seduced, and the train crashed. What experience could have more strongly concentrated his sense of guilt, all the fears and anxieties that kept afflicting after he had made his break with Kate and taken up with troublesome Ellen? The blow from the unconscious, the blow from the outraged forces of Authority, had struck him down.

It must not be forgotten, too, that the railway was in fact the greatest visible force destroying the old world. "To the rail is due principally much of the changed appearance of London," said T. A. Trollope, reviewing the vast difference between the world of his childhood and that of his old age; and he, too, takes up a horror-image ("marvelling at the ubiquitous railway bridges and arches, which seem to return again and again like the recurring horrors of a nightmare dream") to express his early feelings. This attitude is basic in Dickens. The train is both creator and destroyer, emblem of industrial activity.

Then, the train rattled among the housetops, and among the ragged sides of houses torn down to make room for it, and over the swarming streets, and under the fruitful earth, until it shot across the river, bursting over the quiet surface like a bombshell, and gone again as if it had exploded in the rush of smoke and steam and glare.

A little more, and again it roared across the river, a great rocket. (*Our Mutual Friend.*)

Thus, in the conviction of menace from this force, he is feeling the basic anxiety-pressure born from his antagonism to the existing (capitalist) world; and while the fear contributed much to his break up, it also played its part in driving him to the final courageous confrontation of the evil world and all its menace, in *Our Mutual Friend* and *Edwin Drood*.

The increasing anxiety-pressure drove him even more assiduously out on his readings. In 1866 his doctor told him that he was suffering from "irritability of the heart." One of his legs hurt him badly, and he was lame; he was threatened with erysipelas. He drank iron, quinine and digitalis to get his heart contracting healthily. Then he rushed off on another reading tour.

He threw himself more nervously than ever into his performance. Carlyle, who saw the first of the new series of readings, said that he made "a whole tragic, comic, heroic *theatre* visible, performing under one hat, and keeping us laughing—in a sorry way some of us thought—the whole night." Rushing all over Britain, suffering from bad catarrh, he was continually in railway trains. Dolby, the new manager, saw that whenever the train went fast Dickens started writhing with fear. But the tours went on.

The year 1867 opened with another tour of forty-two performances. He kept going with oysters and champagne, but couldn't sleep. His colds went on, and he fought against fainting fits. But he wouldn't stop reading. He even asked local M.P.s and Chatham officers to Gadshill for Christmas to hear him reading. He went on reading in London and in the provinces. He determined to go and read in America. Late in 1867 he crossed the Atlantic once more. He read in city after city and made huge sums. His colds were exhausting, but he refused to give in. He lived on cream and rum for breakfast, sherry-cobbler in the morning, a pint of champagne at three, and an egg beaten up in sherry before the reading; for supper, soup, wine, and (generally) laudanum.

Back at Gadshill, he filled his chalet with glasses, which "reflected and refracted in all kinds of ways the leaves quivering at the windows, the fields of waving corn, and the sail-dotted river." He felt used up. By June he feels that the Christmas story is beyond him: "I cannot raise the ghost of an idea. I am in a positive state of despair." He feels he can only reproduce "the old string of stories in the old inappropriate bungling way." He ended by giving up.

Now he was afraid of getting on horseback. He feared some sort of seizure. He decided to get rid of his pet son Plorn by bundling him off to Australia with a New Testament. Georgina took a strong line; she wanted to get rid of the sons, who couldn't help feeling some partizanship for their mother. Henry, the one son who seemed to have any independent energy, went to Cambridge. "You know you are one of many heavy charges on me," Dickens wrote to him. Charley had gone bankrupt.

Dickens signed a contract for a hundred readings at £8,000; and then, as the prospect of general elections caused a halt in the programme, he took the fatal and revealing step of incorporating the murder scene from *Oliver Twist* in his repertory. He tried the new item out on a special audience in November. He impersonated Fagin, Morris Bolter, Bill Sykes and Nancy, with hypnotic power. Dickens had been warned that if one woman fainted at the murder moment, there would be a rush of hysteria all over the hall; but he refused to be deterred. The morning after the first performance a friend wrote, "I am bound to tell you that I had an almost irresistible impulse upon me to scream and that if anyone had cried out I should have followed."

So the murder went into the list of scenes to be given.

The year 1869 opened with a tour in Ireland, on which Dickens took Georgina with him. Then came the west country. All the while the fascination of acting out the murder was getting stronger. Dolby protested. Dickens put up the weak defence that it had become "a kind of hobby."

They went up to Scotland (and in the train he suffered "thirty thousand shocks to the nerves"); then to Liverpool, and so on. At Birmingham he was delighted at the way workers stopped him in the street and thanked him for his work. At Blackpool a fit of giddiness caught him, and then his left side began to go dead at Chester. A schizophrenic break up was threatening. He had to stop in the middle of the tour and return to Gadshill.

VI

The obsession with the violent murder scene showed that at last he was weakening in the struggle and that his inner conflict was growing knotted into a neurosis. Behind it lay the whole impulse of instability which had driven him into the readings.

Though he was fretting about money, there was no longer any real economic need for his displays, but he couldn't stop. After the Staplehurst accident the process of break-down was speeded up, and his anxieties clotted round the murder scene. He wanted to make the show of himself before the world as a murderer, to take the woman by the throat, and yet himself to be the woman who was strangled. He was enacting out before everyone his inner drama of despair, of hate and frustration.

The social significance of this murder obsession is clarified by some of the papers he had written in the later 1850's, as he was approaching the point of breaking with Kate. Here he shows a deep-rooted sense of existing society as a murder conspiracy. In *The Murdered Person* (1856) he writes fiercely of law and the State as organized to murder people. He takes as example the law of divorce, and describes the advocates of the existing state of things as murderers:

They utter homilies without end upon the good side of the question, which is in no want of them; but, from their exalted state of vision the murdered person utterly vanishes. The tortures and wrongs of the sufferer have no place in their speeches. They felicitate themselves, like the murderers, on their own glowing state of mind, and they mount upon the mangled creatures to deliver their orations. . . .

He goes on to accuse the advocates of Sunday observance, the men who deny the workers a chance of relaxation and entertainmant. They, too, are murderers.

The murdered person—the consumptive, scrofulous, rickety worker in unwholesome places, the wide prevalence of whose reduced physical condition has rendered it necessary to lower the standard of health and strength for recruiting into the army . . . the murdered person, in this phase of his ubiquity, is put out of sight, as a matter of course.

And he accuses Parliament and the State of being the supreme murderer. Enter Parliament any night, he says,

and you will observe the murdered person to be as comfortably stowed away as he ever is at Newgate. What In said to Out in eighteen hundred and thirty-five, what Out retorted upon In in eighteen hundred and forty-seven, why In would have been Out in eighteen hundred and fifty-four but for Out's unparalleled magnanimity in not coming in, this, with all the contemptible ins and outs of all the Innings and Outings, shall be discoursed upon, with abundance of hymns and paeans on all sides, for six months together.

But, the murdered old gentleman Time, and the murdered matron, Britannia, shall no more come in question than the murdered people do in the cells of the penitents—unless, indeed, they are reproduced . . . to show that they were expressly created for the exaltation of the speech-makers.

These statements are important in giving us an insight into the symbolism of murder in Dickens's work. In finding himself driven to enact the Nancy murder before his public he was not following out some chance impulse. As his grip on himself deteriorated and he was no longer able to unpack himself in work, it was inevitable that his show-compulsion should take this form, in which he both revealed his own deepest frustration and at the same time accused society.

His union with the people, his love, was thus also a hatred of Victorian society, the State and its money-ethic of alienation. In the horrible scene that he ached to enact he mimed his final judgment on himself and his world.

VII

Twice or thrice a week, when at Gadshill, he went over to spend the night with Ellen at Windsor Lodge. In his enforced leisure he found the strength to turn back to writing, and *The Mystery of Edwin Drood* was conceived. The first number appeared in April 1869, and to his delight he found himself carried off once more by a story. He had brooded long over a complex mystery, and felt that at last he had devised a watertight tale of horror and suspense which would be able to stand up against the inventions of the capable Wilkie Collins. Above all he had in mind the recently successful work of that writer, *The Moonstone*, which had turned his thoughts to the possibilities in Eastern themes.

The story, set in Cloisterham (Rochester), concerns the disappearance of Drood under conditions that look like murder. There is no mystery about the person responsible for the crime, who is Jack Jasper, the organist. Jasper is madly in love with Rosa Budd and seeks to throw suspicion on Neville Landless. The doubtful points are: Was Drood really killed or did he somehow escape, in order to burst out of the tomb to the confounding of Jasper? Who is Datchery, the odd detective who turns up to haunt Jasper? Is he Drood himself or Helena Landless in disguise? And, most important of all, what is the full motivation of Jasper? Is it simply a mad jealousy, or is the jealousy one aspect of a spiritual derangement of much wider significance?

How the story was to work out in detail has been debated at vast length, but need not concern us here. What we want to know is the meaning of this fragment in Dickens's work, what it adds to our understanding of him as man and artist.

The most interesting theory is that Jasper was in fact a Thug, and that his effort to kill Drood was a sort of ritual murder as well as an act of jealousy. There is much reason to believe that this notion is correct. Beyond doubt, in *Edwin Drood* Dickens is setting him deliberately up against Wilkie Collins and his method of mystery suspense; he has changed his whole method of writing and is trying to regain power and purpose by matching himself with the young writer whose work had been so much in his mind for many years. *The Moonstone* (published in *All the Year Round*), with its background of mystery fermenting in the religious life of India, was certainly one of the objects of his rivalry, but he also had a number of Collins's other books in mind, *No Name* and *The Woman in White*.

We know that he had read and thought about Thuggery. Meadows Taylor, a contributor to his weekly, had written *The Confessions of a Thug*; and in *Le Juif Errant*, by Sue, certainly known to him, a Thug appears as a character. In Thug ritual a victim had to be sacrificed to the goddess Kali in a certain way: he had to be a guest on good terms with the killer, and he had to be strangled by a white silver-weighted scarf thrown on him from behind. Further, the body should be stripped and buried in a hidden place made ready for it.

The careful emphasis which Dickens puts on Jasper's scarf in the murder night is explicable only on the hypothesis that Jasper is a Thug or aspires to become one. (He told Fildes, "I must have the double necktie! It is necessary, for Jasper strangles Edwin Drood with it.") Dickens, in his usual way, prepares for the disclosure of Oriental origins in the mystery by providing many links with the East. Neville and Helena come from Ceylon and are at least to some extent Singhalese; and Drood sneers at Neville, "You are no judge of white men." Drood himself is intending to go out to Egypt, and in his cool semi-insolent way talks about the white man's mission in bringing industrial techniques to the backward races. As an engineer, he is "going to wake Egypt up a little." Above all, Jasper is enigmatically entangled with the East, and it would be no surprise if he were to turn out a Eurasian himself. He is an opium-smoker, in whose consciousness the boundary between actuality and the dream is shifting and unstable. We first meet him in the den of Opium Sal (based on a real person, Lascar Sal) among Orientals; and in the opening paragraph of the novel with extreme felicity Dickens establishes the dream-basis of his consciousness, in which English cathedral quiet and Eastern tumult are madly mingled:

An ancient English Cathedral Tower? How can the ancient English Cathedral Tower be here? The well-known, massive, grey, square tower of its old Cathedral. How can that be here! There is no spike of rusty iron in the air, between the eye and it, from any point of the real prospect. What is the spike that intervenes, and who has set it up? Maybe it is set up by the Sultan's orders for the impaling of a horde of Turkish robbers, one by one. It is so, for cymbals clash, and the Sultan goes by to his palace in long procession. Ten thousand scimitars flash in the sunlight, and thrice ten thousand dancing-girls strew flowers. Then follow white elephants caparisoned in countless gorgeous colours, and infinite in number and attendants. Still the Cathedral Tower rises in the background, where it cannot be, and still no writhing figure is on the firm spike. Stay! Is the spike so low a thing as the rusty spike on the top of a post of an old bedstead that has tumbled all awry? Some vague period of drowsy laughter must be devoted to the consideration of this possibility.

The basic tensions of the novel's theme are there—a strange unapprehended conflict between India and Cloisterham. This new orientation of symbolism shows once more how deeply directed by the historical process was Dickens's choice of subject. Just as he had felt himself driven to America in 1842 in order to find out the full truth of the money-ethic, and to the Continent a few years later to get the feeling of the new expansive world situation, so he now turned his thoughts towards Asia, in a period when the forms of exploitation were rapidly becoming imperialist.

When we grasp this point, I think we can be reasonably sure that Datchery with the obvious wig and hidden hands is Helena Landless in disguise. Early in the book Dickens has planted the information that Helena likes in emergency to dress as a male. Several times she and her brother have run away, and "each time she dressed as a boy, and showed the daring of a man." Her courage and resourcefulness are stressed. Once, in the proofs, Dickens struck out the words, "and she is a truly brave woman," in order not to give the show away too easily. But he left the passage in which she unflinchingly measures herself against Jasper. "You would be afraid of him, under similar circumstances, wouldn't you, Miss Landless?" asks Edwin; and she replies scornfully: "Not under any circumstances." Further, when Rosa collapses and throws herself on Helena's protection, "There was a slumbering gleam of fire in the intense dark eyes, though they were then softened with compassion and admiration. Let whomsoever it most concerned look well to it!" A direct warning that she will be out for Jasper's blood.

Dickens had intended to call her Olympia Heyridge or Heyfort; names obviously intended to bring out her imperious and lofty character. When he turned from their too obviously manufactured look and chose Helena Landless, he cannot have been unaware of the link with Ellen Lawless, but some compulsion drove him into the tell-tale change: the magical feeling for names, the sense that he must play fair with the enigma he was seeking to solve, the perverse wish to give himself away, because then he would learn the truth he desired as well as feared.

Lawless becomes Landless, as if to bring out the way in which the twins with their unbroken wills represent the seekers for the lost heritage.

When we note this itch to bring out directly the relation of Helena to Ellen, we understand further the way in which she goes guising as a man. To some extent the Collins rivalry comes out at this point; for Dickens must have had in mind Collins's novel, *No Name*, which he fervidly admired. In *No Name*, a daughter, who has lost her heritage, is very clever at disguising herself.

She is capable of going a long way beyond the limit of dressing herself like a man, and imitating a man's voice and manner. She has a natural gift for assuming characters, which I have never seen equalled by a woman; and she has performed in public until she has felt her own power, and trained her talent for disguising herself to the highest pitch. A girl who takes the sharpest people unawares by using such a capacity as this to help her own objects in private life; and who sharpens that capacity by a determination to fight her own way to her own purpose which has beaten down everything before it. . . .

This girl of nineteen, Magdalen Vanstone, has clear affinities with Helena Landless, and (if my analysis is right) with Ellen Lawless herself.

There is another angle from which we can approach the motive of the male-clad girl. That Dickens could be warmly stirred by such a motive we know from his excited letter to Forster in 1859 about Miss Wilton (later Lady Bancroft) as Pippo in the burlesque, *The Maid and the Magpie*:

There is the strangest thing in it that ever I have seen on the stage —the boy Pippo, by Miss Wilton. While it is astonishingly impudent (must be, or it couldn't be done at all), it is so stupendously like a boy, and unlike a woman, that it is perfectly free from offence. I have never seen such a thing. She does an imitation of the dancing of the Christy Minstrels—wonderfully clever—which, in the audacity of its thoroughgoing, is surprising. A thing that you cannot imagine a *woman's* doing at all. . . .

So this picture of audacity links with the characterization of the bold Vanstone girl, to beget Helena. And to complete the series we must remember that Ellen had been used to acting boys' parts. The episode which started off her affair with Dickens was based on her exposed "boy's legs" in *Atalanta*.

There is thus a weight of strongly suggestive evidence to suppport the thesis that Helena is Datchery; and in fact a critical examination, purely in terms of the clues afforded by the narrative, establishes her dominant claim for the part of the avenging detective.

But, for my part, I find the most important evidence in the basic idea of the novel. If I am right in saying that *Edwin Drood* provides a fantasy-form describing the imperialist network ensnaring Old England as well as India, and tangling a somnolent cathedral town in a hidden struggle of hate and murder, then Dickens's method would fail unless he showed both the forces of good and evil at work in the representatives of Oriental culture. If Jasper is to be the tormented force of evil, English neurotic and Indian religious murderer, he must be set against some other semi-Indian figure, in whom the regenerative and rebellious energies of the East are incarnated. Clearly that figure is Helena with her deep spiritual comprehension, her fragility and her sinewy resources.

Her extraordinary spiritual insight, working for good, is set against the divided consciousness of Jasper, working for evil. "Did it mean," he asks, "she saw below the surface of his thoughts, and down into their twilight depths?" Both he and she possess clairvoyant or hypnotic powers. Jasper can impress his emotions on Rosa without a word, and Helena is in a kind of direct telepathic rapport with her brother.

Thus Dickens manages with uncanny skill to bring, symbolically, the moral and spiritual problem of imperialism into his English setting. Here, he says, is the real struggle going on under the surface of the dull old decaying township. And as usual, the contemporary theme gains its depth by the tension with conscious and unconscious childhood memories. Cloisterham is Rochester, but the childhood site is now defined almost entirely in charnel graveyard terms. The green of the church playground, where he clasped Fanny, falls away and shows the mouldering bones beneath. This sense of an earth become corrupted with old bones is never let fade out of the narrative. With extreme skill Dickens conjures up the dark scene of decay, the religious gloom and smug emptiness of lives based upon the past; and makes this the counterpart to the Indian superstitions and sophisticated despairs darkening in Jasper's soul. The two evils are fused, and become the externalization of the terrible historical struggle, with its brutal exploitation, its countless deaths by war and famine, its predatory disguises.

It is of interest to compare this picture of a cathedral town with those given by Trollope. We see at once the difference between great art and good minor art. What Bernard Shaw says of Chesney Wold can be applied to Cloisterham. "A leading encyclopedia tells us that Dickens had 'no knowledge of country gentlemen.' It would have been nearer the mark to say that Dickens knew all that really mattered about Sir Leicester Deadlock and that Trollope knew nothing that really mattered about him. Trollope and Thackeray could see Chesney Wold, but Dickens could see through it." Through it, into the human whole in terms of which it alone had meaning.

Here, in the picture of Cloisterham, Dickens reaches his most sustained and sensitive writing. So far from showing any falling away of talent, *Edwin Drood* shows the birth of a new Dickens, whose deepening perception of the human condition and of contemporary struggle is linked with a new subtlety of style—without loss of his demonic power to project character types.

As usual, the symbols of historical process are one in the last resort with the childhood-symbols of loss and union. We can deduce Helena's key part in the novel from her opposition to Jasper; but we can also deduce it from her union with the brother, whom she protects and saves from the evil shadow. From one level we find the heroine turning out yet again a sister-figure: Fanny as she might have been, fused with Ellen as she was and as she might have been. *Drood*, which utters Dickens's deepest sexual fear (his fear of exposure in terms of murder-lust), also reveals his fullest image of perfect brother-sister relationship. And both the fear of exposure and the happiness of union are incarnated in the same figure, Helena.

We can, I think, see three stages in the idea that made up the novel. First, the elements that went into the thwarted love relations of Edwin and Rosa. "Two people, boy and girl, or very young, going apart from one another, pledged to be married after many years—at the end of the book. The interest to arise out of the tracing of their separate ways and the impossibility of telling what will be done with that impending fate." That is, the theme of *Great Expectations* inverted. The chosen pair are really destined for one another; but that bond also brings its own problems of frustration. Somehow the two that came together as children are torn apart by their "fate," their diverging developments. (Once again we find the Estella-figure showing up, at one level, as a sister-image.)

That idea was put out in July 1869. Next month Dickens felt the intuition deepening, growing subtler, baffling direct statement. "A very curious and new idea for my new story. Not a communicable idea (or the interest of the book would be gone), but a very strong one, though difficult to work."

My guess is that at this stage he had the idea of bringing back the "murdered man" to confront his murderer. The notion of a man who thinks he has got away with a crime but is being watched all the while by the "murdered man" or his surrogate certainly had a strong emotional effect on Dickens. In both *No Thoroughfare* (written partly with Collins) and *Hunted Down*, a supposedly dead person turns out to be alive after all; and Dickens may well have toyed with this motive for *Drood*. The traces of it may appear in the rejected titles: *James's Disappearance, Flight and Pursuit, The Disappearance of Edwin Drood, The Flight of Edwin Drood, Edwin Drood in Hiding*.

In *No Thoroughfare* (1867) Vendale travels in Switzerland with Obenreiser, a criminal whom he means to expose but whom he does not know in person. An attempted murder occurs, but Marguerite, Vendale's girl, turns up in time. She thinks, however, that Vendale is dead; she sinks "with both her living hands upon the heart that stood still." Later, however, when the culminating exposure arrives, "supported on Marguerite's arm —his sunburnt colour gone, his right arm bandaged and slung over his breast—Vendale stood before the murderer a man risen from the dead."

The effect is merely a matter of melodramatic phraseology; but it at least reveals the fascination of the motive of the resurrected dead man who accuses and vindicates. Much the same feeling underlies the part of Rokesmith in *Our Mutual Friend* (and, in a different relation, that of the elder Rudge in *Barnaby*).

But it seems clear that, even if Dickens had played about for a while with the idea of keeping Drood alive and bringing him back into the story to accuse the man who thought he had committed murder, he soon abandoned it; and gave a twist to the motive. He turned it from a melodramatic device to one of spiritual significance; the risen man was now to rise in the driven soul of the murderer.

It seems that we must interpret along these lines the frontispiece drawing made by C. A. Collins at Dickens's dictation. There the representation of Jasper with the lantern confronting the immobile figure of a young man depicts "the ghost of Edwin as seen by Jasper in his half-dazed and drugged condition," to use Katie Dickens's words. Or Helena Landless "dressed as Datchery." The second alternative is possible, but even so the dreadful moment of confrontation would be for Jasper a spiritual resurrection, in which the advent of the murdered man marks the break into a new level of consciousness, a new pang of growth.

VIII

For it seems clear that Dickens meant to attempt a thorough exploration of the problem of divided consciousness in Jasper. And at this point we cannot miss the close relation of the theme to Dickens's own predicament. He, whom the readings were driving close to schizophrenia and who was tormented by the problem of holding Ellen's love, had put a great deal of himself into the picture of Jasper, the frustrated artist and lover. All the agony of loss and jealousy which he felt before the young— Ellen and Wilkie Collins—bursts out in Jasper's characterization.

Dickens had been trying to gain a magnetic point of contact with the people through the readings; all accounts pay tribute to the hypnotic quality of his powers of personal projection. Earlier he had attempted to find in actual hypnotism (animal magnetism) a roadway into the deepest spiritual secrets of another; to gain through hypnosis the contact which he could not gain through love.

These aspects of himself appear openly in Jasper, who seeks to hold Rosa through his powers of hypnotic suggestion; and this element in him, which tries to overcome isolation by direct mesmeric projections of himself, is tied up with his whole condition of divided consciousness, in which opium plays a part. The end of the book was to consist somehow of the terrible moment when the divided levels of Jasper's consciousness came together. Thus, the problem of resolution was to be boldly tackled.

How successful Dickens would have been in this very difficult problem we cannot tell, since he died before he reached it. As I understand the artistic and psychological issue here, there was no question of the simple Jekyll and Hyde split. Dickens was not trying to infer that Jasper was unaware of the murder in his normal states of consciousness. Rather, Jasper lives in an uneasy oscillation of states which continually fall away into a chaotic anxiety; he tries by opium to break through into a satisfying vision, he aspires to an exalted state in which a ritual certainty of purpose is possible, but neither his "normal states" as a respectable inhabitant of Cloisterham nor his abnormal states of opium and murder-power are stable. What he has to face is the conscious movement into his abnormal possessions, the sane confrontation of his motives.

What was guiding Dickens, however, in his attempt to explore the divisions of Jasper's soul, was no doubt the principle laid down by Collins in *The Moonstone* and which Dickens rephrased in *Drood*: "As in some cases of drunkenness, and in others of animal magnetism, there are two states of consciousness which never clash, but each of which pursues its separate course as though it were continuous instead of broken (thus, if I hide my watch when I am drunk, I must be drunk again before I can remember where), so Miss Twinkleton has two distinct and separate phases of being." He is writing humorously; but the apparent casualness is quite in the key of his method for preparing the reader to meet serious reapplications of the motive.

Forster says that Dickens told him the theme was to be "the murder of a nephew by his uncle," and that originality was to lie in the review of the murderer's career by himself after his exposure. "The last chapters were to be written in the condemned cell, to which his wickedness, all elaborately elicited from him as if told of another, had brought him." Somehow Jasper was to retrace his steps through the labyrinth of his abnormal fantasies and to come out at the end into the shattering realization of his futility, his total failure.

Perhaps one might almost say that Dickens died because he couldn't dare to reach this point in the story. His artistic and social consciousness had leaped far ahead of his world, and he was trying to do something that is still to be achieved after Dostoevsky and Strindberg, after Freud and the Surrealists.

One personal point. Forster had been told by Dickens that the ring was to betray Jasper. Grewgious had given the ring to Edwin with the words, "Her ring. Will it come back to me? My mind hangs about her ring very uneasily to-night. But this is explainable. I have had it so long, and I have prized it so much. I wonder. . . ."

Her ring. Remember that for some thirty years Dickens had religiously worn Mary Hogarth's ring. It was the token of his safe contact with the desired angelic spirit; and of his deep guilt-fear.

Behind the theme of the maddened Jasper, the frustrated lover and artist, who hovers in his impotent hatred round the world of youth (Edwin, Rosa, Neville, Helena), there lies Dickens's sense of nearing death, of a total inability to grapple any longer with the love relationship he had demanded from Ellen. The Ring, the magical point of union, is being abdicated, given up, taken away by the young. In it lies the clue to his betrayal, the exposure before the world and the final defeat of death. He looks out on Wilkie Collins and on Ellen, the two young people who have so much of time and activity ahead, and he is rent with fear and anger. Ellen, in whom he had hoped to find a return to the pure sources, the Edenic garden, has become Helena-Datchery, the hidden watcher and betrayer. The strain of hiding for ten years from the multitudinous eyes of the world has ended by turning the love accomplice into the secret accuser.

And by an odd chance we can detect in the choice of the name Edwin Drood the emotion of bitter envy towards Wilkie which I have suggested. (I am not inferring any overt drama of jealousy towards either Ellen or Wilkie; I mean merely that these two, looming largest in his emotional life, inevitably symbolized, in the depths of his spirit, the enemies, the ravishers, the favoured ones who were given the treat while he was being sent out into the cold.) We happen to know that a young aspiring journalist, Edwin Drew, had written to Dickens asking about his chances in London, and that Dickens in reply did his best to put him off. "On no account try literary life here. Such an attempt must lead to the bitterest disappointment." Under these altruistic warnings it is not hard to see the pattern of fear and resentment. Edwin Drew stood for the younger generation knocking on the door. Via the forms James (Edwyn) Wakefield, Edwin Brude, he mixed somehow with Trood (landlord of the Falstaff Inn opposite Gadshill) and became Edwin Drood, the careless youth able to get away with the things that Jasper-Dickens so passionately and vainly desires.

Some of the papers written during the 'sixties help us to grasp the state of mind that Dickens had reached. Thus, *The German Chariot*, which begins with a talk between himself and his child-self, goes on to recount a death-obsession. He goes to the Paris Morgue. "I never want to go there, but am always pulled there." One Christmas Day he finds there an old, grey man with water dripping over his face; on New Year's Morning he finds a murdered boy. Now he encounters

a large dark man, whose disfigurement by water was in a frightful manner comic, and whose expression was that of a prize-fighter who had closed his eyelids under a heavy blow, but was going immediately to open them, shake his head, and "come up smiling." O, what this large, dark man cost me in that bright city.

He tells of his haunting by the form. He goes bathing in the river and feels it coming towards him, contaminating the water. He gets out, sick. "Some morsel on my plate looked like a piece of him." He sees boxers and one of them is the man. In shop-window reflection he sights the foul ghost, "and instantly I was sickened again." At the theatre the same thing happened, and in the street.

He then breaks into an appeal for consideration of children, and insists that to force them into doing what they fear creates fixed images of terror. Force a child into "a lonely bedroom against its will, and you had better murder it."

Another essay, *Houselessness*, which tells of his night wanderings, records the sort of heightened dream-consciousness that came over him at such moments of exhaustion and loneliness. Twice he goes into a coffee-house near Bow Street, and sees a man "in a high and long snuff-coloured coat and shoes, and, to the best of my belief, nothing else but a hat." This man took a cold meat pudding out of his hat and "stabbed it, over-hand, with the knife, like a mortal enemy; then took the knife out, wiped it on his sleeve, tore the pudding asunder with his fingers and ate it all up." This pudding-stabber was a "most spectral person . . . whose figure promised cadaverousness, but who had an excessively red face, though shaped like a horse's."

On the second occasion of my seeing him, he said, huskily, to the man of sleep, "Am I red to-night?"

"You are," he uncompromisingly answered.

"My mother," said the spectre, "was a red-faced woman that liked drink, and I looked at her hard when she laid in her coffin, and I took the complexion."

Somehow, the pudding seemed an unwholesome pudding after that, and I put myself in its way no more.

Here we meet the ogre-fears of childhood in tangled dream-form, become one with a general sense of horror of the world. This is the crude material with which Dickens wrestles as he builds up his full dramatization in *Our Mutual Friend*, and then, with a sharp turn in comprehension, in *Edwin Drood*.

Drood, with its incomparable picture of social decay, leaps far ahead of its world. *Our Mutual Friend* fights that world, and is still within recognizable reach of its terms of battle; but *Drood* does not make that sort of attack. It begins with a dreadful assumption of decay, of a total rot of bourgeois values, and then stages its dream-picture of imperialist conflict on an earth of ghosts and mouldering bones. At the same time it reaches forward into artistic problems, psychological problems, that ran far ahead of the resources of the novel at that time.

Whether Ellen was giving Dickens any direct cause for jealousy, or whether he was merely suffering from a general fear of inability to hold her, we do not know. In any event he was feeling a bitter sense of age, a resentment at being excluded from the world of youth. The last essay in *The Uncommercial Traveller*, written shortly before *Drood*, gives away the unusual bitterness that had come over him. He tells of his anger at hearing some girls talking loosely; how he followed them and forced a policeman to take the loudest-voiced in charge, then turned up at the court and insisted on the magistrate proceeding with the summons. His account makes clear that both policeman and magistrate were unwilling to act, and that the magistrate was not a little shocked at finding the humanitarian Dickens insistent in such a matter. We can explain it only as a sharp resentment against the sexuality bubbling over in the girls.

This event helps us to understand the extent to which his sex fears and frustrations entered into the picture of the maniac Jasper. It also helps us, with *Drood*, to understand the complex of forces driving him into the exhibition of himself in the murder scene at the readings.

The minor characters in the novel, Durdles or Miss Twinkleton, Sapsea or Honeythunder, Mrs. Crisparkle or Grewgious, are drawn with all the old mastery, though keeping a more restrained place within the general framework than usual. One character in particular, Honeythunder, is of importance for the understanding of Dickens's attitudes. In him the satire on the meddling philanthropist comes to a head, and in doing so it enlarges its sphere of reference in ways that Dickens could hardly have guessed at. The way in which an original love of man has become ossified into hatred, and the way in which this hatred draws its sanctions from the original love, is brilliantly represented; and the picture raises a fundamental moral problem for all persons engaged in necessary democratic activities.

. . . You were to love your brother as yourself, but after an indefinite interval of maligning him (very much as if you hated him), and calling him all manner of names. Above all things, you were to do nothing in private, or on your own account. You were to go to the offices of the Haven of Philanthropy, and put your name down as a Member and a Professing Philanthropist. Then, you were to pay up your subscription, get your card of membership and your riband and medal, and were evermore to live upon a platform, and evermore to say what Mr. Honeythunder said, and what the Treasurer said, and what the sub-Treasurer said, and what the Committee said, and what the Vice-Secretary said. And this was usually said in the unanimously carried resolution under hand and seal, to the effect: "That this assembled Body of Professing Philanthropists views, with indignant scorn and contempt, not unmixed with utter detestation and loathing abhorrence"—in short, the baseness of all those who do not belong to it, and pledges itself to make as many obnoxious statements as possible about them, without being at all particular as to facts.

From one angle such a passage expresses the fear of the individualistic Radical when faced with problems of revolutionary organization—the fear of loss of individuality in the disciplines necessary to united democratic action. But from another angle it raises a valid issue, the need for incessant psychological self-scrutiny so that the participant keeps aware of the narrow line between united action based on the democratic carrying out of agreed policy and surrender of individual responsibility by mechanical reference to decisions outside his control. Between true brotherly union and the use of forms of union to give social disguise to egotistic power cravings and paranoically inclined fears.

Finally, there is the farewell note that broods all over this book. The precision of much of its writing gives the effect of a backward glance which seeks to grasp all the details in a beloved and significant scene before it is too late. We feel the shadow of Dickens wandering in the dusk among the tombs and the bursts of hidden song, wandering by the Medway and noting the banks of seaweed:

an unusual quantity had come in with the last tide, and this, and the confusion of the water, and the restless dipping and flapping of the noisy gulls, and an angry light seaward beyond the brown-sailed barges that were turning black, foreshadowed a stormy night. In his mind he was contrasting the wild and noisy sea with the quiet harbour of Minor Canon Corner.

This precision is a dream-precision, and the shadow walks among the stones and leaves of childhood. End and beginning are coming together, first and last things, in the solution of the enigma, the healing of the split in consciousness:

Christmas Eve in Cloisterham. A few strange faces in the streets; a few other faces, half strange and half familiar, once the faces of Cloisterham children, now the faces of men and women who come back from the outer world at long intervals to find the city wonderfully shrunken in size, as if it had not washed by any means well in the meanwhile. To these, the striking of the cathedral clock, and the cawing of the rooks from the cathedral tower, are like the voices of their nursery time. To such as these, it has happened in their dying hours afar off, that they have imagined their chamber floor to be strewn with the autumnal leaves fallen from the elm trees in the Close: so have the rustling sounds and fresh scents of their earliest impressions revived when the circle of their lives was very nearly traced, and the beginning and the end were drawing close together.

IX

The connection between *Edwin Drood* and *Macbeth* is of interest; for among other things it helps to bring out the

extraordinary unity of basic imagery throughout Dickens's life
—the enduring effect of his childhood impressions. He tells us
that when he was six he was taken to the theatre at Rochester,
where he saw *Macbeth* and was indelibly affected by the witch-
horror, the murder and its nemesis. Then a couple of years
later he was given the special treat of seeing Grimaldi, the
clown. One of Grimaldi's main acts was an interpretation (in
clown's dress) of the dagger scene from *Macbeth*. "A dead
silence pervaded the whole house, and young and old seemed
to vibrate with the effect upon the imagination."

Later, when he came to write, one of the first *Boz* sketches
tells humorously of a *Macbeth* performance. In *Nickleby* the
star Snivillicci can do anything "from a medley dance to Lady
Macbeth"; and in *Dombey* at Miss Tox's lodgings "the most
domestic and confidential garments hung like Macbeth's banners
on the outward walls," while at Florence's wedding "the amens
of the dusty clerk appear, like Macbeth's, to stick in his throat
a little."

In *Copperfield* the *Macbeth* reference begins more seriously to
mingle with the novel's theme. Steerforth throws off a twinge
of despair. Why that being gone, I am a man again, like Macbeth.
And now for dinner! If I have not Macbeth-like broken up the
feast with most admired disorder." The butcher-boy with whom
David fought at Canterbury comes darkly up in memory "like
the apparition of an armed head in *Macbeth*."

Macready, whom Dickens so much admired as an actor, was
famous for his Macbeth. He had taken charge of the Dickens
children during Charles's first United States tour; and in *Lying
Awake* Dickens wrote of a night when sleep "seeming to be a
thousand miles further off than Niagara," he made up his mind
to think about slumber but was at once whirled off to Drury
Lane, where he saw "a great actor and a dear friend of his
playing Macbeth and heard his apostrophizing the death of
each day's life."

As the murder obsession strengthened its grip on Dickens,
the *Macbeth* image got more and more control. In the Birmingham address given in the midst of writing *Drood*, he referred
to "the apparition of the externally armed head in *Macbeth*."
Macready himself responded to the Sykes–Nancy scene in the
readings as "equal to two *Macbeths*," to Dickens's delight. And
there were three references in *Drood* itself to *Macbeth*. "No one
of these quotations is flung casually into the flow of the narrative, but each is linked with a nerve centre of the novel." As a

title for the meeting of Drood, Jasper and Landless on the Christmas Eve of murder, Dickens took the quotation, "When shall these three meet again?" When Grewgious is entrusting the ancestral ring to Edwin, one of the waiters drags his foot after him like "Macbeth's leg when it accompanied him off stage to the assassination of Duncan"—a reference to the leg-play invented by Macready. The dinner (suggesting Macbeth's part as host), with its ominous background evokes from Dickens the response of the *Macbeth* image of murder-guilt. Thirdly, there is the passage telling how Crisparkle sets off to the weir after the murder, "as confident of the sweetening powers of Cloisterham Weir as Lady Macbeth was hopeless of all those of the seas that roll." In the weir he is to find tokens of the lost Drood.

A direct connection is here established with childhood fears, such as those which come out in the account of Mary Weller's stories. The Canon is standing in a closet on the stairs as he is drawn off on the trail that leads to the weir, to the first evidences of murder; and Dickens carefully adds in his notes that he "remembered as a child" the very closet.

Further, it has been suggested that Opium Sal has many of the characteristics of the Weird Women. She appears in the prologue of the novel as the figure of evil who unlocks dark potences in men; she confronts the doomed Edwin in the same way as the witches confront Macbeth and Banquo, on the road to the murder. Her enigmatic warning does not deter Edwin any more than those of the witches deter Banquo or Macbeth. Dickens, like Shakespeare, seeks to create a dusk atmosphere of evil for the deed of blood. "A strange dead weight was in the air. The clouds were copperous. The winds were rising. The sky was angry. The water was troubled." When he brings Jasper in his dark dreams muttering side by side with Opium Sal, he is deliberately building a new image of hell, of the victim tormented in the witch glare and bestial spell. "Look down! Look down! See what lies at the bottom there. . . . Look at it. That must be real. It's over." Like Lady Macbeth he is the prisoner of the murder-moment. She cries, "Nor time nor place did then adhere, yet you would make them both—they've made themselves." He cries, "Time and place are both at hand."

In the way in which the *Macbeth* images thus come out as the organizing factors in Dickens's last work, after having haunted him for some fifty years, we find an extraordinarily impressive example of the emotional unity of his creative life. Only a few years before he began *Drood*, in an essay on revisiting Rochester

(*Uncommercial Traveller*, XI), he had described how the sight of the old theatre revived his childhood memory of *Macbeth*.

Many wondrous secrets of Nature had I come to the knowledge of in that sanctuary; of which not the least terrific were, that the witches in *Macbeth* wore an awful resemblance to the Thanes and other proper inhabitants of Scotland; and that the good King Duncan couldn't rest in his grave, but was constantly coming out of it, and calling himself somebody else.

Here, in this jesting passage, we have one of the clues to *Drood*. Edwin Drood is the figure who rises up, unable to rest in his grave (as the frontispiece design done at Dickens's dictation shows); he is the childhood memory in which both the secret of paradisiac happiness and of the murder done ceaselessly to life are hidden. And in the shifting skein of lights and shadows the faces change, and the problem of identity, which is also a problem of union, is ceaselessly agitated.

There is yet another work with which it is useful to compare *Drood*—Bulwer Lytton's *A Strange Story*, which had been written for Dickens's magazine in 1860–61. This powerful symbolist romance had in turn drawn on Dickens. Thus, Mrs. Poyntz, who stands for fate in the form of relentless social forces, takes an important trait from the women of the revolution in *A Tale of Two Cities* (published so recently before in the same magazine): she knits as she contemplates the action she dominates, and this knitting is an emblem of her fate-power.

In this tale, as in *The Coming Race*, Bulwer makes an imaginative effort to grasp the new concepts of transformation emerging in science, from biology to physics; and in the final scene, where Margrave in the Australian wilds summons up the power of renewal to his own destruction, Bulwer Lytton uses symbolism closely related to that of Dickens in *Bleak House*.

In my final scene I suppose an atmosphere extremely electrical—there is spontaneous combustion in the bush, the soil is volcanic, there is trembling of the earth. (Letter to Forster.)

So here, too, we meet the notion of "spontaneous combustion" to express the supreme moment of change in man and society, the dangerous moment which can become either renewal or destruction. That moment destroys Margrave with its terrific invocation of spiritual or elemental forces, but it releases the heroine Lilian into a fuller life.

Bulwer Lytton discussed the inner meaning of his tale with

Dickens, and Dickens was certainly much impressed by the allegory which put into exciting form the theme of hidden forces in men. Margrave, the totally unscrupulous seeker of personal satisfaction and renewal at the expense of others, has his clear link with Jack Jasper. He exerts an hypnotic influence over Lilian in the same way as Jasper over Rosa; he has his close connections with the East and its magics; he gets rid of those who stand in his way by means of the Strangler. This Strangler is definitely stated to have been an Indian and a Thug.

He was believed by them to belong to that murderous sect of fanatics whose existence as a community has only recently been made known to Europe, and who strangle their unsuspecting victim in the firm belief that they thereby propitiate the favour of the goddess they serve.

So the strangling motive, which appears in rationalized form in Drood, appears here in openly symbolic terms, and the final escape of the hero Fenwick from the whole terrifying snare of evil arrives with his defeat of the Strangler.

Before I could turn, some dark muffling substance fell between my sight and the sun, and I felt a fierce strain at my throat. But the words of Ayesha had warned me; with one rapid hand I seized the noose before it could tighten too closely, with the other I tore the bandage away from my eyes, and wheeling round on the dastardly foe, struck him down with one spurn of my foot. His hand, as he fell, relaxed its hold on the noose; I freed my throat from the knot, and sprang from the copse into the broad sunlit plain.

In *A Strange Story* the struggle of Fenwick with Margrave for control of Lilian is allegorical; it lacks the sexual content of the struggle of Jasper with Drood for Rosa. But despite many differences between the two books, there is yet a strong link. In trying to objectify artistically his inner conflict in 1869–70, Dickens revives his memory of the imagery of evil, of the whole battle for human renewal, in *A Strange Story*, and carries over some of it for his own purposes. The motive of drug-taking, the extension of the imagery of struggle from the Victorian money-world to the connected turmoil of greed and fear in the eastern spheres of imperialism, he had borrowed from Wilkie Collins; the yet deeper symbolism of the upheaval, schism and renewal in the human soul, he owed in part to Bulwer Lytton.

In *A Strange Story* the desperate fight put up by Margrave is to defeat death; and Dickens's re-use of the Thug motive is tangled up with the death-fear that must have been heavy over him in 1869–70, merged indistinguishably with his fear of failure and defeat in love.

There is yet one more piece of evidence which backs up my analysis of Datchery. In reading Lady Lytton's *Cheveley* (1839), I lighted on the name Datchet, and at once, knowing how susceptible Dickens was to names and their associations, I wondered if Datchet would turn out to play the part of detector, whether he would be the person to expose and ruin De Clifford (Bulwer). For this book could not but be well known to Dickens. It had caused its sensation by putting Rosina Bulwer's case against her husband, the writer who (apart from Carlyle) most interested Dickens among all contemporary English writers; it had a funny and virulent picture of Forster as Fuzboz; and it must often have come to his mind as he reflected that Bulwer's family life had broken up and yet Bulwer had managed to keep his social and literary position. There was thus a good case for supposing that the names in the story would contain a certain amount of emotional significance for him and that Datchet might turn out to be Datchery.

To my surprise, the events of the story more than justified this dim suspicion. De Clifford (Bulwer) has seduced and ruined a girl Mary, who bears a child, goes temporarily mad, and is coupled with her old father (another example of the Old Man–Young Girl theme.) De Clifford finally frames a case against the father, who flees with Mary. Arrested and put on trial, the Old Man and Mary are suddenly vindicated by the arrival of Datchet in court. Datchet produces evidence of De Clifford's complicity. De Clifford rides off furiously, is thrown by his horse, and killed.

Datchet is thus the instrument who exposes the wicked novelist and shows him up as a vile seducer as well as a callous tyrannizer over his long-suffering wife (Rosina's dream-picture of herself, which is, however, far more like the facts of Kate Dickens). And when we recall that Dickens's deep terror of railway accidents had communicated itself to driving and riding, so that he had to give up such exercises, the emotional relevance of the tale grows even stronger. It seems clear that *Cheveley*, read with much interest and brooded over later as his own domestic circumstances grew more strained, had seemed to pose his own problem and to present the accusation against him. The exposure by Datchet, with its resulting shock-death, is thus exactly paired off by the point reached in *Edwin Drood*, where Datchery makes his marks of satisfaction, and the shock-death that promptly followed that point—a shock-death which, coming on the anniversary of Staplehurst, re-enacted both the railway accident and the horse accident.

A strange foreshadowing, this tale of *Cheveley*; and yet it fits so well into the whole pattern that it cannot be without significance. I suggest that as Dickens went on working at the *Drood* theme, elements from *Cheveley* were half-recalled or unconsciously affected his mind; in particular his use of the name Datchery for the exposer was derived from an unconscious reminiscence of *Cheveley*, and helped to intensify the pattern of fear.

X

Edwin Drood was never to be finished. The pressures of anxiety were too great. Dickens had scarcely found this return to his creative faculty than he was longing to get away from it, back to direct contact with the people. Away from the painful effort to define psychologically and artistically the sources of discord, the deep tensions between himself and society. Away into the direct miming of the murder impasse, with its accusation and its appeal to pity.

He promised to give twelve more readings, beginning January 1870; and opened at a rented house in London with a show of the "murder" at three o'clock with the morning for friends. The actors and actresses present were astounded, and his pulse went up from 72 to 112. Afterwards, he spent ten minutes on a sofa, wrestling for breath. But he went on with the series at St. James's Hall, with electrifying effect. On March 15th he read for the last time. "From these garish lights I vanish now for evermore with a heartfelt, grateful, respectful, and affectionate farewell." Weeping, he stumbled off. In all he had cleared about £45,000.

In February George Hogarth died and was buried in Kendal Green cemetery, with the once-beloved Mary Hogarth. In March Dickens found that the symptoms of physical break-up were recurring; he could read only the right-hand half of the names over the shops. His left hand was now generally in a sling. His speech had been getting confused; in the last readings his son noted that he said "Pickswick" or "Picnic" or "Peckswicks" for "Pickwick."

The bad effect of the "murder" scene on his health had been clear from the very first, and his friends had tried vainly to dissuade him from going on with it; but he could not resist its morbid excitement. He kept on referring to it as if it were an actual murder. "The foot goes on famously. I feel the fatigue in it (four Murders in one week) but not overmuch. It merely aches at night." He loved to note its terrifying effect. "B. had a seat behind the screen, and was nearly frightened off it, by the murder. Every vestige of colour left his face when I came off, and he sat staring over a glass of champagne in the wildest way." "I am glad you are coming to the Murder on the second of March." "I am sitting at a side-window looking up the length of Princes Street, watching the mist change over the Castle and murdering Nancy by turns." To Mary Boyle: "The crime being completely off my mind, and the blood spilled, I am (like many of my fellow-criminals) in a highly edifying state to-day." At Clifton, "I should think we had a dozen or twenty ladies taken out stiff and rigid, at various times. It became quite ridiculous."

He himself was aware of the connection between his agitated state and the Staplehurst accident.

At Chester last Sunday I found myself extremely giddy, and extremely uncertain of my sense of touch, both in the left leg and left hand and arms. . . . I had an inward conviction that whatever it was, it was not gout. I also told Beard, a year after the Staplehurst accident, that I was certain that my heart had been fluttered, and wanted a little helping. That the stethoscope confirmed; and considering the immense exertions I am undergoing, and the constant jarring of express trains, the case seems quite intelligible.

But nothing short of serious breakdown and the insistence of the doctors stopped him; and even then, after the period of rest in which he began *Drood*, he madly returned to murder-mime that was shattering him.

We can now better understand the forces closing in on him and killing on June 9, 1870, the anniversary of the accident. The murder-exposure of the mime had conclusively wrecked his health and brought about the first stages of a schizophrenic paralysis as expression of hopelessly unresolved inner conflict. But against this he had struggled in *Drood* to grasp artistically what was at stake in the anguish rending him. He had projected himself as Jasper, the frustrated lover and artist, who murdered the youth who supplanted him—but all in vain.

Helena-Ellen turned into the exposer, the enemy worming out the truth which will force Jasper-Dickens into the position of recognized guilt where he must bring together his divided levels of consciousness, his dream-self and his everyday-self. Where, then, will the moment of intolerable pressure emerge? Surely at the point when Datchery-Helena gets indisputably on his trail, and the exposure is inescapable.

That, anyhow, is the point where he died; the point where he broke off the narrative. That was the point when he could no longer go on living. He died of sheer spiritual strain and shock.

Politically, he maintained his essential principles to the end. The statements of his last year express his boundless faith in men, his boundless hatred of Parliament and the State. His shrewdness of insight, which had made him prophesy the American Civil War some twenty years before it happened, appears in his forecast of the Paris Commune. Writing in May 1869, he said:

I don't know how it may be with you, but it is the fashion here to be absolutely certain that the Emperor of the French is fastened by Providence and the fates on a throne of adamant expressly constructed for him since the foundations of the universe were laid. He knows better, and so do the police of Paris, and both powers must be grimly entertained by the resolute British belief, knowing what they have known, and doing what they have done through the last ten years. What Victor Hugo calls "the drop-curtain, behind which is constructing the great last act of the French Revolution," has been a little shaken at the bottom lately, however. One seems to see the feet of a rather large chorus getting ready.

XI

We have now reached the end of the story. How may we best sum up Dickens's achievement? In a career which takes in such a huge span of human change and manages to give artistic expression to that change, there are endless points of interest, which demand explication. Many of these points have been touched on in the narrative. Here we must concentrate on certain essentials.

First, there is the aspect already mentioned: the huge span which Dickens covers. Very few writers on his work seem to be even vaguely aware of the remarkable inner development which it reveals. If dimly conscious of a deepening gloom in the later works, they put it down to irritability or unhappiness in the domestic sphere. Criticism of Dickens has so far been very largely at the level which Shakespearean criticism clung to before 1800. Dickens is not of Shakespeare's stature; but the comparison is not altogether inept. For Dickens is the first writer in England after Shakespeare (except Blake) who is centrally and continuously aware of the problem of dissociation.

He begins in a pre-industrialist world, partly borrowed from childhood fantasy and partly borrowed from eighteenth-century novelists like Smollett. He moves step by step into the hell of the actual world, always consolidating his position by the building-up of significant symbols that grasp the basic plight of men. The fusion of these symbols and the realistic depiction of the world goes on all the while, till it reaches the major definitions of *Bleak House*, *Little Dorrit*, and *Our Mutual Friend*—with *Great Expectations* as the more personal commentary on the situation, and *Edwin Drood* as a masterly epilogue which sets out the tensions of the next phase of life and art.

Even Balzac, Dostoevsky, or Tolstoy cannot show such an orderly progression of penetrating definitions illuminating the fate of man under capitalism in all its aspects. This progression it is that makes the comparison with Shakespeare necessary and relevant.

We can put the claim in another way. Dickens defines in his work all the pangs of national growth from the first stages of an emerging petty-bourgeois (still implicating many pre-industrialist elements of festival fellowship and hospitality) right on up to the point of conflict beyond which lies the full egalitarian harmony that transcends all existing relationships. Thus his work spans the whole process of nationhood, and defines the various conflicts and tensions of that process, the discovery of dissociation and the alienation of man from his fellows and his own essence, the stages of struggle against the dissociative forces, and the intuition (uttered in symbolic forms) of the resolving unity. He and Blake are still the prophets of our epoch.

What I am discussing is not any explicit statement of ends, but the total direction of a definition: the artistic integration. For in such an integration the term *artistic* is always to be equated with the term *human*. Dickens (with Blake) is the writer who gives full expression to the human forces caught up in the throes of national development, moving powerfully from folk-levels to the resolving and unifying levels of socialism, and, in between, defining all the complex conflicts of love and fear, dissociation and integration. Blake, in the primary period of uprooting, gave deep poetic expression to the whole arc of transformation; Dickens, coming in the secondary phase, gave an extended novel-expression to the same arc. Now, as we reach the end of the arc, we can pick up their struggle anew, understand it at last, and find the forms that carry it forward through the decisive final phase.

Yet this steady unfolding of the fate of dissociated man in terms of dynamic imagery which looked forward beyond the dissociation, was made by a writer who managed to keep a general popularity in the Victorian world. How can we speak of the revolutionary virtue and integrity of a man who remained a best seller to Victorian audiences?

That question goes to the heart of the terrible strain that tugged at Dickens all his life after the first simple burst of creative energy. He gained his popularity, his union with the Victorian audience, at a moment of general upheaval and transition. He drew on popular sources and on the eighteenth-century novelists, and built up a world of bonhomie and hospitable happiness, a nostalgic picture which consoled and heartened in a callous society. Almost at once (even before he had finished *Pickwick*) he had discovered the other side of the picture and begun introducing it into his passionate imagery. His readers felt in his work, not only the consolations of a lost Eden (ultimately the family bosom), but also the pang of loss, the imagery of all the fears they felt in a world not understood, a world busily bent on excluding them from all satisfactions of love and peace.

Here lay the function of Dickens's sentimentality—an expression of the overwrought emotions of men at this difficult moment of loss and thwarted development. I have explored the psychological mechanism of this sentimentality in Dickens, its relation to his childhood, to Fanny and his mother, to Mary Hogarth and Mary Weller. But what gave that mechanism its social and artistic import was the way in which it set him in immediate union with the vast homeless pang of the people in the convulsions of change. Without it he would never have laid the basis for his unity with the mass audience and his capacity to grasp the inner structure of historical crisis. Its weakness lay in the tendency to smudge out conflict in the fathomless pang of the tear, the intolerable sense of a shared loss. But it was humanly sound while the astringent gusto of his delight in life and his savage hatred of greed and oppression accompanied it.

Thus in the earlier stages of his work he built that strong basis of union with his public that was able to weather the difficult strains of the later years.

If we can imagine him somehow having written *Little Dorrit* in the 'fifties without the preceding works, we can see that he would never have managed to get the work across to the general public as he did. If he had managed to get it published, it would have been furiously rejected on all sides.

The story I have told makes clear how bitterly hard he found it to keep on writing almost from the very start. All the themes which stirred his creative faculty had at their core a deep-going antagonism to the major trends of respectable society. Being built as he was, having reached expression by the road he had, he could neither set himself simply into opposition with the trends about him, nor accept them in any terms used by their exponents. He remained a lone fighter—and in that there may be detected his petty-bourgeois origins. But if we see only that, we see little. His lone fighting derived in the long run from his need to fight for a concept of unity that lay far ahead and had no hope of actualization in his world. On the one hand, he stands for all the constructive and brotherly elements going to build up the nation; on the other hand, he is too aware of the actual contradictions and distortions everywhere in the contemporary situation to take any obviously partisan position. He speaks for the soul of the struggle, and therefore for a future in which the existing contradictions will be humanly resolved. For this fully human resolution he is an uncompromising fighter, a consistent partisan.

Hence the enormous strain he felt from the moment he introduced the prison episode into *Pickwick*. (Personally, much of the strain expressed itself as a fear of exposure as a jail-bird's son, who had worked in a blacking factory; but this fear was only a rationalization of a much deeper conflict between himself and society.) He had to keep his union with the struggling, broken, aspiring human being of his world, and yet he had to speak in terms of a resolving unity which did not yet possess the means of actualizing itself. If he failed on either count, he failed as an artist—and also went bankrupt. Hence the important part that financial responsibilities play in his life (with far-reaching effects on his work, its themes and its characters). He had to go on making money, but he could not write powerfully unless he remained true to himself, and if he remained true to himself he threatened to lose his public by too explicit attack on the ruling values of society.

Therein lies the tug-of-war that made him so restless, so hectically happy or unhappy, so unable to find any secure personal relationships, boisterously expansive and yet always aware of a cold reservation.

When, however, the utmost has been said about his compromises, confusions, and obliquities, there remains as the central dynamic of his work a critical vision which we can only call revolutionary, since it draws its creative virtues from a fundamental rejection of existing values. Bernard Shaw has well brought out this point. "Dickens never regarded himself as a revolutionist, though he certainly was one. His implacable contempt for the House of Commons . . . never wavered." He points out that Thackeray could write as fiercely about the ruling classes, and yet Thackeray remained a bourgeois; for he had a basic agreement on social doctrine with the persons he reviled. Dickens had a basic disagreement. "*Little Dorrit* is a more seditious book than *Das Kapital*." A pardonable exaggeration.

XII

I have already sketched the way in which Dickens's work grew up out of ferment of popular forms and forces. *The key nature of such popular elements is to be found in the emphasis on the notion of transformation and on all images or characters that seem to embody the transformative processes.* Dickens found his deepest contact with these elements through his subtle and pervasive use of the day-dream, the childhood fantasy. It is because he always fuses the fantasy with realism that he redeems realism from its bourgeois distortion (naturalism) and shows himself an outstanding upholder of the great creative tradition which the triumph of the bourgeoisie threatened. The mass tradition is one of fantasy, moving between dream-image and poetic symbol; naturalism (i.e. realism minus fantasy) is historically the bourgeois form of expression. Dickens captures this form and refuses it with fantasy, orientates it towards the concept of transformation.

It is precisely the great creative power in Dickens which has been belittled by those who, one way or another, employ a naturalistic critique—Taine or G. H. Lewes in Dickens's own day, or E. M. Forster in ours. Taine thought Dickens's image-making power to be monomaniacal; Lewes called it hallucinative. ("Dickens once declared to me that every word said by one of his characters was distinctly *heard* by him; I was at first not a little puzzled to account for the fact that he could hear language so utterly unlike the language of real feeling, and not be aware of its preposterousness; but the surprise vanished when I thought of the phenomena of hallucination.") Forster finds Dickens's world flat and three-dimensional—i.e. is perfectly blind to the spiritual depths from which Dickens's characters emerge with their dynamic energies. Such an attitude is quite logical if one has no sense whatever of the creative unity of a Dickens novel. Then what could one see but a crowd of galvanic marionettes, strange figures of theatric violence wandering in a mad and yet prearranged void? Forster by his comment gives away that he himself lives in an utterly unreal world, in which the knowledge of the key factor in experience, without which all experience is essentially unmeaning and pettily personal, is totally missing. Dickens is the poet who knows simultaneously what alienation and union mean in capitalist society.

Barker Fairley says of Goethe's *Faust*, in reply to Santayana's complaint that Faust does not develop: "The development is in the poem as a whole, not in its supposed hero." The point is equally true of Dickens's important novels. The comment that his characters are marionettes, bright, exciting, over life-size, has its slight measure of truth, in so far as it points to the folk-elements of humour and symbolism in his work; but in the form in which it is usually made (with the implication that the people lack Soul or Inwardness), it shows a sad lack of response to Dickens's creative method and its importance for the post-1830 world. Like Goethe, he makes a fundamentally lyrical approach, and this means that his figures are not Shakespearean persons realized individually but fitting into a single symbolic conception, or Ibsen characters in whom the pattern of unconscious memory is psychologically united with naturalism as both fate and revelatory liberation. His people are lyrical images which gain profundity and symbolic significance through their relation to a total concept, a total movement, born out of a personal tension. The Shakespearean and Goethean methods are equally valid; the virtue of either depends on the extent to which the personal tension is realized in unity with the environing pressures of history. Dickens, from this angle, shows up as

416

a creator of the highest order; and to call his people flatly three-dimensional is to miss the terrific inwardness of the whole concept which reacts on each single figure, giving it a depth of emotional overtones.

The best statement of his method is perhaps that made by himself in later years:

It does not seem to me to be enough to say of any description that it is the exact truth. The exact truth must be there; but the merit or art in the narrator, is the manner of stating the truth. As to which thing in literature, it always seemed to me that there is a world to be done. And in these times, when the tendency is to be frightfully literal and catalogue-like—to make the thing, in short, a sort of sum in reduction that any miserable creature can do in that way—I have an idea (really founded on love of what I profess), that the very holding of popular literature through a kind of popular dark age, may depend on such fanciful treatment.

That goes to the very heart of the problem. In a "popular dark age"—an age when the mass audience reasserts itself but in situations of the direst self-alienation—the carrying on of the vital popular elements, fantasy and imagery of dream-transformation, is the only way in which to keep alive the great tradition of art and to defeat the bourgeois dissociation of naturalism.

Here Dickens turns out, in his own way, to be making exactly the same kind of protest as the great Romantic and Symbolist poets—though he was inevitably unaware of the relation. Those poets proclaimed the need for a new organic integration in art and life, and, in a society falling away into worse dissociations, they fought to act as pathfinders towards the harmonies that men would need in completing their revolt against the dehumanizing pressures. By his fantasy-method Dickens picks up all that has been most poetically vigorous in our tradition, re-creates it on a new level, and sets his dynamite inside the bourgeois form, the novel. Into the novel he blasts the poetic tradition (which includes Shakespeare and folk-tale, transformative images on the high tragic level or at the folk-level of marvel, burlesque, dream-tale). He thus completes on a grand scale the work which the Gothic novel, the novel of fantasy and sensibility, the *roman noir*, had begun.

Bulwer Lytton, in 1845, in his preface to *Night and Morning*, had given the best contemporary statement of what was at issue. "The vast and dark Poetry around us—the Poetry of Modern Civilization and Daily Existence, is shut out from us in much, by the shadowy giants of Prejudice and Fear. He who would arrive at the Fairy Land must face the Phantoms." *The vast and dark Poetry around us, the Poetry of modern civilization and daily existence*: those words go to the very heart of the artistic problem, and they reveal the link between the work of Bulwer and Dickens and that of the French symbolists. But though Bulwer had done his best, the proud claim with which he continues can only be truly taken into the mouth of Dickens: "Betimes, I set myself to the task of investigating the motley world to which our progress in humanity has attained, caring little about misrepresentation. I incurred what hostility I provoked, in searching through a devious labyrinth for the footprints of Truth."

XIII

Now, if what I have said is true, what becomes of his influence? If his attitudes are fundamentally revolutionary, do they peter out in misconceptions, falsifications—till Chesterton can get away with a picture of him as a roaring loon of gusto, or Forster can seem to sniff validly at his tremendous universe of creation as at a flat shadow-show? Or does his work find devious ways, in the rapidly extending and complicated situation of world capitalism, to reassert its basic energy and stir further artistic developments along the same lines?

If one looks at England, it seems at first glance as if Dickens's influence does indeed peter out. Clearly, he has a strong effect, directly or indirectly, on the post-1848 novelists of Victorian England, the Brontës, Trollope, Collins, Reade, George Eliot; but they move, on the whole, steadily towards naturalism. Enough of the grand tradition remains in their work to give it breadth, dignity, fullness; but the weakening side of their definition shows up in the epigones who succeed them. Dickens's influence seems fairly well quenched.

True, he entered powerfully into the lives of writers like Swinburne and William Morris, though he did not directly affect their styles. More importantly, he had a strong effect on Ruskin, helping to bring about the redirection of his energies from art criticism to a method which embraced both art and social problems in a single concept of integration. *Unto this Last*, the decisive work of revolt by Ruskin, reveals this effect of his. But still we are far from finding any successor in the realm of fiction who carries on his work.

The successor is, however, there: George Bernard Shaw, who

has abundantly paid tribute to the decisive impact on his life of works like *Little Dorrit* and *Our Mutual Friend*. I do not wish here to enter into any examination of the strengths and weaknesses of Shaw; but even a cursory glance shows that his great virtue has been the fact that throughout his work he is aware of people as living in capitalist society. This it is which marks him out from all the other writers of his period in England. And this virtue he owed first to Dickens, and then to Marx. Dickens gave him the vision of what the alienating pressures meant, and Marx gave him intellectual confidence.

Other writers, from Gissing to Wells, owed much to Dickens; but they did not share the fully penetrative sense that Shaw had of Dickens's essential meaning.

Dickens's influence has then been by no means negligible in Britain; but it is to the European novel in general that we must look for the full fertilizing results of his work. In France and even more in Germany he helped to broaden the sphere of the novel; but it was in Russia and Scandinavia that he found his natural kinsmen. For there it was that a number of factors made possible the rebirth of the novel as a great tragic medium. Through Dostoevsky and Strindberg, on whom he had a profound effect at key moments of their development, his influence broadly enters the whole European stream.

Here were writers who were able to carry on in terms of the post-1860 situation his awareness of what self-alienation meant, and to apply in various ways his method of fantasy-projection and dream-process. (Strindberg's novels, in which Dickens's influence is paramount, must be recalled here.)

To examine the new forms, the new tensions, which his ideas and methods assume in Dostoevsky and Strindberg, would require another book; but I must emphasize the kinship to bring out the part which he played in the European developments since 1850. They lacked his broad resolutions, but they carried on his definition of the *alienation of man from man, man from himself*, in a capitalist society.

It is because I believe that the revaluation of Dickens's work and influence can yet play a very important part in the cultural struggle of to-day, that I have written this study. The "dark popular age" is still with us, is with us, indeed, to an extent that Dickens could not have guessed at. Mass-media like radio and cinema make incomparably more pressing the problem of transmuting naturalistic and decadent forms with a new life, a poetic life which will utter the truth of the human condition and recapture tradition. Dickens is the master who has shown how this can be done; his method is more relevant to-day than ever.

I do not mean that we should start trying to write novels like Dickens's or ape his tricks of style. I mean that we should realize his fundamental method of fusing dream-process and realism in terms of essential human conflict, and find our own ways of relating this method to contemporary issues.

Dickens is still ahead of us.*

XIV

And so we come back to the June day when the strains pulled him to pieces. Though he had had to give up his readings, he had not given up intentions of appearing in private theatricals once more. Not long before, he had told a friend that his lifelong ambition had been to have complete charge of a great theatre; now he produced three plays at a show given at Lady Freake's on June 2nd, with his daughters in leading parts. In May 1869, he had made his will, which, as its first item, left £1,000 to Ellen; and now on June 2, 1870, he added a codicil leaving *All the Year Round* to Charley. (He left almost £100,000 in all, showing how unnecessary had been the toils that shortened his life.)

On Monday, June 6th, he walked once more over to Rochester with his dogs, and leant on the fence before Restoration House. This house had appeared in *Great Expectations* as Miss Havisham's House.

I had stopped to look at the house as I passed; and its seared red-brick walls, blocked windows, and strong green ivy clasping even the stacks of chimneys with its twigs and tendons, as if with sinewy old arms, had made up a rich attractive mystery, of which I was the hero. Estella was the inspiration of it, and the heart of it, of course. . . .

I mention this in this place, of a fixed purpose, because it is the clue by which I am able to be followed into my poor labyrinth.

* Mr. J. B. Priestley has pointed out to me that Charley Chaplin is the last direct carrier of the Dickens tradition. He uses the tension of day-dream and actuality, develops the full pathos of the excluded individual, and has in many ways the same mixture of strength and weakness as Dickens. Chaplin, we should remember, came out of the last remnants in England of the stage and music-hall tradition that had meant so much to Dickens.

Now he stood looking in fascination at this place; and the people who noticed him said that the house would appear in the next instalment of *Edwin Drood*. And so it did; in the last instalment he ever wrote, as "The Vinery" (after the open space before the house, known as "The Monk's Vineyard").

The House of Love, the House of Childhood.

Next day he drove to Cobham Wood. In the evening he hung up Chinese lanterns in the recently added conservatory.

On Wednesday he worked at *Edwin Drood* in the chalet. At the dinner-table he told Georgy that for an hour he had been feeling ill. He stood up and almost fell over. She caught him in time and tried to help him over to the sofa. He muttered, "On the ground."

These were his last coherent words. He sank into a kind of coma, dying about six in the evening next day. Mamie and Katie were called in from London as soon as he was found to have suffered a stroke, and Katie went back to tell her mother. But it was not Kate Dickens who came in haste to the house of death; it was Ellen Ternan.

The last words he had written were those with which *Edwin Drood* ends—the passage where Datchery, having had his talk with Opium Sal, feels at last that he has definite evidence against Jasper the murderer. "I mention this in this place, of a fixed purpose, because it is the clue by which I am able to be followed into my poor labyrinth."

Appendix

NOTE ON BULWER LYTTON'S CONCEPT OF ART EXPRESSION AS A TRANCE CONDITION

I include the following note on Bulwer Lytton's aesthetic because it helps us to understand Dickens and his work—*Edwin Drood* in particular. Dickens had never worked out anything like so definite a notion of creative process, and the papers in which Lytton formulated his viewpoint were late (in the 'sixties) so that they could not have affected Dickens's development in its earlier formative phases. However, though the lights are sharper in Lytton's statement of position, there were elements in Dickens which corresponded to that position; partly through the direct influence of Lytton in conversation and writing, and partly through the extent to which they both drew on the Gothic aspects of Romanticism.

The concept of Trance in Lytton is of special import if we are to understand Jasper in *Drood*. Dickens shared many of Lytton's influences; both men knew Elliston and were deeply interested in mesmerism and clairvoyance; both saw in spiritualism, not a revelation from another world, but a chance of getting clues to the workings of the human unconscious. Jasper's drug-induced trance states are thus certainly in Dickens's symbolism one aspect of artistic experience —but an aspect which has become perverted, leading to evil and disintegrative trends, sundering what it should join. (That is, the emotional dissociation of Jasper has its art-equivalent in Naturalism.) Hence the deep meaning that was to attach itself to the account of Jasper's facing himself.

Lytton's ideas help to give us an idea of Dickens's artistic climate as nothing else can.

It is difficult to construct any clear aesthetic theory from Bulwer's scattered pronouncements; but a certain amount of coherent sense can be made out.

He knew the German Romantics, poets, and thinkers well. Carlyle, some nine years older than Bulwer, confessed that only less praise should go to Bulwer than to himself for having stimulated and fed the early Victorian hunger for German culture.

It is therefore, no doubt, directly to Goethe and Hegel as well as to lesser German writers, that Bulwer went for his aesthetic idiom; and he drew very little on Coleridge and his acclimatization of the ideas of the organic process of poetry.

First, he affirms the perpetual upflow of forms of reverie (dream-images, evanescent fantasy-gleams) out of the unconscious on to the edge of consciousness. He cites Kant in support of the belief that in dreams the movement of thought is extremely rapid and that it is for this reason dreams are so difficult to remember. He considers that Kant understates in saying, "We can dream more in a minute than we can act in a day." And adds, "So much is suggested in so small a point of time, that, were it in my power to transcribe all that passes through my mind in any given half-hour of silent reverie, it would take me years to write it down." Herein lies the reason for the great difference between the imagination of a work and the work as it gets written down. "We may, indeed, give the general purport of a meditated argument; the outlines of a dramatic plot, artistically planned, or of a narrative of which we have painted on the retina of the mind the elementary colours and the skeleton outlines. But where the boundless opulence of idea and fancy which had enriched the subject before we were called upon to contract its expenditure into sober bounds? How much of the fairy gold turns, as we handle it, into dry leaves? And by a tyranny that we cannot resist, while we thus leave unuttered much that we had designed to express, we are carried on mechanically to say much of which we had not even a conscious perception the moment before the hand jotted it down, as the inevitable consequence of the thought out of which another thought springs self-formed and full-grown."

Again he expresses the gap between the fullness and complexity of the art form as projected in reverie and the comparative dryness and thinness of the art product.

"All thoughts, and perhaps in proportion to their gravity and scope, lose something when transferred from contemplation into language, as all bodies, in proportion to their bulk, lose something of what they weighed in air when transferred to water.

"Musing over these phenomena in my own mind, whereby I find that, in an art to which I have devoted more than thirty years' practice and study, I cannot in any way adequately accomplish my own conception; that the typical idea within me is always far, infinitely far, beyond my power to give it on the page the exact image which it wore in space; that I catch from the visible light but a miserable daguerreotype of the form of which I desire the truthful picture—a caricature that gives indeed features, and lines, and wrinkles, but not the bloom, not the expression, not the soul of the idea which the love in my own heart renders lovely to me."

He says that "this wondrous copiousness of thought . . . escapes from me, scattering into spray as a cataract yields but drops to the hand that would seize it amidst its plashes and fall."

In this unseizable fullness of the image he finds a pledge of the future. "For Man, every present contains a future. I say not with Descartes, 'I think, therefore I am,' but rather, 'I am, therefore I think; I think, and therefore I shall be.'" (This future he imagines, following Chalmers in his Bridgewater Treatise, as an immortality off the earth; but his logic would apply equally to an earthly future of continually realized potentiality.)

To canalize the vast flow of reverie certain forms of activity are needed, certain tricks or gestures which simultaneously release and control the flow. He relates these release-controls of the writer, the orator, the artist, with the methods used by Braid of Manchester, who hypnotized patients by making them stare at a lancet-case held by his finger and thumb.

Lesser intelligences cannot control the release-mechanisms, but are lost between the burst of dream-imagery and the actual details of living. "It is only the poet of immense grasp and range that, seizing on all these material elements of earth, carries them aloft into his upper air, held there in solution, as the atmosphere above us holds the metals and the gases, and calling them forth at his easy will, to become tangible and visible, through luminous golden vapour; as, at the magic of the chemist, gases burst into light from the viewless space; or, in a ray of the sun, are discovered the copper and the iron which minister to our most familiar uses."

Here he has to some extent reversed his first-cited position, which emphasized the impossibility of holding the richness of the aesthetic intuition in anything like completeness. Now he emphasizes the extent to which the creative process can successfully transmute the intractible material with which it begins, into something luminously new and strange—something which yet to critical analysis can reveal the primary ingredients persisting inside the transmutation.

Perhaps the reason why he does not notice the change in his attitudes lies in the undetected duality of his conception of reverie. On the one hand it is the dream-flow of unseizable speed and opulence; on the other hand it encloses a "typical idea." And by the typical idea he means, as other statements of his prove, the archetypal pattern which gives universality and aesthetic unity to the intuition. Reverie, in so far as it is the dynamic dream-flow, leaves a sense of defeat and weakness; in so far as it sets into action the creative faculty, it provides a shaping and transformative mechanism, in which resides triumph and strength.

But this duality of meaning is never noted by Bulwer. From another angle, however, he brings out the contrast of passive and active elements in the creative process. He discusses the achievements of the clairvoyant, and then opposes to them the work of the poet—"the normal clairvoyance of the imagination."

The feats of mediums in mesmeric trance he finds capricious and uncertain. "Although a somnambulist tells you accurately to-day the cause of an intricate disease or the movements of your son in Bombay, he may not be able to-morrow to detect a cold in your head, or tell you what is done by your next-hand neighbour." The more remarkable "the advice or predictions dictated by this mystical second-sight," the more careful we need to be in placing any every-day reliance upon it.

"No man has sacrificed more for the cause of mesmerism than

Dr. Elliotson, and perhaps no man would more earnestly warn a neophyte—startled by his first glimpse of phenomena, which, developed by the priesthood of Delphi, once awed to subjection the luminous intellect of Greece—not to accept the lucky guesses of the Pythian for the infallible response of Apollo."

For reliable marvels, capable of an infinitely stabler extension, he declares that he has only to look to his library. The poets and scientists provide "instances of normal clairvoyance immeasurably more wonderful than those erratic gleams of lucidity in magnetic sleep, which one man reveres as divine and another man disdains as incredible."

The poet habitually sees "through other organs than his eyes." He improves by practice, whereby the medium at the end of his days is merely a fitful instrument of a power that shows no deeper insight into reality.

"Whereas the clairvoyance of the somnambule has solved no riddle in nature, added no invention to art, the clairvoyance of wakeful intellect has originated all the manifold knowledge we now possess—predicted each step of our progress—divined every obstacle that encumbered the way—lit beacons that never fade in the wastes of the past—taken into its chart the headlands that loom through the future." Here indeed the future held in the unexhausted potentiality of the creative image is entirely an earthly one. Bulwer has forgotten his Bridgewater Treatises.

He goes on, "Every art, every craft that gives bread to the millions, came originally forth from some brain that saw it first in the typical image. Before the very paper I write on could be fashioned from rags, some musing inventor must have seen in his lucid clairvoyance the idea of a thing that was not yet existent. It is obviously undeniable that every invention added to our uses must have been invented before it was seen—that is, its image must have appeared to the inventor 'through some other organ than his eyes.' "

Again he halts on an undetected duality of concept. By poetic clairvoyance he means both the active comprehension of the "typical idea"; but he also means realistic vision reaching beyond the mere bounds of circumstance. "The gift of seeing through other organs than the eyes is more or less accurately shared by all in whom imagination is strongly concentred upon any selected 'object, however distant and apart from the positive experience of material senses." Thus, Richardson, the prim printer, realizes the inner and the outer man of the libertine Lovelace; and Shakespeare expresses the dizziness of samphire-picking through he may have never seen a cliff.

In all this there is the imagination of realistic penetration, but hardly that of the Typical Idea. Bulwer goes on to claim realistic clairvoyance. He had often, he says, minutely described places in his books without having seen them. If later he actually visited the places, he never once found, "after the most rigid scrutiny, that the clairvoyance of imagination had deceived me." And he adds, "I am not sure, indeed, that I could not describe the things I imagine more exactly than the things I habitually see. I am not sure that I could not give a more truthful picture of the Nile, which I have never beheld except in my dreams, than I could of the little lake at the bottom of my own park, on the banks of which I loitered out my schoolday holidays.

"The truth really seems to be, that the imagination acquires by custom a certain involuntary unconscious power of observation and comparison, correcting its own mistakes, and arriving at precision of judgment, just as the outward eye is disciplined to compare, adjust, estimate, measure, the objects reflected on the back of its retina."

The whole question of the Typical Image and its power of creating the New seems forgotten. Indeed, Bulwer goes on to define the imagination as merely "the faculty of glassing images." A kind of crystalline space of pure perception free of time and space but always seeing what is actually there. "Where the imagination is left clear from disturbing causes—no confusing shadows cast upon its wave from the shores that confine it—there, with an equal fidelity, it reflects the star that is aloof from it by myriads of miles, or the heron that has just soared from the neighbouring reeds."

This movement of the realizing imagination is continual, a going out from the self into the world and into other persons. "Genius in the poet, like the nomad of Arabia, ever a wanderer, still ever makes a home where the well or the palm tree invites it to pitch the tent. Perpetually passing out of himself and his own positive circumstantial condition of being into other hearts and into other conditions, the poet obtains his knowledge of human life by transporting his own life into the lives of others."

First, the poet "establishes his inquisitive impassioned sympathy with Nature: affected by her varying aspects with vague melancholy or mysterious joy. Thus, all great poets commence with lively and sensuous impressionability to natural objects and phenomena, though the highest order of poets, in proportion as life unfolds itself, ascend from sympathy with groves and streams to sympathy with the noblest Image of the Maker—spiritual, immortal Man! and man's character and man's passions, man's place and fate in creation. . . ."

Thus he seeks to define the movement of imaginative union by which the poet enters into the life of nature and of men. The Clairvoyance of the Normal, which is essential to all human growth, but which is most intense and comprehensive in the poet.

But the problem of the New is still not faced. Does the act of union merely give the poet the power to know and combine various forms or elements in new ways? Yes, says Bulwer. Art "may be said to create when it combines existent details into new wholes." Both Nature and Art work with given elements or forces; but Art has the distinction that with it the act of creation involves at once the infusion of "life and intellect." And "it is only in proportion as the life thus bestowed endures beyond the life of man, and the intellect thus expressed exceeds that which millions of men can embody in one form, that we acknowledge a really great work of Art." In such a work the poet "has created a form of life which the world did not know before."

The point at which the difference between a mere combination of given elements and a new form comes about is not at all clearly indicated. Bulwer is simply making an empirical distinction. The works that endure must have the new vitalizing element, or they would die; the works with the new vitalizing element must endure, or they wouldn't have it. All that is tautological and does not help us far.

But he has read too much Hegel and Goethe to be gravelled for long at this point. He knows that Hegel has defined Art as "essentially destined to manifest the general." Not the generalized canon of a pseudo-classical art from which the vitality of particular existences has been banished; but the order of an art in which general and particular are dialectically opposed and united. Art is the resolution of the contradictions that clash in daily experience. "The necessity of the beau-ideal in art is derived from the imperfections of the real," he cites Hegel as saying. "The mission of art is to represent, under sensible forms, the free development of life, and especially of mind."

The free development of life. Here at last is a term which promises to reconcile the dream-flow with the conscious activity, the realizing union with the Typical Idea. And in Goethe's notion of Symbol he hopes to find the key for the working-out of the fusion of the opposites.

Goethe had said of the drama, "to be theatrical a piece must be symbolical; that is, every action must have an importance of its own, and must lead to one more important still." This symbolism, Bulwer argues, will be most potent when, as in the plays of Shakespeare, there is the most intense conflict and union between "truths the most subtle, delicate, and refining in the life and organization of men" and "the elements which humanity has most in common."

As a more recent example of symbolism he takes Goethe's own *Wilhelm Meister* where the story of events is merged with "the inward signification of an artist's apprenticeship in art, a man's apprenticeship in life." *Don Quixote* and *Gulliver's Travels* are other works that unite "an interior symbolical signification with an obvious popular interest in character and incident."

Thus the realizing union, which moves out from the self into Nature and other persons in the clairvoyance of the normal, becomes one with the Typical Idea, which introduces a new organizing centre into life, a new total pattern.

Bulwer may therefore be said to overcome the conflict in his thought and achieve something of a consistent aesthetic. But he never managed to bring a fully critical focus to bear on his terms and definitions, on the relations of his thought. His attempt to make a comprehensive statement staggers and stumbles, and he only succeeds in getting at his goal by some drastic short cuts:

"[Art's] base is in the study of Nature—not to imitate, but first to select, and then to combine, from Nature those materials into which the artist can breathe his own vivifying idea; and as the base of Art is in the study of Nature, so its polish and ornament must be sought by every artist in the study of those images which the artists before him have already selected, combined, and vivified; not, in such study, to reproduce a whole that represents another man's mind, and can no more be born again than can the man who created it; but again to select, to separate, to recombine—to go through the same process in the contemplation of Art which he employed in the contemplation of Nature; profiting by all details, but grouping them anew by his own mode of generalization, and only availing himself of the minds of others for the purpose of rendering more full and complete the realization of that idea of truth and beauty which has its conception in his own mind.

"For that can be neither a work of art (in the aesthetic sense of the word) nor a work of genius in any sense of the word, which does not do something that, as a whole, has never been done before; which no other living man could have done; and which never, to the end of time, can be done again. . . ."

The essays from which these passages are taken were written in 1862–63; and represent a highly important attempt, at a dark and difficult moment of English culture, to restate the main positions of the great Romantic critics and writers on aesthetics. Bulwer was not unaware of the work done by Coleridge; but he did not grasp its full virtue; he was thus prevented from gaining just that insight into the full organic nature of art-process which he lacks.

But this weakness is probably inevitable. We could not expect the gains of Coleridge to be directly inherited by the Victorians. The failure of the great poetic tradition in England after Shelley and Keats meant that the main struggle to advance awareness of the transformative nature of poetry had passed over to Baudelaire and the symbolists in France. Bulwer was stating as much as was assimilable in England of the 1860's.

And he was adding something new in his own way. His efforts to use the material of clairvoyance and hypnotism in order to illuminate the creative process were important, and showed correctly the lines along which the new poetic attack on the contemporary world must proceed. His deep curiosity as to the unconscious processes of the spirit (which he shared with his friend Dickens) was fruitful in leading him on to intuit the new orientations, the new idioms and methods which poetry would have to acquire if it was to confront the darkening world of Victorian capitalism.

Thus, in his 1845 preface to *Night and Morning*, he had already touched on the problem which, from Baudelaire on to Tzara and Eluard, was to obsess French poets. He speaks as a novelist, but what he says has even greater relevance for the poet. But in Victorian England the poets had recoiled from the tremendous task that Bulwer outlines, and it was left for the novelists, above all for Dickens, to carry on the advance into new human tracts.

"Long since, in searching for new regions in the Art to which I am a servant, it seemed to me that they might be found lying far, and rarely trodden, beyond that range of conventional morality in which Novelist after Novelist had entrenched himself—amongst those subtle recesses in the ethics of human life in which Truth and Falsehood dwell undisturbed and unseparated. The vast and dark Poetry around us—the Poetry of Modern Civilization and Daily Existence, is shut out from us in much, by the shadowy giants of Prejudice and Fear. He who would arrive at the Fairy Land must face the Phantoms. Betimes, I set myself to the task of investigating the motley world to which our progress in humanity has attained, caring little what misrepresentation I incurred, what hostility I provoked, in searching through a devious labyrinth for the foot-tracks of Truth."

Those are great words, which could not have been uttered except by a man with a deep insight into the real creative problem of his day. "The vast and dark Poetry around us, the Poetry of Modern Civilization and Daily Existence." Those few words set the whole basic problem for the post-Romantic poet, and explain Bulwer's fascinated interest in things like hypnotism—an interest more than shared by Dickens, who in his relations with Mrs. De la Rue is clearly trying to use the hypnotic contact for a love-exploration of the depths in another personality, which he wants desperately to reach and from which he feels barred away by all prevailing forms of communication.

As the Surrealists have felt in dream and automatic writing, so Bulwer feels in clairvoyance and hypnotism; a hitherto disregarded power, which yet lies at the root of creative energy and which is shared by everyone. In making his claims for creative energy, he is thus implicating the common man in a new way and preparing the way for a new kind of art, in which universality will be regained through the fight against the dominant dissociations of a self-divided society. This new kind of art, based on a new kind of release-control, will be that which breaks through all the lies and distortions, and which realizes "the vast and dark Poetry around us."

Notes

I

I.—See also the full-face photo of Mrs. Dickens in Miss Storey's book.

III.—*Letter about Mary Weller*. Note that he assumes her death—compare what is later said of the death-wish.

VII.—At the foot of Chatham Hill stood "The Malt Shovel" with a notice that reappears on the "Pegasus Arms" (*Hard Times*): "Good malt makes good beer. Walk in, you'll find it here." C. D.'s account of the Mudfrog Association holds many respected Chatham names: Waghorn or Sowster the Beadle. For the Falstaff Inn and the country round see *Uncommercial Trav., Tramps*. For the Rochester sunset, *Copperfield*, Chap. XIII, and *Amer. Notes*, Chaps. XV and XVI.

The school dame seems to reappear in Mr. Wopsle's Great Aunt (*Great Exp.*); Capt. Cuttle likes *The Voice of the Sluggard* (cf. *Chuzzlewit*, IX). Jane Bonney appears in *Nickleby*; the Abudah story is cited in the *Haunted Man* and *U.C.*, Chap. XIV.

"Merriest games . . ." is from *The Child's Story* (1852); the pirates, *A Holiday Romance*.

VIII.—He had no sympathy with the Oxford Movement. Harriet Martineau gave up his *Household Words* (to which she'd contributed) because he would allow no favourable word for anyone under Catholic influence; then published a story holding up the Catholic priesthood to contumely. The *Child's History* strongly supports the idea of suppressive action against Catholicism and political reaction in general; and he wrote it to save his children from error. "I don't know what I should do if he were to get hold of any Conservative or High Church notion," he said of his eldest son, Charley; "and the best way of guarding against any such horrible result is, I take it, to wring the Parrot's neck in the very cradle." He saw the danger as "Here, more Popery, there, more Methodism—as many forms of consignment to eternal damnation as there are articles. . . . These things cannot last."

On the other hand, there is the panegyric of the Bible in *Dombey*; and the Bible reading of humble characters, Betty Higden, Little Nell, etc. He wrote a simple version of the N.T. for his children, omitting all theology and treating Joseph as Christ's father. Ruskin (*Fors Clavigera*) says C. D. had no belief in "heaven." In 1861 C. D. cites this joke: "A charity boy persisted in saying to the inspector of schools that Our Saviour was the only forgotten son of his father, and that he was forgotten by his father before all worlds, etc., etc., in an Athanasian and Theological Dogmatism."

Consistently he fought the idea that "moral" regeneration must precede social betterment; he always wanted sanitation first, and said education was useless without such things. He quarrelled with Cruikshank over the latter's exclusively moral interpretation of drunkenness.

2

I.—*Camden Town*. Prominent in his early works. Bob Cratchit lived there, and Jemima Evans. Traddles lodged there with Micawber. Toodles had a friend in Staggs Gardens, "Camberling" town. Heyling, in *Pickwick*, runs his victim down in Little College St., Camden Town, "a desolate place surrounded by fields and ditches."

Barber. Original of Pol Sweedlepipe (?). *Soho* in its early days appears in *Tale of Two Cities*; Ralph Nickleby lives in Golden Square.

Huffam's region. The area round Church Street keeps turning up in the novels (*Dombey, Great Expectations*—also Quilp's wharf in *Old Cur. Shop*), and is particularly prominent in the late *Our Mutual Friend*. Huffam seems to have given many features to Cuttle, Peggotty, and other sailors. In visiting him, Charles often passed the dropsical tavern, "The Six Jolly Porters."

Covent Garden. Then a centre of harlots.

II.—*Periodicals*. The *Portfolio* was born 1823 and lasted some three years. Other such productions were *The Mirror, The Vehicle*.

Lant Street. The family reappear as the Garlands in *Old Cur. Shop*. *Pickwick* deals with the street: which is the street also of Dick Swiveller.

The Perils, etc. This tale has a Mr. Commissioner Pordage, an old Rochester name.

Rats. Rat-swarming was a common horror feature in the dreadfuls which C. D. read. E.g. ". . . a lingering death in the stifling vault, to be gnawed by rats. The prospect of such a doom was simply awful. . . . A scampering might have been heard, a few sharp squeaks and then once more the army of foul and disgusting rats returned to the charge, raging for the blood of their human foes." Chap. 3, *The Blue Dwarf*, by Percy B. St. John.

III.—*Urinary trouble*. It has been suggested that John had suffered from venereal disease and that the fact had much to do with Dickens's horrors—a possible but unproved thesis.

IV.—*Johnson Street*. Micawber lived there with Traddles as lodger.

School. Cruikshank lived in this street later and died there. *Jones* was the original of Creakle. *Taylor* the English master was a constant flute player: (?) original of Mr. Mell. The usher who took writing, maths., English, some of the Latin, mended pens and (being the most gentlemanly person in the establishment) called at homes of sick boys, no doubt mixed with an idealized portrait of C. D. himself to fashion Nich. Nickleby, and the gruff man-of-all-works with a kind heart, who nursed the boys during an epidemic of scarlet fever, is (?) Phil Squad of *Bleak House*.

431

Tobin was later one of C. D.'s amenuenses.

Miller and His Men. Produced 1811, revived 1835; held a fascination for C. D. all his life; many refs. in his books and letters. "We knew it by heart, every word of it," says P. Fitzgerald. Some twenty years later it was revived again, and C. D. insisted on taking young P. F. There was extreme disillusion. "The whole was stupid, dull, and heavy to a degree, so at last, about the second act, Boz rose slowly and sadly, and said 'he could stand it no longer.' I really think he was grieved at having his old idol shattered, and perhaps was mortified."

This episode was in many ways allegorical of C. D.'s attitude to his childhood.

For its popularity among children, see Sgt. Ballantyne's *Some Experiences of a Barrister's Life*, Chap. II. (Other passages in this book of interest for C. D. are Chap. IV on Laing; Chap. XI on the Shakespeare Club).

3

I.—*Blackmore*. Ellis of the firm was great snuff-taker, seems Mr. Perker of *Pickwick*. B. said he recognized in *Pickwick* and *N. N.* many persons and events of the office. On the books were Weller, Mrs. Bardell, Rudge, Newman Knott (a hard up gent. often in the office: Newman Noggs).

Potter. In *Making a Night of It*, and *Misplaced Attachment*, by Boz.

Polygon. Here Godwin and Mary Wollstonecraft lived—C. D. seems not to have known it. Skimpole and family lived here, with many Spanish refugees walking about in cloaks. Skimpole's house was very dilapidated, two or three area rails gone, water-butt broken, bell-handle pulled off, etc. The old St. Pancras Church nearby figures (with body snatching) in *Tale of Two Cities*. Boz tells of the clerk population of Somers Town pouring through (cf. Lowton of *Pickwick*).

Legal Types. Vholes, Heep, Dodson and Fogg, Sampson Brass, Spenlow, Jorkins, Tulkinghorne. Almost all scoundrelly and repulsive.

Boz has a sketch of the St. Bart. disputes: *Doctors' Commons*.

II.—*Fitzroy Square*. The family's movements from 1831 to 1833 are somewhat complicated. They go to Norfolk St., F. Sq., then to Margaret St.; then to Fitzroy St., and on to Bentinck St.

III.—*True Sun*, owned by Murdo Young and Laman Blanchard.

Mirror. Gladstone in 1877 said it was for years superior to Hansard. Barrow's house at Norwood: (?) home of Spenlow in *D. C. W.* Harness says that when Joseph Hume in 1834 complained his speeches weren't faithfully reported in *Times*, Barrow put C. D. on to him, and Hume soon called *peccavi*.

Stanley. Later, dining with Gladstone, C. D. found himself in the same room and told his host; Lord Derby, present, also had his version of the meeting. (He sent Stanley a copy of *Boz*, reminding him of the interview; though he damned his politics, he wasn't above trying to use him.)

Black. Mill wrote in his *Autobiography*: "I have always considered Black as the first journalist who carried criticism and the spirit of reform into the details of English institutions. Those who are not old enough to remember those times can hardly believe what the state of public discussion then was."

IV.—*Private Theatricals*. Box's *Mrs. Joseph Porter*, which describes all the disorder and miseries.

The next letter to Kolle after the Monday protest encloses 14s. for cigars to go to H. Bramwell, one of the cast, later judge and peer. Scenery was by Austin, Mitton, Kolle. "The Band will be numerous and complete under the direction of Mr. E. Barrow."

Love. See letter to T. Powell, August 2, 1845, about his brother Augustus. C. D. refuses to interfere in A.'s loves. "I broke my heart into the smallest pieces, many times between thirteen and three-and-twenty. Twice I was very horribly in earnest; and once I really set upon the cast for six or seven long years, all the energy and determination of which I am the owner. But it went the way of nearly all such things at last, though I think it kept me steadier than the working of my nature was, to many good things for the time. If any one had interfered with my very small Cupid, I don't know what absurdity I might not have committed. But having plenty of rope he hanged himself, beyond all chance of restoration."

Forster (end of chap. 3) cites letter at time of *Dombey* when C. D. was selecting church for marriage of Florence and visited the city churches, recalling time he went out of shower with Angelica (Maria) into a church in Huggin Lane, and begged that their marriage should take place there. "And O, Angelica, what has become of you, this present Sunday morning when I can't attend to the sermon; and, more difficult question than that, what is become of me as I was when I sat by your side." Note how he relives his own life in fantasy in marrying off his heroine, and sees his past self as a detached person.

Also his paper on birthdays about the unsent letters to Mrs. Beadnell asking for Maria's hand. Maria "pervaded every chink and crevice of my mind for three or four years."

Mr. Beadnell. Two more letters, Dec. 11, 1854: "I am at this moment pledged to several readings . . . several large towns . . . all tearing at me like so many zoological creatures before dinner." And Dec. 15, 1859, about a Mlle Blanche who wants facilities for translating his books.

4

I.—*O'Thello*. Georgina objected to Kitton reproducing a page; Langdon also gives one. Note the Boz amateurs play *Othello*. In a letter to Kolle, 1834 (March–April), C. D. mentions he hopes to place the *O.* manuscript in K.'s hands and jokes about what he'll do if a lottery ticket wins ("money or freehold houses").

Holland. Had served under Bolivar. Only one issue under new editor had appeared. By printing young authors, he built up the paper and sold at a profit by auction, 1835.

The Red Rover. Only at the end does the theme of American Independence emerge; but the general picture might well have led to an argument on the Americans. The book, I think, had a strong effect on Dickens, helping to build his image of *Shipwreck* as social and personal crisis (especially Chap. XXIV, the account of the child found with dying mother on the wrecked ship). There is one remarkable phase which shows how Cooper responded to the dream-symbol, "the tones of an oracle—the whisperings of fancy—the very words of truth! It was a strange and persuasive voice."

II.—*Chronicle.* Estab. 1769, twenty years before *Times*, but had declined. E. bought it for £17,000 to turn into Liberal paper. Joseph Parkes, one of powers behind political scene (sort of chief Whig agent) helped Black and engaged Beard.

Five pounds was journalist minimum, agreed by all papers but *Times.* Parkes wanted a polemical policy: thunder against *Times.* The Eatonswill editors are Stirling and Black.

Times beat *M. C.* by a day over Edinburgh report and called its account "By Express." C. D. thereafter set out to show what express could be.

Lodgings. Those at Buckingham St. are the ones that Copperfield takes from Mrs. Crupp.

IV.—*Bristol and Bath* occur in *Pickwick*, but Bath (with its footmen's swarries) much more in detail.

V.—*Reviews of Sketches.* They were praised in *Lit. Gazette, Sun, Sunday Times, Satirist, Sunday Herald, Athenaeum.* Forster noticed it in *Examiner. Chambers's Edinburgh Journal* said that unless he were to "fall off very miserably," he could hardly fail to become "a successful popular author."

Whitehead. Later famous for *Richard Savage* (printed in *Bentley's M.,* 1841–2).

Originals of P. Characters. Much industry has been put into tracing these. Buzfuz is Serg. Bompas; Jingle is C.'s old pal Potter; Nupkins is Laing the London magistrate who comes again into *Oliver.* Many Chatham figures appear: the Fat Boy is James Budden, whose father kept the "Red Lion." (Four names come from the minutes of the case in which the Duke of York in 1827 was accused of giving promotions on the recommendation of his mistress, Mary Anne Clarke: Wardle, Dowler, Lowton, and Mary Anne Clarke.)

The "Leather Bottle" at Cobham was a special favourite of C. D. all his life. Dingley Dell was probably Cob Tree Hall, near Maidstone.

Lord Jeffrey seems the first to have compared Pickwick and Sam with Don Quixote and Sancho.

P. Chronology. Set in 1817; but Jingle refers to the July Revolution, and so C. D. made the time 1830, then in the list of errata set it back to 1827.

P. Appeal. At this phase C. D. appeals to all classes alike and lays the basis of national popularity on which he builds his struggle. *Pickwick* was liked by the common reader, but also by Lord Denman, Chief Justice Campbell, Sir. B. Brodie, Miss Craven (author of *Récit d'une Soeur*), Miss Mitford.

VI.—*Origins of Pickwick.* I have dealt cursorily in the text with this matter as it has been treated far beyond its importance. In 1849 Seymour's widow pub. a pamphlet to claim P. for her husband, who she said got the idea in 1835, and but for a severe illness would have written as well as illust. the book himself. C. D. replied that all S. had contributed was "the sporting tastes of Mr. Winkle." It has, however, been claimed that S. drew "Pickwick" in some comic etchings long before the *Papers* began, and put Winkle and the Fat Boy in one of his threepenny sketches. No doubt true, but really irrelevant.

Buss. Very soon after he successfully illustrated Mrs. Trollope's *The Widow's Marriage*, and then *Peter Simple*.

Reporting. About a month before the P. contract he reported the opening by Lord Melbourne of the Licensed Victuallers' School in Kennington.

Sunday. Timothy as pseudonym may be a jest at Timothy R. Matthews, free lance clergyman of Bedford, well known in Chelsea area, who gave out Sparks.

Hook. Colburn gave up the idea, put Hook on to the *New Monthly*, from which S. C. Hall resigned; later the *N. M.* was sold to Ainsworth. C. D. got the *Miscellany* through the advocacy of Hogarth.

VII.—*C. D.* may have played a part ((?) one of the waiters) in *Strange Gent.* In 1843 a revival of the *Village C.* was proposed; Dickens begged that it be dropped, as he had written it and the farce "in a fit of damnable good nature" without the least "regard for reputation." But in July 1836 he eagerly told Hullah that Hogarth had been with Braham, who "spoke highly of my works and fame" and wanted to be first to introduce him "as a dramatic writer." And he offered *V. C.* to Macready in 1838.

The *Strange G.* was revived 1873, but withdrawn at family displeasure. (In 1836, Feb., he told C. and Hall he wanted it published. Next year it did appear. His comments in the ded. of *V. C.* show he took its "success" very seriously.)

Room 23. Is the name chosen because Charles was 23 in 1835, the year when he was successfully wooing Kate?

Words. Note the previous quotations about the associative fascinations of letters and words—in 1, III; 2, I; 2, II.

VIII.—*Doughty St.* Sydney Smith had lived there when chaplain at the Foundling Hospital.

Country love. Chelsea was then full of tulip gardens and nurseries, avenues of lime and chestnut.

Sophy Wackles (*Old Cur. Shop*) lived there and her Cheggs was a market-gardener.

XIII.—Charles gave each issue of *P.* up to No. 14 to Mary inscribed, "Mary Hogarth from hers most affy. Charles Dickens." Mary's second name, Scott, came from Sir Walter.

Farm. Home of Linnell and visited by Blake.

Funeral. Day before he wrote to Chapman. "I feel that as to-morrow draws nigh, the bitterest part of this calamity is at hand. I hope that for that one day at all events I may be able to bear my part in it with fortitude and console those about me—it will be no harder trial to anyone than myself." To Ainsworth he wrote, "I have been so much unnerved and hurt by the loss of the dear girl whom I loved after my wife, more deeply and fervently than anyone on earth, that I have been compelled for once to give up all idea of my monthly work, and to try a fortnight's rest and quiet." The *Misc.* also announced, "The melancholy domestic affliction which Mr. Dickens has just sustained prevented the possibility of any mental exertion for the present number."

The biographers have all failed to see the terrible revelation of guilt-fear in his emotion. Examples are: "A pathetic business, this lovely girl's death," Straus. Wright sees the insult to Kate, but no more. "A gentle epitaph," etc., Una Pope-Hennessy.

IX.—*Parliament.* Note how he begins *Pickwick* with a debunking satire on parliamentary method; he continues the same attitude to p. method in his account of The Finches of the Grove (*Great Exp.*) and of *Our Vestry* (*H. Words*, 1852). In *Our Home Friend* (*H. W.*) the typical member is the "Member for Verbosity."

Bulwer. Plumer Ward was half-way house between fashionable romance and political novel. In his *De Vere* and *Tremaine* he took Balzac's *Petits Ménages* as model and set out to pique curiosity as to the actual figures behind his stories. (There is thus a link with the seventeenth–eighteenth-century *Chroniques Scandaleuses* which grew out of the heroic romance.) In *Tremaine* Cleveland was Chatham, and the theme was the evil effects of party spirit on the individual. Ward leads on to Disraeli and Bulwer. "He stands, with his remote and cultured gravity, at the junction between the philosophic fiction of 1780 to 1810 and the school of novel writing . . . from 1830 to 1850" which "with more or less elaboration or satire, dealt in actuality," M. Sadleir.

Bulwer in his *England and the English* insisted on the violent political effect which the fashionable novel of the 1820's had as an unconscious exposure of aristocratic society.

Sketches. James Grant of *Morning Advertiser* had pioneered, dealing with such subjects as the Marshalsea and its chum system. Dickens's new touch was the concentration on character.

Audience. The 1830's (following the strong and often violent working-class journals of the 1820's) saw a start in self-educative lower-class productions pioneered by Chambers's *Edinburgh J.* aiming to present knowledge in its "most cheering and captivating aspects." (See Mark Rutherford.) In a few weeks the sales rose to 30,000; then soon to 80,000. This rep. an extension of audience from previous improving periodicals; and was followed by the *Penny Mag.* (Soc. for Diff. of Useful Knowledge) and *Saturday Mag.* (S.P.C.K.), which was short-lived.

Cheap magazines published long extracts of Dickens's novels (e.g. *Cleave's Gazette* did *Nickleby*).

Hook. He influenced Dickens: in his *Gilbert Gurney* appear Jingle and Daly, the Judge, the lion-hunting ladies, etc.

Egan. From *Life in London*, "the Fat Knight who meets Corinthian Tom at the village of Pickwick: the King's Bench changed to the Fleet, and the archery match changed to the shooting party." (Una P.-H.)

S. Smith. He first resisted Dickens's charm, but gave in after Mrs. Nickleby. "My friends have not the smallest objection to being put into a number, but on the contrary would be proud of that distinction; and Lady Charlotte, in particular, you may marry to Newman Noggs."

Sterne. Charles claimed to know *The Sent. Journey* by heart (*The Holly Tree Inn*). Sterne had a primary influence on Bulwer in his "Caxtons" period.

Popular Taste. The Salisbury Square School of popular fiction (close in type to *The Police Gazette*) showed the general hunger for violence. Some boys wrote to T. Frost, "If you don't give us a good highwayman story we shan't take your publication any longer. So take notice." Signed: Jack Sheppard, Dick Turpin, Claude Duval, etc. In the 40's he read popular cheap fiction to find what to write (e.g. *Varney the Vampire*; *Ada the Betrayed*; *The Lady in Black*, whose brother had been hanged for forgery and who wandered before the bank, waiting). It will be obvious that both Dickens and Wilkie Collins (also Bulwer, Ainsworth, and Lefanu) had certain affinities with this genre.

Gothic Novel. Very strong in influence on the early work of Bulwer, Ainsworth, and Dickens alike. "Dickens notably illustrates the continuity of what has been roughly labelled as the Gothic element in romantic literature," E. A. Baker.

5

I—*Macready.* His father, too, had been jailed for debt, and M. had to go straight to the stage from Rugby—no university.

Forster. "I regarded him as a bitter personification of Whiggery that was natively instinct with hatred of everything like Chartism, living or dead," *The Life of Thomas Cooper, Written by Himself.*

II.—*Smithson*. T. Mitton's partner. Mrs. S. was sister of T. J. Thompson, another early friend. S. is the Yorkshireman mentioned in *N. N.* preface. He died 1844 and Dickens attended his funeral on Good Friday.

Light track. The sunset track as death appears in *What Christmas Is* (1851): "The winter sun goes down over town and village; on the sea it makes a rosy path, as if the sacred tread were fresh upon the water."

III.—*Portraits*. 1837, Cruikshank and S. Lawrence (who also did Kate; C. D.: "I shall assign her to you as you think proper"). Cruikshank put several portraits of Charles in his illustrations. In 1848 Maclise did a companion picture of Kate for his one of Charles used as frontispiece for *N. N.*

Piracies. The Posthumous Papers of the Cadgers' Club, . . . of the Wonderful Discovery Club, formerly of Camden Town, etc. G. W. M. Reynolds wrote books on *Pickwick in France*, and *in America*. When only eight issues were out of Dickens's story, F. Yates put on *The Peregrinations of Pickwick* at the Adelphi, and the play was published, done in the provinces and at the Surrey. April 1837 saw *The Pickwick Club* of E. Stirling played; July, *Sam Weller* at the Strand, by W. T. Moncrieff, who pirated also Scott, Lytton, and in his preface to this play congratulates himself on extending *P.'s* popularity.

For account of *Nicholas N.* at the Ambigu-Comique, see Thackeray's papers. Stirling adapted *N. N.* for the Adelphi. Moncrieff, too, printed with an insolent ded. to Dickens. Stirling also wrote *The Fortunes of Smike*. (1840.)

Quarterly Review. Charles remarked, "I hope I may truly say that no writer ever had less vanity than I have; and that my only anxiety to stand well with the world in that capacity, originated in my authorship being unhappily my trade, as it is happily my pleasure." *Pickwick* was much criticized for its laxities. One critic deplored its lack of "gentlemanlike accomplishment."

IV.—*Sketches of Young Gents*. Mr. and Mrs. Chirrup are Mr. and Mrs. W. Hall; their friend is E. Chapman.

Shakespeare Dinner. Late at night on the Saturday Dickens rode off with Forster, but already with news of near 50,000 sales.

Twickenham. Meagles lived there; the *N. N.* duel is at Petersham; the Kenwigs' excursion to Eel Pie Island; Oliver and Sikes stop at a pub in Isleworth on their burglary expedition.

Burdett. One of the first to hail Dickens as great champion of the poor. He was Miss Coutts's father.

V.—*Paul Clifford* is also a *roman a clé*: Gentleman George is George IV, Fighting Attie is the Duke of Wellington, Old Bags is Lord Eldon, etc. (Hazlitt, Godwin, Ebenezer Elliott all praised it strongly.) The vogue for such "scandalous chronicler" is shown by the remark in *Cheveley* about young girl novel-readers who at once wrote to London for the 'Key' (!) of every fashionable novel that came out, and got the names by heart.

This common habit of using real people helps to explain Dickens's method, though he added his own new creative verve to the direct caricature-copying.

Note that Dickens was not the only writer who worked at more than one novel at a time. Bulwer continually did so (*Aram* and *Godolphin*, *Lucretia* and *The Caxtons*, *Pausanias* and *K. Chillingly*).

VI.—*Publics*. The sense of divergent "publics" appears in comments like the following: "If I write a red-hot Puseyite story, I know exactly to whose care it ought to be confided; if a Low Church novel, where it would receive a hearty welcome," says one of the heroines of Emma Jane Worboise (a popular Low Church writer). Bulwer in his *England* differentiated between Public and People (public being a more limited class relation).

Richardson in a mild way was a precursor; by issuing *C. Grandison* in separate volumes he worked up the young ladies to write in.

X.—*N. N. originals*. Davenport seems V. Crummles, Miss D. the Infant.

Death. Ex. of C. D.'s burlesquing of his own themes, the mockery of the death-bed scene in Nicholas's play.

6

I.—*Broadstairs*. A letter to F. is a long jest on the death-wish, death-potence he wields. "I am doubtful whether it will be a murder, a fire, a vast robbery, or the escape of Gould, but it will be something remarkable, no doubt. I almost blame myself for the death of that poor girl who leaped off the monument upon my leaving town last year. She would not have done it if I had remained, neither would the two men have found the skeleton in the sewers.

II.—*Little Nell*. F. claimed to have suggested the death, as Nell was too pure to enter ordinary life. Even if this is true, C. D. would have merely taken it for the outward sign that he must face up to the ordeal of repeating Mary's death in his work.

Tong, where she died, was known to C. D. through staying there for one night at the Bell Inn in 1838—horses were changed there for the London–Chester mail.

Further light on the Victorian emotion about "pure dying girls" could be thrown by a study of Ruskin—especially interesting is his preface to *The Story of Ida*, by F. Alexander (1883): "Here is a real passage of human life, seen in the light that Heaven sent for it." The *Story* is an account of a "pure dying" Italian girl, who dies of a broken heart (and, perhaps, insanitary living conditions).

Clock. Note opening of *David C.* where his birth is one with the clock-voice, as if this mechanism of Time was the father-power of birth. Also, the paper about old Humphrey where C. D. climbs into the bowels of St. Paul's clock—"London's Heart": "When it should cease to beat, the City would be no more." Here he is at the core of power. "The great heart of London throbs in its giant breast." It "regulates the progress of the life around"; and the image is of a mechanical ogre "grinding the base to powder." By entering it, he feels himself one with all men, even "the meanest wretch that passes."

Rhymes. R. H. Horne pointed this out. At moments he seems imitating Young, e.g. "What words can paint tremendous truths like these?" (*M.C.*, chap. XLVII).

Stage Versions of O.C.S. Somebody turned *M. H.'s Clock* into a "domestic drama" two months after it started. Stirling made a play of *O.C.S.* in Nov. 1840.

Carlyle's Influence. Even Trollope shows an awareness of him (see Dr. Pessimist Anticant in *The Warden*, 1855); Rutherford tells of the excitement and tears of joy as he and his fellows read Carlyle, feeling privileged at being alive at the same time as he. (George Eliot and Lewes took Trollope to visit Carlyle in 1861, and he and the Carlyles got on well together.)

Walt Whitman well summarized the feeling: "As a representative figure, a literary figure, no man else will bequeath to the future more significant hints of our stirring era, its basic paradoxes, its din, and its struggling parturition periods. . . . Himself more of a French Revolution than any of his volumes."

Elliotson. Thackeray ded. *Pendennis* to him for having saved his life. Accompanying C. D.'s deep interest in mesmerism, etc., was a strong dislike of spiritualism. He once took the conjuror Houdin to a séance, and Houdin outdid all the medium's tricks.

Townshend was poet and antiquarian; appreciated Clari (C. D. didn't); said to be original of Cousin Pheenix.

Songs. Pitt was no doubt the pilot whom Sir L. Dedlock regretted.

Picnic Tales. He wrote his *Lamplighter* as a story for it. The book earned £300 for the widow.

Reputation. Dickens was still considered low: note the back-handed compliment by Lockhart (*Quarterly*, May 1843), who puts Hook and Dickens together. Hook "is to the upper and middle life of that region (contemporary English society) what Dickens is to its low life."

VII.—*Maypole.* "King's Head" at Chigwell: "the greatest place in the world. . . . Such a delicious old inn opposite the churchyard."

Bulwer's Night and Morning. Fanny, with her wild snatches of song, is closer to Barnaby than Nell. It is of interest that the old man is once compared by Bulwer with a raven. "The old man clawed them [coins] up, chuckling and talking to himself; and, rising with great alacrity, hobbled out of the room like a raven carrying some cunning theft to its hiding place."

In the episode of Gawtrey's death while trying to escape the police there is reminiscence of Sikes's death in *Oliver*.

7

I.—*Poe* called on Dickens in New York after leaving his essay on *Barnaby Rudge* and his *Tales of the Grotesque*. Poe hoped to get his stories published in England, and C. D. promised to inquire. Next November he wrote to Poe, "They have one and all declined the venture." Poe and C. D. do not seem to have taken at all to one another, though Poe had a deep respect for Dickens's work. (*Dickensian* (1940), pp. 109, 163; (1943) p. 21; (1946) p. 79.) It is likely that Poe's *Raven* in part was inspired by *Barnaby Rudge*.

II.—*Tom Beard* was invited to hear Forster read the first chapter of *American Notes*. Charles wanted encouragement.

III.—*Maclise* told Charles about Frith's sketches of the girls in *Barnaby*, and Charles commissioned two pictures. Maclise painted (with Etty, etc.) frescoes in the Pavilion at Buckingham Palace; and Sept. 1843, C. D., Kate, Macready went to see them. Maclise's 1843 drawing of C. D., Kate, and Georgy is an excellent representation of the trio—Georgy plumply assured, Kate prettily lowering her head.

Browning. His *Blot on the 'Scutcheon* was read by Dickens in manuscript and deeply admired.

Chuzzlewit. Mrs. Harris is a midwife in Richardson's *Pamela*. Trollope, of all writers, introduced Mrs. Gamp in his *The Three Clerks*.

Finance. It seems to me likely that Dickens had in mind the Independent West Middlesex Assurance Co., which R. Nicholson exposed in articles in *The Town* (esp. Sept. 19, 1840, issue). Also, the mock company set out in the same paper as "The Long Range Gold-Finding Company, California."

V.—*Toasting Dream*. The cannibal theme was no doubt reinforced by the story of Sweeney Todd, written by T. Prest for Edward Lloyd as *The String of Pearls* (*A Romance*) and quickly famous. Dickens could hardly have missed reading it or seeing it on the stage. The victims were turned into pies of Mrs. Lovett's shop. The cannibalistic note is lusciously stressed by Prest—the "delicious gravy that defied description," "the tender, veal-like tastiness of the meat," "the fat and lean so artistically mixed." After the disclosure, "How the throngs of persons recoiled—what a roar of agony and dismay there was! How frightfully sick about forty lawyers' clerks became all at once, and how they spat out the gelatinous clinging portions of the rich pies they had been devouring."

Cannibalism by wrecked sailors is a theme stretching from Marryat's sea stories to Géricault's great picture, *The Raft of the Medusa*. It occurs in *Famine Abroad* (*Household Words*, Jan. 16, 1858). Compare the whole *Bill of Fare* and the fantasy cited later from

The Uncommercial Traveller. The acute smell-associations, noted in the text have a paranoic element.

VI.—*Carol.* "Who can listen to objections regarding such a book as this?" Thackeray.

Royal Academy Dinner, 1844. Charles spoke at it—a speech "rather pompous and shapely . . ." said Brookfield, "in a rather sonorous, deep voice."

Unitarianism. In 1844 the Little Portland Street congregation gave the Rev. E. Tagart a service of plate; C. D. wrote the inscription, calling Unitarianism "the religion which has sympathy for men of every creed, and ventures to pass judgment on none."

J. Overs. A poor carpenter, dying, for whose collection of stories Dickens wrote a preface. He also helped the widow and children. (Dr. Ellerton had been very kind to Overs.) J. D. Burn dedicated to Dickens his *Autobiography of a Beggar-Boy*, a remarkable account of poverty and gradual political education. (1855.)

Begging Letters. Dickens was much afflicted by these. He prosecuted one writer, whose wife, however, appealed so piteously he gave up the case.

8

I.—*Father.* "The longer I live, the better man I think him," Charles declared. J. D. ("a gentleman of most convivial stamina," as Latimer of the *Western Times* described him) acted as intermediary between Exeter and London. "On Jan. 29th he brought down an express edition of the paper (*Daily News*) containing Peel's speech on the Corn Law Repeal to Exeter by rail, left copies at 143 Fore Street, posted on by chaise to Plymouth, drove back the same afternon, looked in for a chat with Latimer at about seven, and then caught the night train back to town." (R. S. Lambert.)

On the tombstone Dickens described him as having a "zealous, useful, cheerful spirit." Odd glimpses of J. D. we get as follows: May 1841, involving "congenial tempests" and saying he must soon leave Devon for Paris "to consolidate Augustus's French"; and Sept. 1844, having been for a couple of months in the Isle of Wight with Fanny and having gone back with her to Manchester.

Cricket. "The last time we went to the theatre was in 1922, to see Dickens's *Cricket on the Hearth*; Ilyitch (Lenin) was already bored after the first act. Dickens's middle-class sentiment began to get on his nerves . . ." and he walked out. (Krupskaya.) A Lyceum version appeared Dec. 1845; by Jan. 1846 versions were being acted at twelve London theatres. Dramatized versions brought out the "middle-class sentiment" and minimized the rebel leaven.

Turner. At Niagara in 1868, Charles wrote: "Everything in the magnificent valley—buildings, forest, high banks, air, water, everything—was made of rainbow. Turner's most imaginative drawing in his finest day has nothing in it so ethereal, so gorgeous in fancy, so celestial."

Dickens's main *faux pas* in the sphere of art was his attack on the pre-Raphaelites (on Millais in particular); but we must remember that he was politically opposed to any idealizations of the past (which he linked with Catholic, Tractarian, and Young-England Tory propaganda), so that he no doubt was too antipathetic to the whole idea of pre-Raphaelitism to consider what the movement meant in art-terms. Still, the attack showed his philistine Achilles heel.

II.—*Macbeth* (in connection with dream). Note how common references, at crucial points, are to Macbeth (e.g. 10, I in the excuses to Maria); compare what is said later in connection with *Drood*.

III.—*Chimes*. Alderman Cute was based on Sir Peter Laurie, etc.

IV.—*Italy*. At Florence he called on Mrs. Landor, met Mrs. Trollope and Augustus. At Genoa he shrank from a public hanging.

VII.—*Prostitutes*.—Letters to Hullah (Dec. 1847 and Sept. 1848) deal with singing lessons for the reclaimed girls (to be sent to colonies).

VIII.—*Work*. Difficulties, "coupled with that craving for streets, so thoroughly put me off the track," he thought of giving up the Christmas book. Then he started work, and "I was last night in such a state of enthusiasm about it that I think I was an inch or two taller."

His bad art-taste appears in the duelling bronze frogs that he brought from London to stand on his writing-desk—an accessory of inspiration for many years.

IX.—*Mrs. Gamp*. He wrote a laboured account of the Manchester play visit, putting it into the mouth of Mrs. Gamp. (Cf. his effort to resurrect Pickwick and the Wellers in *Humphrey's Clock*.)

Criticism. Thackeray (Titmarsh) was parodying writers in *Punch*, and the proprietors (Bradbury and Evans) quashed the one on Dickens (certainly at Charles's own request).

March 1848. Charles, Forster, handsome Leech, and portly jovial Lemon rode over Salisbury Plain and visited Stonehenge and Hazlitt's Winterslow. A November project for "Blackgang Chine, in the Isle of Wight, with dark winter cliffs and roaring scenes" fell through; but at the turn of the year he decided on "some old cathedral town we don't know." So they went to Norwich and Stanfield Hall (seat of a recent crime) with "a murderous look that seemed to invite such a crime."

Fanny's Death. Maria Beadnell (now Mrs. Winter) called, but there was no personal meeting.

Walter Gay. Dickens intended to make him go on the loose, but grew afraid.

Florence Dombey. Dickens perhaps drew on Mrs. Inchcape's *Simple Story*.

I.—*Yarmouth.* C. D. seems to have visited the area before 1849.

Mary Boyle. Soon became "my dearest Meery," and a flirtatious air was maintained. She sent fresh buttonholes (even in America) for every reading.

II.—*Presence.* "So I saw her [his mother] afterwards, in my sleep at school—a silent presence near my bed. . . ." (*Copperfield*); cf. the early tale of the murderer.

Micawber. Burly, oval-headed Thomas Powell contributed traits.

Copperfield. Once started, he wrote this book with special ease, and he had a special fondness for it.

Mr. Dick. Note that Dickens signed letters "Dick." Mr. Dick, with his sister-obsession and his fool-qualities, belongs to the Pinch-Barnaby series.

III.—*G. A. Sala.* One of Charles's most brilliant young men, who played an important part in founding the new journalism.

Madmen. A Frenchman called, excused himself, "You must be visited every day by princes, statesmen, scholars, writers, artists, and even madmen." "Yes, madmen! madmen! madmen! they alone amuse me," cried Dickens, and pushed the visitor out.

H. Martineau. She had attacked *Oliver Twist*; four years later Mrs. Trollope's *Jessie Phillips* was probably an attack on her. C. D. was to get his attack in with the philanthropists of *Bleak House*.

Hair-combing. This obsessional act shows a sense of defilement (guilt).

V.—*Dead Girl.* The Christmas story for 1851 has an outburst about the "dear girl—almost a woman" who dies. "O look upon her now! O look upon her beauty," etc.

Skimpole. Dickens tried to make amends to Leigh Hunt, by apology, and by essays. (1855 and 1859.)

Double of Lord Chancellor. Can Dickens have got the idea of a "double" of the Lord Chancellor from R. Nicholson, who established the Judge and Jury Society at the Garrick's Head in 1841 and became famous as "Lord Chief Baron Nicholson"? See his cheerful autobiography for his disreputable career. "Even attorneys, when seeing me, say, 'Well, my lord!' " (The autobiography has a long account of life in debt-jails.)

VI.—*Trade Unions.* As an example of the very friendly attitude of *Household Words* to working-class organizations, take *The Blue-Jacket Agitation* on April 5, 1851. In the account of a rising of foresters in the Forest of Dean (August 9th) against enclosure, the hero is even the one who vainly proposed violent resistance to the troops. In *Strike!* (Feb. 6, 1858) the right to strike is defended and extensions of the principle are suggested.

Throughout the 'sixties a stubborn trade union fight went on. The building trades were agitated, 1861-2, by a fight against the cruel hour system. The London Trades Council emerged. A National Miners' Conference was held in Leeds, 1863. Then the International Working Men's Association was formed in 1864, with the aid of Marx.

In Sheffield (1859, 1861, 1866) cases of violence occurred; and the *Daily News* demanded, "The unions must be stamped out as a public nuisance." But, instead, after the 1868 General Election, a Trade Union Bill gave legal protection to the T.U. funds for the first time. Working-class feeling about the American Civil War, and the struggle in Italy, Poland, Hungary, did a great deal to educate the movement.

VIII.—*Stephen.* The working-class bewilderment, well expressed in *Stephen Blackford*, had been previously dealt with by Mrs. Gaskell in *Mary Barton*. Mary's father is a shrewd, kindly, hard-working weaver—a seeker of the "right way"; near the end of his life he says, "it's a hard one for a poor man to find." He was taught to read, but given no books. Hearing of the Bible, he read it, and was more bewildered than ever. "They all spoke up for it, and went and did clean contrary."

This trail, from *Mary Barton* and *Hard Times*, leads to George Eliot's *Felix Holt*, Mark Rutherford's novels, and E. Lynn Linton's *Joshua Davidson, Christian and Communist*.

In 1854 (Dec. 17th) Dickens wrote to Wilkie Collins, "I am so sorry at heart for the working people when they get into trouble, and have their wretched arena chalked out for them with such extraordinary complacence by small political economists, that I have a natural impulse upon me, almost always, to come to the rescue— even of people I detest, if I believe them to have been true to these poor men."

See Jackson (p. 281) for Mr. Justice Maule's judgment in 1857 in a divorce case very like Stephen's, which created the agitation leading to the first Divorce Law in England—and for the probabilities that Maule was influenced by Dickens.

A slight anticipation of the anti-Gradgrind satire will be found in Lady Bulwer's novel of 1839.

The interest of the *Household Words* original of *Hard Times* is that it shows Dickens fascinated by a tale of uncompromising revolt, absorbing it into his own set of values and tensions, refashioning it. The original plain choice of revolt and love becomes one of hopelessly entangled and divided decisions; but the first dynamic remains underneath. The simple forest-choice (in a feudal world) is strangely complicated in the industrial city; but revolt and love are still the touchstones of virtue, manhood.

II

I.—*Sons.* By 1859 C. D. had managed to disperse the boys—Walter was in India; Frank in Hamburg; Alfred, Sydney, and Harry were at school in Boulogne; Flora at Southsea. Charley was out all day (and in May next year went to Hong Kong). Katie went to see her mother occasionally; Mamie seldom; Georgina never.

Thackeray. The deep lack of sympathy burst out now in the quarrel over Yates (who had criticized Thackeray and who was excluded from the Athenaeum). The episode is of interest only in showing the intransigent mood of Dickens.

Thackeray hated both Bulwer and Dickens. Statements such as the following must have made him writhe: "we are scarcely among those who consider Thackeray as a mere ill-natured imitator of Dickens. . . . Their great distinction consists in this—that Dickens is a man of genius and Thackeray a man of talent. Dickens is a poet, Thackeray a man of the world. . . . Thackeray shows what we are, but gives the idea of scoffing and satisfaction. . . . Dickens is an enthusiast—Thackeray a cynic by nature; and 'tis whispered that the very fashion which he despises owns him for a slave." A. B. Richards (1851), *Poems, Essays and Opinions,* I.

Katie. The only one of the children with any real self-respect, she wrote "a life of her father, clearing her mother of false accusations made at the time of their separation" (Miss Storey); but she later burned it. "I told only half the truth about my father," she said, "and a half-truth is worse than a lie; for this reason I destroyed what I had written. But the truth must be told when the time comes."

See Miss Storey (Chap. X) for her resolve to go on the stage and C. D.'s keen opposition. Katie ends, "I know things about my father's character that no one else ever knew; he was not a good man, but he was not a fast man, but he was wonderful."

Katie, reading later a letter in which Georgina called her "intolerant," said, "Aunty was not quite straight, and I often stood up to her; that is why she called me 'intolerant.' To build up the reputation of one big person you often have to knock down the reputations of a lot of little people. My father, with all his greatness, was what Aunty called me—'intolerant'." (G. Storey.)

II.—For the letter written by Mrs. Thompson (Kate's aunt) to a friend in Scotland, referring to Ellen, see Ralph Straus, *Dickensian* (1946) p. 21.

He felt the weakness of English culture next to the French, in much the same vein as Dickens. In 1865 he wrote, "I'm sick of England and the English, and would give ten years of my life had I been a native of this great nation of literature and art, rather than one of the people whose literature is now 'robbery ill-concealed'..."

And strangely for one without any political understanding (though he had read Mill and Ruskin), he had something of a sympathetic attitude to the Commune. ("Half the Communists were honest, single-minded, pure-hearted men; the other half infernal scoundrels who would have burnt their own mothers for a franc and a half a day." The division he makes is ultimately the split in his own "petty-bourgeois" views: one half aspiring to an "idealized" aspect of the revolution, the other half afraid of violence and struggle. Here, in a simple way, is something of the conflict inside Dickens.)

The Coleman passage is cited by E. Watts Phillips, p. 51.

III.—*London.* "The streets are hideous to behold, and the ugliness of London is quite astonishing." (Feb. 1856.)

IV.—*Slight Jingle.* Manette reversed is Tenam, not unlike Ternan. These details may seem trifling; but close scrutiny has convinced me of the complex associative play in Dickens's name-formations.

V.—*Middle-class Audience.* One can judge how rapidly Dickens parts from the more respectable middle-class by reading the works of E. Sewell (*Amy Herbert,* 1844) and C. Yonge (with her great success, *The Heir of Radclyffe,* 1853) where the pious family glorification, with religious tinges and twinges, is worked out. Dickens, like Jerrold, belonged to a cruder generation. Jerrold's *Mrs. Caudle's Curtain Lectures* (from 1845) shows the Dickensian sense of the frantic discord behind the respectable screen.

VI.—*Tale of Two Cities.* The body-snatching theme was suggested by an article in *H. W.* (April 3, 1858), *Use and abuse of the Dead.* It is a sort of symbolic doubling of the main motif of Returned from the Dead.

Carton–Darnay. There is a case (in *Sgt. Ballantyne's Experiences,* Chap. XIII) where a man is acquitted through a dramatic production of someone very like him. As Dickens knew Ballantyne, he had doubtless heard the story; but his liking for twins (e.g. in *Our Mutual Friend,* where they play an important part in the unmasking of evil) had deeper roots—compare Wilkie Collins's *Woman in White.*

Watts Phillips: Artist and Playwright, by E. Watts Phillips (1891), written after *The Dead Heart* had regained popularity through Irving's revival. W. P. had several points of similarity with Dickens: he disliked English Sundays and loved Paris (". . . dances and other amusements being prohibited, especially on a Sunday, by a Christian and humane legislature," he writes from Paris).

He visited the Morgue in Paris and wrote a long letter on a drowned betrayed girl. He wrote satirical sketches (e.g. *Thoughts in Tatters, by the Ragged Philosopher*) and about 1854–5, *The Wild Tribes of London,* an account of the slums, including Ratcliffe Highway and Seven Dials (which was dramatized by one Travers).

VII.—*Great Expectations* starts in the Cooling Marshes, with Miss Havisham's house in Rochester. (The marshes appear in *Bleak House,* Chap. XXVI.)

Bill Bailey was a special favourite of Swinburne's (with Mrs. Gamp). The theme of imprisonment (isolation) appears in a letter to Wilkie Collins (Sept. 6, 1858) about a projected Christmas story, the subject to be a man who tries to cut himself off—but, "You are in it, to be of it." "So you get yourself into a false position the moment you try to sever yourself from it."

Australia. In 1862 C. D. was rather eagerly considering requests to read in Australia—and the writing of an *Uncommercial Traveller Upside Down.* (For the turn of interest to Australia from 1849 onwards, see *Dickensian,* 1946, pp. 75–7.) Note the setting of the crisis in Bulwer's *A Strange Story* in Australia.

12

II.—*Young girls.* That the Genoa house and Gadshill Place should become girls' schools was surely the symbolically correct thing—the right setting for the ghost of Charles.

Adah Isaacs Menken. The American actress notorious for her Mazeppa act (in tights, with blouse and trunks): Forster mentioned her friendship with Dickens (during the 60's) in his first edition, then suppressed it. She had affairs with many men (including Dumas, *fils*, and probably Swinburne); it seems unlikely that much occurred between her and Dickens.

Sense of strain. It is hard to see any marks of the scientific crisis (Lyall, Darwin, etc.) of the 50's and 60's in C. D.'s works, though it may have helped indirectly to increase his sense of a world breaking up; but his essential sense of crisis was personal, social.

IV.—*Politics.* Dickens (though he hated slavery so fiercely) wavered at the outset of the Civil War under the pressure of propaganda for the chivalrous South against the dollar-greedy North. His worst political misjudgment, however, was his support of Eyre in Jamaica (1865–7): he accepted Carlyle's attitude, which was essentially imperialist. He was led into this by his hatred of the Nonconformists, the "Exeter Hall Gang."

But there was no truth in the rumour that the attacker of privilege, titles, and the toady tree, was ready to accept a baronetcy in the last months of his life. ("And here we might have been drinking confusion to Baronetcies, and resolving never to pluck a leaf from the toady tree, till this very small world shall have rolled us off," to Wilkie Collins, April 30, 1856.)

Blackpool (1869). A touch of his old spirits appeared. Walking to the railway station, his hat blew off. Some Preston men caused "summonses to be served on him for compensation and disappointment on the grounds that they had seen him on the sands at Blackpool 'kicking his hat about as if he had been a boy!'"

Patronage. In Sept. 1869, he again attacked patronage at the Birmingham Institution as "a curse to England," and was pleased that most of the 500 members (some women) were wage-earners. Cf. the letter to Charley from the U.S.A. saying that the locals in his cricket club must have the right to manage their own affairs, insisting on democratic discussion, and attacking patronage.

Workers (1870, Charley on visit to Birmingham), "I was continually stopped by men reeking with sweat and grimy with dirt to ask me, 'Is that Charles Dickens? Is that Charles Dickens?' "

When Charley drove to the office shortly after the funeral, the cabby said, "Your father's death was a great loss to all of us, and we cabbies were in hopes that he would soon be doing something to help us."

Ashton Dilkes on the day of the death was buying tobacco; a worker with bag of tools came in, bought twopence worth of screw-tobacco, and said, "Dickens is dead. We have lost our best friend."

VI.—*Murder*. In *Murderous Extremes* he sees the passive reliance on the law as a kind of murder of personal resource.

Train. His tendency to personalize trains appears in many of his works: thus, "The locomotive post offices with their great nets—as if they had been dragging the country for bodies. . . ." (*Houselessness*.) "The engine would blow and heave and perspire," etc.

Our Mutual Friend. Dramatized as *Dustman's Treasure* in 1866 at Britannia Theatre.

Drood. After examining the theories that try to make Datchery out as Drood, Bazzard, Grewgious, Tartar, or merely a hired detective, I feel there is little doubt that Helena is the guiser. On the Datchery issue there is a lot of sense in H. J(ackson), *About Edwin Drood*, and W. Robertson Nicoll, *The Problem of Edwin Drood*. There may be something in the idea that Jasper had seduced (even murdered, the previous Christmas) a daughter or friend of the opium woman; in any event there was certainly something more to come out about the relations of Jasper and this woman.

Drood is linked with Bulwer's *Eugene Aram* (1831) by its element of tragic irony. Jasper kills Drood under the delusion that Edwin and Rosa are to marry, whereas they have broken apart; Aram is drawn into a murder for money, and at once gets a legacy; while he takes no advantage of his plunder. "Just Heaven! when they told me, I thought I heard the devils laugh out at the fool who had boasted wisdom. . . . No, it was for this, for the guilt and its penance, for the wasted life and the shameful death—with all my thirst for good, my dreams of glory—that I was born. . . ." But Jasper's awakening to the truth was to implicate a much deeper net of good and evil than Aram's. Still, *Aram* is one of the elements underlying *Drood*.

The Drug. The visual effects suggest cannabis indica or mescal rather than opium. Note that Wilkie Collins took to drugs.

Macbeth. I was myself working out the relation of *Macbeth* to *Drood* when I found the idea in Edwin Charles, and well worked out by Howard Duffield in the *Dickensian* (1934), pp. 263-71. It is from him that I quote, and my exposition closely follows his.

Woman in White. Based on a real episode, when a woman in white rushed out of a villa near Regent's Park, screaming. Collins, with his brother and Millais, saw her; and he followed her. She was Caroline, who became his mistress. Later she married someone else

Wilkie Collins attended the wedding; then came and told Katie Dickens all about it, ending, "I suppose you could not marry a man who—" "No, I couldn't," she broke in. (G. Storey.)

VII.—*Thugs*. Dickens mentions Thugs in 1857 in relation to a garotting epidemic in London; he probably knew E. Thornton's *Illustrations of the History and Practices of the Thugs* (1837) where the victim's having no gold is mentioned. He must have known C. Kingsley's *Yeast*, where Lancelot, repudiating Catholicism, cries out to his cousin who wishes to emulate the flagellations of Mary of Oignies, "Such a decision would have better pleased Kali the murder-goddess of the Thugs!" (Here Thuggery is equated with religious-sexual perversion: a relation richly in *Drood's* key.)

For Thug division of personality see J. L. Sleeman cited E. Wilson, *Wound and Bow*, 93 ff. : further, H. Duffield, *Amer. Bookman* (Feb. 1930); and A. Boyd (*Humanistic Studies*, IX, Washington Univ.), who shows Jasper as an hypnotist like Dickens; (Jasper "wills" Crisparkle to go to the weir.)

J. de Mille published a Thug novel *Cord and Creese* in U.S.A. in 1869.

VIII.—*Swinburne*. "I remember one occasion on which he made us all into a kind of *tableau* out of *Dombey and Son*—himself taking the part of Mrs. Skewton in her Bath Chair! There was a consultation as to who should be Carker—whoever could show the best set of teeth. I was eager to qualify for the part, and put on a tremendous grin. . . . He says in a letter to me so late as 1901. . . . 'Never shall I forget the monthly appearance of the first of his books I was old enough to take in—*Bleak House*, which ran through two of my years at Eton and was apt to interfere with my work rather seriously on the first of each month. Don't I remember how I used to scuttle up to town to Ingalton's after morning school . . ?" (D. Leith). He writes to his mother of reading aloud his work, "It is *very* fascinating, and I don't wonder it killed Dickens. The intoxicating circle of faces . . ."

Strindberg. "In August Strindberg's *Twenty-nine answers to George Bröckner*, written in May 1897, when he was forty-eight, to the question 'What English author do you place highest?' he replied 'Dickens.'

"Strindberg first read Dickens in Swedish translation when, as a youth, he lived in the Stockholm house of Dr. Lamm, a Jewish doctor of medicine and a great lover of the arts. Strindberg was for a time his assistant and tutor to his sons, before he had any notion that he was destined to become a writer. The emphasis in Dickens on the degradation of poverty and the humiliation of unhappy childhood must have appealed at once to Strindberg, for he too was obsessed by these phenomena.

"When in the late seventies, after writing his first half-dozen plays, Strindberg turned his pen to fiction, he began to study Dickens more closely. Discussing Strindberg's early stories, Dr. Martin Lamm says: 'The descriptions of nature are fabulized and personified like those of Dickens or H. C. Andersen.' Certainly Strindberg relates landscape and domestic interiors to character and action in the same way as Dickens, and in his later work he too endows inanimate objects with a life of fantasy and symbolism.

"Strindberg himself acknowledged that Dickens directly inspired his first novel *The Red Room*, in which he castigates a state of society with which he always found it impossible to come to terms. The title of this novel was the name of a coterie to which Strindberg had, as a journalist, belonged. He tells us that he had a notion of forming a 'Swedish Pickwick-Club' which would, we may infer, have been in sharp contrast to *The Red Room* the keynote of which was hopeless cynicism.

"Strindberg was often cynical, but never, fundamentally, hopeless. Like Dickens he was a born reformer, and he destroyed only in the compelling desire to make room for something better. Like Dickens, too, he had a great tenderness for children and a large fund of sentimentality. From the Englishman he drew his taste for caricature, but his type of humour differed greatly from his model's. Humour with Strindberg was always a grim mask for a grimmer truth, and he shows no sign of having really appreciated this aspect of Dickens's genius. Nor was Strindberg's attack on society ever just part of a vast canvas—it was the whole picture."

I owe this note to the kindness of Miss Elizabeth Sprigge, who mentions also that M. Lamm's biography (1940) deals fully with the close relation of Strindberg and Dickens. Dr. G. Ahlström points out that Strindberg cited *Pickwick* at the head of his important satire *The New Kingdom*. And in his great crisis before his final period Strindberg says that it was the re-reading of Dickens's *Christmas Tales* that restored his serenity, his faith in man, his creative energy.

IX.—*Train fear*. On April 25, 1870, Maclise died. Dickens wrote, "I at Higham had the shock of first reading at a railway station of the death of our old dear friend. What the shock would be, you know." A further fear-association.

Readings. Forster, for once in the right, had strongly opposed the murder scene and quite alienated Dickens's affections. A "painful correspondence" ensued; and in the last two years the breach was deep. "God forgive me, but I cannot get over the mania for proprietorship which is rampant in Palace Gate House," Charles told Georgy.

Mrs. Dickens. In 1879 Kate Dickens was getting ill (cancer); one Sunday morning she fell in the street. A passer helped her up, and, when she thanked him very gratefully, said, "I am only a working man, madam." She answered, "You could not be anything better."

Katie said to Miss Storey, "My poor mother was afraid of my father. She was never allowed to express any opinion—never allowed to say what she felt."

Death. There seems a clue to the meaning of his last words in the scene at the end of Book II, *Hard Times*: Louisa confesses to her father the lovelessness of her marriage and the way she has fallen under another man's spell. She says she is not sorry or ashamed. " 'All that I know is, your philosophy and your teaching will not save me. Now, father, you have brought me to this. Save me by some other means.' He tightened his hold in time to prevent her sinking on the floor, but she cried out in a terrible voice, 'I shall die if you hold me! Let me fall upon the ground!' " (That is, a return to mother-earth.) Compare Kierkegaard's last words (with their faecal rejected-self note).

XI.—*Work method.* "If you want your public to believe in what you are writing, you must believe in it yourself. I can as distinctly see with my own eyes any scene which I am describing as I see you now; and, indeed, on one occasion when I had shadowed a certain course for one of my characters to pursue, the character took possession of me, and made me do exactly the contrary to what I had originally intended." (To C. Collins.)

"For some time there was no sound to be heard in the room but the rapid working of the pen, when suddenly he jumped up, went to the looking-glass, rushed back to his writing-table, and jotted down a few words; back to the glass again, this time talking to his own reflection, or rather to the simulated expression he saw there, and was trying to catch before drawing it in words, then back again to his writing. After a while he got up again, and stood with his back to the glass, talking softly and rapidly for a long time, then looking at his daughter, but certainly never seeing her, then once more back to his table, and to steady writing until luncheon time." (Mamie Dickens.) This account shows the strong mime element in his method.

André Maurois sees in the fury of mask-faces in Dickens's work a personification of his need to escape a *tête-à-tête* with his own soul. The usual quarter-truth.

Fears. Of course many people knew of Ellen. Thackery at the outset said in the Garrick that Dickens left his wife for an actress, and got a furious letter. Browning seems to have known. Dickens wrote to a woman friend to be discreet, as it would be a blow for Ellen if things came out. "She could not have the pride and self-reliance which (mingled with the gentlest nature) has borne her, alone, through so much." He specially didn't want her sister, Fanny, Mrs. Trollope, to know, as she was "infinitely sharper than the serpent's tooth." Oddly, something of the tale was told in a play by John Garraway in Australia in the mid-nineties, a one-acter set in Manchester during the production of *The Frozen Deep*, but showing Dickens disillusioned and saved in time. (Thackeray in his hate had a keen eye for Dickens's set-up. Thus, earlier, he wrote of seeing at Ryde, "the great Dickens, with his wife, his children, his Miss

Hogarth, all looking abominable coarse and vulgar and happy": *his* Miss Hogarth!)

Dickens's influences. It is, perhaps, not surprising to learn that when Gissing first came to London his main thought was to trace out the sites of Dickens's novels; it is, however, no doubt something of a shock to find a writer like Huysmans devoted to Dickens and haunted by his world, his people—so much so that he once set out to journey to London; but being early for his train, drove to a restaurant frequented by English people, had a hearty Dickensian meal, and then went home. He felt that after that he could live at ease in the world of the Dickensian imagination. Why go to England? "I can always read Charles Dickens." But the story astonishes us only because of our false and limited picture of Dickens's work.

Dickens had important effects in U.S.A.—first to some extent through Poe; more firmly through a deep-seated influence on the later "realists." Thus, "During Norris's childhood it had been the custom of his mother to read aloud to her family night after night, from one or other of the novels of Dickens." (E. Marchand, *Frank Norris, a Study*.) (Note the strong Dickensian element in Norris's characters, e.g. Old Grannis, Miss Baker, Aunt Wess, Grossman, Hoover.)

Dostoevsky even had his own Little Nell—the Nellie of *Insult and Injury*, a character which enables us clearly to evalue the closeness and the difference between the two writers. During his imprisonment, Dostoevsky found Dickens with special force. "Even the books that were offered to him he hardly ever accepted; only in two cases (they were *David Copperfield* and *The Pickwick Papers*) did he show any interest in the books, or take them to hospital with him," Mem. of Martyanov, in *Letters of F. M. Dostoevsky* (1917), translated by E. C. Mayne. Gogol was not uninfluenced by Dickens.

Ellen Ternan. She lived till 1914, marrying Rev. G. W. Robinson in 1876: he became Principal of the High School, Margate.

Note on Balzac. In 1847, Balzac, depressed, read *The Cricket*, and wrote, "This little masterpiece is without a fault. . . . It has given me the idea for a book." Dickens is silent about Balzac, save that he wrote from Paris, after B.'s death, of "people who pass their time with Balzac and Sand, and criticise English works for their uninteresting heroes." But add Forster's comment in the *Life* (Dickens cannot, like "that great story-teller" B., leave morality out and treat a passion as part of the life-force), and Wilkie's review of Werdet's *Portrait Intime* in *All the Year Round* (1859) which praises very highly B. in his prime, but calls his later works admirable yet "needlessly and horribly repulsive." We surely see Balzac much discussed by C. D. after 1859, envied and (in part) berated, but helping to free him for his last period.

INDEX

455

E 3